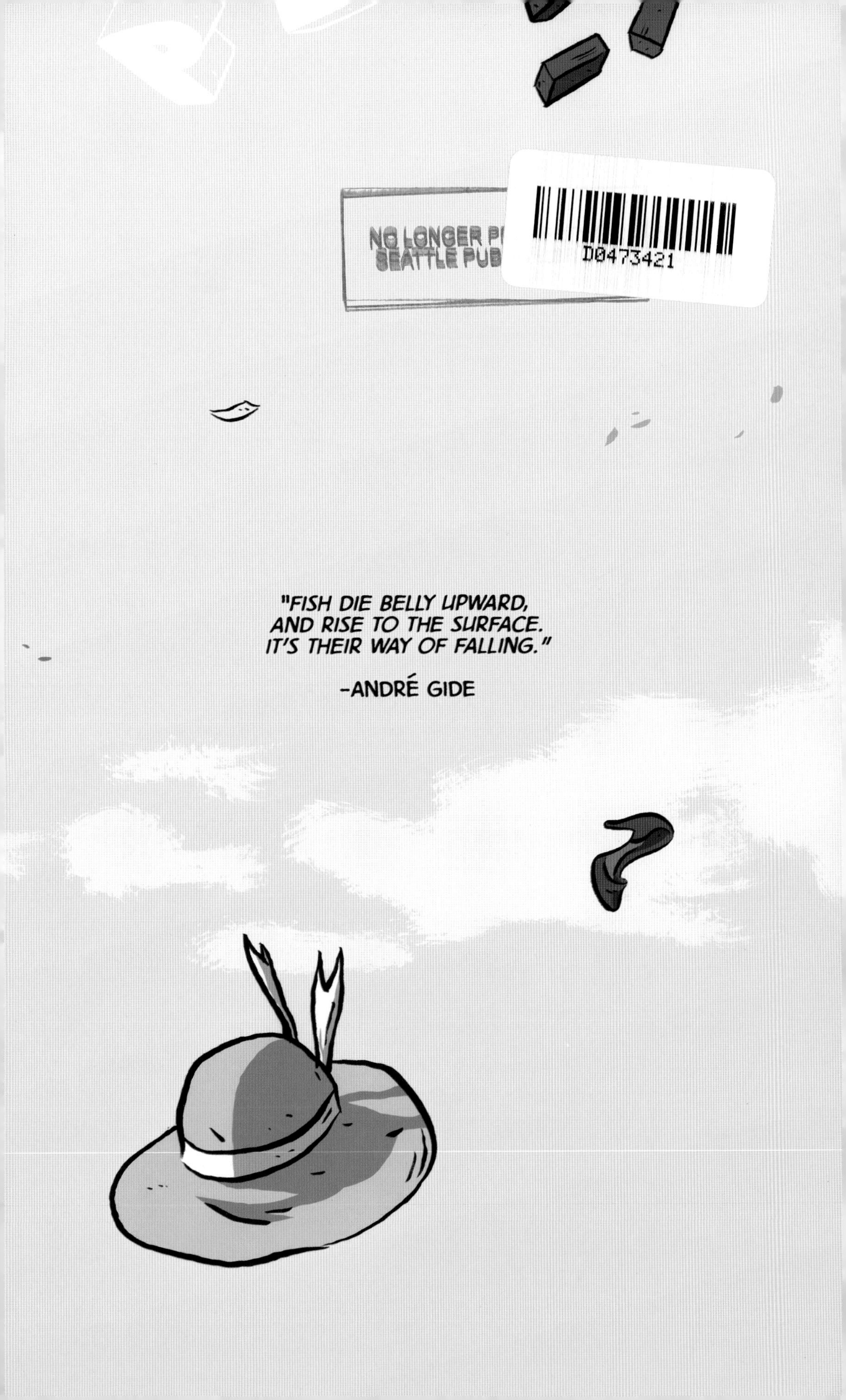

*"FISH DIE BELLY UPWARD,
AND RISE TO THE SURFACE.
IT'S THEIR WAY OF FALLING."*

-ANDRÉ GIDE

PRINTED IN CHINA BY IMAGO
FIRST EDITION
DESIGN BY SHERWIN TJIA

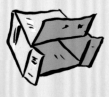

ISBN 978-1-77262-040-5
LIBRARY DATA (CIP) AVAILABLE FROM
LIBRARIES AND ARCHIVES CANADA

CONUNDRUM PRESS
WOLFVILLE, NS, CANADA
WWW.CONUNDRUMPRESS.COM

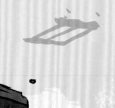

DISTRIBUTION IN CANADA
BY LITDISTCO

DISTRIBUTION IN USA AND UK
BY CONSORTIUM

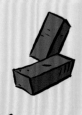

CONUNDRUM PRESS ACKNOWLEDGES
THE FINANCIAL ASSISTANCE OF
THE CANADA COUNCIL FOR THE ARTS,
THE GOVERNMENT OF CANADA,
AND THE NOVA SCOTIA CREATIVE INDUSTRIES
FUND TOWARD THIS PUBLICATION.

NOVA SCOTIA

THE AUTHOR ACKNOWLEDGES
THE CANADA COUNCIL
FOR THE ARTS.

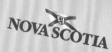

Canada Council for the Arts
Conseil des arts du Canada

Canada

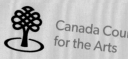

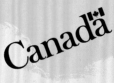

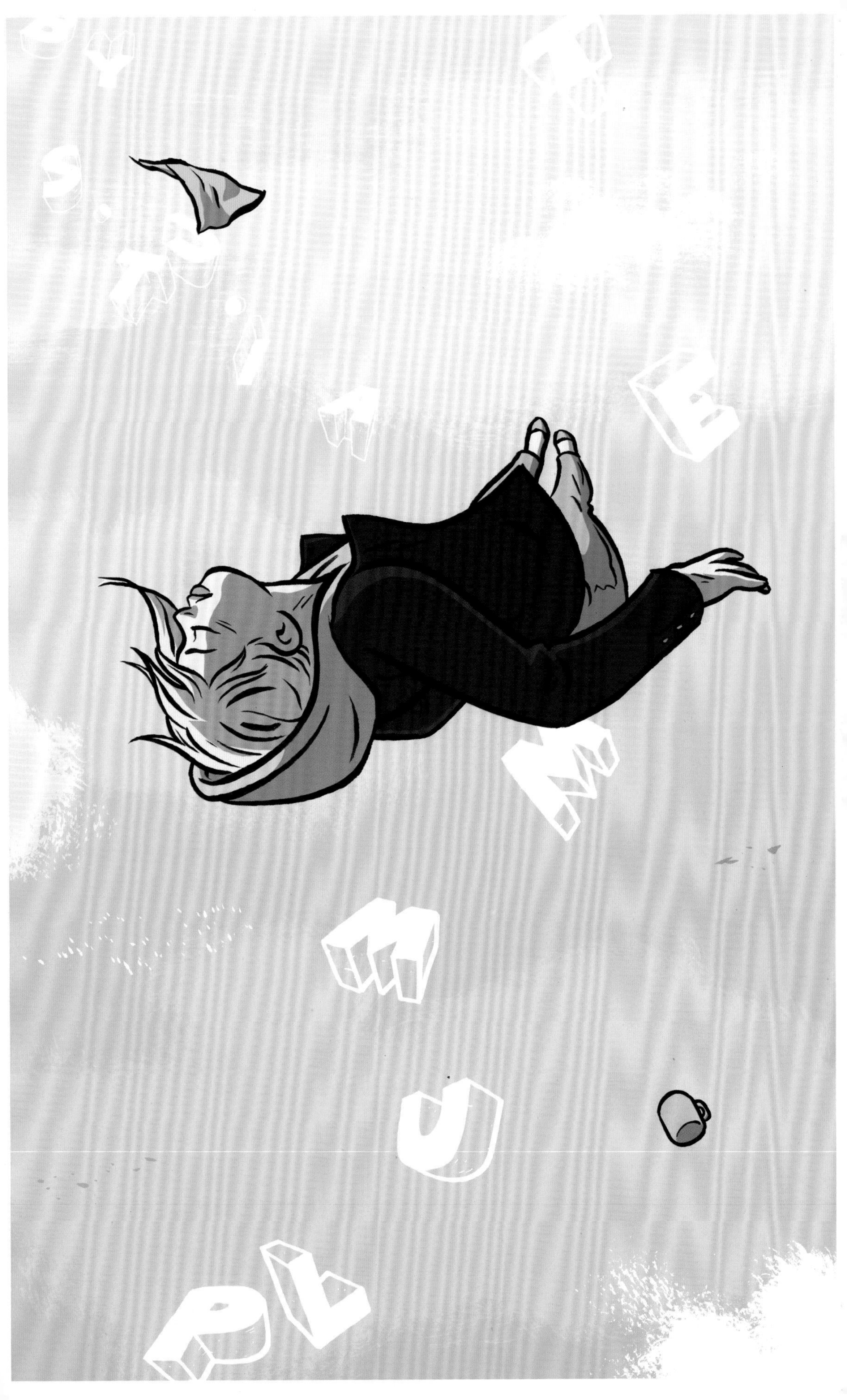

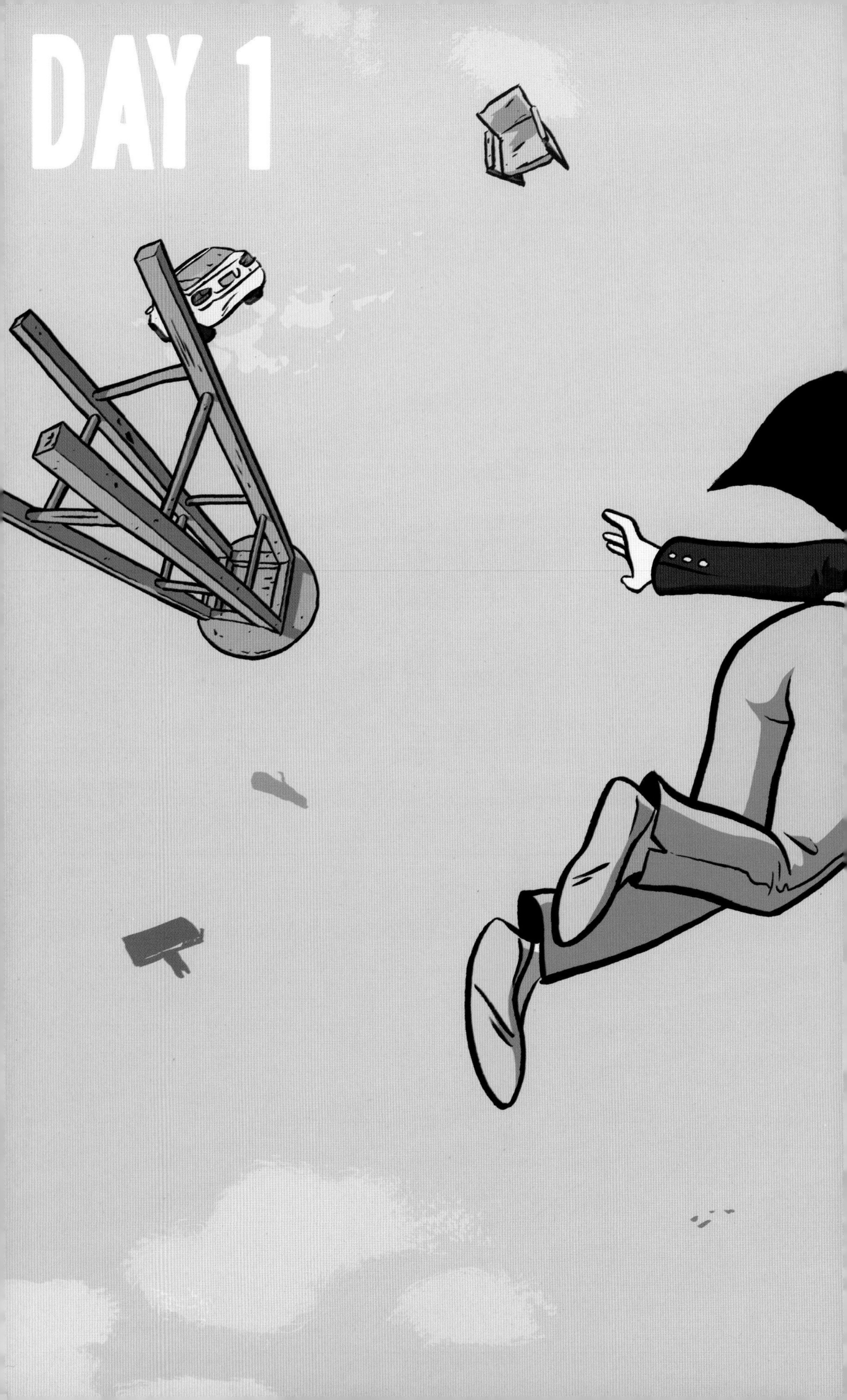
DAY 1

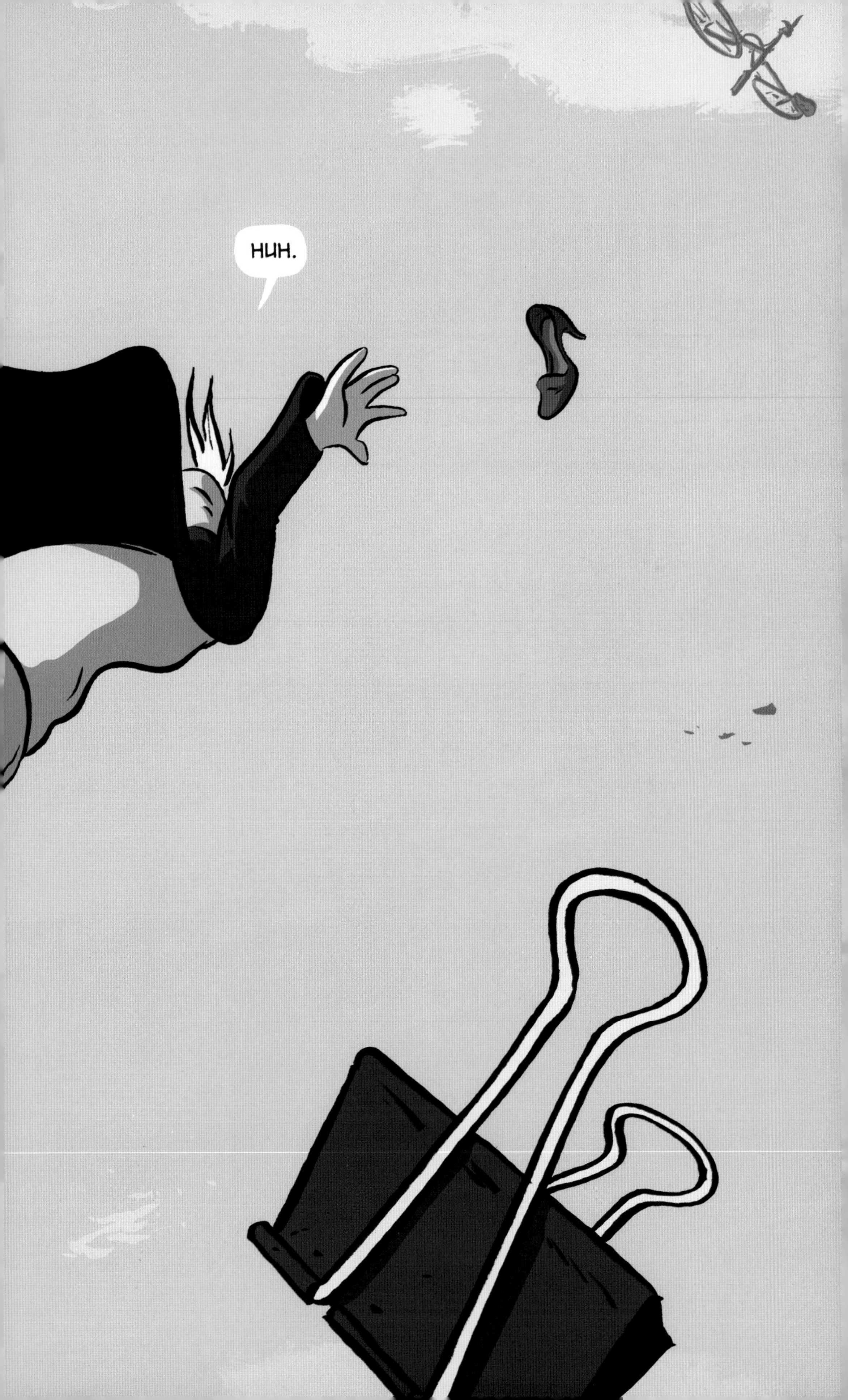
HUH.

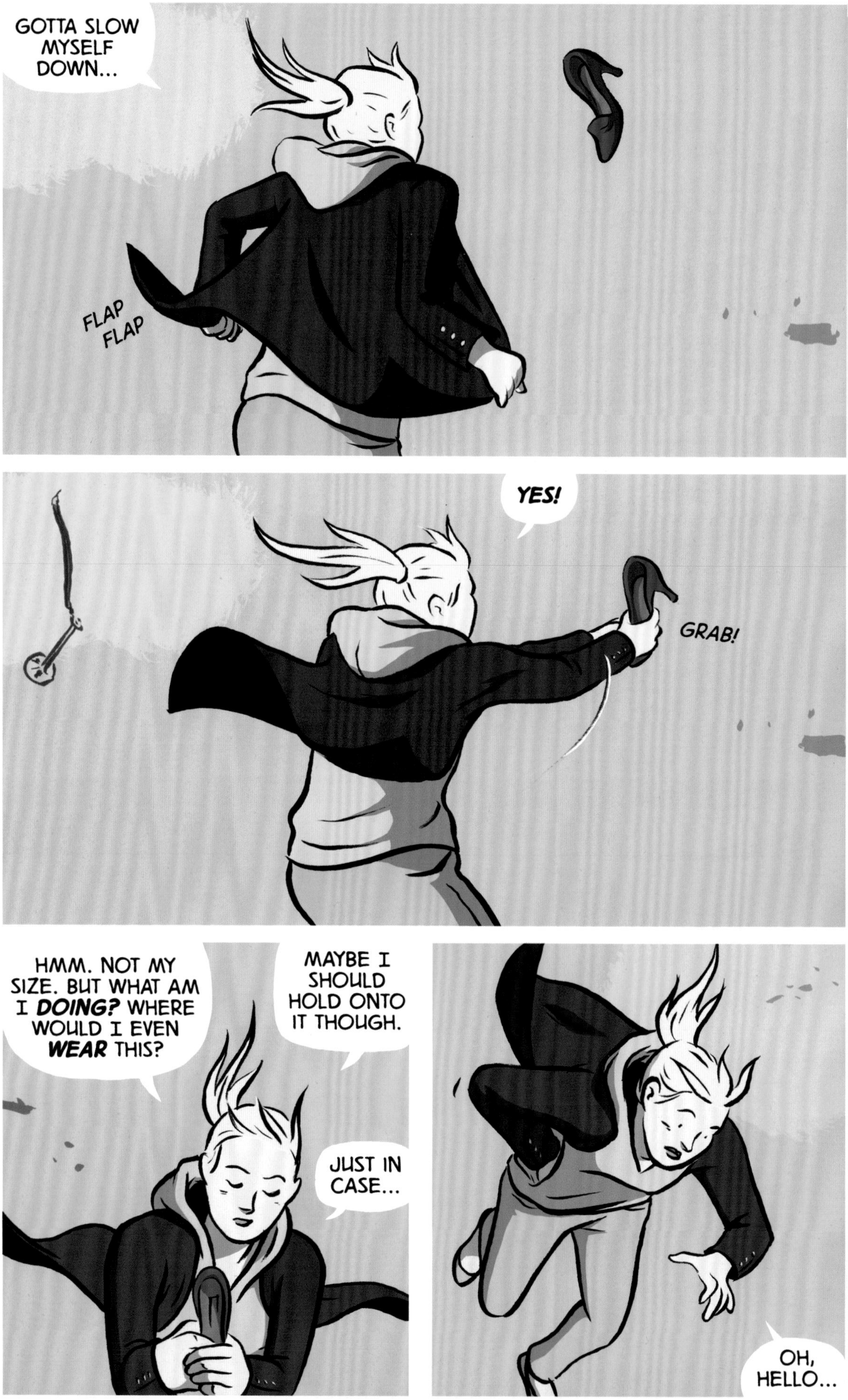
GOTTA SLOW MYSELF DOWN...
FLAP FLAP
YES!
GRAB!
HMM. NOT MY SIZE. BUT WHAT AM I **DOING?** WHERE WOULD I EVEN **WEAR** THIS?
MAYBE I SHOULD HOLD ONTO IT THOUGH.
JUST IN CASE...
OH, HELLO...

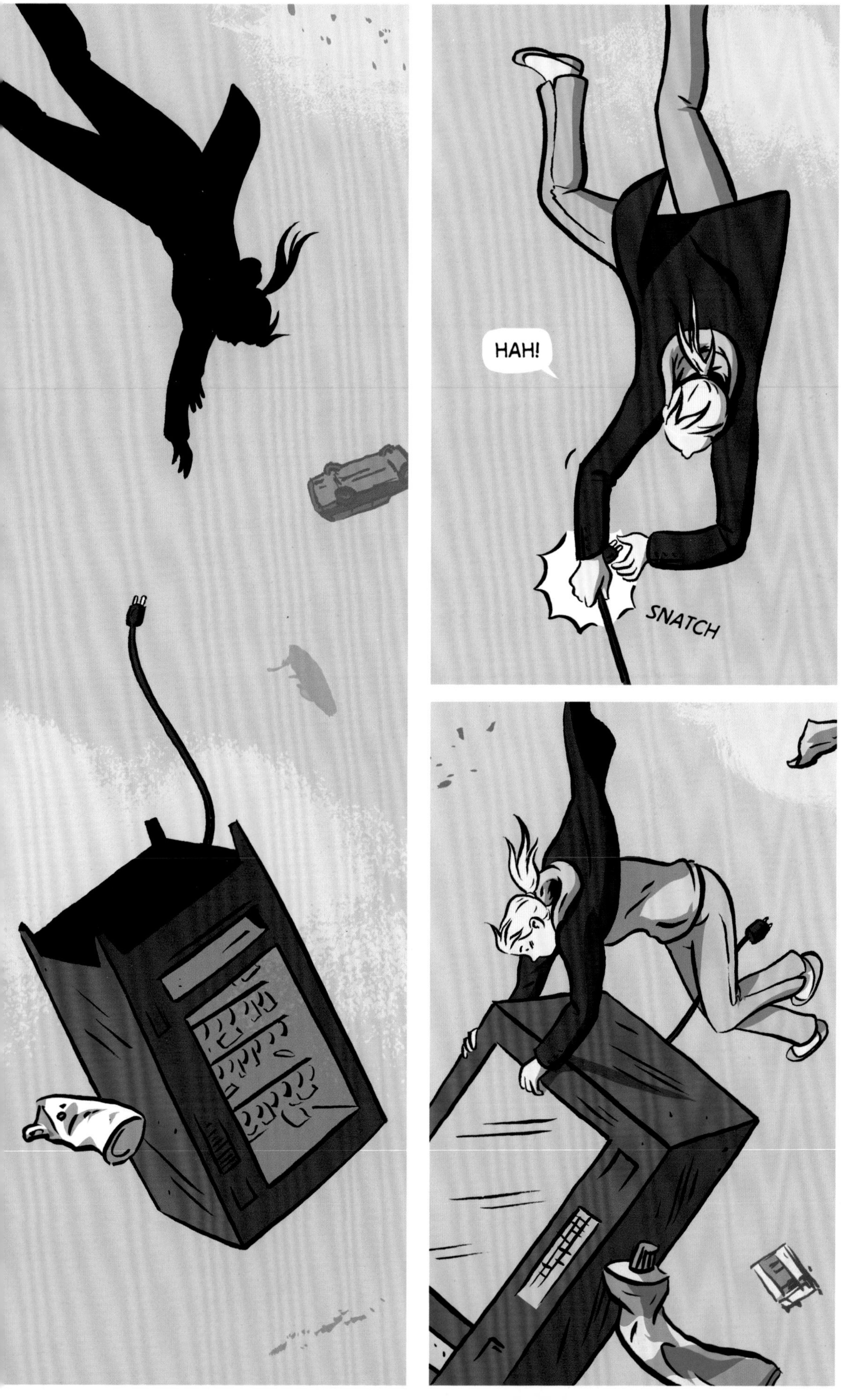
HAH!
SNATCH

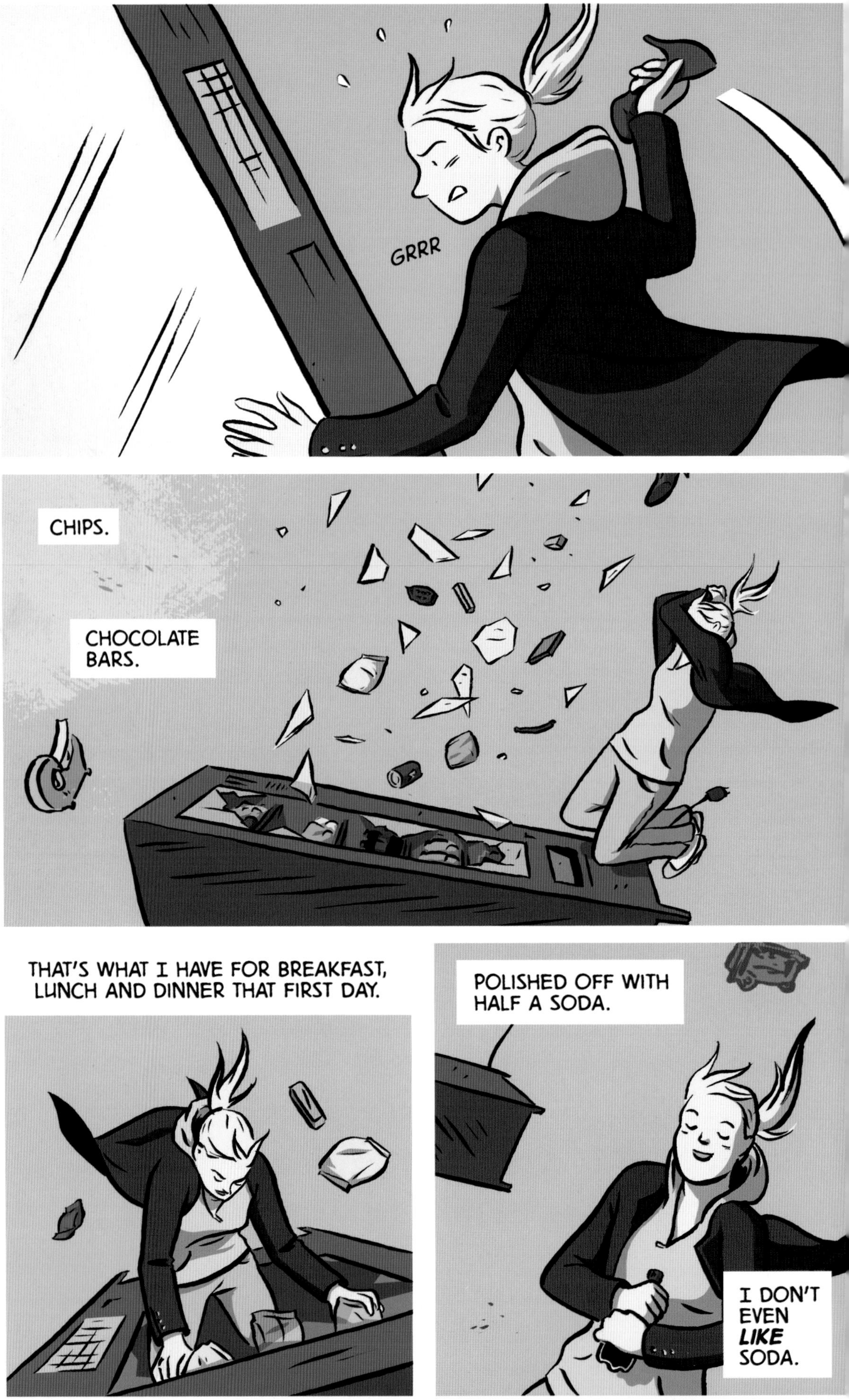
GRRR
CHIPS.
CHOCOLATE BARS.
THAT'S WHAT I HAVE FOR BREAKFAST, LUNCH AND DINNER THAT FIRST DAY.
POLISHED OFF WITH HALF A SODA.
I DON'T EVEN *LIKE* SODA.

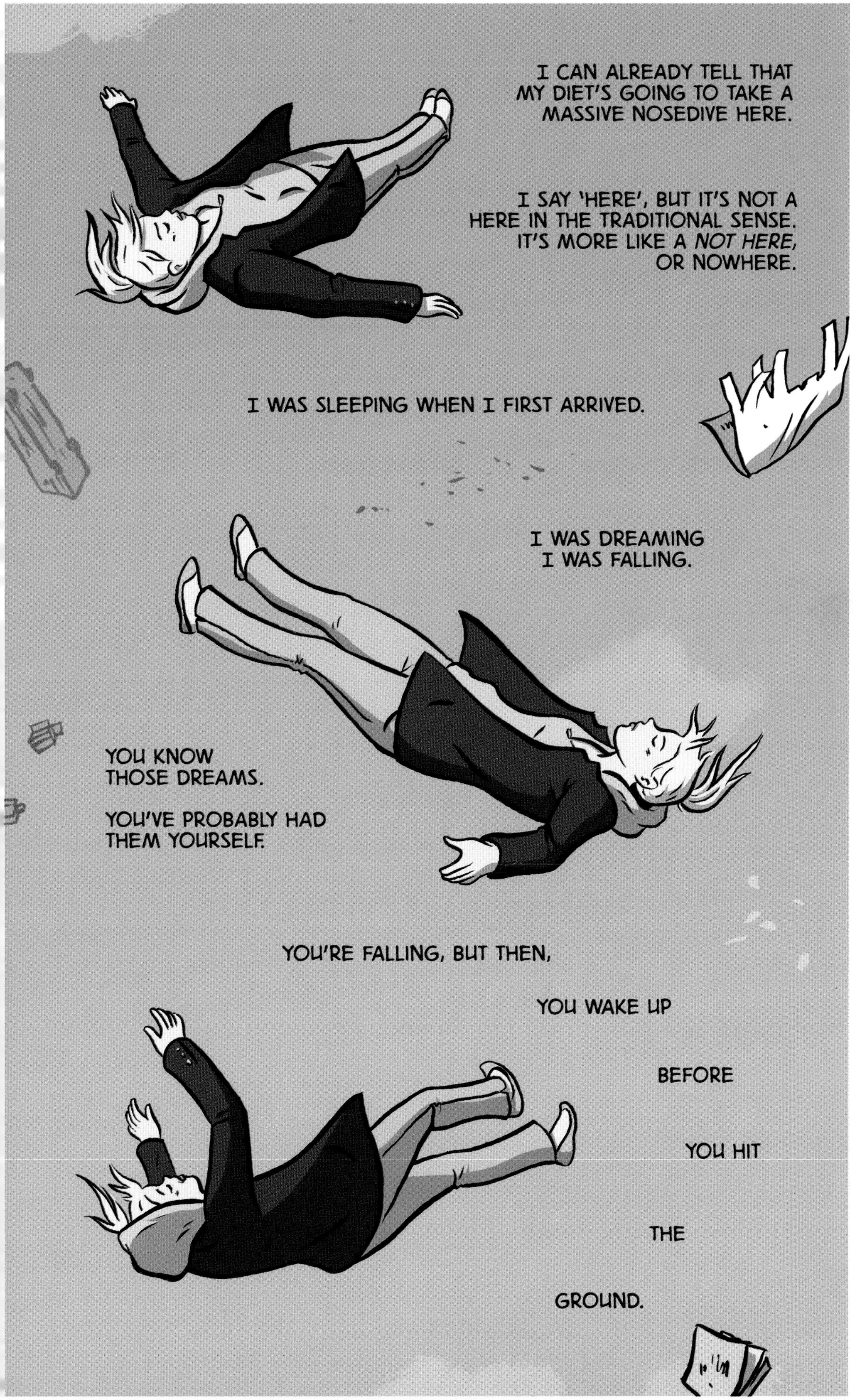
I CAN ALREADY TELL THAT MY DIET'S GOING TO TAKE A MASSIVE NOSEDIVE HERE.
I SAY 'HERE', BUT IT'S NOT A HERE IN THE TRADITIONAL SENSE. IT'S MORE LIKE A *NOT HERE,* OR NOWHERE.
I WAS SLEEPING WHEN I FIRST ARRIVED.
I WAS DREAMING I WAS FALLING.
YOU KNOW THOSE DREAMS.
YOU'VE PROBABLY HAD THEM YOURSELF.
YOU'RE FALLING, BUT THEN,
YOU WAKE UP
BEFORE
YOU HIT
THE
GROUND.

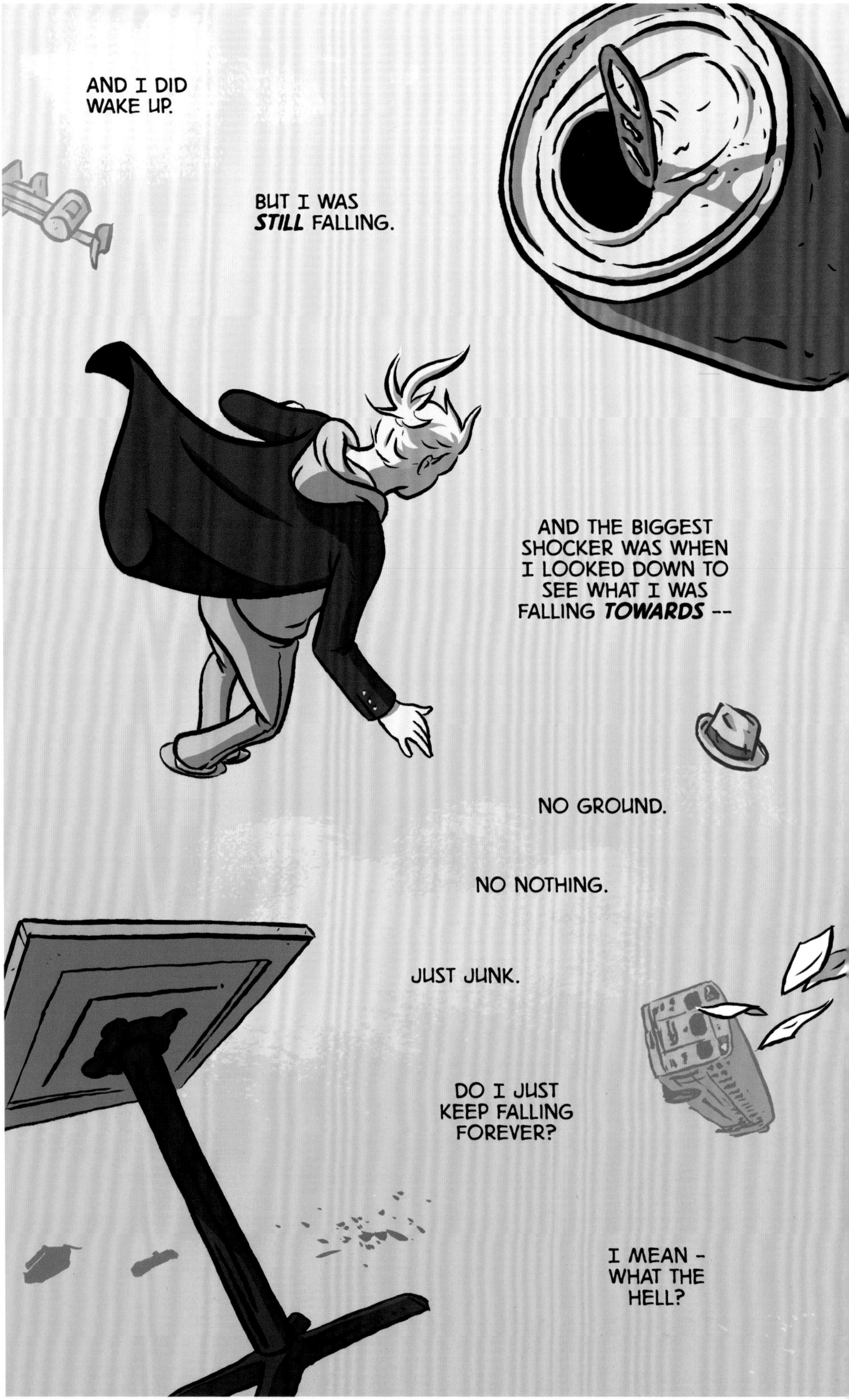
AND I DID WAKE UP.
BUT I WAS *STILL* FALLING.
AND THE BIGGEST SHOCKER WAS WHEN I LOOKED DOWN TO SEE WHAT I WAS FALLING *TOWARDS* --
NO GROUND.
NO NOTHING.
JUST JUNK.
DO I JUST KEEP FALLING FOREVER?
I MEAN - WHAT THE HELL?

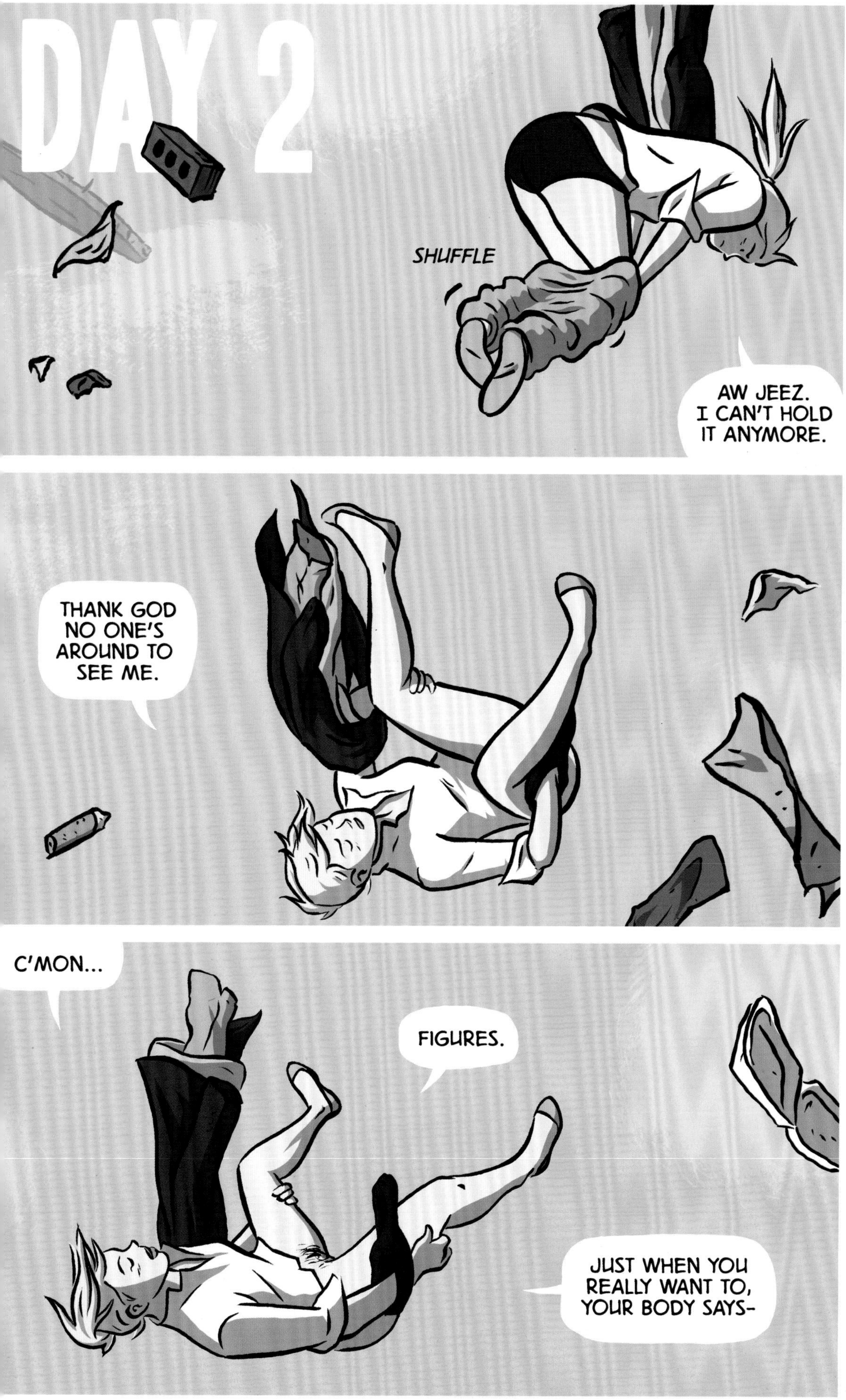
DAY 2
SHUFFLE
AW JEEZ. I CAN'T HOLD IT ANYMORE.
THANK GOD NO ONE'S AROUND TO SEE ME.
C'MON...
FIGURES.
JUST WHEN YOU REALLY WANT TO, YOUR BODY SAYS-

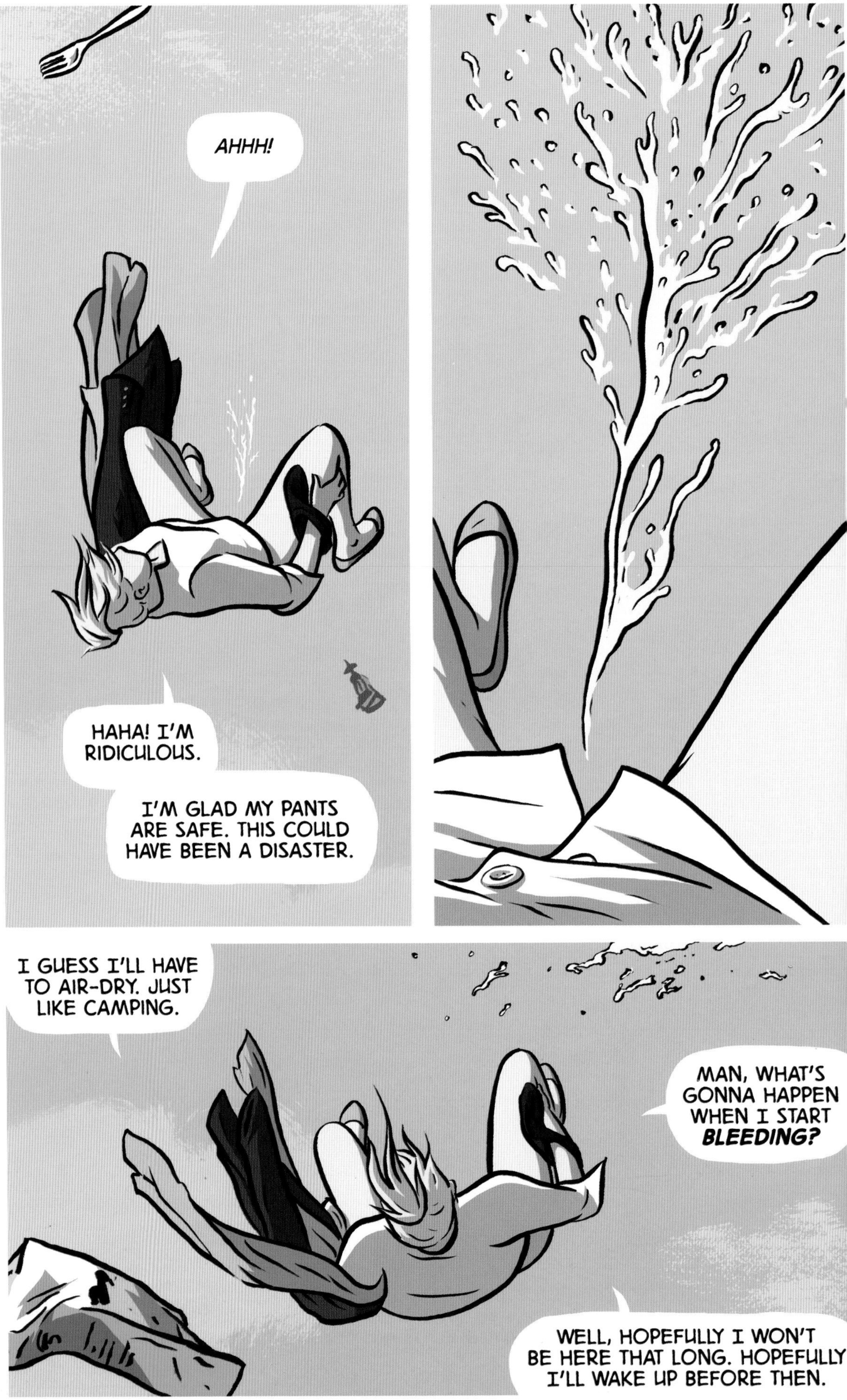
AHHH!
HAHA! I'M RIDICULOUS.
I'M GLAD MY PANTS ARE SAFE. THIS COULD HAVE BEEN A DISASTER.
I GUESS I'LL HAVE TO AIR-DRY. JUST LIKE CAMPING.
MAN, WHAT'S GONNA HAPPEN WHEN I START *BLEEDING?*
WELL, HOPEFULLY I WON'T BE HERE THAT LONG. HOPEFULLY I'LL WAKE UP BEFORE THEN.

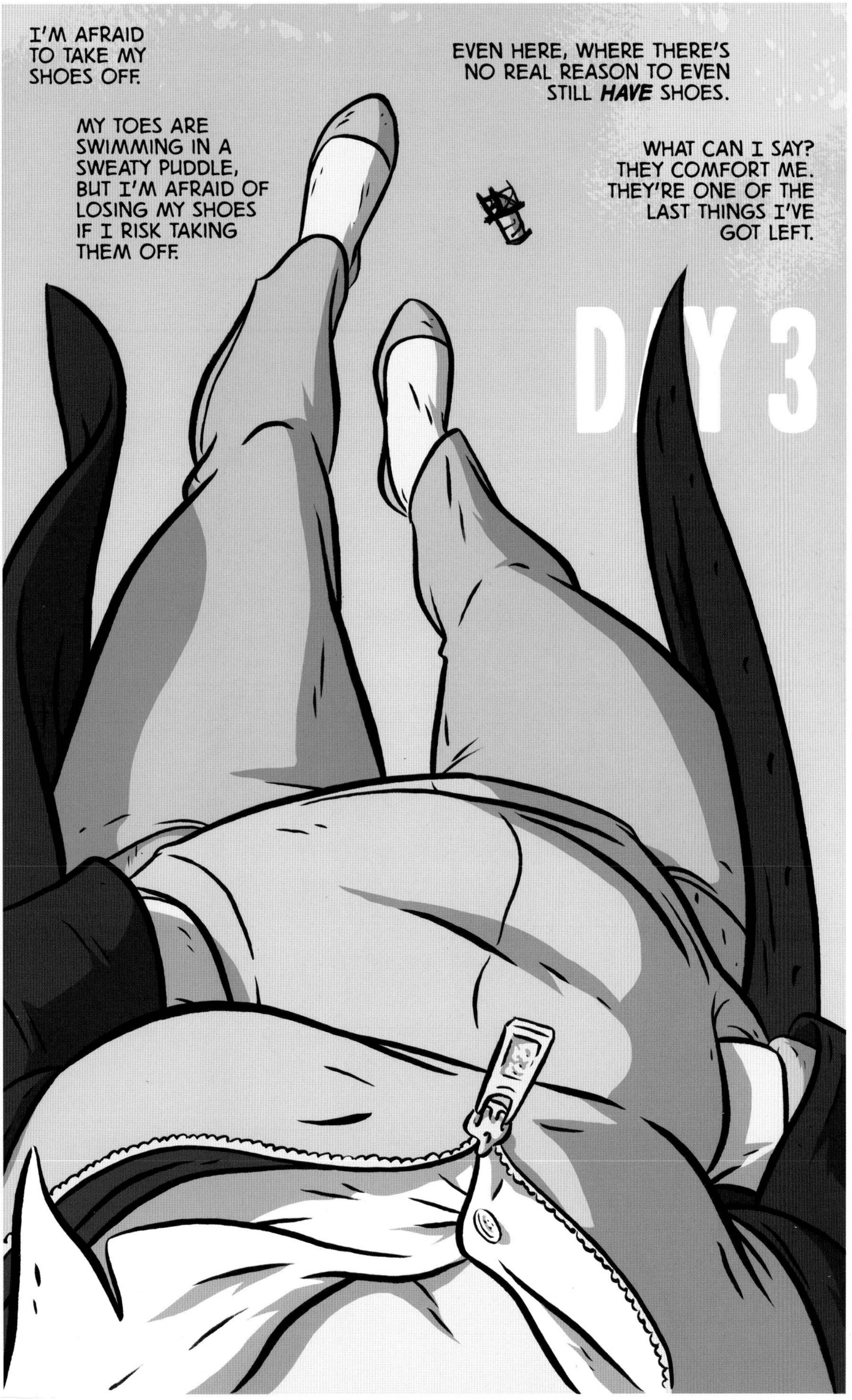
I'M AFRAID TO TAKE MY SHOES OFF.
MY TOES ARE SWIMMING IN A SWEATY PUDDLE, BUT I'M AFRAID OF LOSING MY SHOES IF I RISK TAKING THEM OFF.
EVEN HERE, WHERE THERE'S NO REAL REASON TO EVEN STILL *HAVE* SHOES.
WHAT CAN I SAY? THEY COMFORT ME. THEY'RE ONE OF THE LAST THINGS I'VE GOT LEFT.
DAY 3

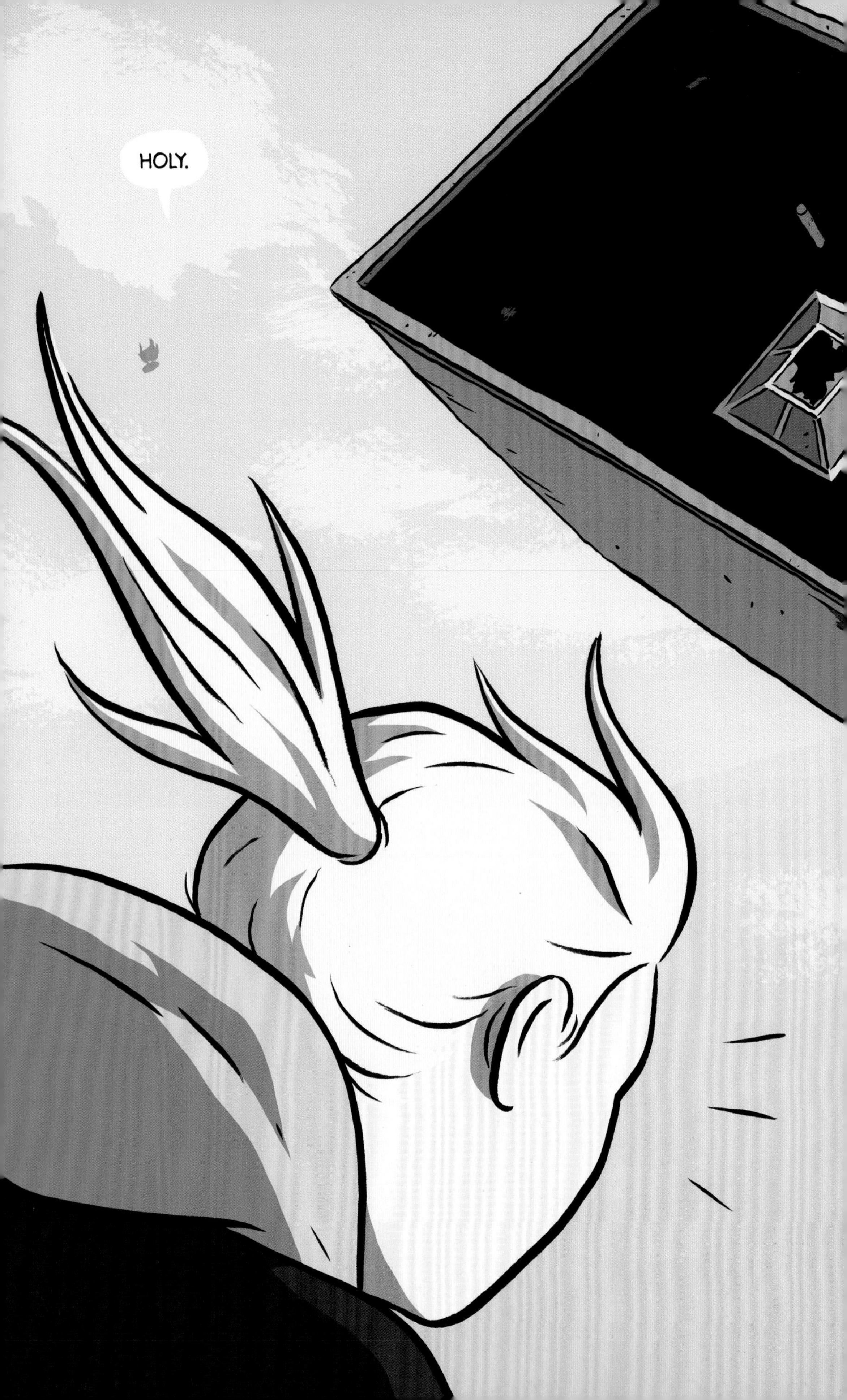
HOLY.

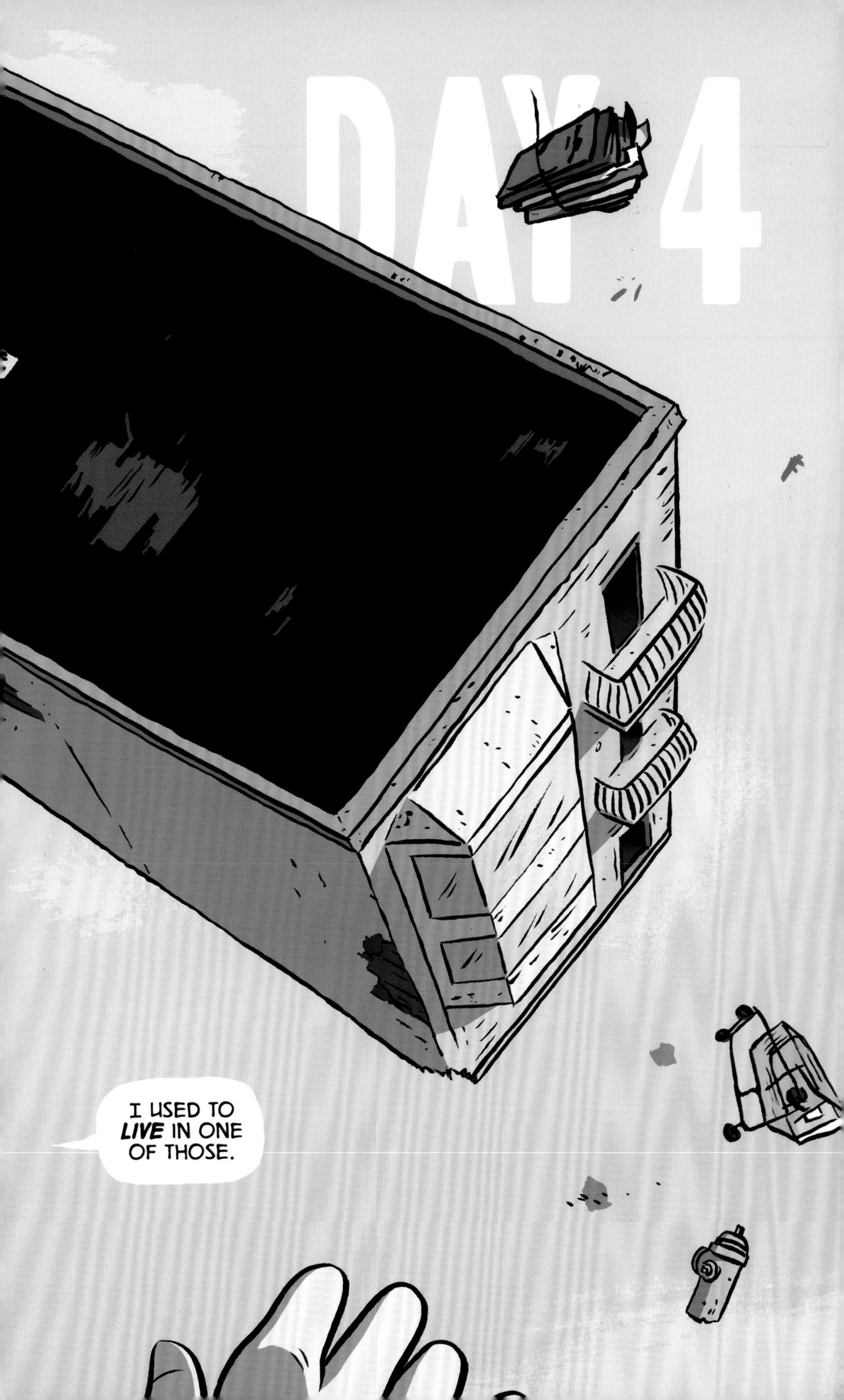
DAY 4
I USED TO *LIVE* IN ONE OF THOSE.

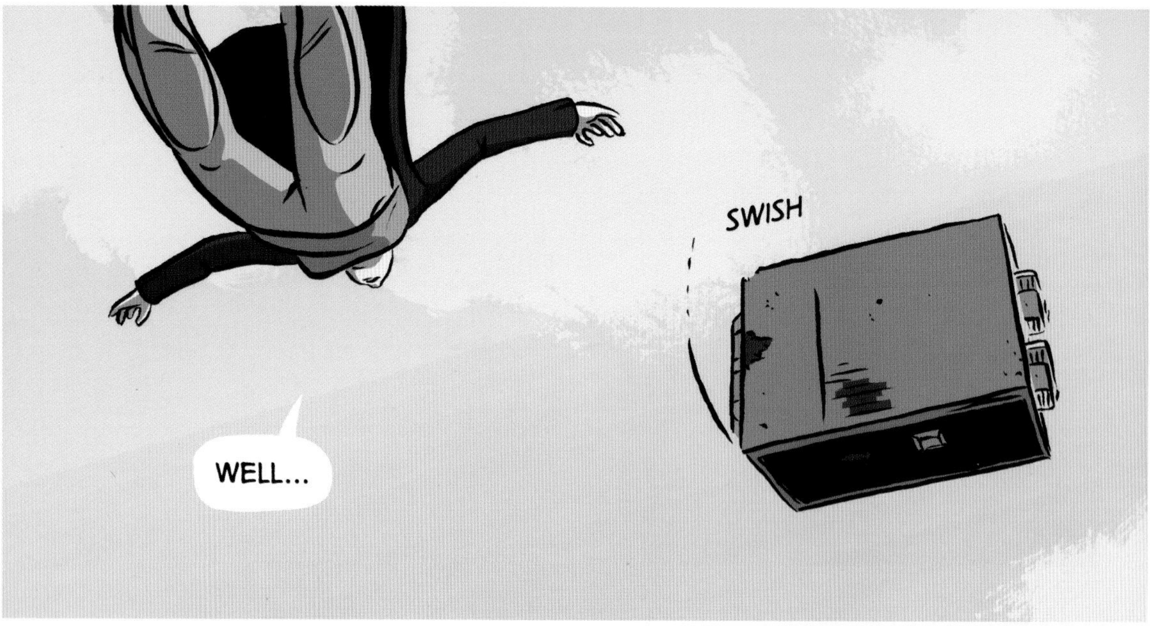
SWISH
WELL...
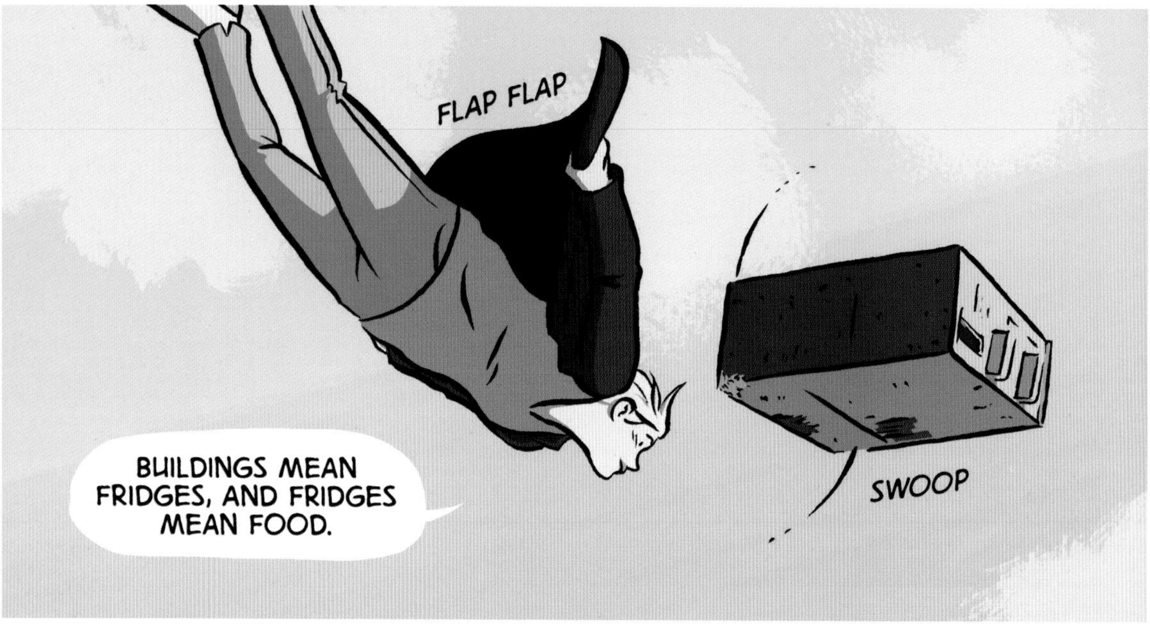
FLAP FLAP
BUILDINGS MEAN FRIDGES, AND FRIDGES MEAN FOOD.
SWOOP
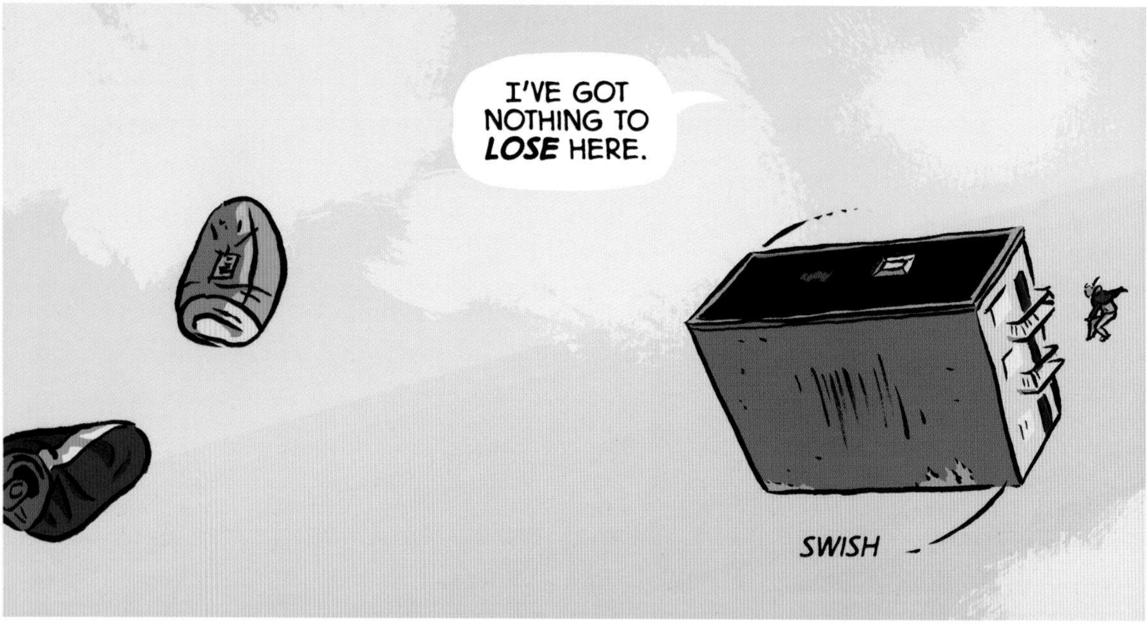
I'VE GOT NOTHING TO LOSE HERE.
SWISH

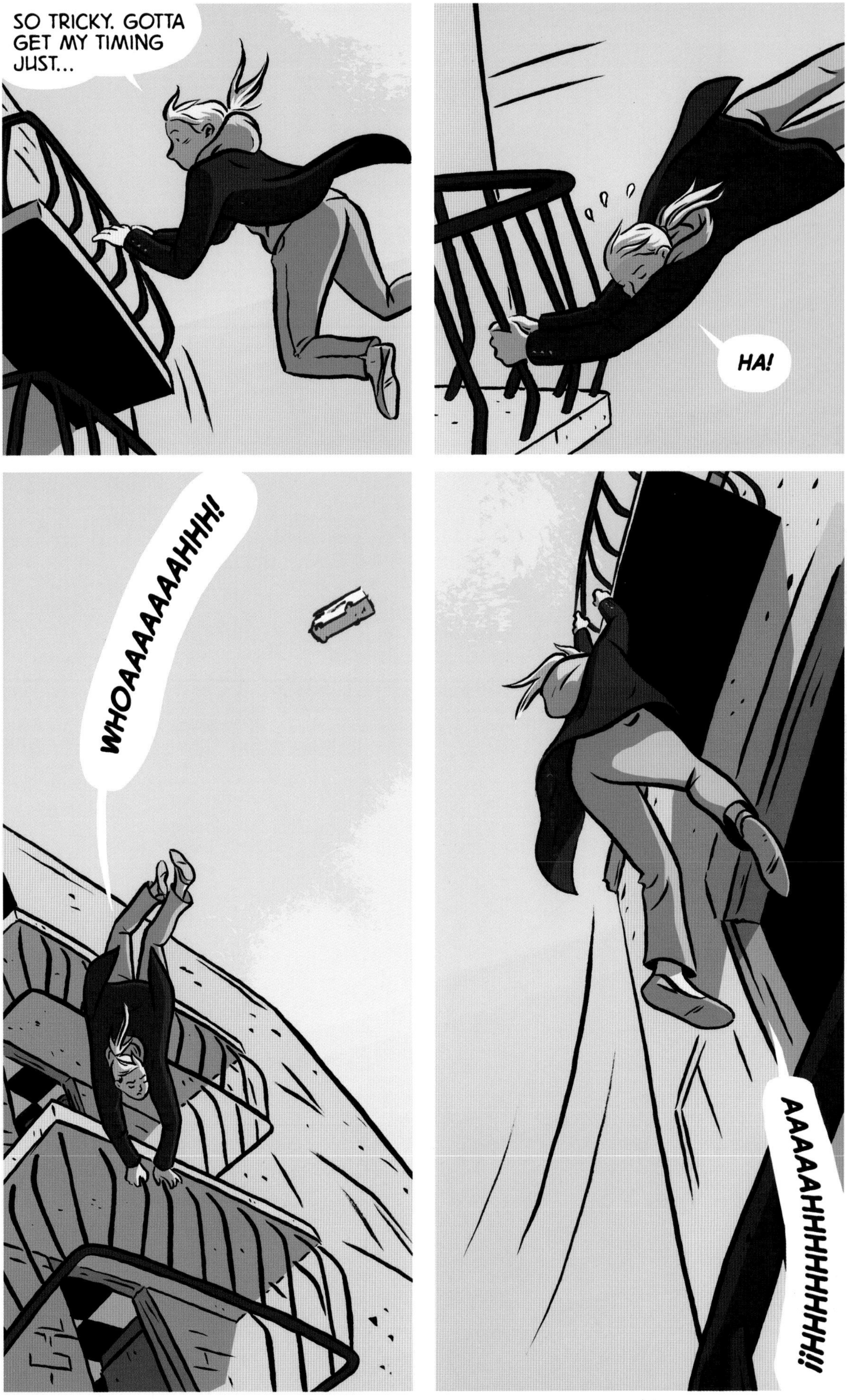
SO TRICKY. GOTTA GET MY TIMING JUST...
HA!
WHOAAAAAAAHHH!
AAAAAAHHHHHHHH!!!

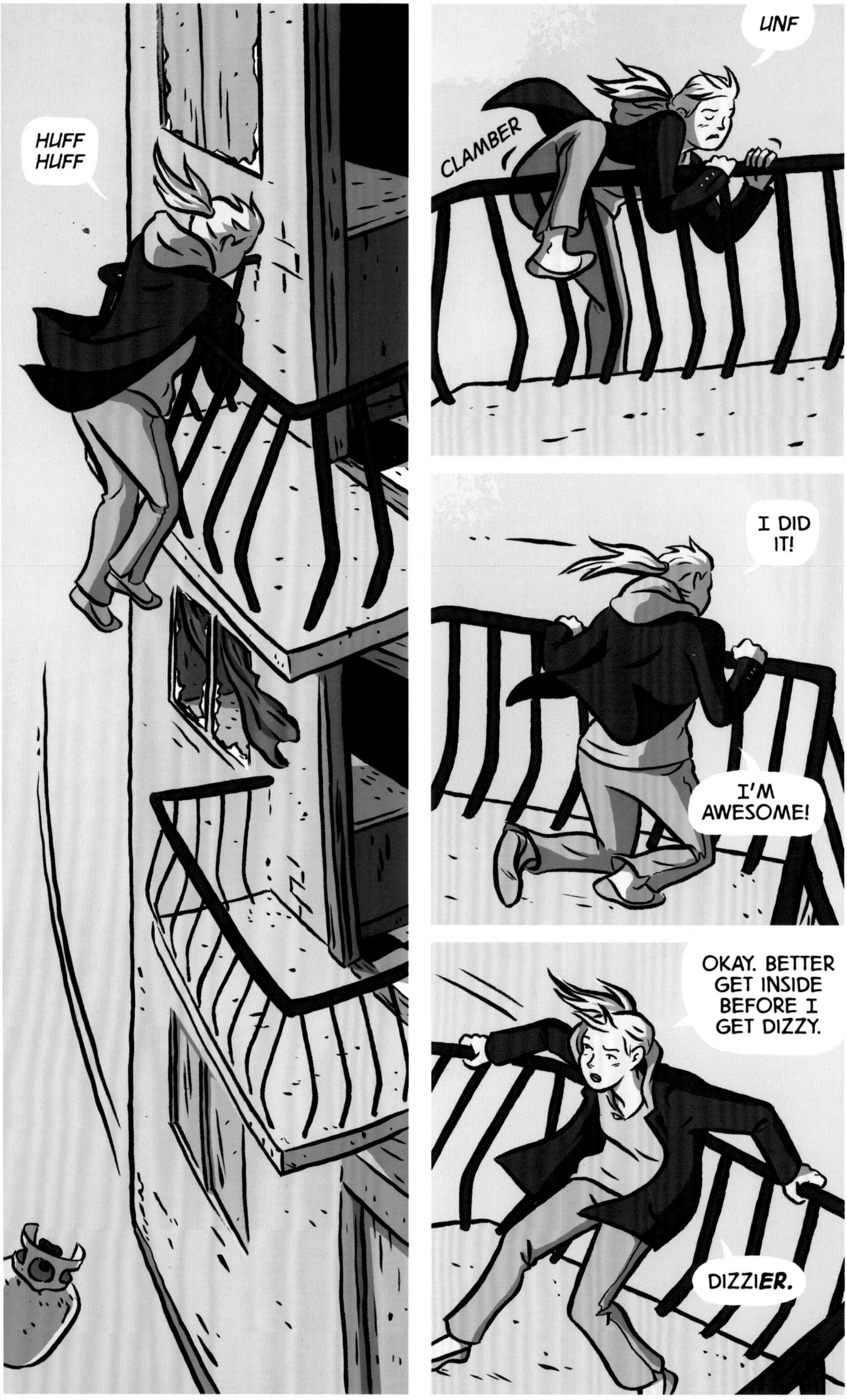
HUFF HUFF
UNF
CLAMBER
I DID IT!
I'M AWESOME!
OKAY. BETTER GET INSIDE BEFORE I GET DIZZY.
DIZZIER.

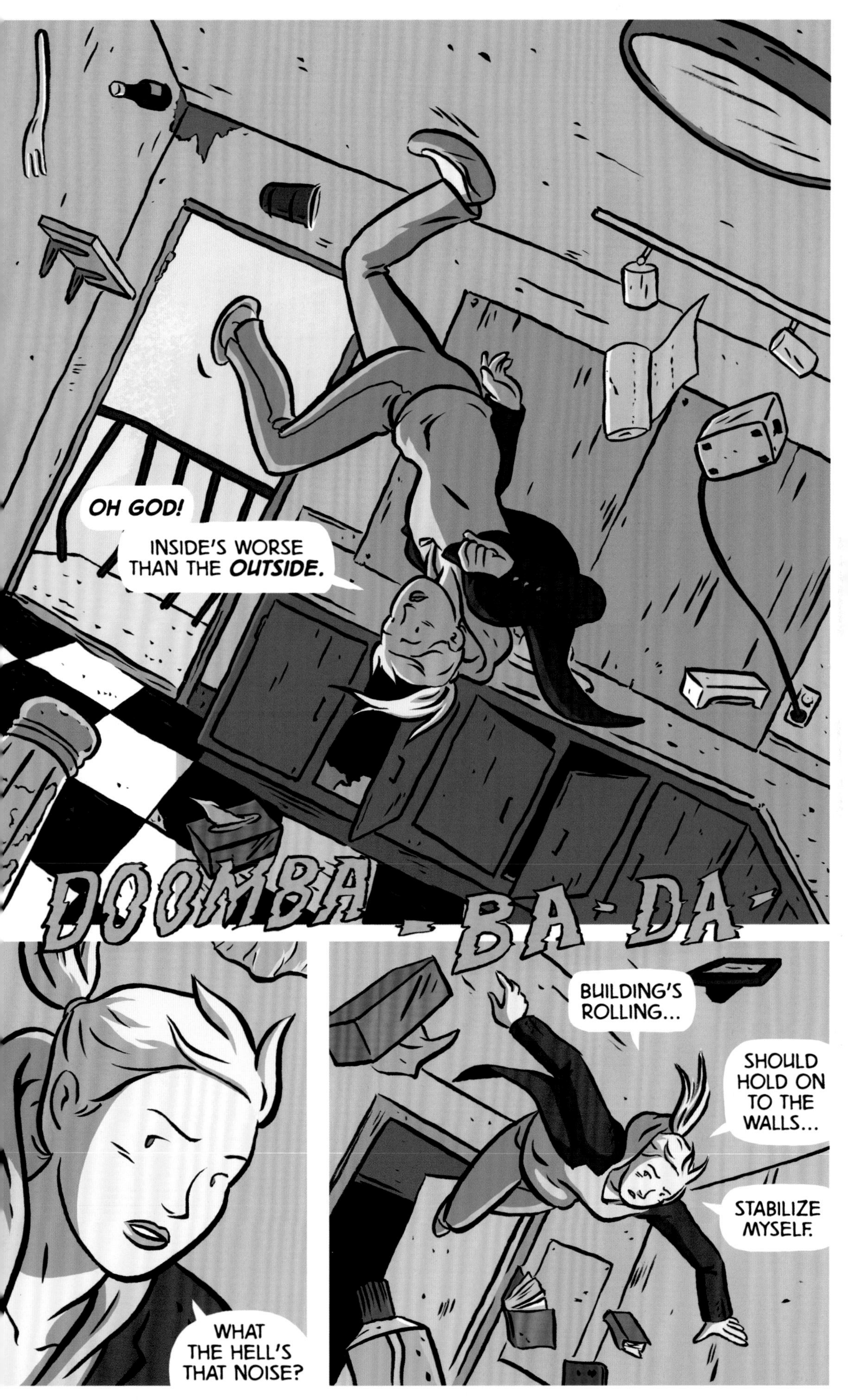
OH GOD!
INSIDE'S WORSE THAN THE *OUTSIDE.*
DOOMBA - BA - DA -
WHAT THE HELL'S THAT NOISE?
BUILDING'S ROLLING...
SHOULD HOLD ON TO THE WALLS...
STABILIZE MYSELF.

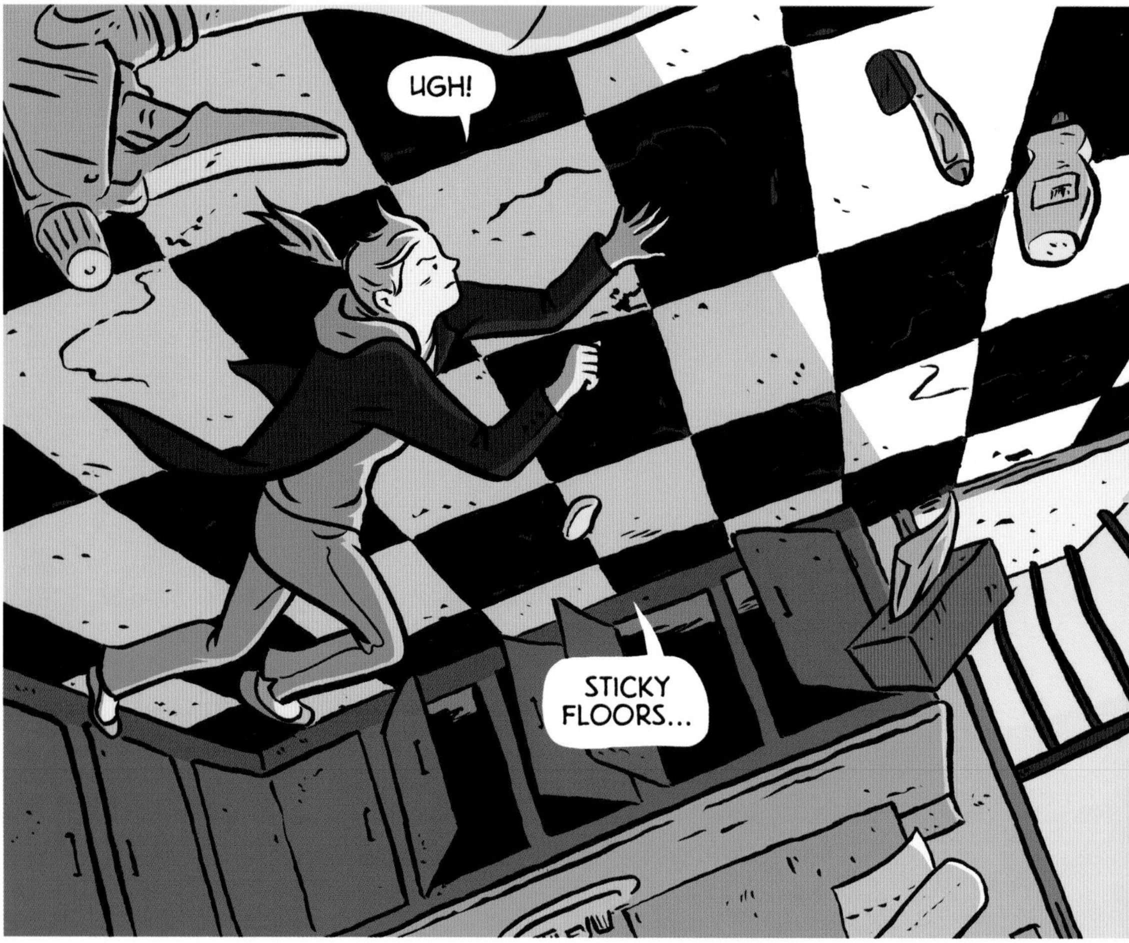
UGH!
STICKY FLOORS...

THIS WHOLE TIME I'M GETTING MORE AND MORE NAUSEOUS. MY ADVICE: DON'T EVER HANG OUT IN A SOMERSAULTING TRIPLEX IF YOU CAN POSSIBLY HELP IT.

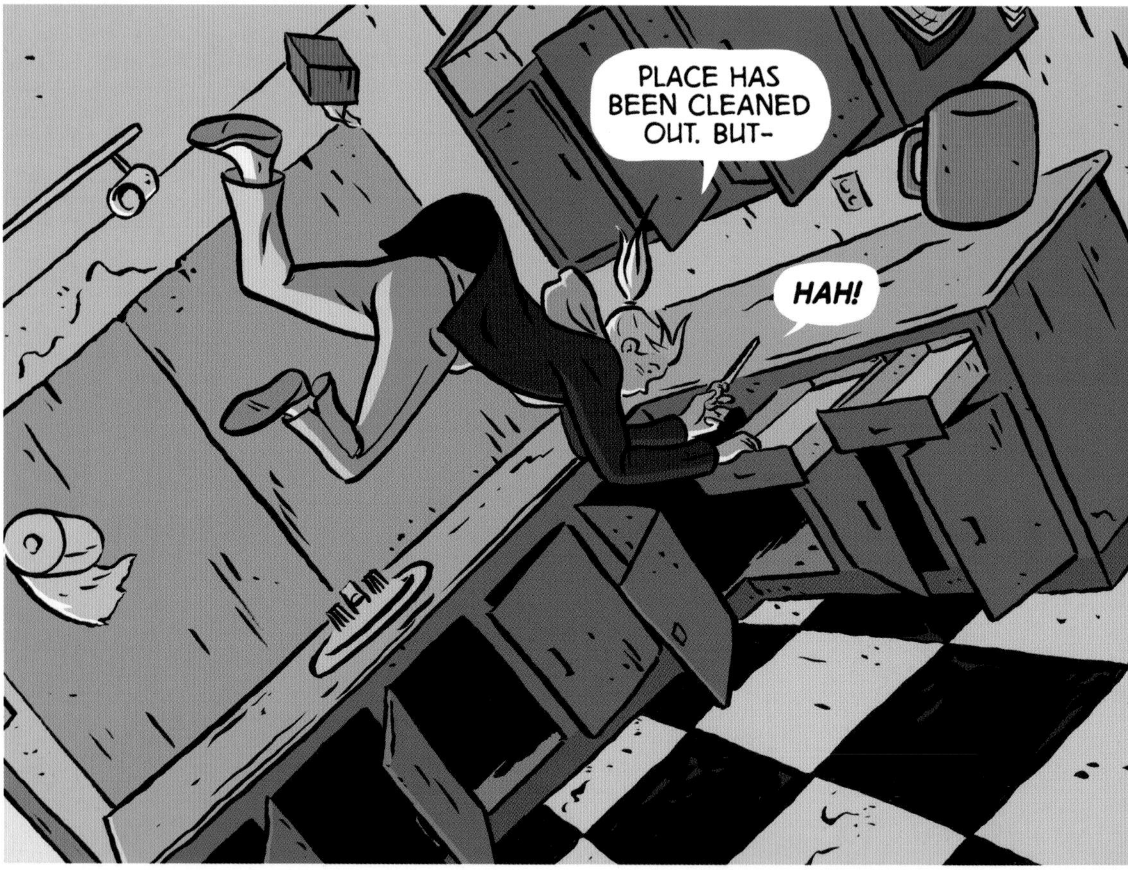
PLACE HAS BEEN CLEANED OUT. BUT-
HAH!

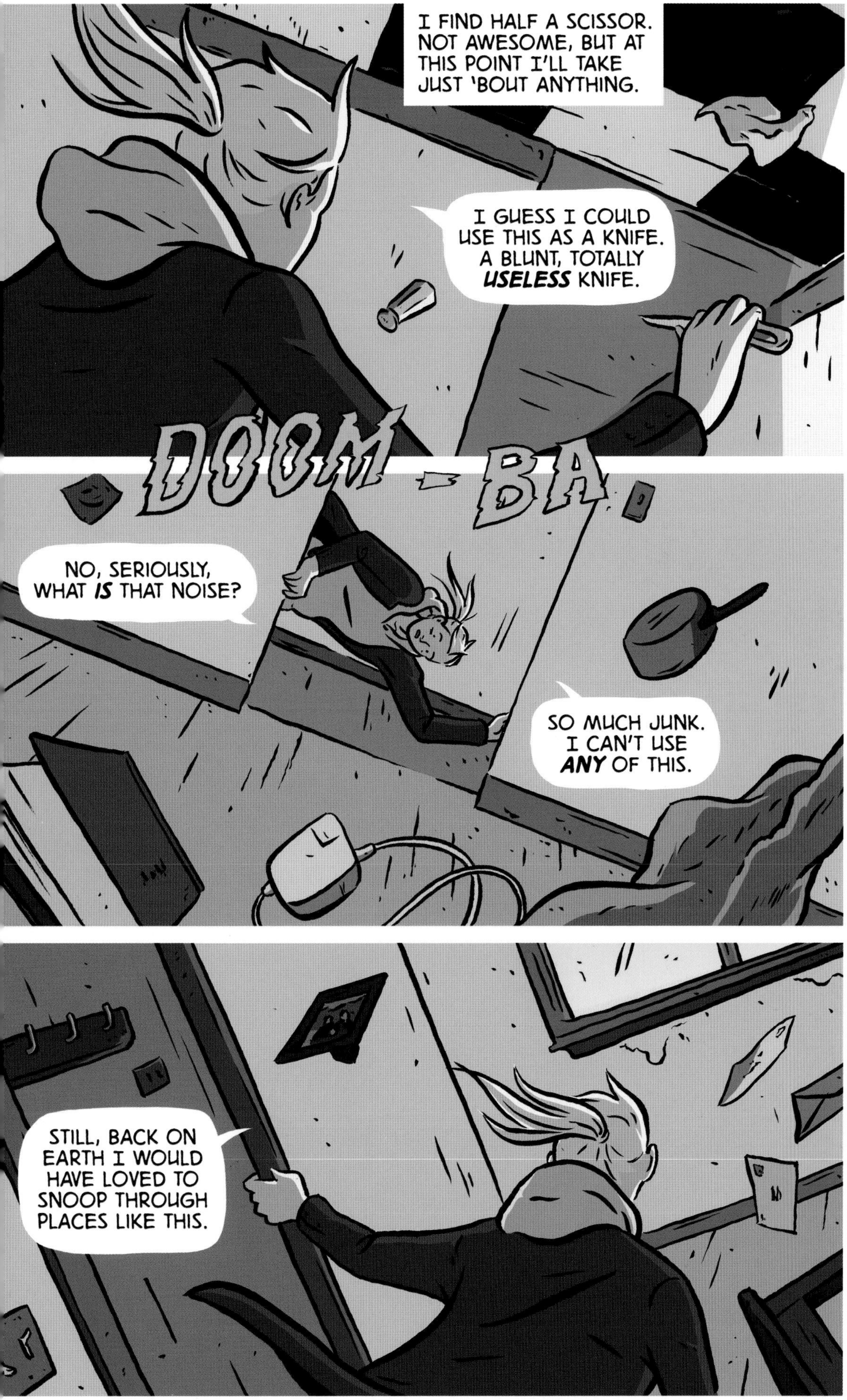
I FIND HALF A SCISSOR. NOT AWESOME, BUT AT THIS POINT I'LL TAKE JUST 'BOUT ANYTHING.
I GUESS I COULD USE THIS AS A KNIFE. A BLUNT, TOTALLY ***USELESS*** KNIFE.
DOOM-BA
NO, SERIOUSLY, WHAT ***IS*** THAT NOISE?
SO MUCH JUNK. I CAN'T USE ***ANY*** OF THIS.
STILL, BACK ON EARTH I WOULD HAVE LOVED TO SNOOP THROUGH PLACES LIKE THIS.

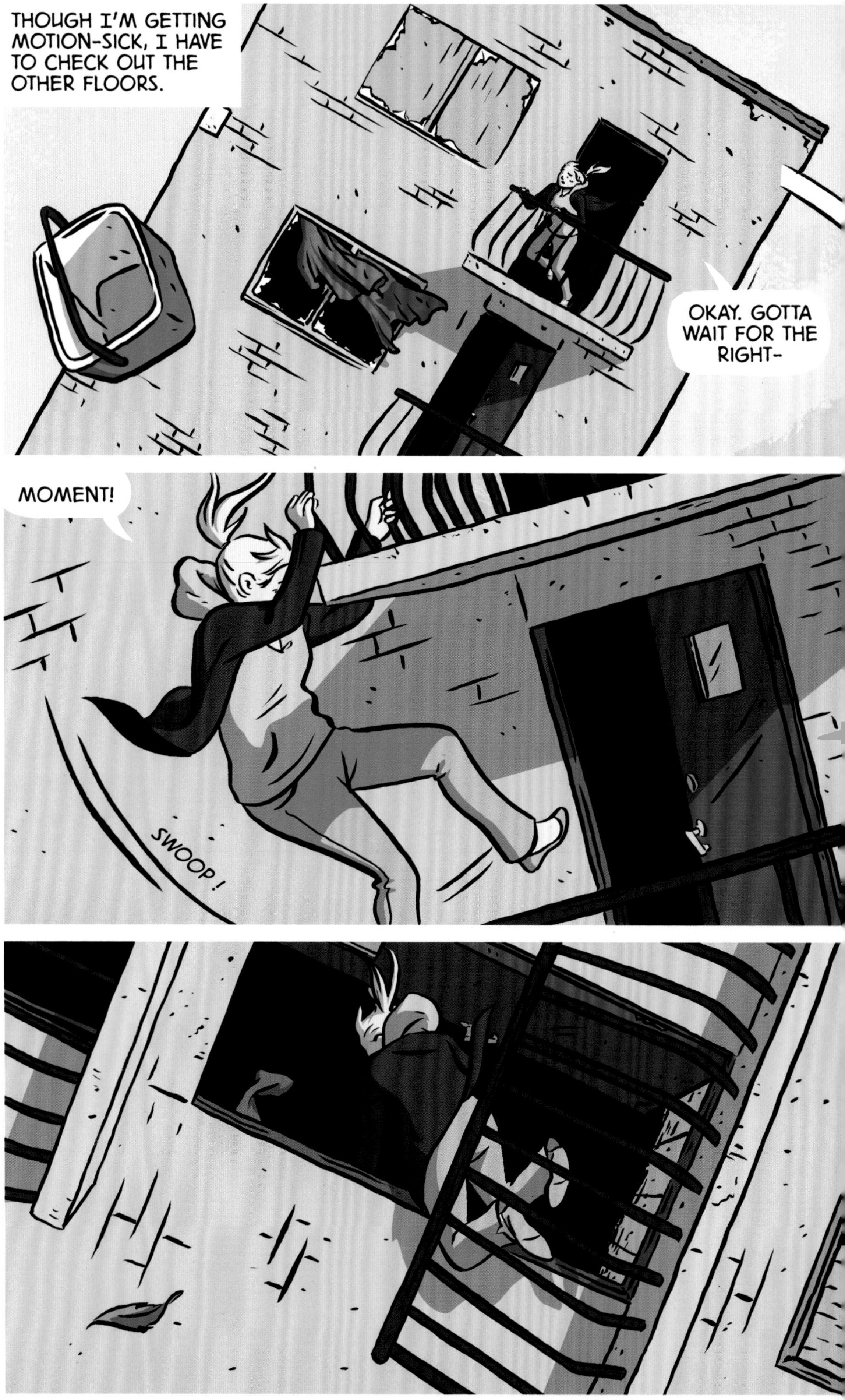
THOUGH I'M GETTING MOTION-SICK, I HAVE TO CHECK OUT THE OTHER FLOORS.
OKAY. GOTTA WAIT FOR THE RIGHT-
MOMENT!
SWOOP!

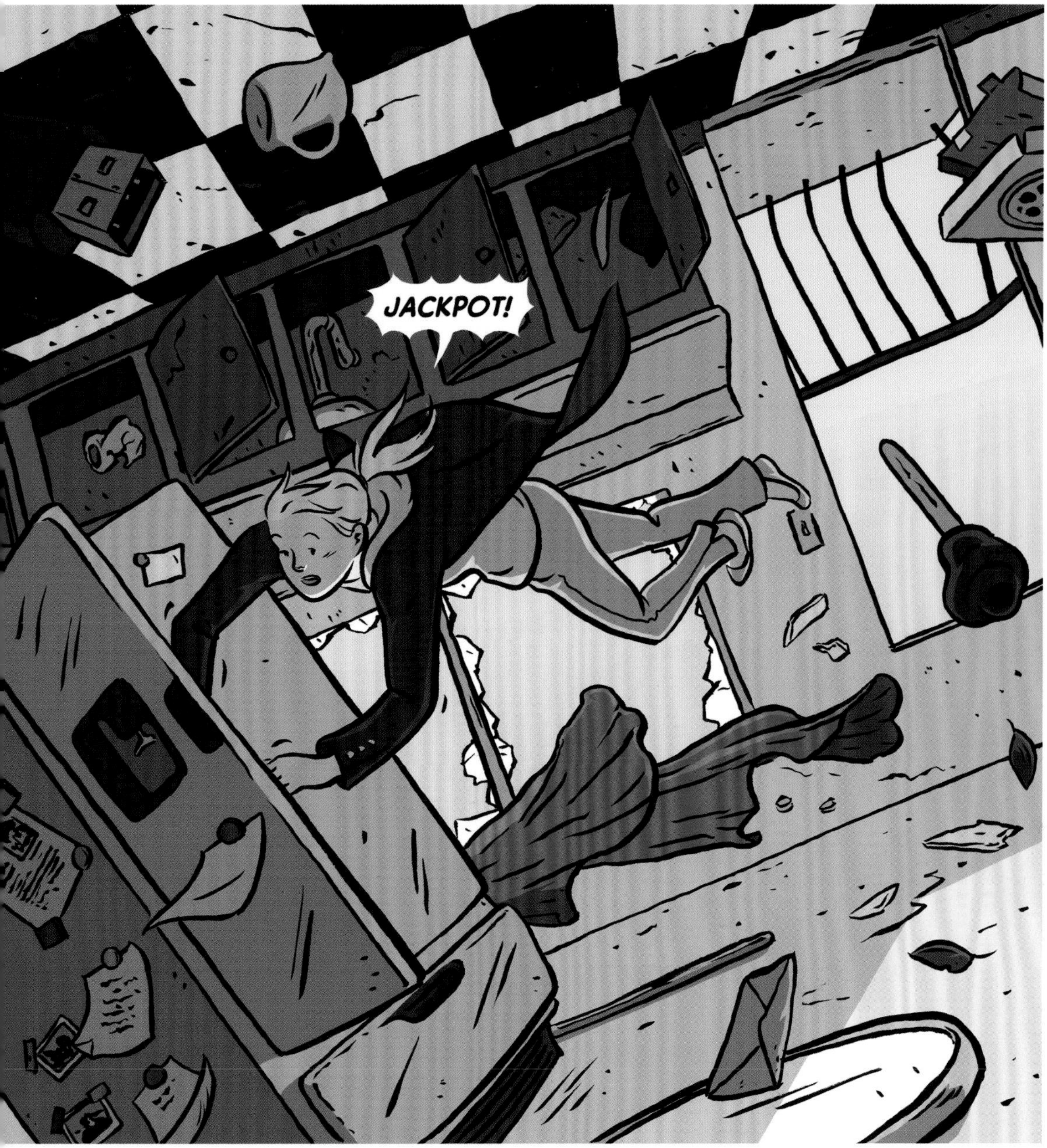
JACKPOT!

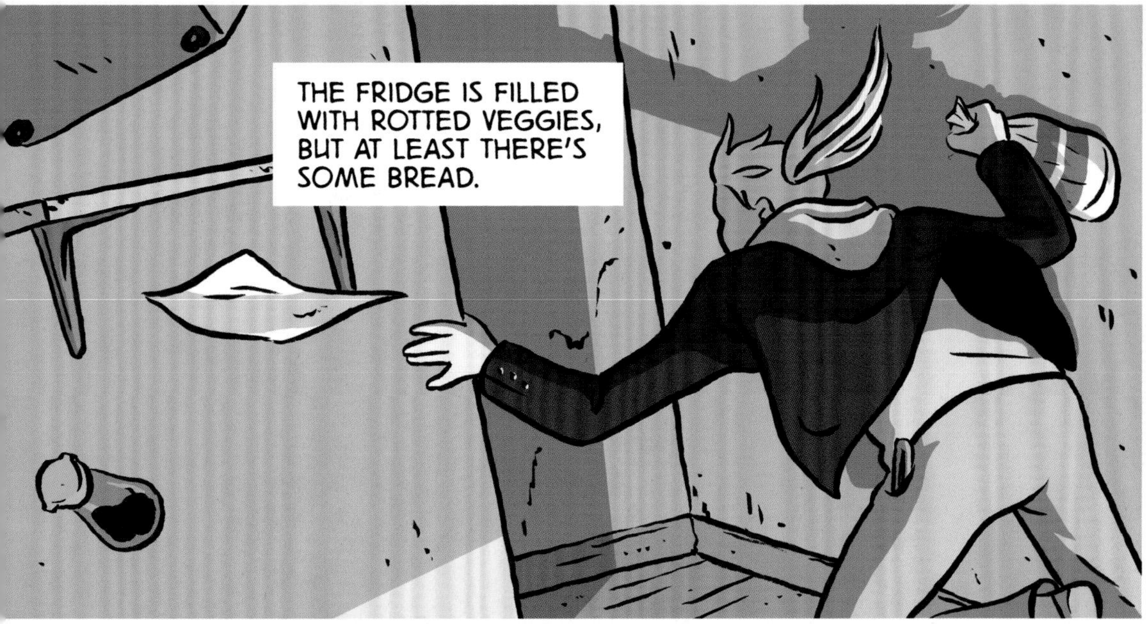
THE FRIDGE IS FILLED
WITH ROTTED VEGGIES,
BUT AT LEAST THERE'S
SOME BREAD.

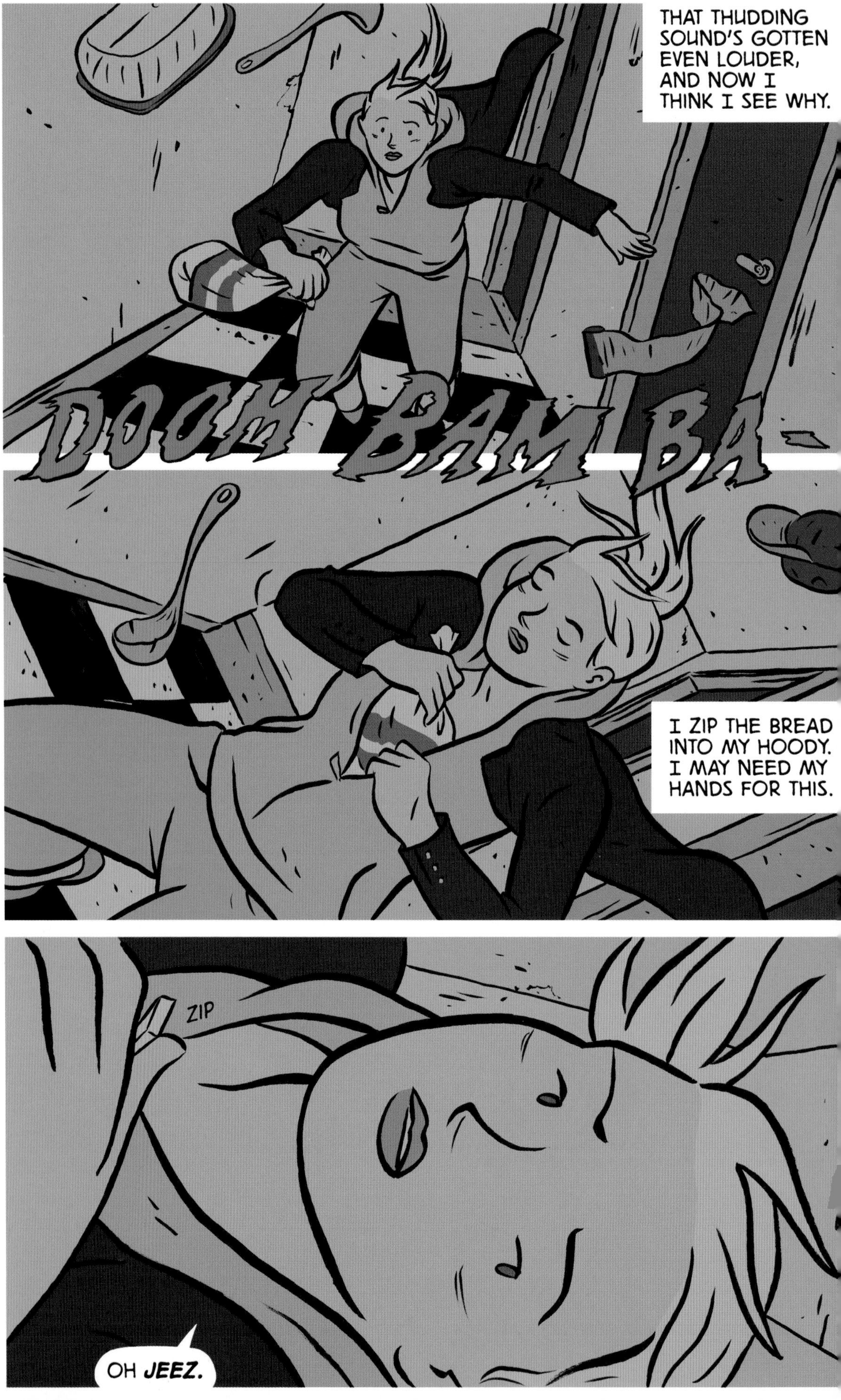
THAT THUDDING SOUND'S GOTTEN EVEN LOUDER, AND NOW I THINK I SEE WHY.
DOOM BAM BA-
I ZIP THE BREAD INTO MY HOODY. I MAY NEED MY HANDS FOR THIS.
ZIP
OH JEEZ.

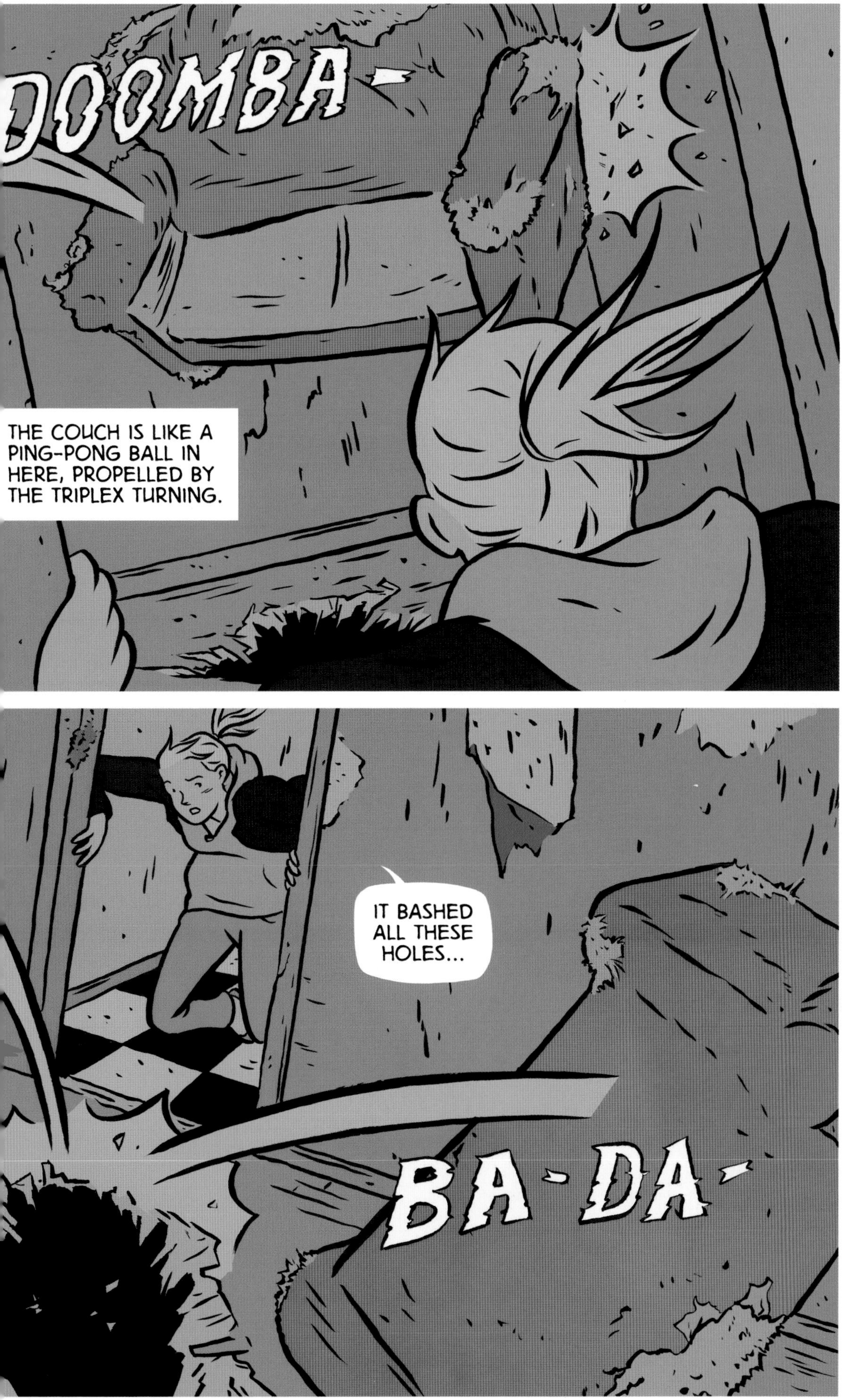
DOOMBA-
THE COUCH IS LIKE A PING-PONG BALL IN HERE, PROPELLED BY THE TRIPLEX TURNING.
IT BASHED ALL THESE HOLES...
BA-DA-

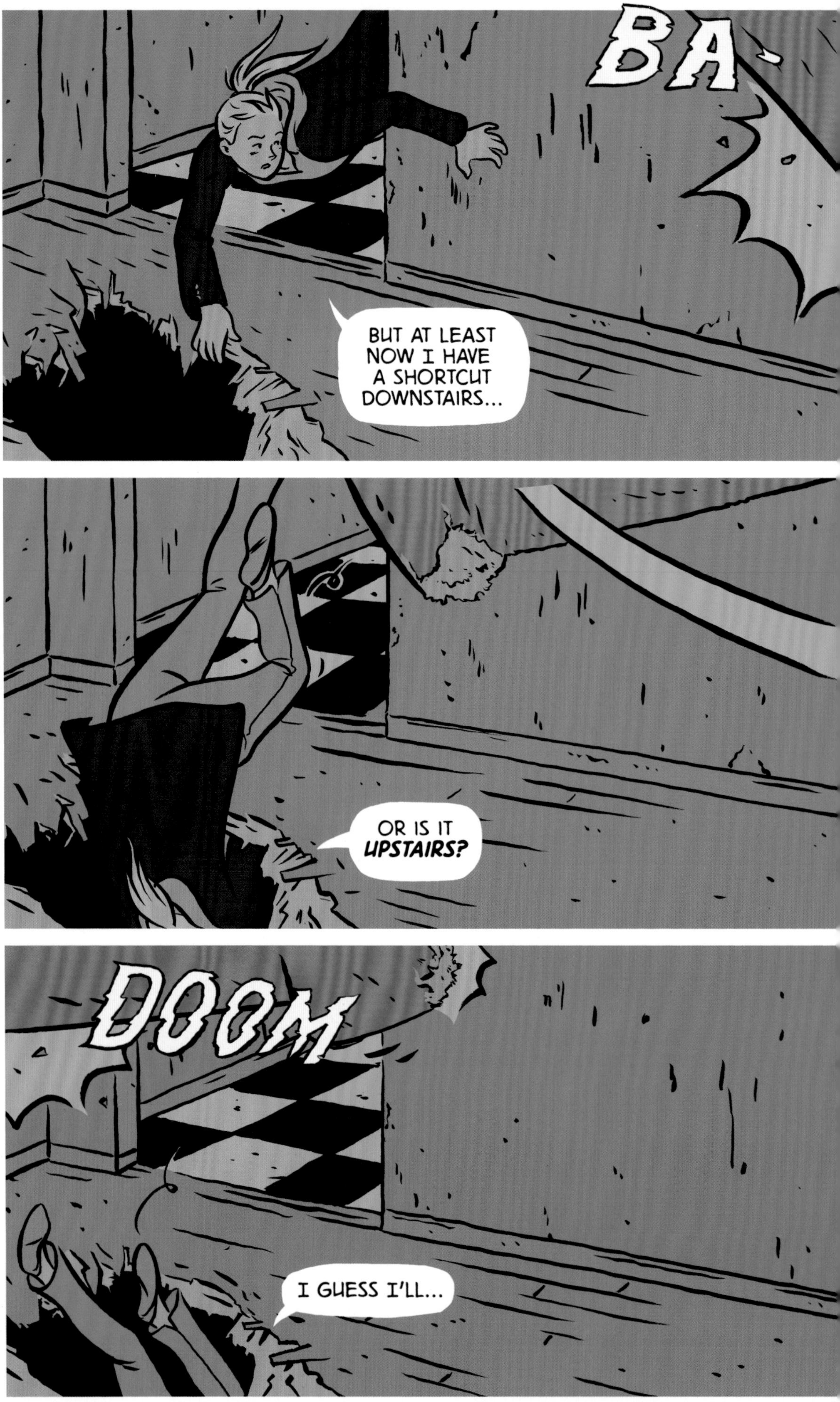
BA-
BUT AT LEAST NOW I HAVE A SHORTCUT DOWNSTAIRS...
OR IS IT ***UPSTAIRS?***
DOOM
I GUESS I'LL...

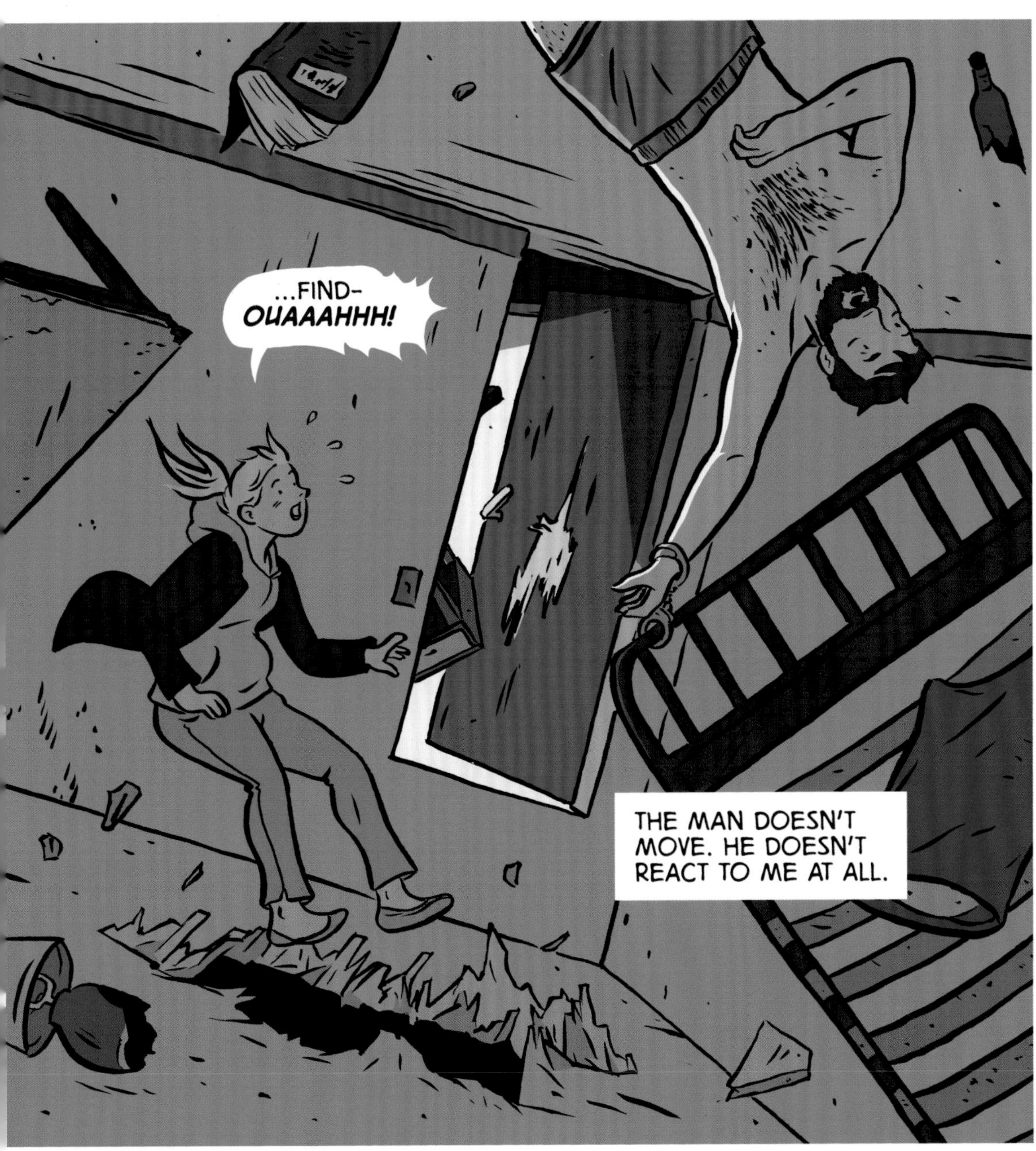
...FIND-
OUAAAHHH!
THE MAN DOESN'T MOVE. HE DOESN'T REACT TO ME AT ALL.
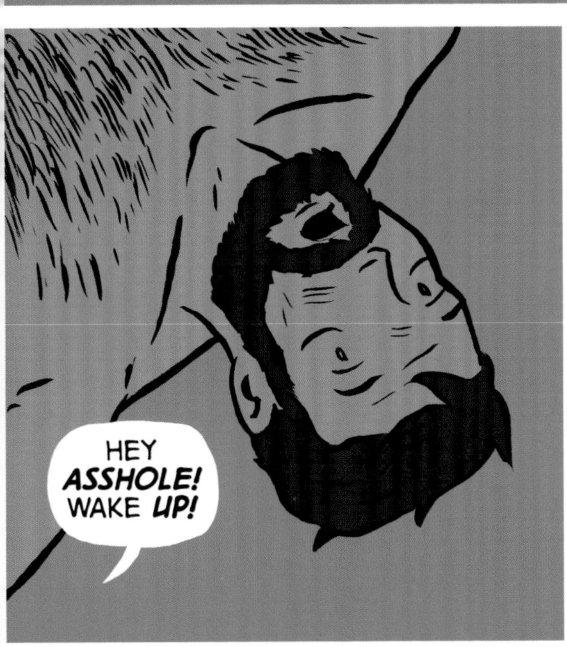
HEY ASSHOLE! WAKE UP!
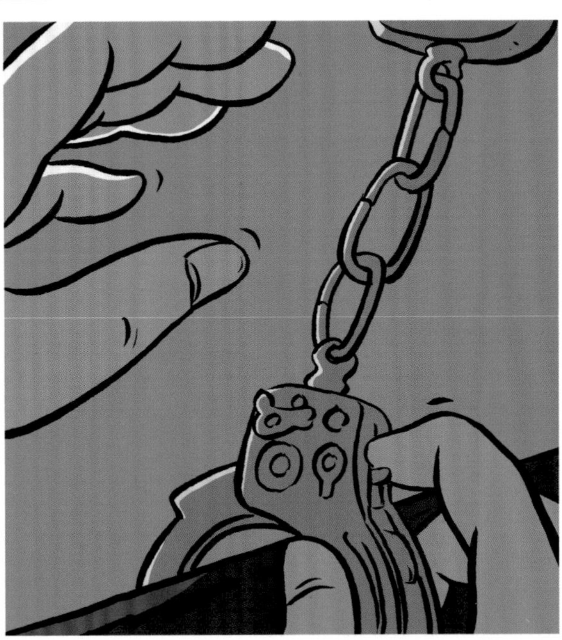

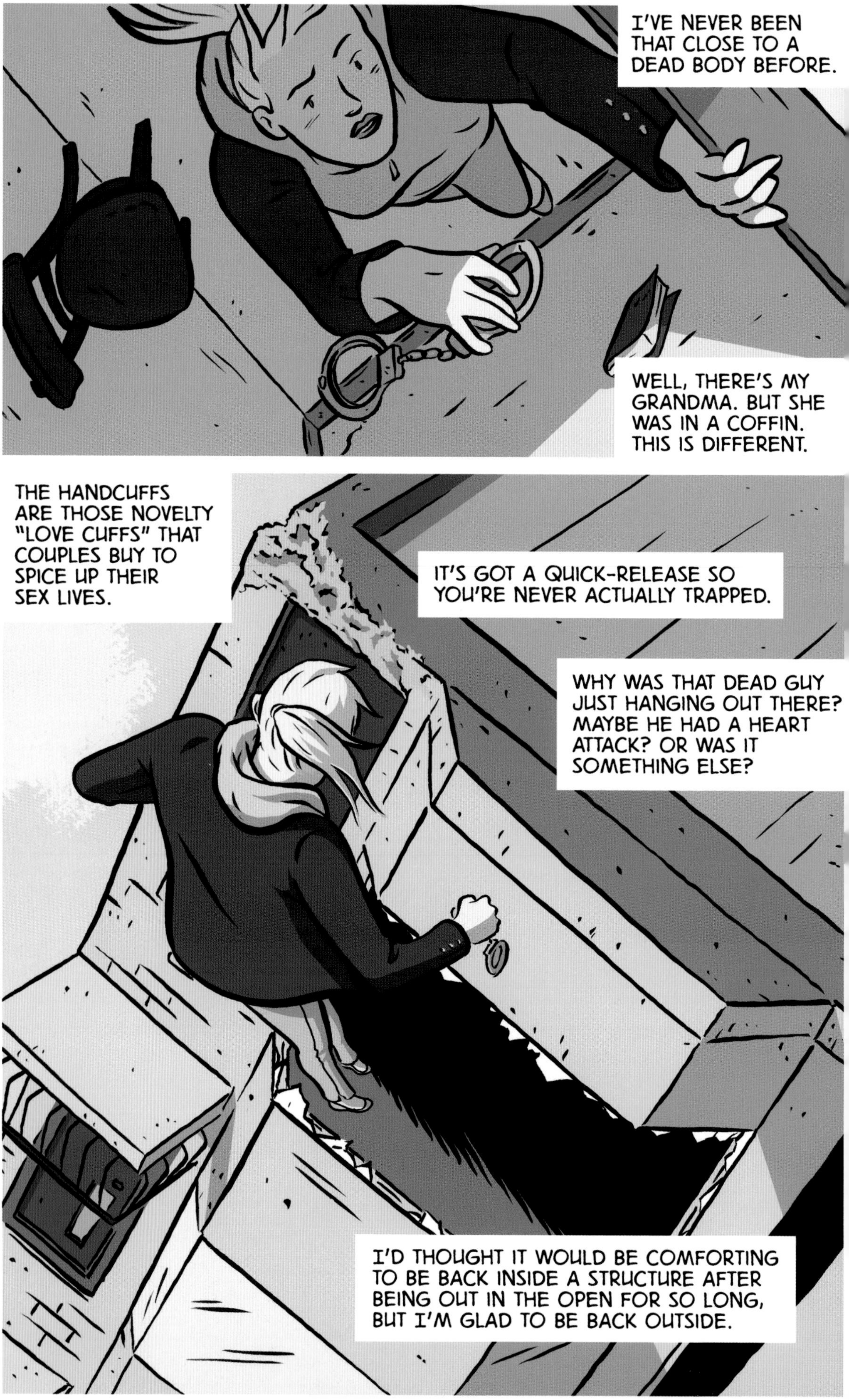
I'VE NEVER BEEN THAT CLOSE TO A DEAD BODY BEFORE.
WELL, THERE'S MY GRANDMA. BUT SHE WAS IN A COFFIN. THIS IS DIFFERENT.
THE HANDCUFFS ARE THOSE NOVELTY "LOVE CUFFS" THAT COUPLES BUY TO SPICE UP THEIR SEX LIVES.
IT'S GOT A QUICK-RELEASE SO YOU'RE NEVER ACTUALLY TRAPPED.
WHY WAS THAT DEAD GUY JUST HANGING OUT THERE? MAYBE HE HAD A HEART ATTACK? OR WAS IT SOMETHING ELSE?
I'D THOUGHT IT WOULD BE COMFORTING TO BE BACK INSIDE A STRUCTURE AFTER BEING OUT IN THE OPEN FOR SO LONG, BUT I'M GLAD TO BE BACK OUTSIDE.

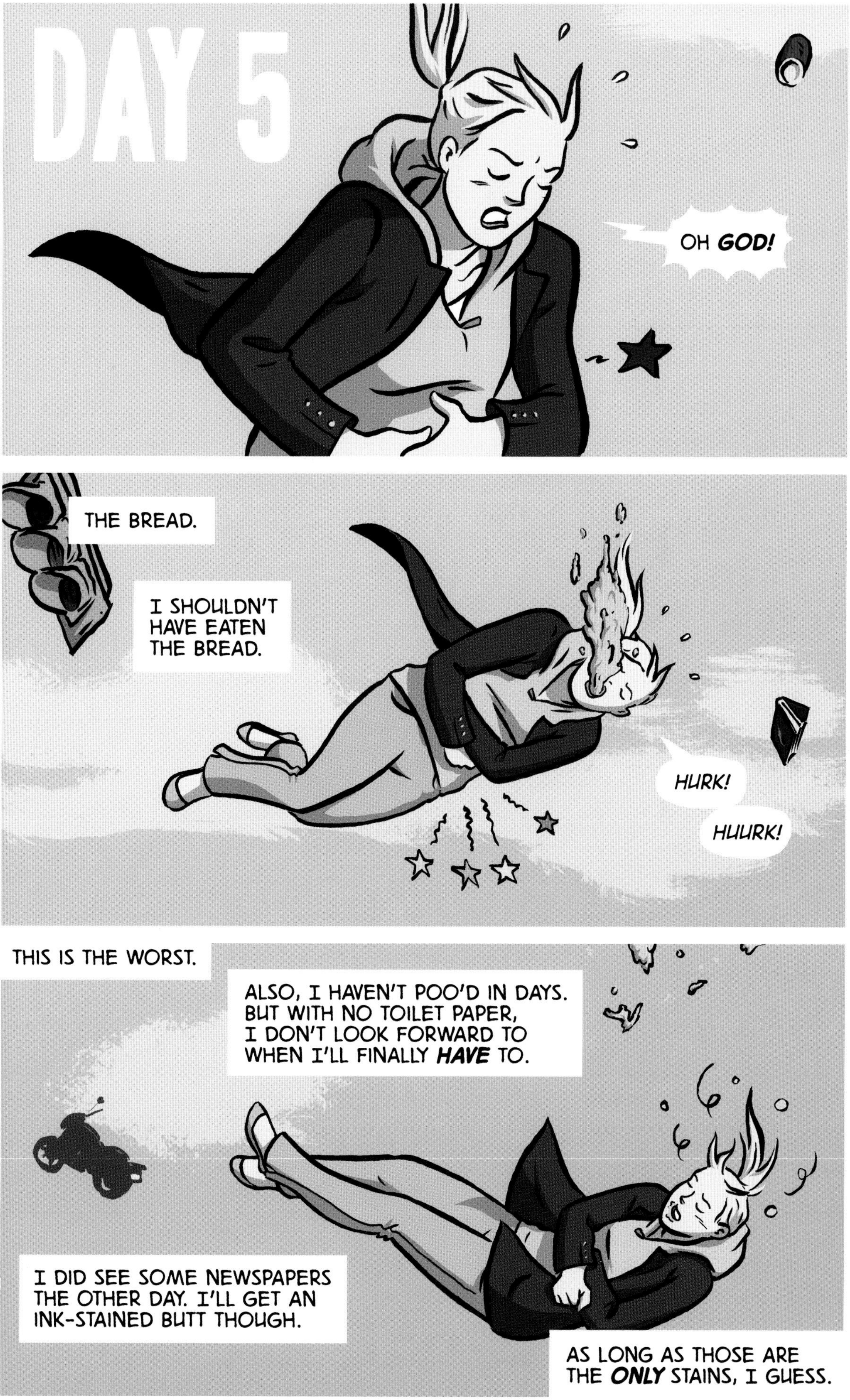
DAY 5
OH GOD!
THE BREAD.
I SHOULDN'T HAVE EATEN THE BREAD.
HURK!
HUURK!
THIS IS THE WORST.
ALSO, I HAVEN'T POO'D IN DAYS. BUT WITH NO TOILET PAPER, I DON'T LOOK FORWARD TO WHEN I'LL FINALLY *HAVE* TO.
I DID SEE SOME NEWSPAPERS THE OTHER DAY. I'LL GET AN INK-STAINED BUTT THOUGH.
AS LONG AS THOSE ARE THE *ONLY* STAINS, I GUESS.

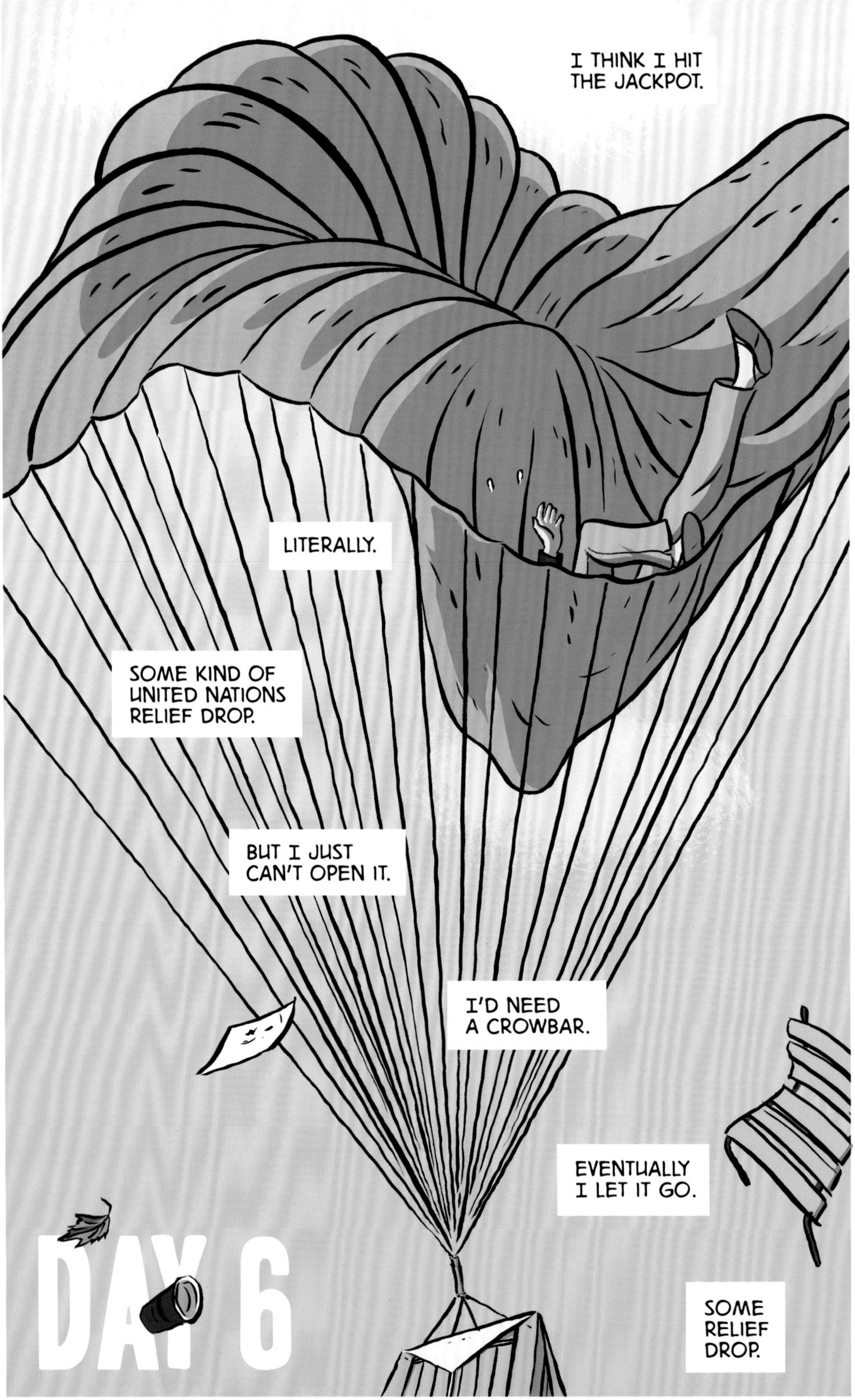
I THINK I HIT THE JACKPOT.
LITERALLY.
SOME KIND OF UNITED NATIONS RELIEF DROP.
BUT I JUST CAN'T OPEN IT.
I'D NEED A CROWBAR.
EVENTUALLY I LET IT GO.
DAY 6
SOME RELIEF DROP.

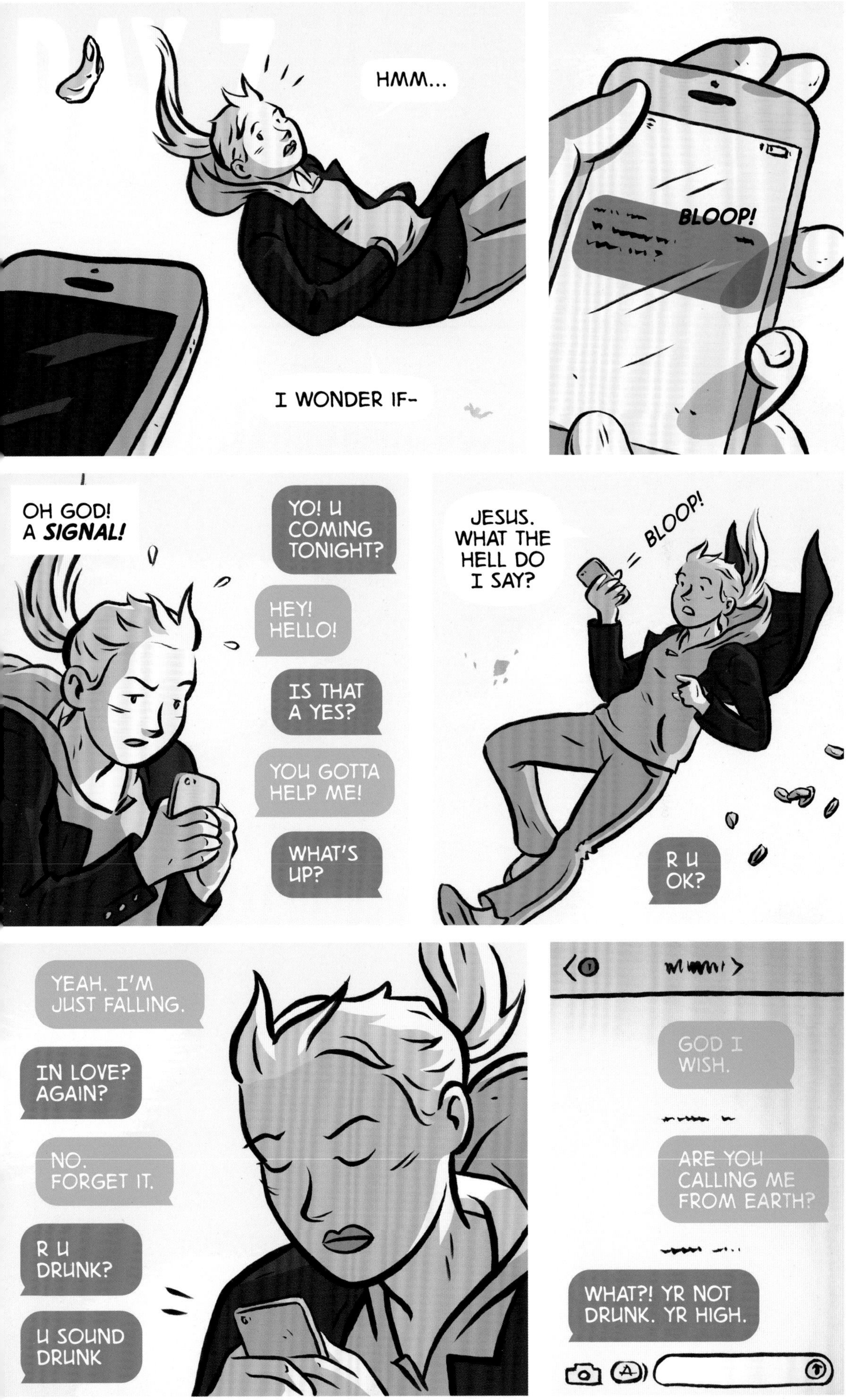
HMM...
I WONDER IF-
BLOOP!
OH GOD! A **SIGNAL!**
YO! U COMING TONIGHT?
HEY! HELLO!
IS THAT A YES?
YOU GOTTA HELP ME!
WHAT'S UP?
JESUS. WHAT THE HELL DO I SAY?
BLOOP!
R U OK?
YEAH. I'M JUST FALLING.
IN LOVE? AGAIN?
NO. FORGET IT.
R U DRUNK?
U SOUND DRUNK
GOD I WISH.
ARE YOU CALLING ME FROM EARTH?
WHAT?! YR NOT DRUNK. YR HIGH.

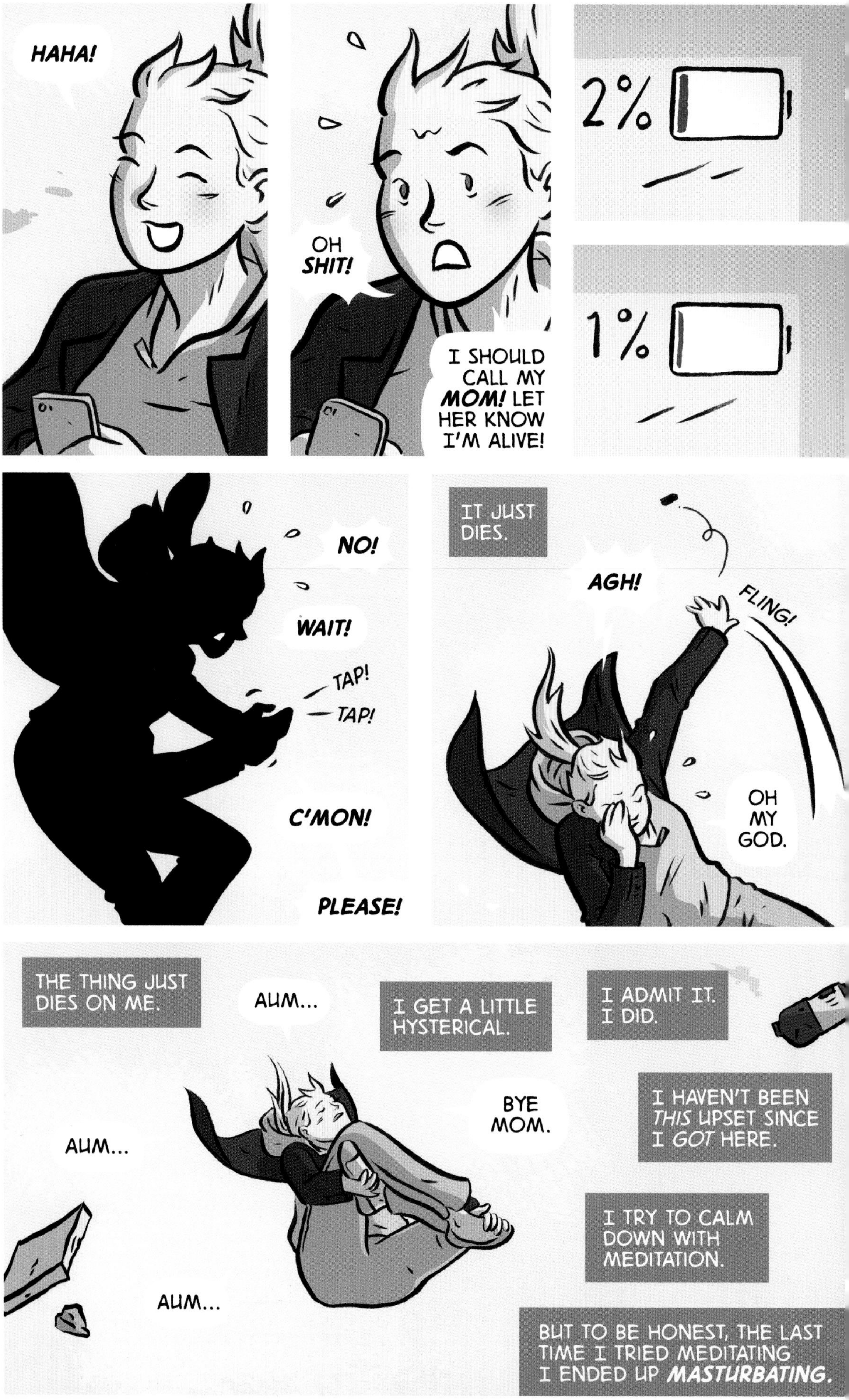
HAHA!
OH SHIT!
I SHOULD CALL MY MOM! LET HER KNOW I'M ALIVE!
2%
1%
NO!
WAIT!
TAP!
TAP!
C'MON!
PLEASE!
IT JUST DIES.
AGH!
FLING!
OH MY GOD.
THE THING JUST DIES ON ME.
AUM...
I GET A LITTLE HYSTERICAL.
I ADMIT IT. I DID.
BYE MOM.
I HAVEN'T BEEN THIS UPSET SINCE I GOT HERE.
AUM...
I TRY TO CALM DOWN WITH MEDITATION.
AUM...
BUT TO BE HONEST, THE LAST TIME I TRIED MEDITATING I ENDED UP MASTURBATING.

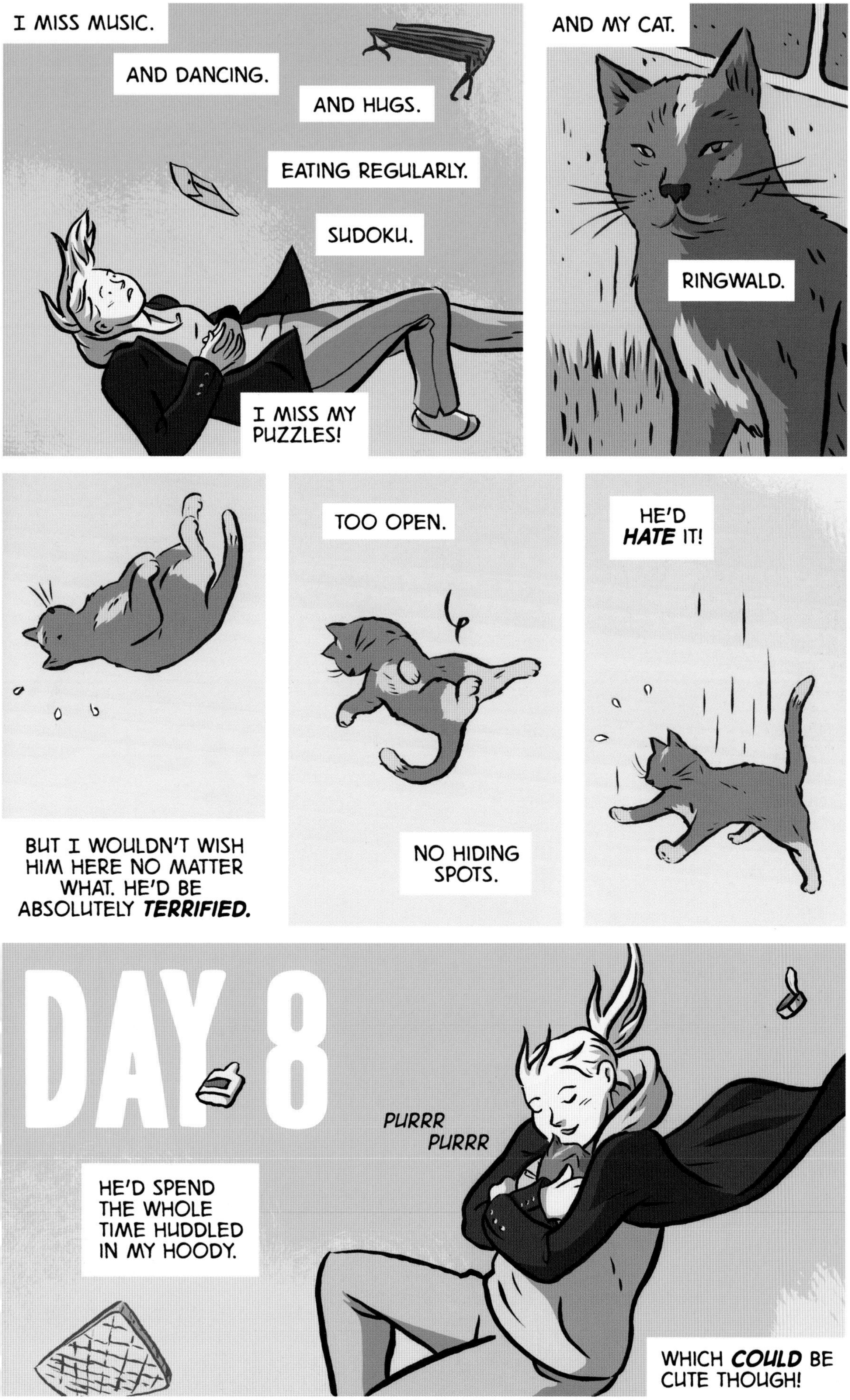
I MISS MUSIC.
AND DANCING.
AND HUGS.
EATING REGULARLY.
SUDOKU.
I MISS MY PUZZLES!
AND MY CAT.
RINGWALD.
BUT I WOULDN'T WISH HIM HERE NO MATTER WHAT. HE'D BE ABSOLUTELY ***TERRIFIED.***
TOO OPEN.
NO HIDING SPOTS.
HE'D ***HATE*** IT!
DAY 8
PURRR
PURRR
HE'D SPEND THE WHOLE TIME HUDDLED IN MY HOODY.
WHICH ***COULD*** BE CUTE THOUGH!

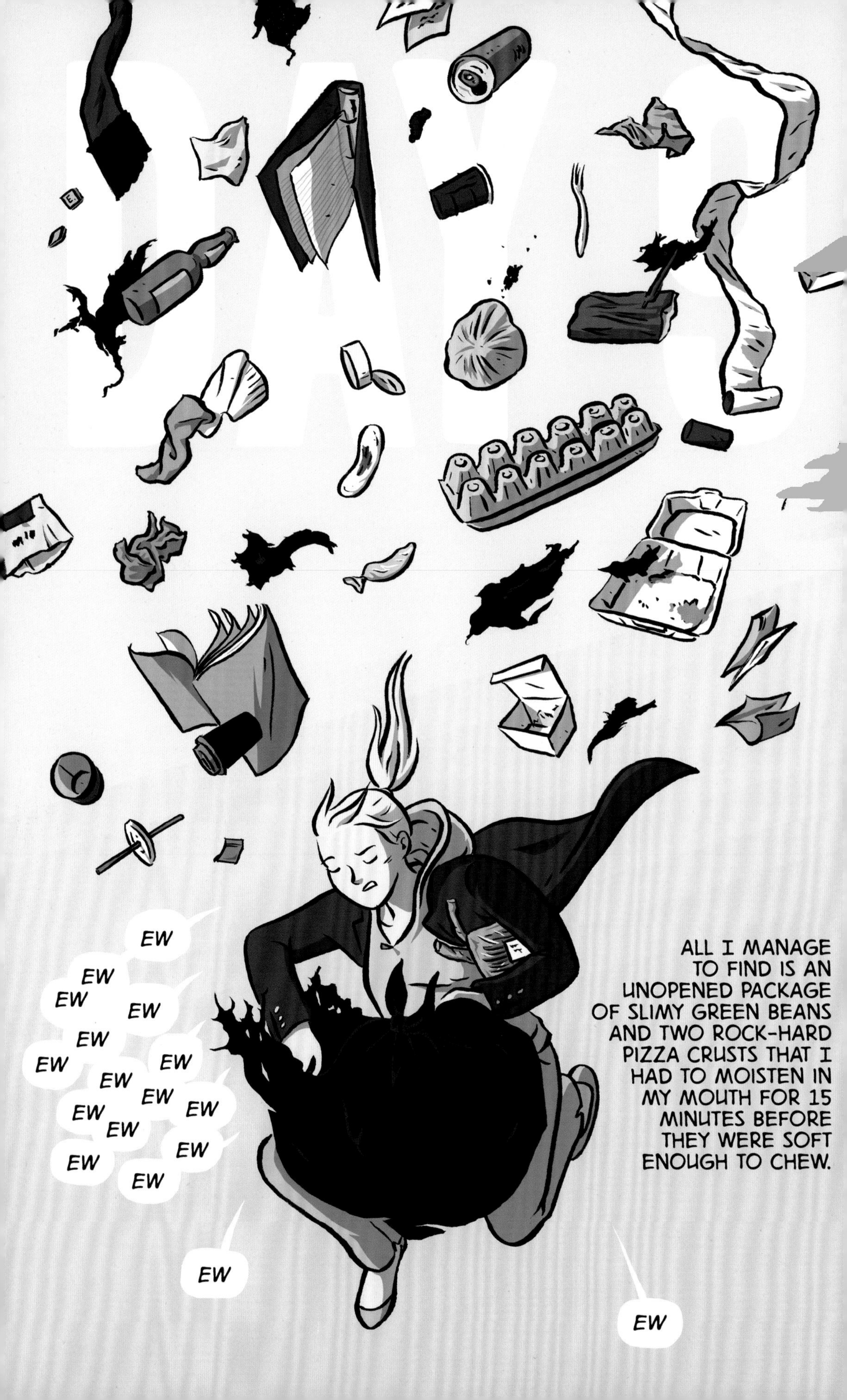
DAY 9
EW
EW
EW
EW
EW
EW
EW
EW
EW
EW
EW
EW
EW
EW
EW
ALL I MANAGE TO FIND IS AN UNOPENED PACKAGE OF SLIMY GREEN BEANS AND TWO ROCK-HARD PIZZA CRUSTS THAT I HAD TO MOISTEN IN MY MOUTH FOR 15 MINUTES BEFORE THEY WERE SOFT ENOUGH TO CHEW.
EW
EW

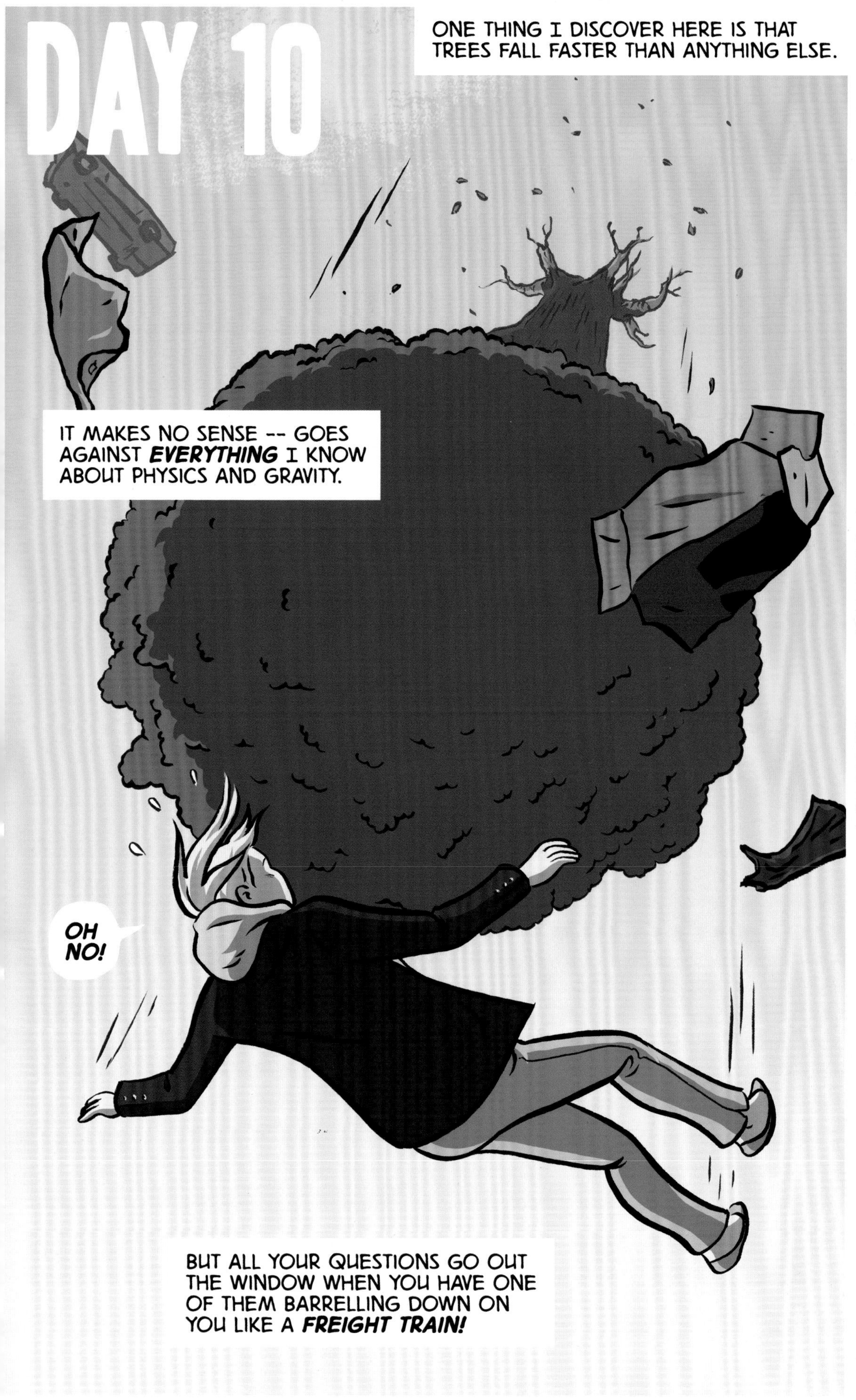

DAY 10
ONE THING I DISCOVER HERE IS THAT TREES FALL FASTER THAN ANYTHING ELSE.
IT MAKES NO SENSE -- GOES AGAINST ***EVERYTHING*** I KNOW ABOUT PHYSICS AND GRAVITY.
OH NO!
BUT ALL YOUR QUESTIONS GO OUT THE WINDOW WHEN YOU HAVE ONE OF THEM BARRELLING DOWN ON YOU LIKE A ***FREIGHT TRAIN!***

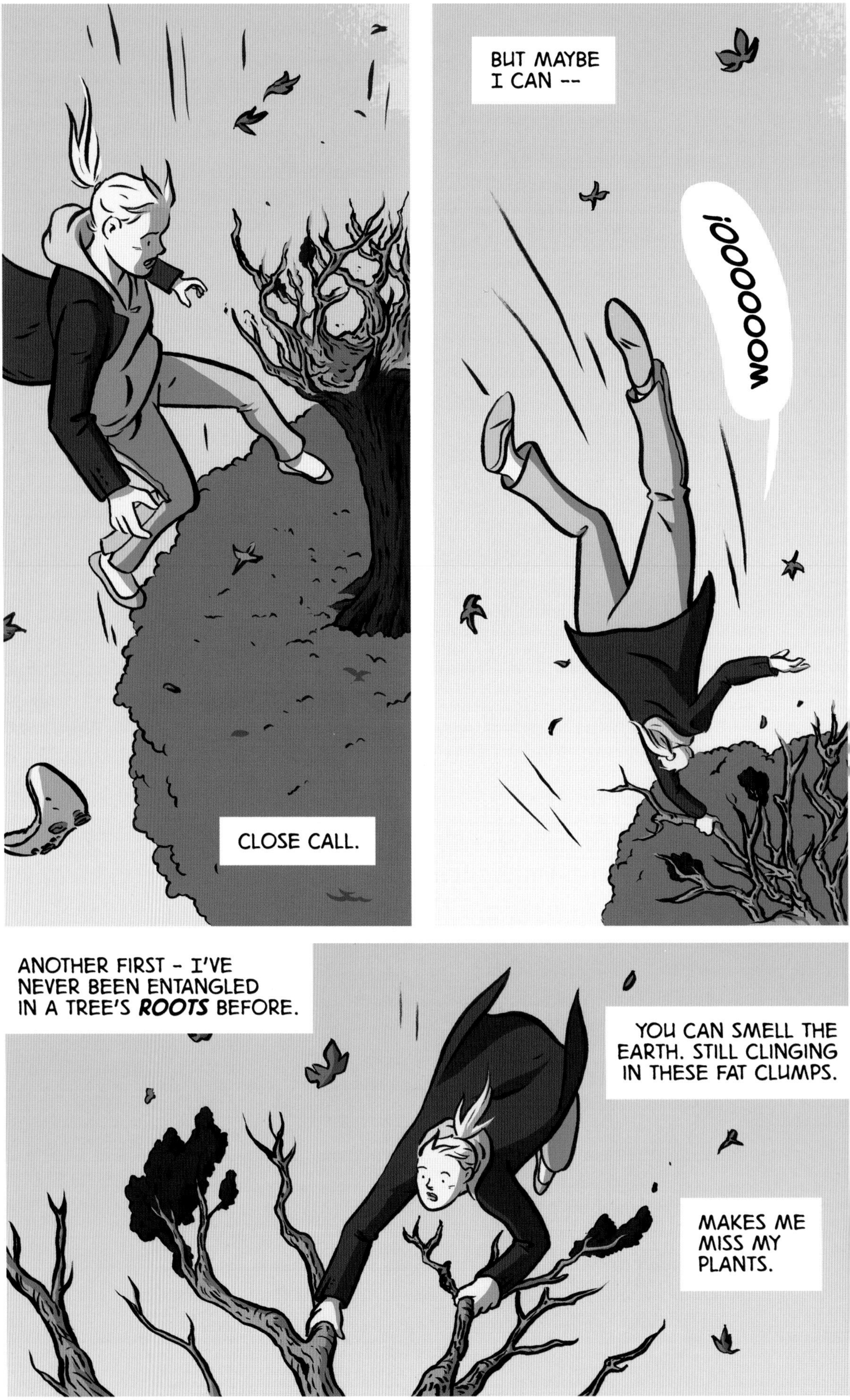
CLOSE CALL.
BUT MAYBE I CAN --
WOOOOOOO!
ANOTHER FIRST - I'VE NEVER BEEN ENTANGLED IN A TREE'S ***ROOTS*** BEFORE.
YOU CAN SMELL THE EARTH. STILL CLINGING IN THESE FAT CLUMPS.
MAKES ME MISS MY PLANTS.

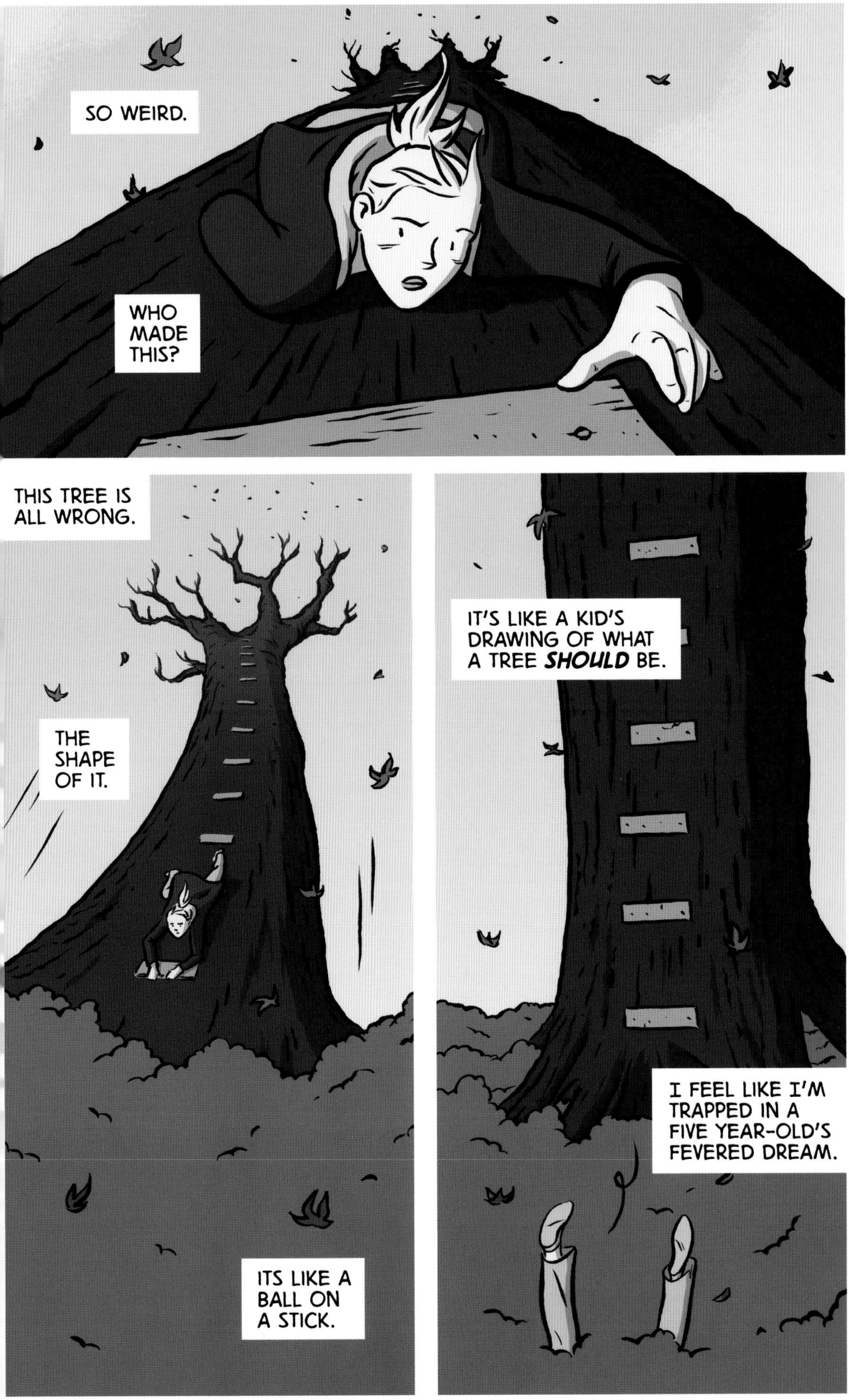
SO WEIRD.
WHO MADE THIS?
THIS TREE IS ALL WRONG.
THE SHAPE OF IT.
ITS LIKE A BALL ON A STICK.
IT'S LIKE A KID'S DRAWING OF WHAT A TREE *SHOULD* BE.
I FEEL LIKE I'M TRAPPED IN A FIVE YEAR-OLD'S FEVERED DREAM.

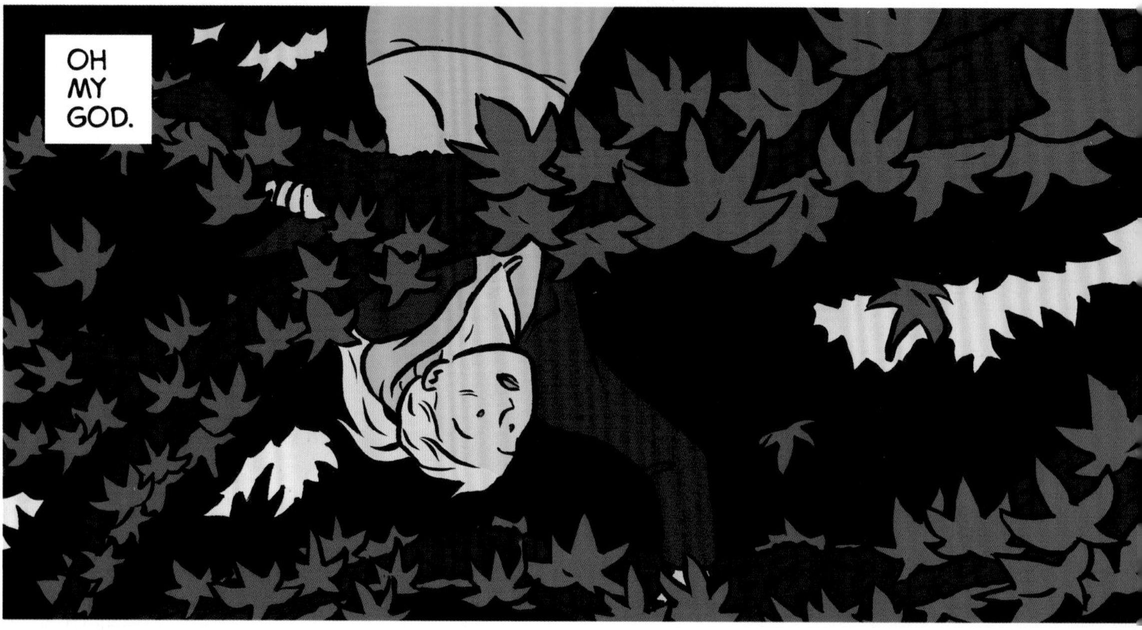
OH MY GOD.
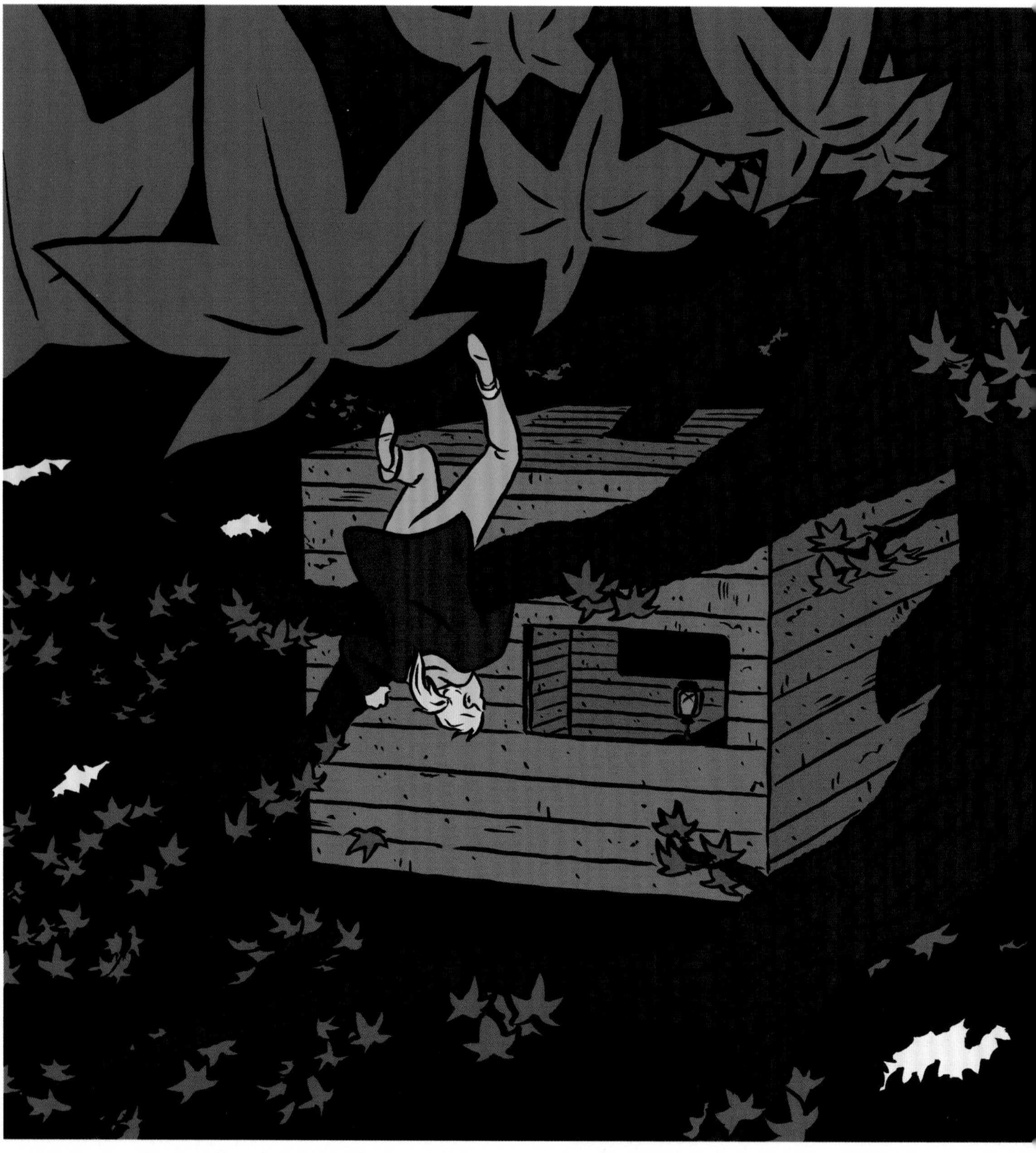

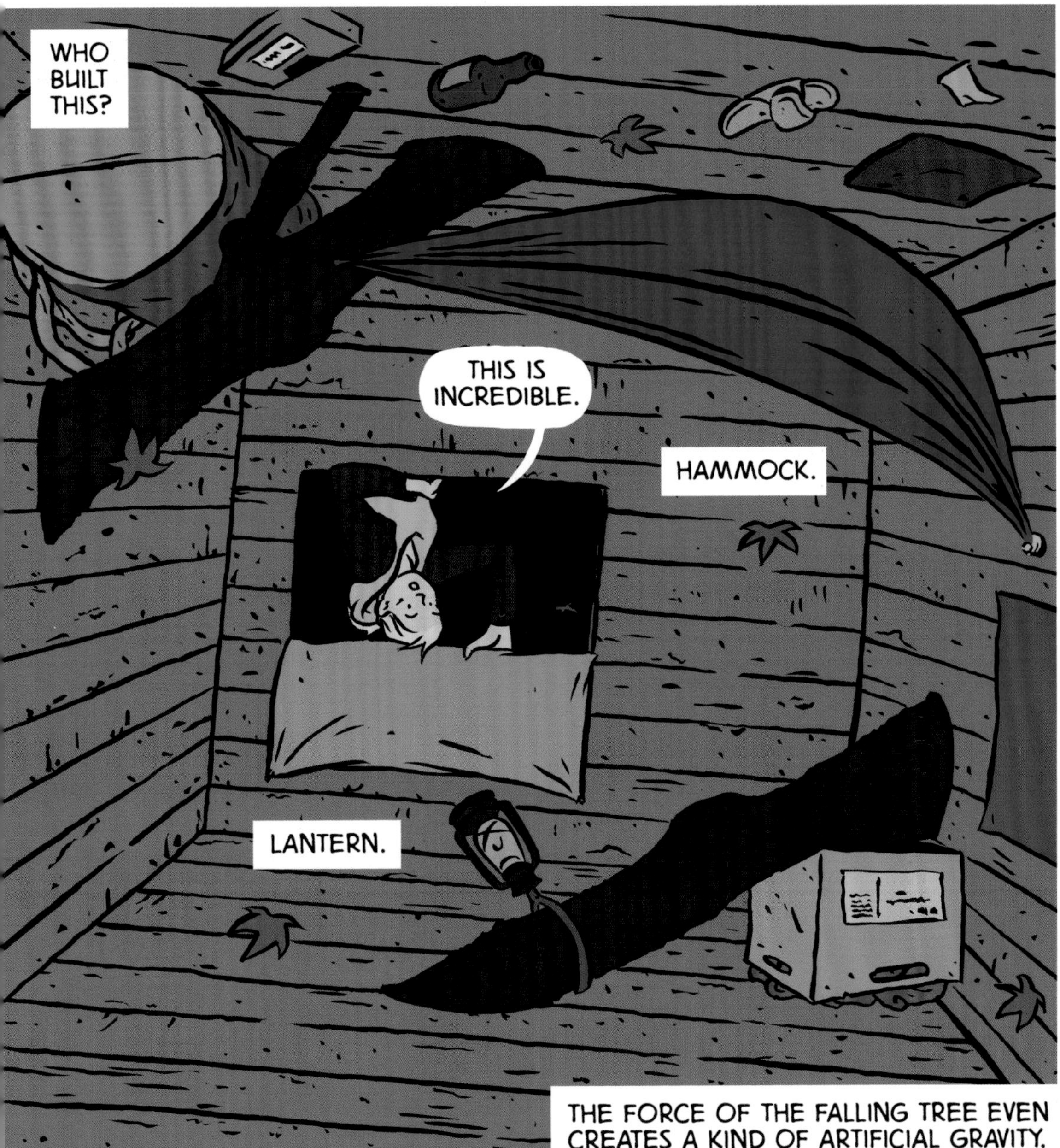
WHO BUILT THIS?
THIS IS INCREDIBLE.
HAMMOCK.
LANTERN.
THE FORCE OF THE FALLING TREE EVEN CREATES A KIND OF ARTIFICIAL GRAVITY.
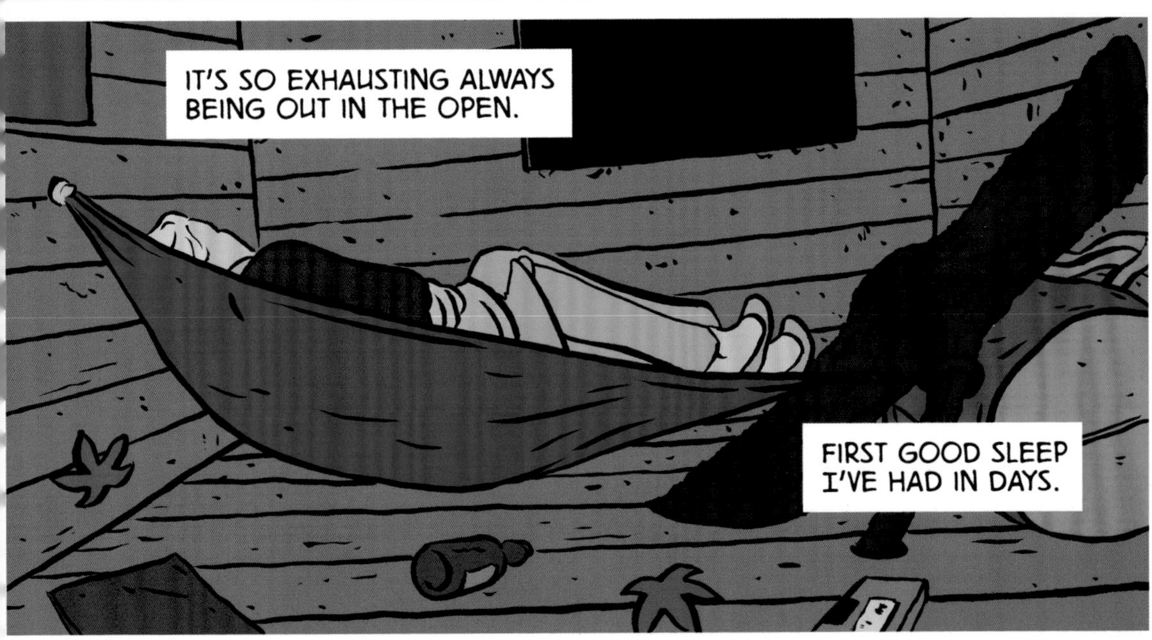
IT'S SO EXHAUSTING ALWAYS BEING OUT IN THE OPEN.
FIRST GOOD SLEEP I'VE HAD IN DAYS.

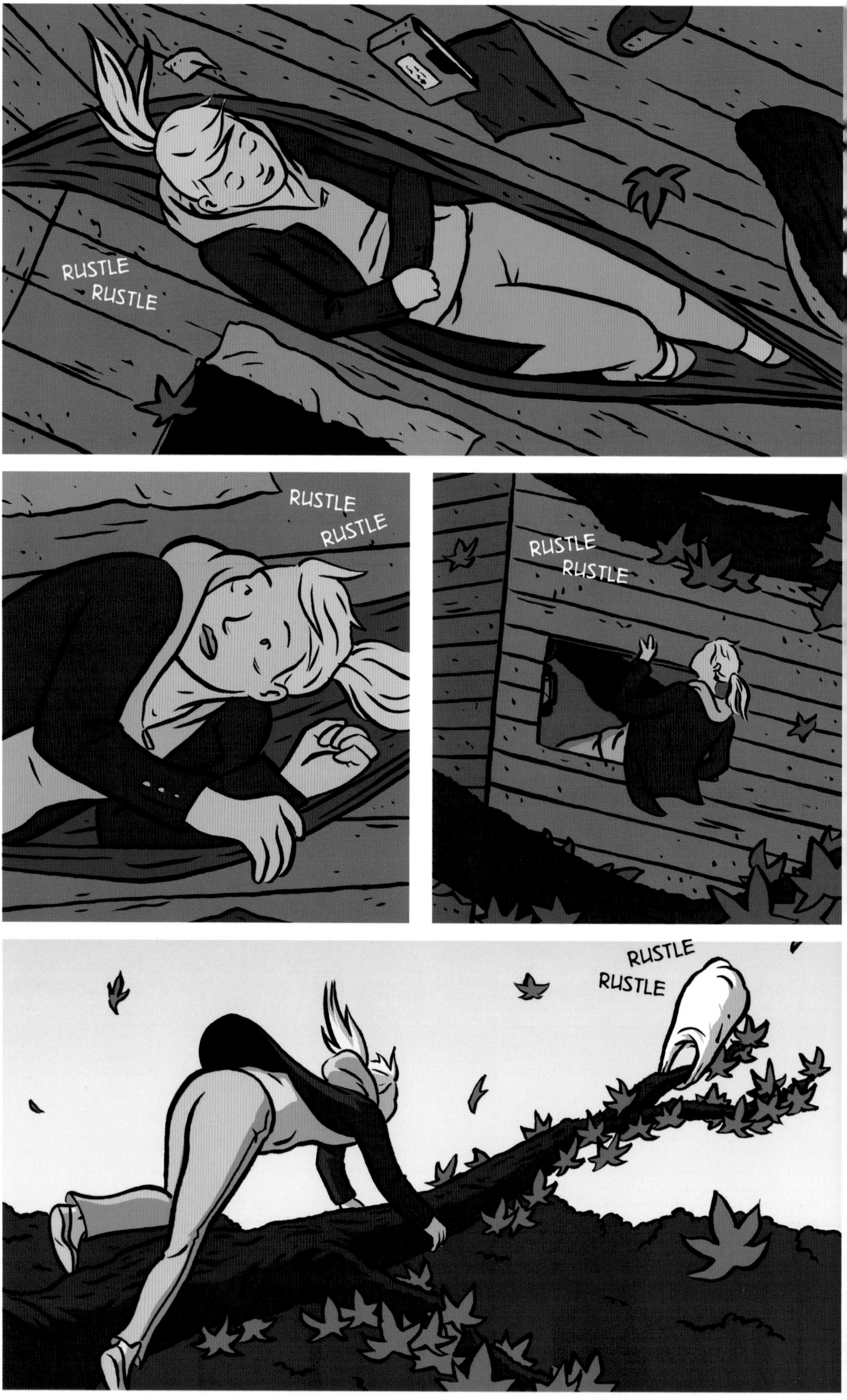
RUSTLE
RUSTLE
RUSTLE
RUSTLE
RUSTLE
RUSTLE
RUSTLE
RUSTLE

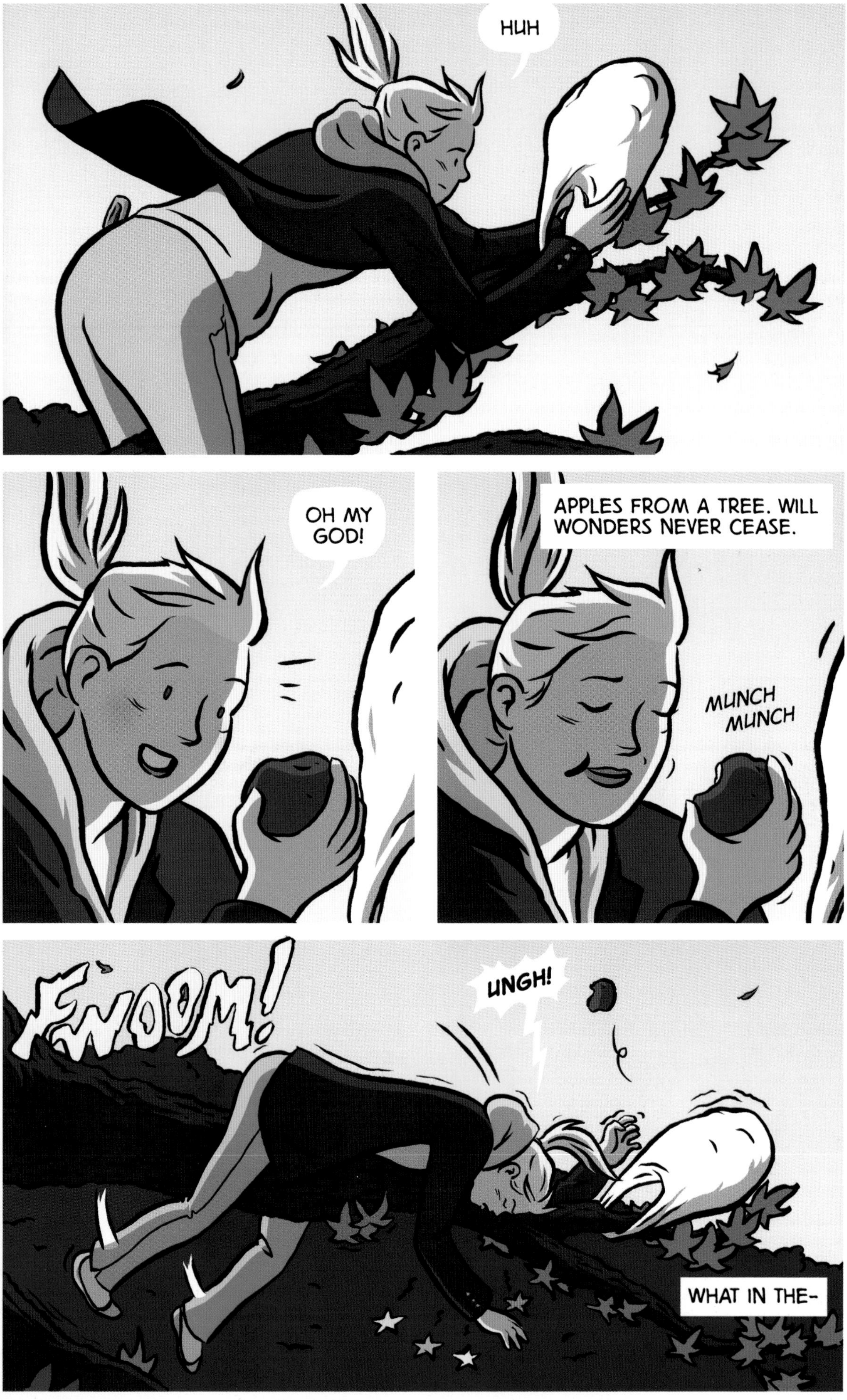
HUH
OH MY GOD!
APPLES FROM A TREE. WILL WONDERS NEVER CEASE.
MUNCH MUNCH
FWOOM!
UNGH!
WHAT IN THE-

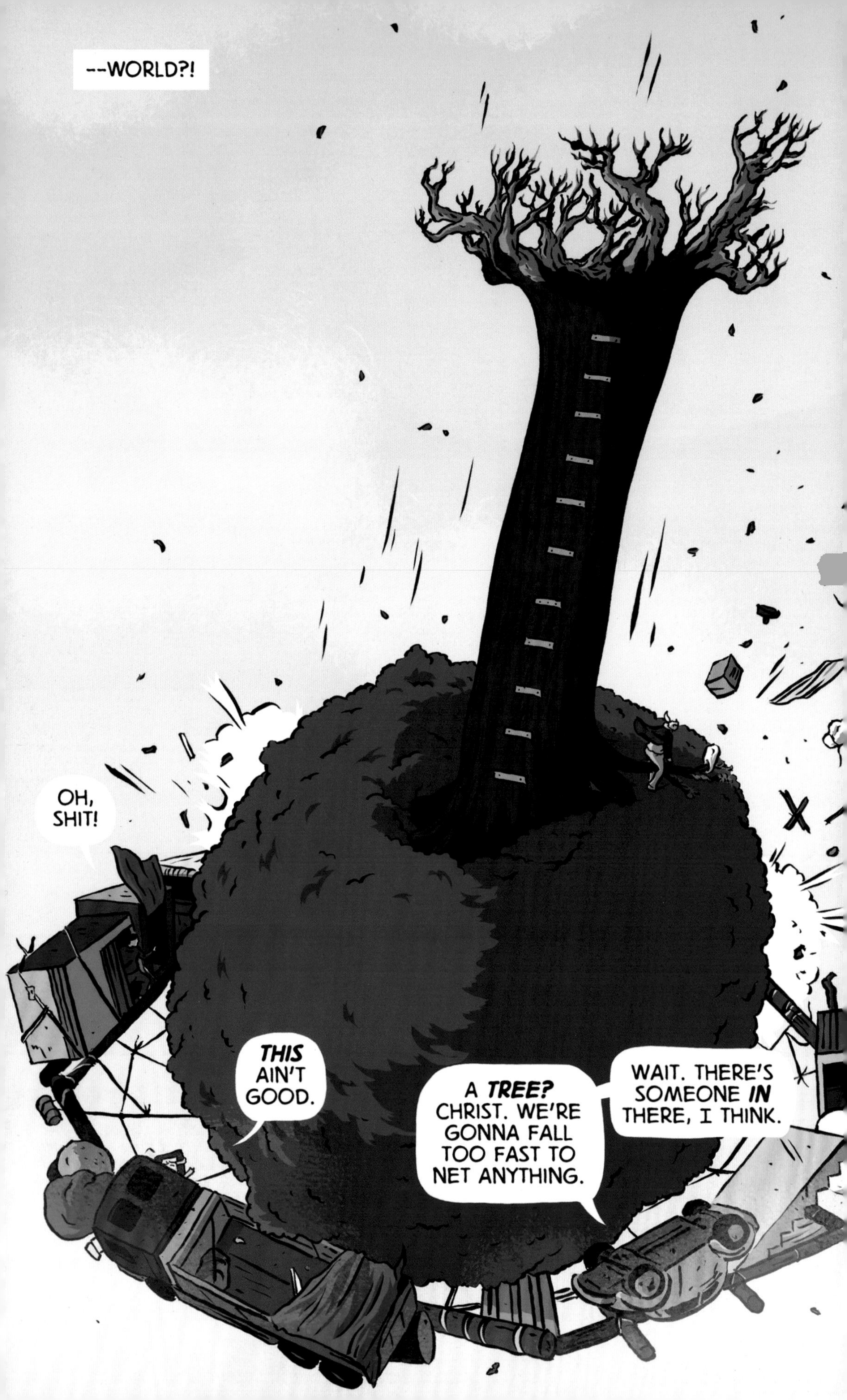
--WORLD?!
OH, SHIT!
THIS AIN'T GOOD.
A TREE? CHRIST. WE'RE GONNA FALL TOO FAST TO NET ANYTHING.
WAIT. THERE'S SOMEONE IN THERE, I THINK.

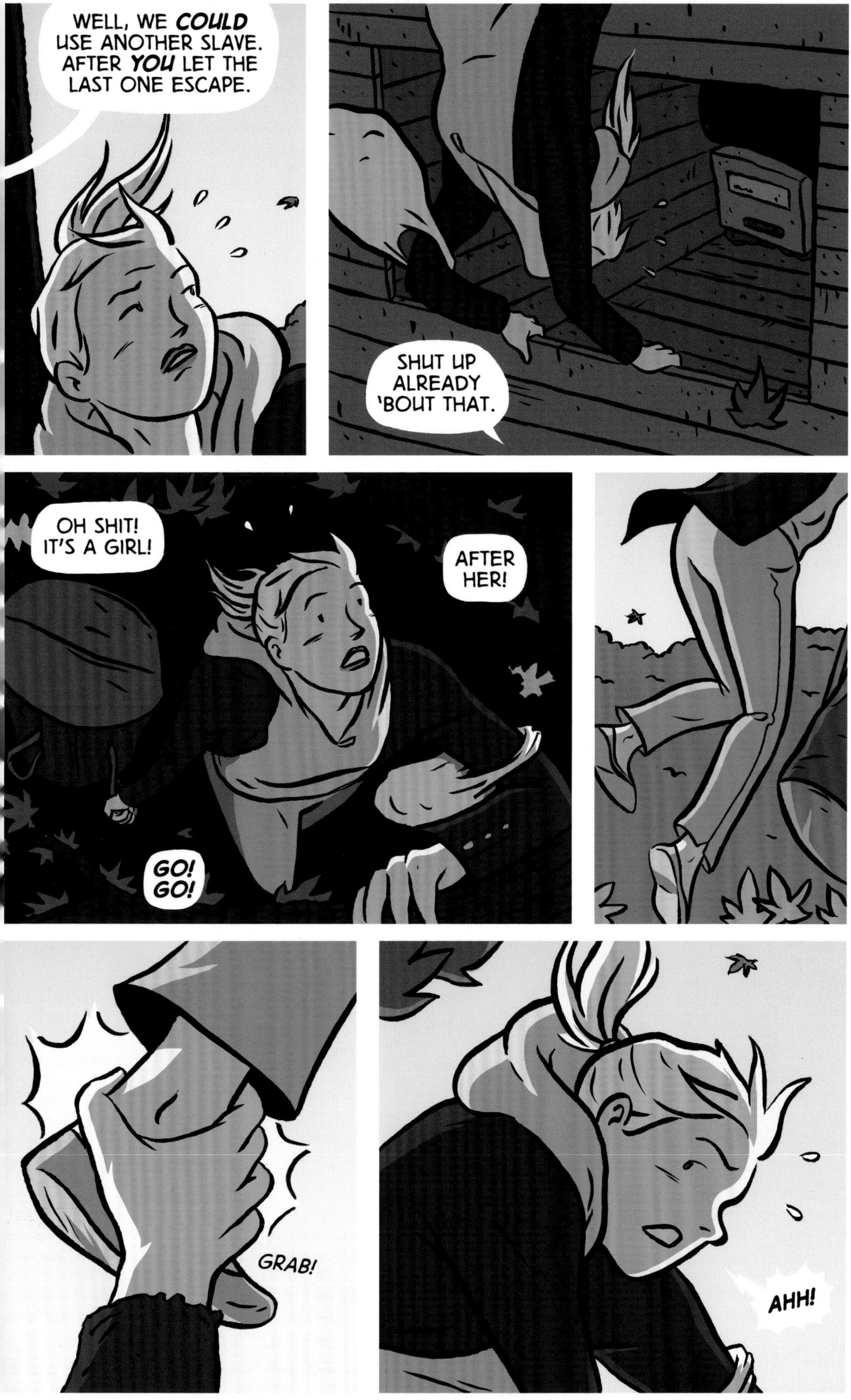
WELL, WE COULD USE ANOTHER SLAVE. AFTER YOU LET THE LAST ONE ESCAPE.
SHUT UP ALREADY 'BOUT THAT.
OH SHIT! IT'S A GIRL!
AFTER HER!
GO! GO!
GRAB!
AHH!

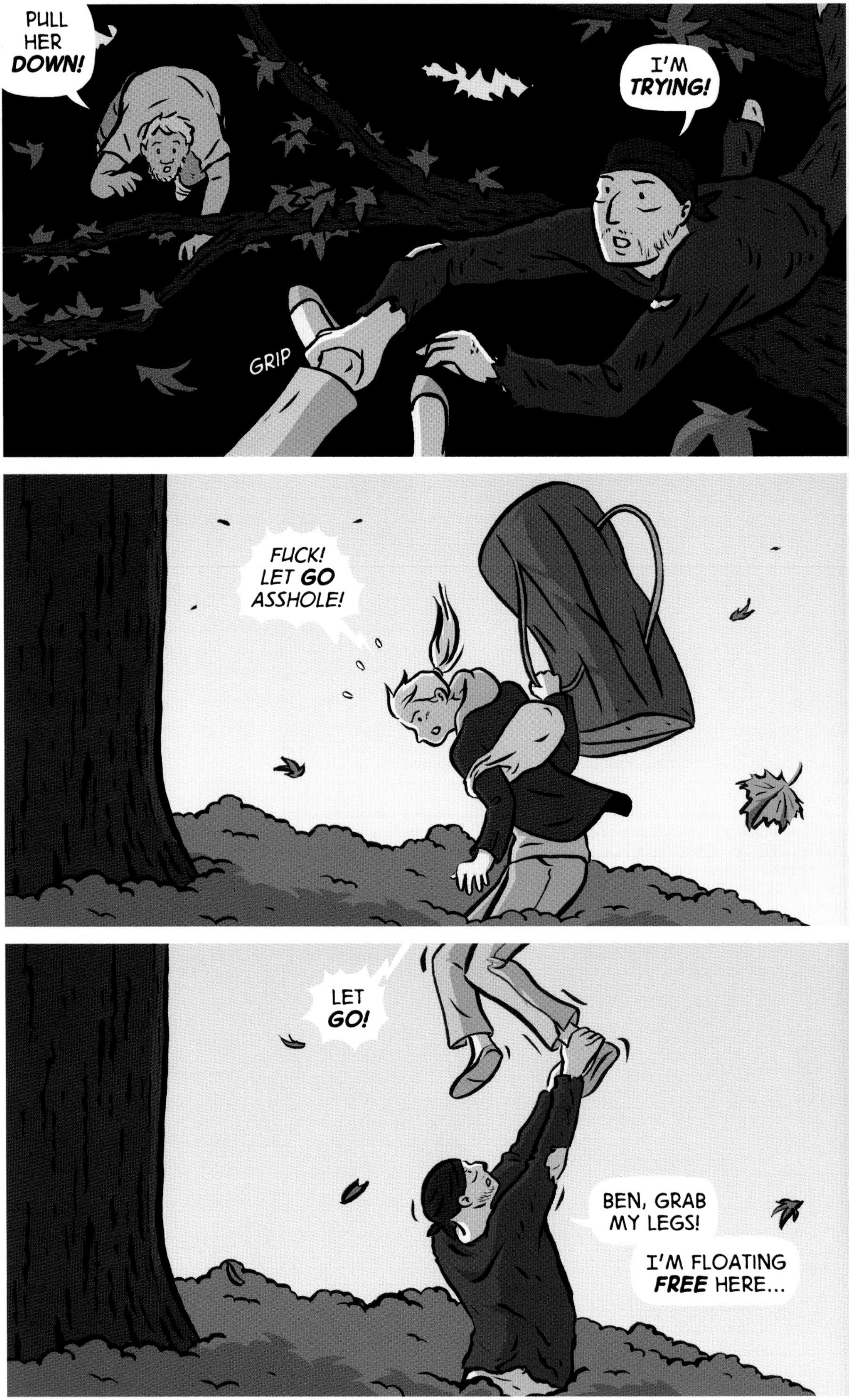
PULL HER DOWN!
I'M TRYING!
GRIP
FUCK! LET GO ASSHOLE!
LET GO!
BEN, GRAB MY LEGS!
I'M FLOATING FREE HERE...

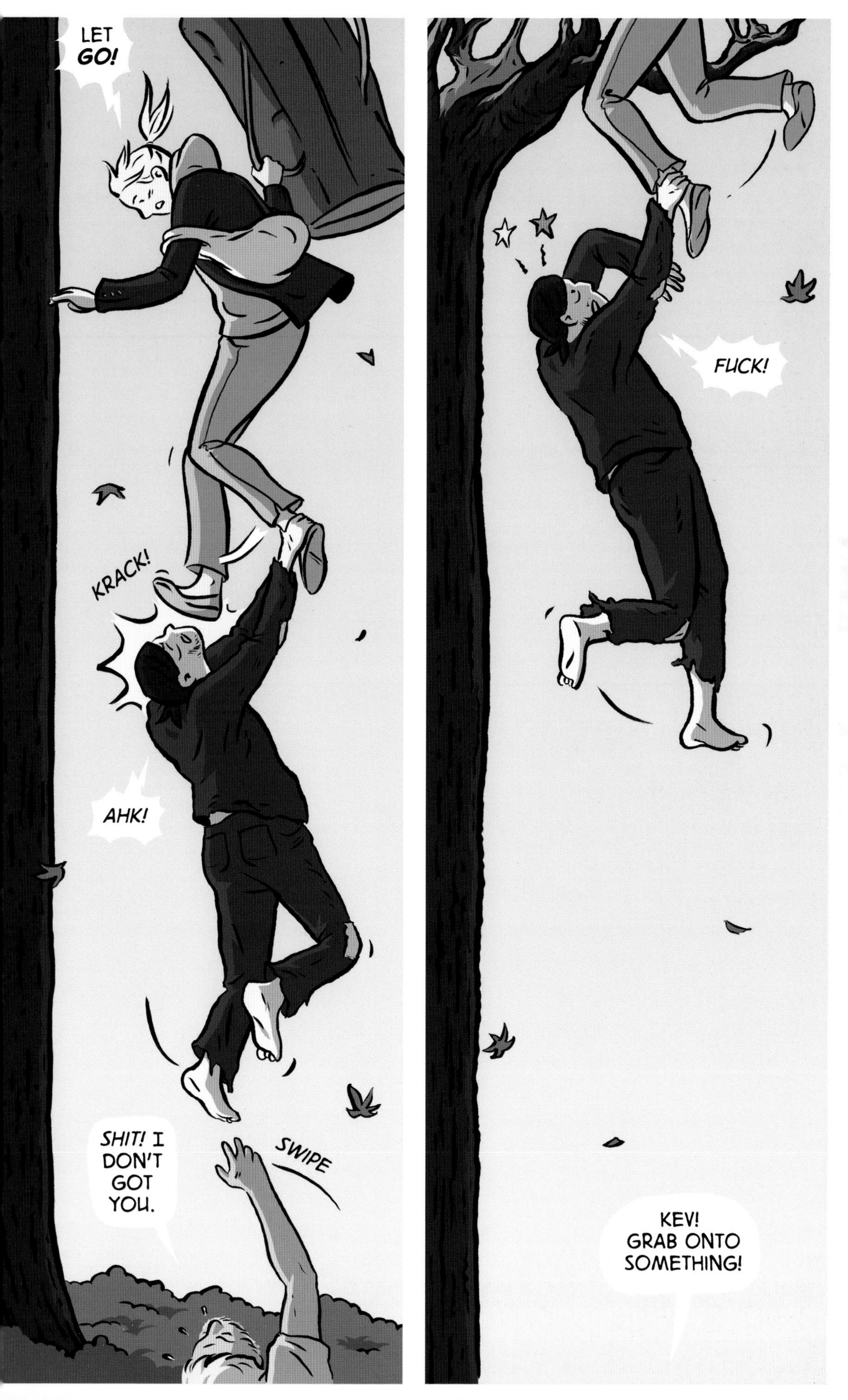
LET GO!
KRACK!
AHK!
SHIT! I DON'T GOT YOU.
SWIPE
FUCK!
KEV! GRAB ONTO SOMETHING!

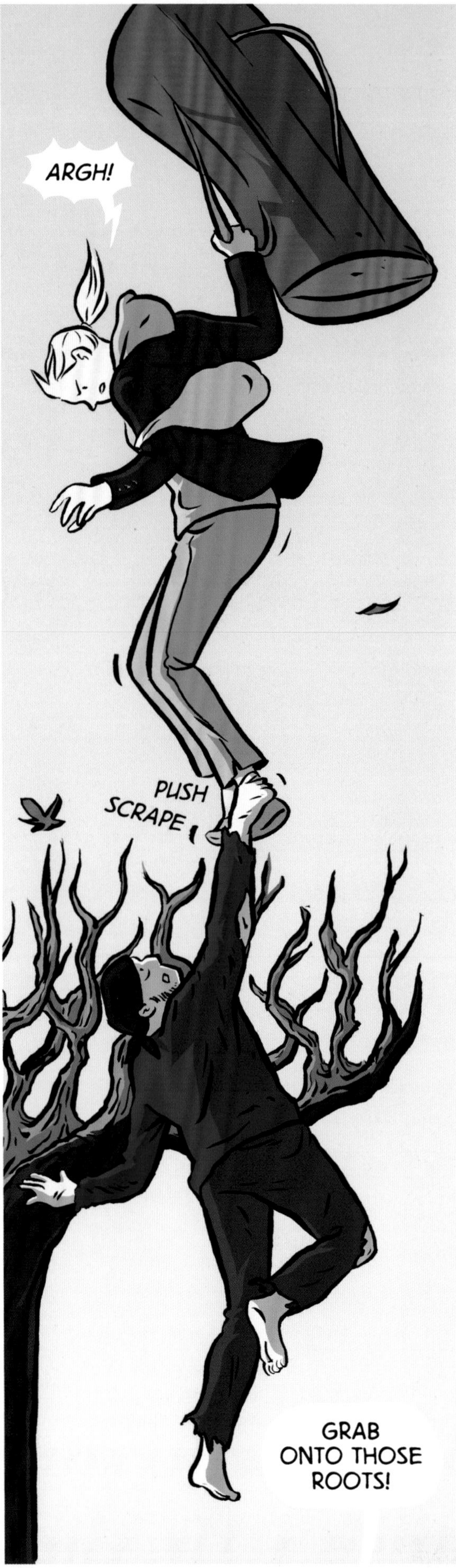
ARGH!
PUSH
SCRAPE
GRAB ONTO THOSE ROOTS!
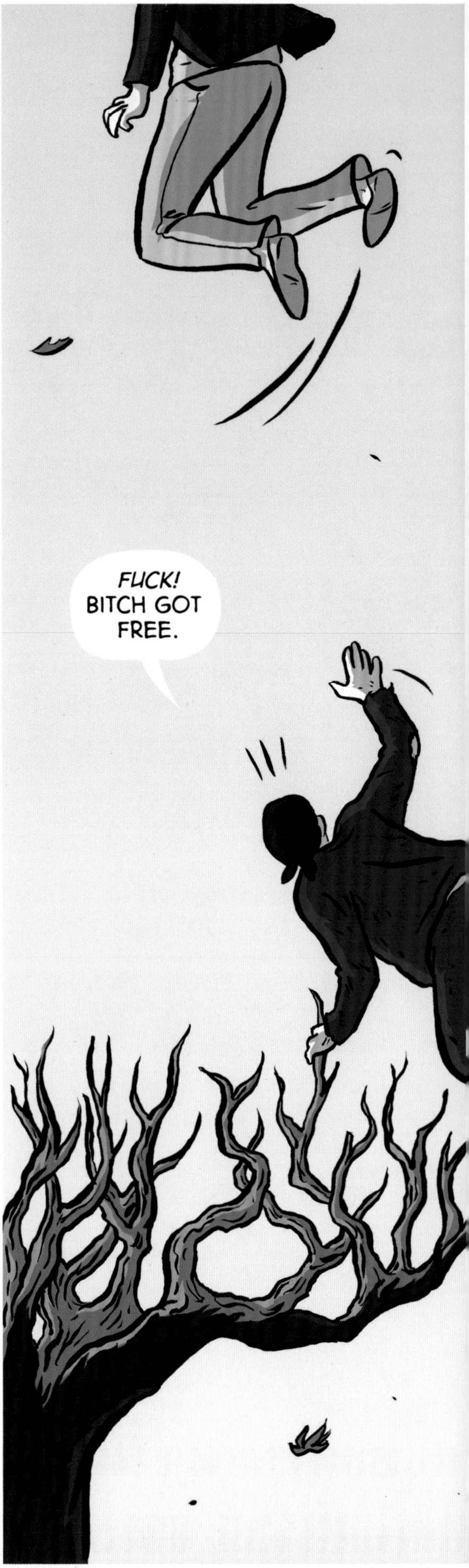
FUCK! BITCH GOT FREE.

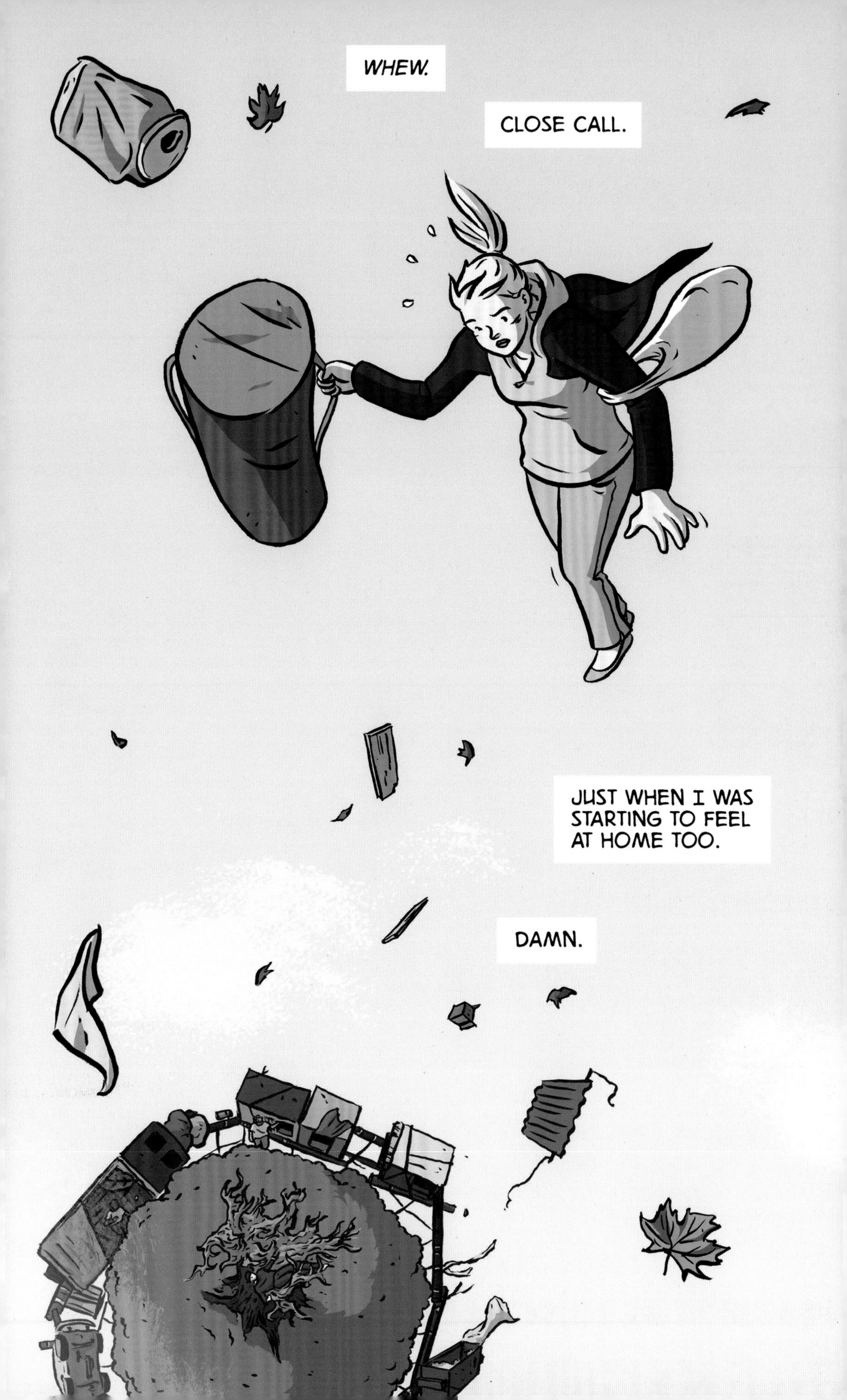
WHEW.
CLOSE CALL.
JUST WHEN I WAS STARTING TO FEEL AT HOME TOO.
DAMN.

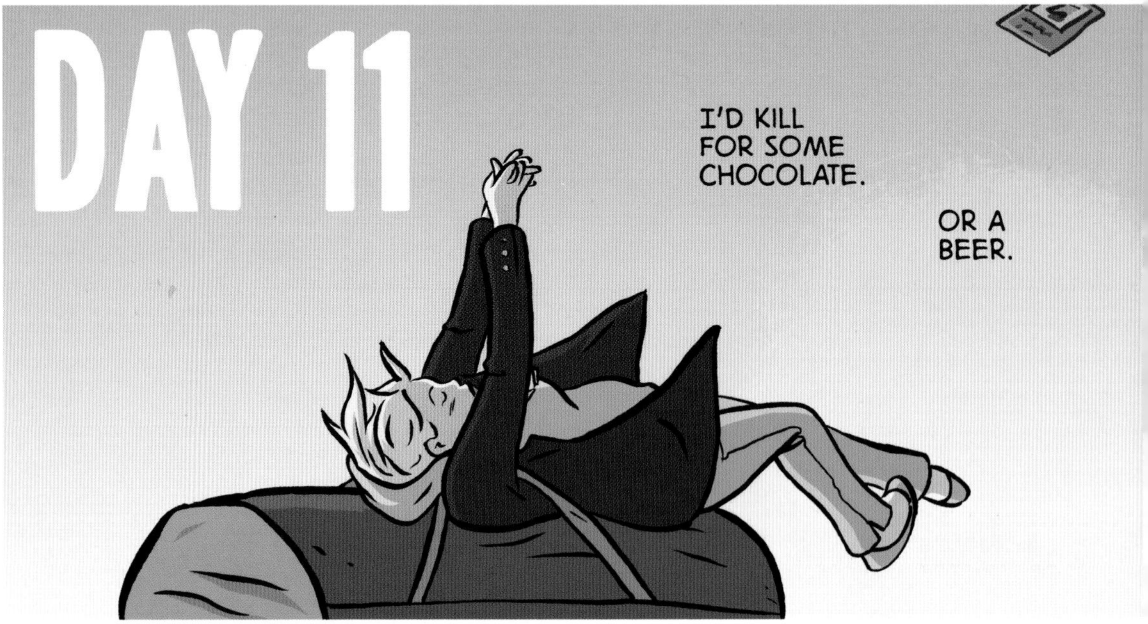
DAY 11
I'D KILL FOR SOME CHOCOLATE.
OR A BEER.

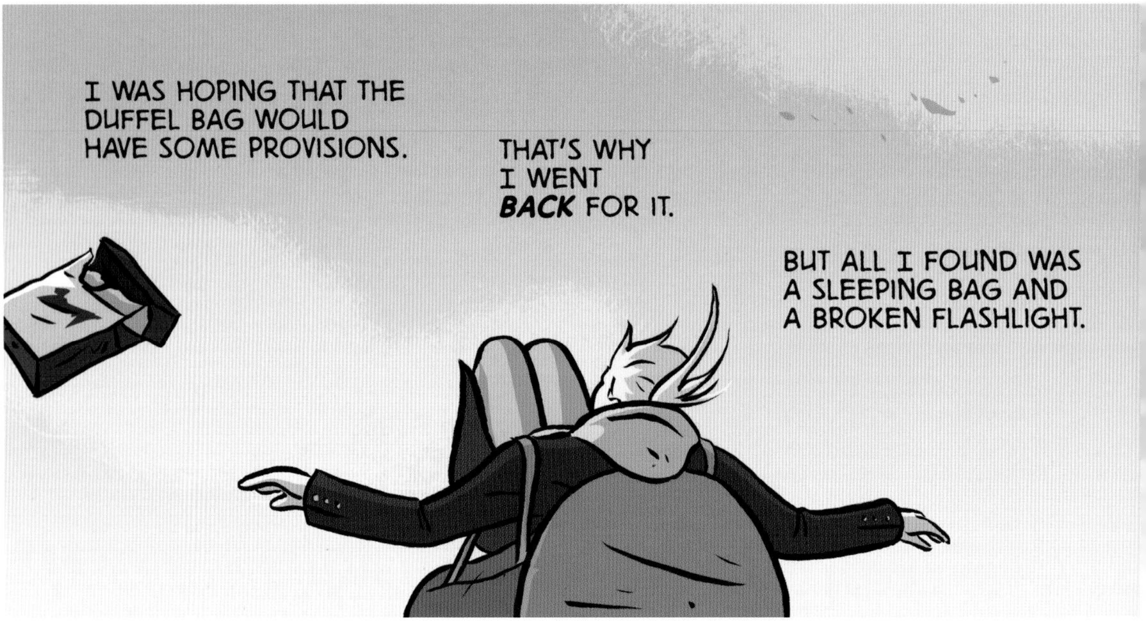
I WAS HOPING THAT THE DUFFEL BAG WOULD HAVE SOME PROVISIONS.
THAT'S WHY I WENT *BACK* FOR IT.
BUT ALL I FOUND WAS A SLEEPING BAG AND A BROKEN FLASHLIGHT.

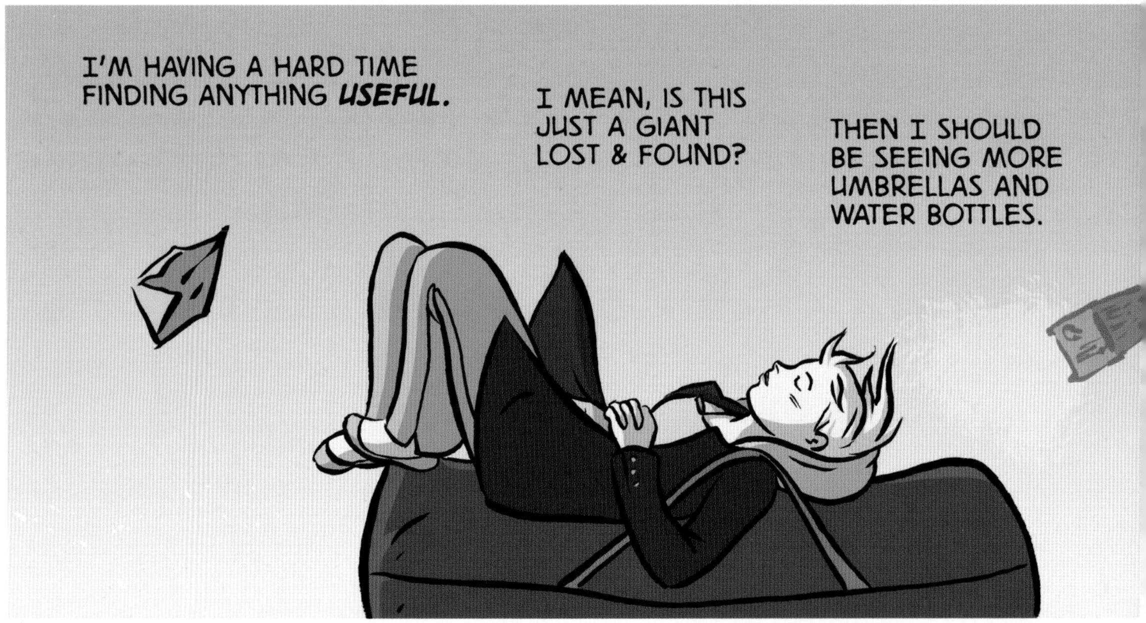
I'M HAVING A HARD TIME FINDING ANYTHING *USEFUL.*
I MEAN, IS THIS JUST A GIANT LOST & FOUND?
THEN I SHOULD BE SEEING MORE UMBRELLAS AND WATER BOTTLES.

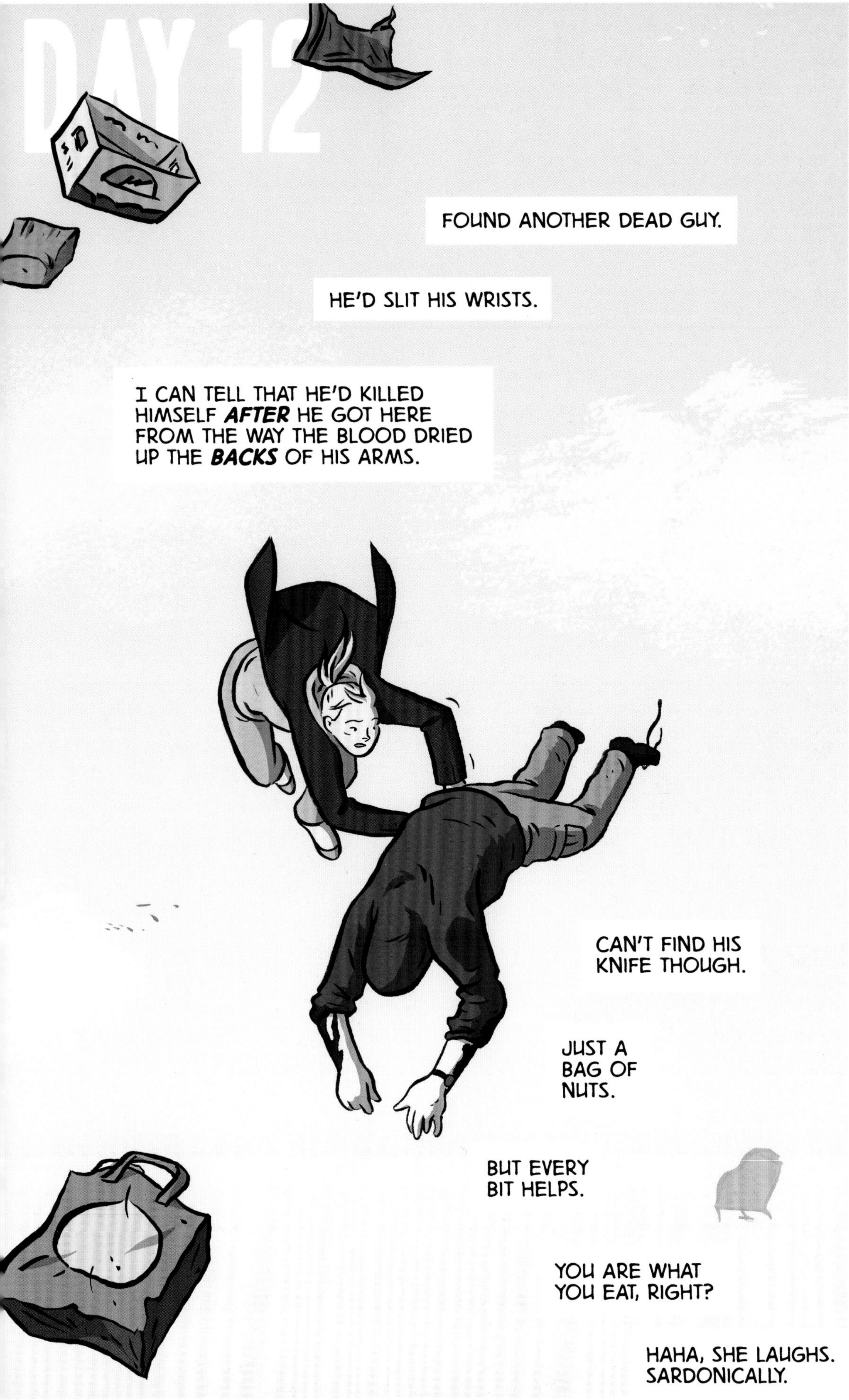
DAY 12
FOUND ANOTHER DEAD GUY.
HE'D SLIT HIS WRISTS.
I CAN TELL THAT HE'D KILLED HIMSELF AFTER HE GOT HERE FROM THE WAY THE BLOOD DRIED UP THE BACKS OF HIS ARMS.
CAN'T FIND HIS KNIFE THOUGH.
JUST A BAG OF NUTS.
BUT EVERY BIT HELPS.
YOU ARE WHAT YOU EAT, RIGHT?
HAHA, SHE LAUGHS. SARDONICALLY.

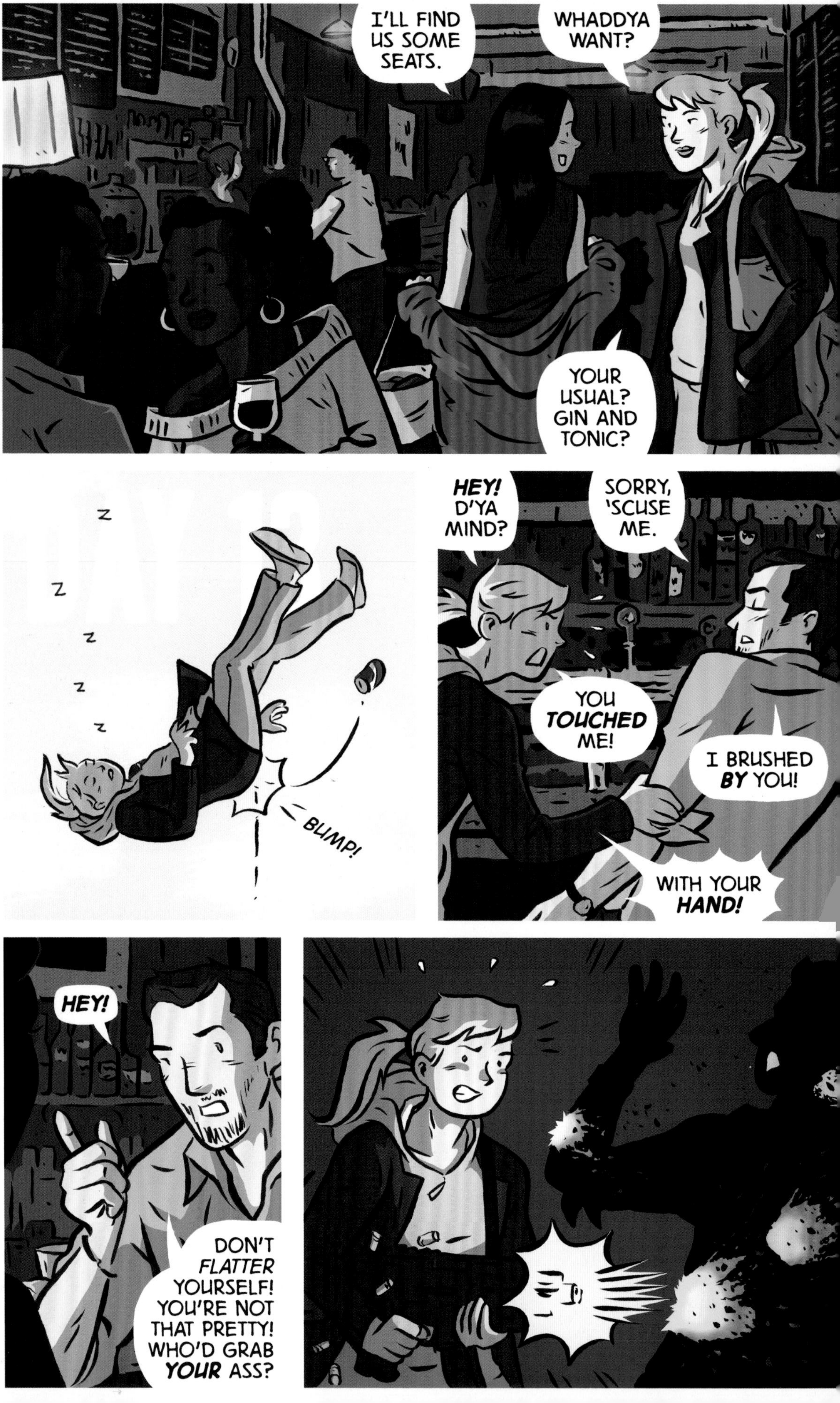
I'LL FIND US SOME SEATS.
WHADDYA WANT?
YOUR USUAL? GIN AND TONIC?
Z
Z
Z
Z
Z
BUMP!
HEY! D'YA MIND?
SORRY, 'SCUSE ME.
YOU TOUCHED ME!
I BRUSHED BY YOU!
WITH YOUR HAND!
HEY!
DON'T FLATTER YOURSELF! YOU'RE NOT THAT PRETTY! WHO'D GRAB YOUR ASS?

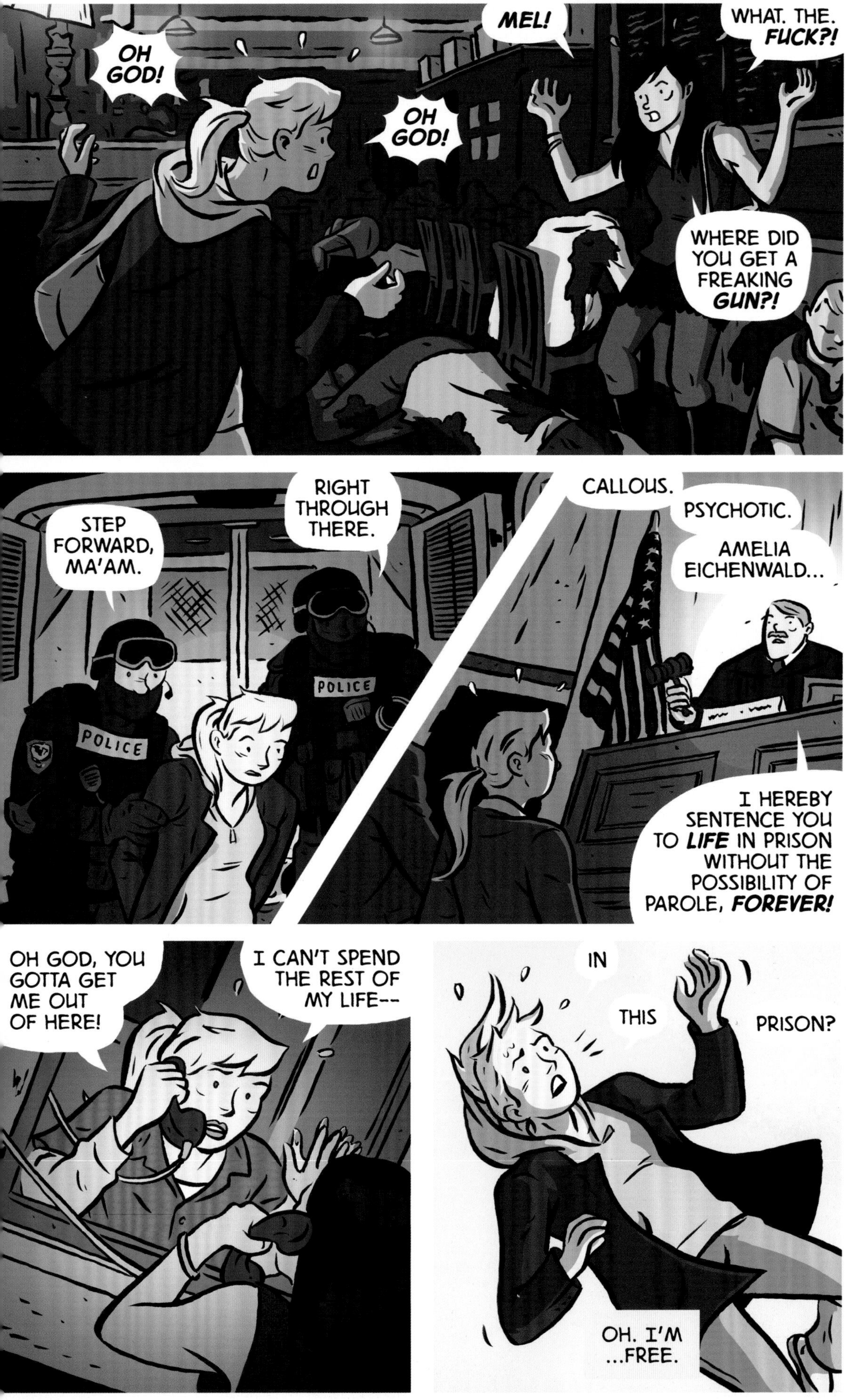
OH GOD!
OH GOD!
MEL!
WHAT. THE. *FUCK?!*
WHERE DID YOU GET A FREAKING *GUN?!*
STEP FORWARD, MA'AM.
RIGHT THROUGH THERE.
POLICE
POLICE
CALLOUS.
PSYCHOTIC.
AMELIA EICHENWALD...
I HEREBY SENTENCE YOU TO *LIFE* IN PRISON WITHOUT THE POSSIBILITY OF PAROLE, *FOREVER!*
OH GOD, YOU GOTTA GET ME OUT OF HERE!
I CAN'T SPEND THE REST OF MY LIFE--
IN
THIS
PRISON?
OH. I'M ...FREE.

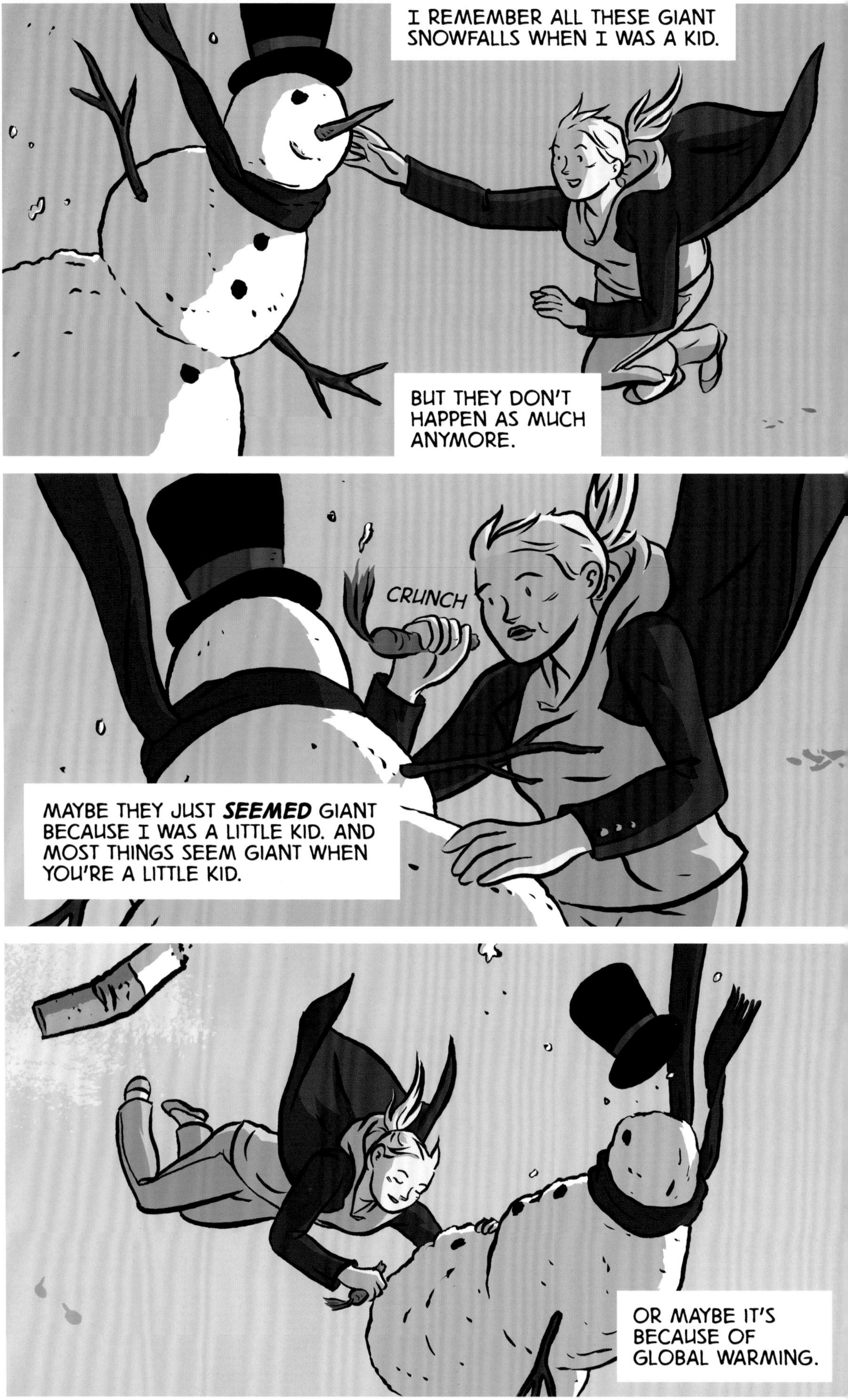
I REMEMBER ALL THESE GIANT SNOWFALLS WHEN I WAS A KID.
BUT THEY DON'T HAPPEN AS MUCH ANYMORE.
CRUNCH
MAYBE THEY JUST ***SEEMED*** GIANT BECAUSE I WAS A LITTLE KID. AND MOST THINGS SEEM GIANT WHEN YOU'RE A LITTLE KID.
OR MAYBE IT'S BECAUSE OF GLOBAL WARMING.

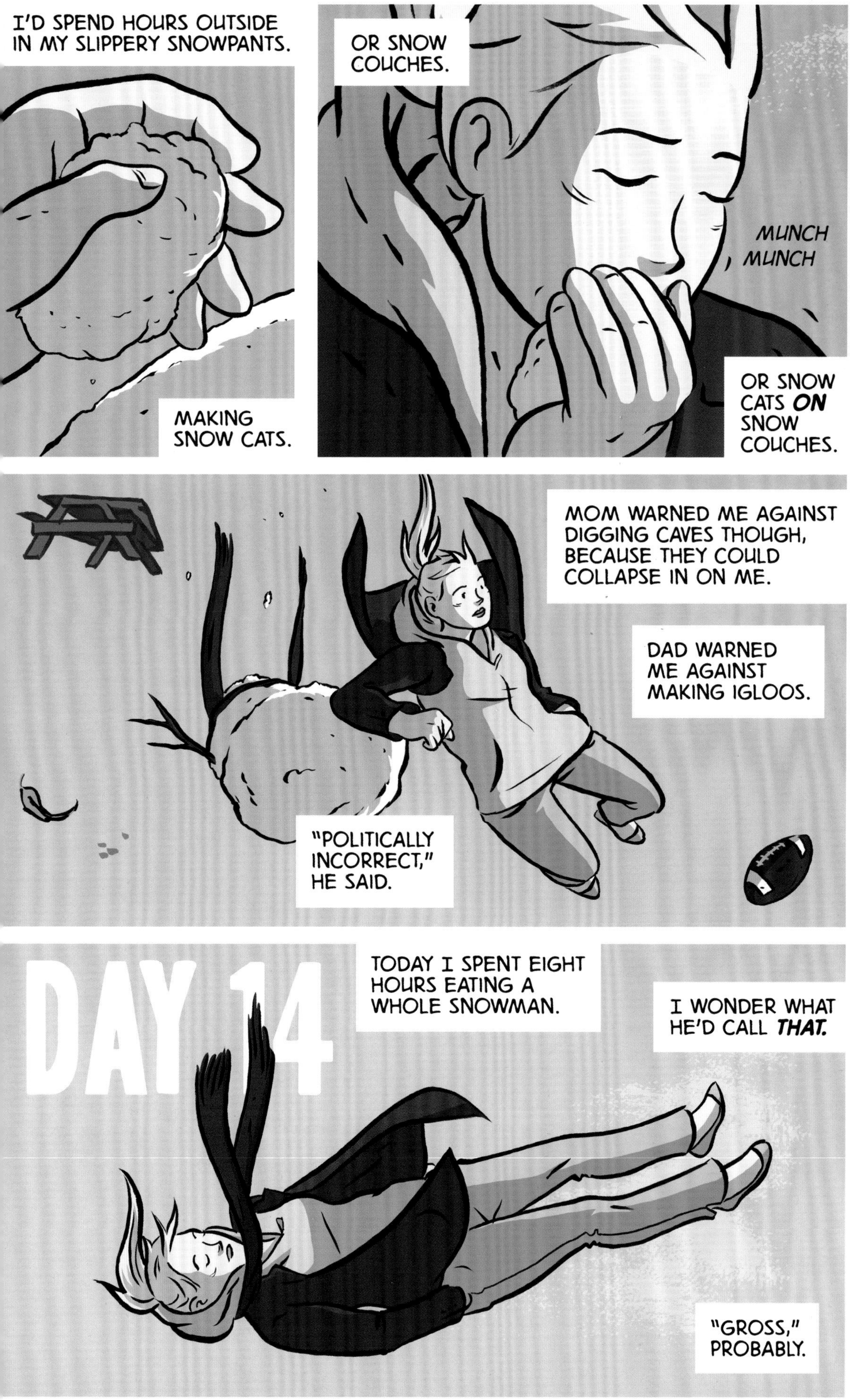
I'D SPEND HOURS OUTSIDE IN MY SLIPPERY SNOWPANTS.
MAKING SNOW CATS.
OR SNOW COUCHES.
MUNCH
MUNCH
OR SNOW CATS **ON** SNOW COUCHES.
MOM WARNED ME AGAINST DIGGING CAVES THOUGH, BECAUSE THEY COULD COLLAPSE IN ON ME.
DAD WARNED ME AGAINST MAKING IGLOOS.
"POLITICALLY INCORRECT," HE SAID.
DAY 14
TODAY I SPENT EIGHT HOURS EATING A WHOLE SNOWMAN.
I WONDER WHAT HE'D CALL ***THAT.***
"GROSS," PROBABLY.

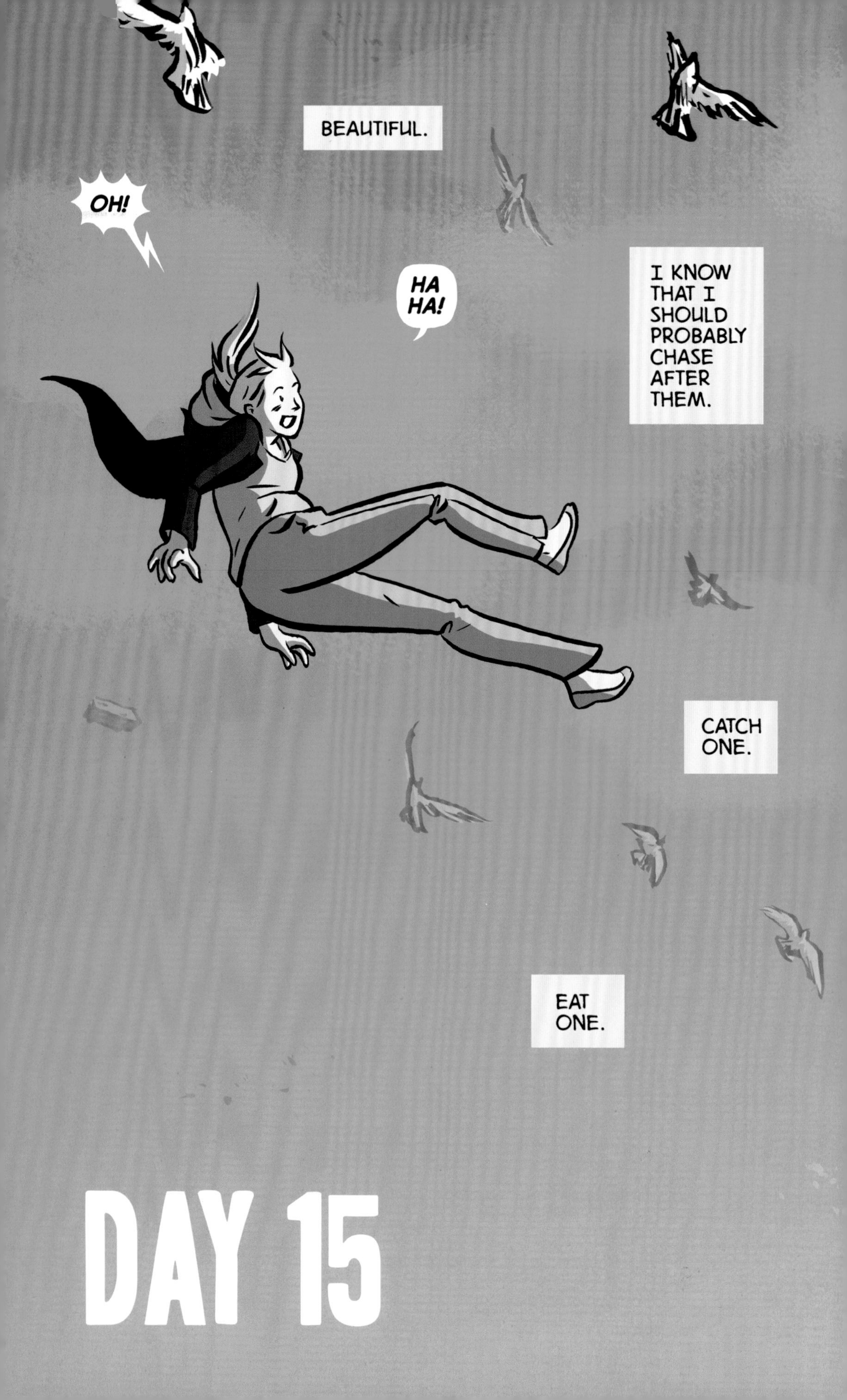
BEAUTIFUL.
OH!
HA HA!
I KNOW THAT I SHOULD PROBABLY CHASE AFTER THEM.
CATCH ONE.
EAT ONE.
DAY 15

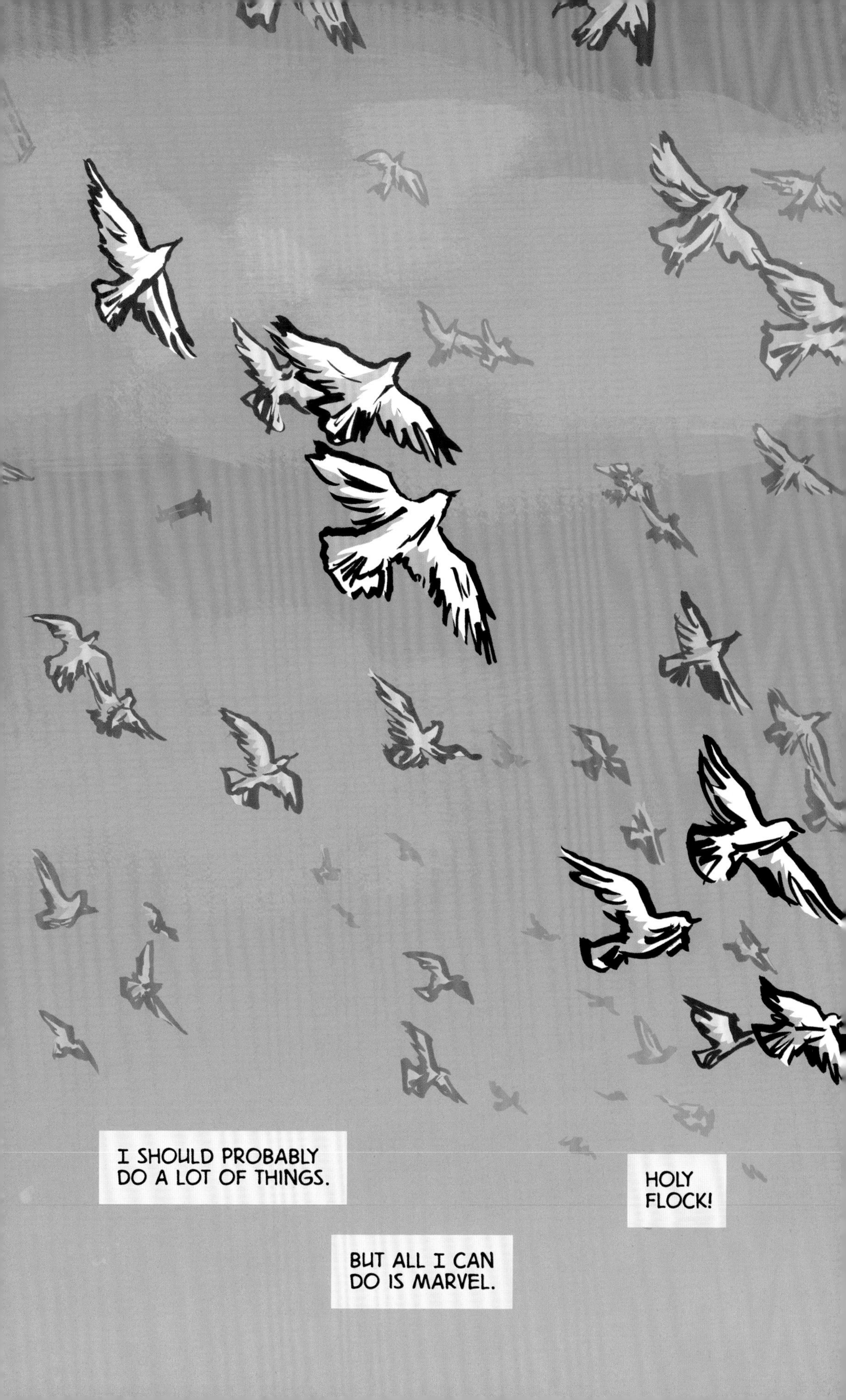
I SHOULD PROBABLY DO A LOT OF THINGS.
HOLY FLOCK!
BUT ALL I CAN DO IS MARVEL.

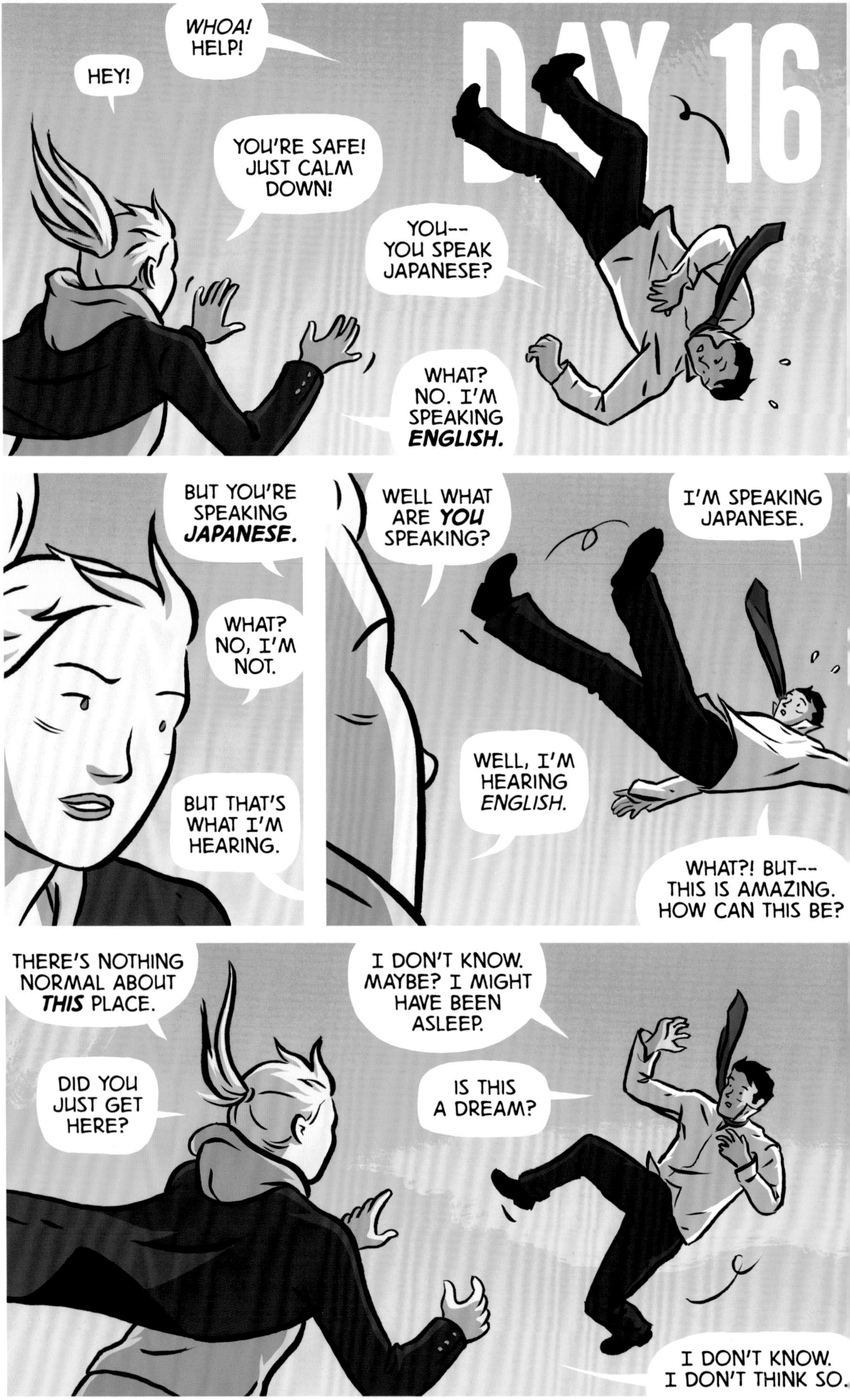
DAY 16
HEY!
WHOA! HELP!
YOU'RE SAFE! JUST CALM DOWN!
YOU-- YOU SPEAK JAPANESE?
WHAT? NO. I'M SPEAKING ENGLISH.
BUT YOU'RE SPEAKING JAPANESE.
WHAT? NO, I'M NOT.
BUT THAT'S WHAT I'M HEARING.
WELL WHAT ARE YOU SPEAKING?
I'M SPEAKING JAPANESE.
WELL, I'M HEARING ENGLISH.
WHAT?! BUT-- THIS IS AMAZING. HOW CAN THIS BE?
THERE'S NOTHING NORMAL ABOUT THIS PLACE.
DID YOU JUST GET HERE?
I DON'T KNOW. MAYBE? I MIGHT HAVE BEEN ASLEEP.
IS THIS A DREAM?
I DON'T KNOW. I DON'T THINK SO.

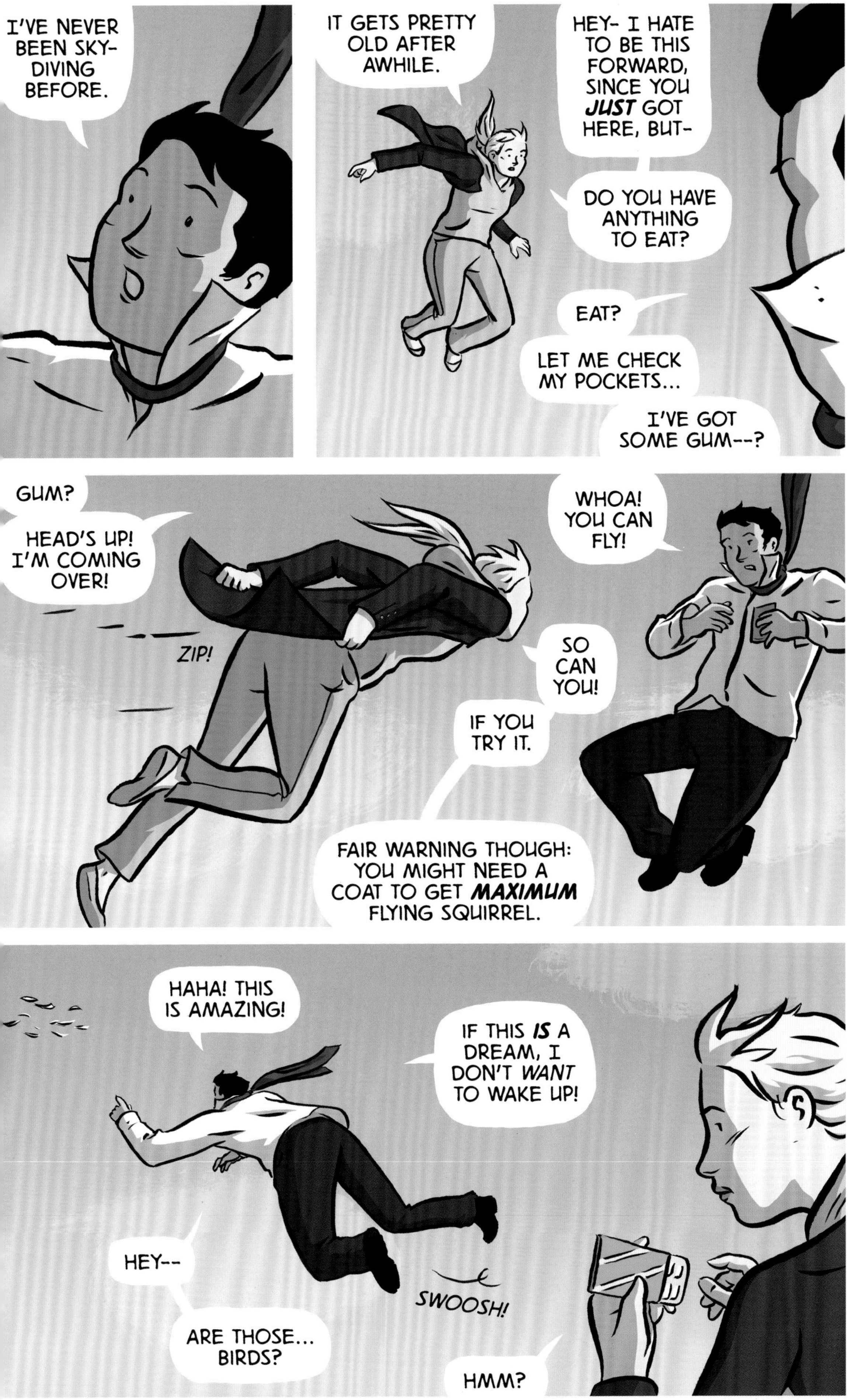
I'VE NEVER BEEN SKY-DIVING BEFORE.
IT GETS PRETTY OLD AFTER AWHILE.
HEY- I HATE TO BE THIS FORWARD, SINCE YOU *JUST* GOT HERE, BUT-
DO YOU HAVE ANYTHING TO EAT?
EAT?
LET ME CHECK MY POCKETS...
I'VE GOT SOME GUM--?
GUM?
HEAD'S UP! I'M COMING OVER!
ZIP!
WHOA! YOU CAN FLY!
SO CAN YOU!
IF YOU TRY IT.
FAIR WARNING THOUGH: YOU MIGHT NEED A COAT TO GET *MAXIMUM* FLYING SQUIRREL.
HAHA! THIS IS AMAZING!
IF THIS *IS* A DREAM, I DON'T *WANT* TO WAKE UP!
HEY--
SWOOSH!
ARE THOSE... BIRDS?
HMM?

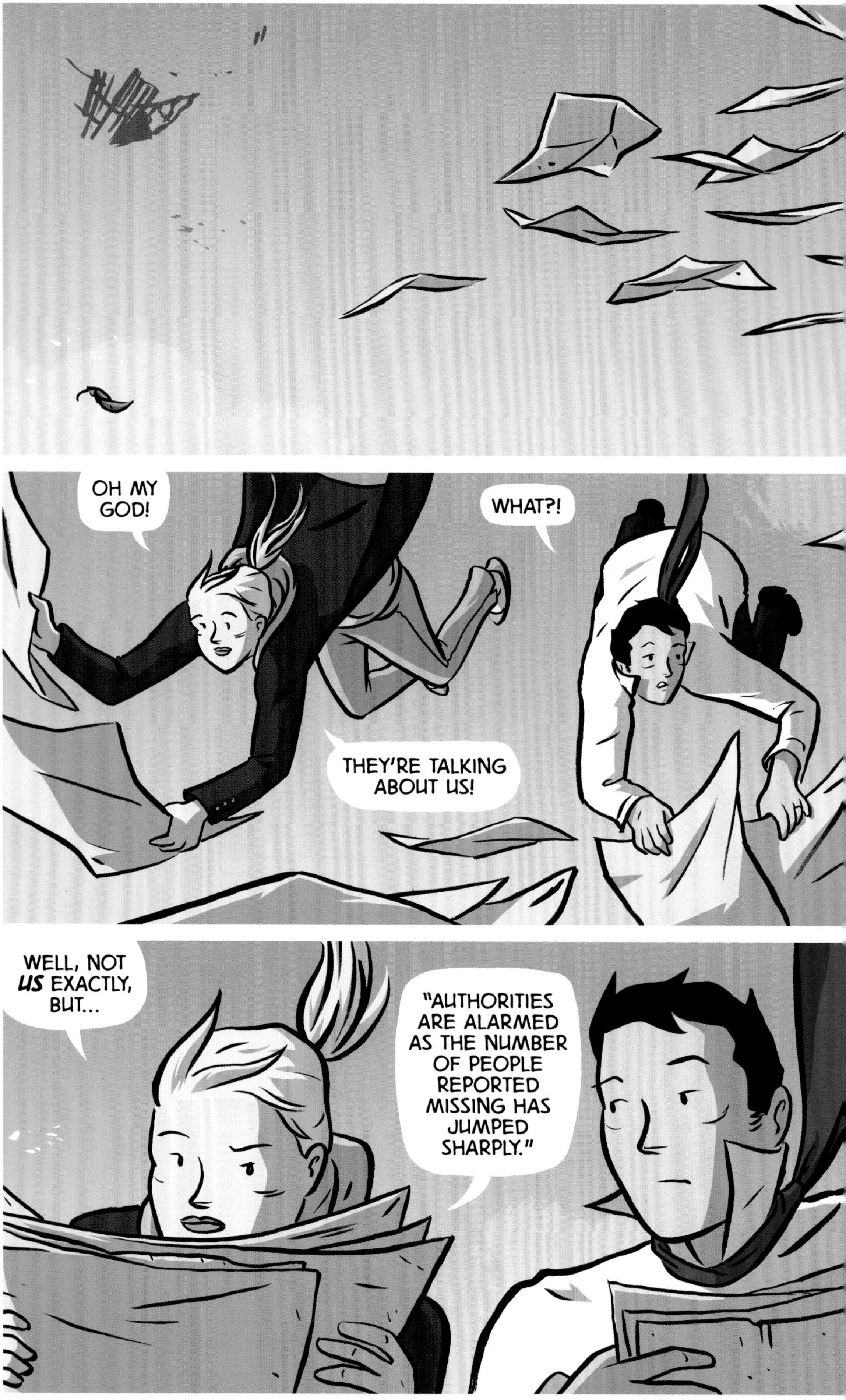
OH MY GOD!
WHAT?!
THEY'RE TALKING ABOUT US!
WELL, NOT *US* EXACTLY, BUT...
"AUTHORITIES ARE ALARMED AS THE NUMBER OF PEOPLE REPORTED MISSING HAS JUMPED SHARPLY."

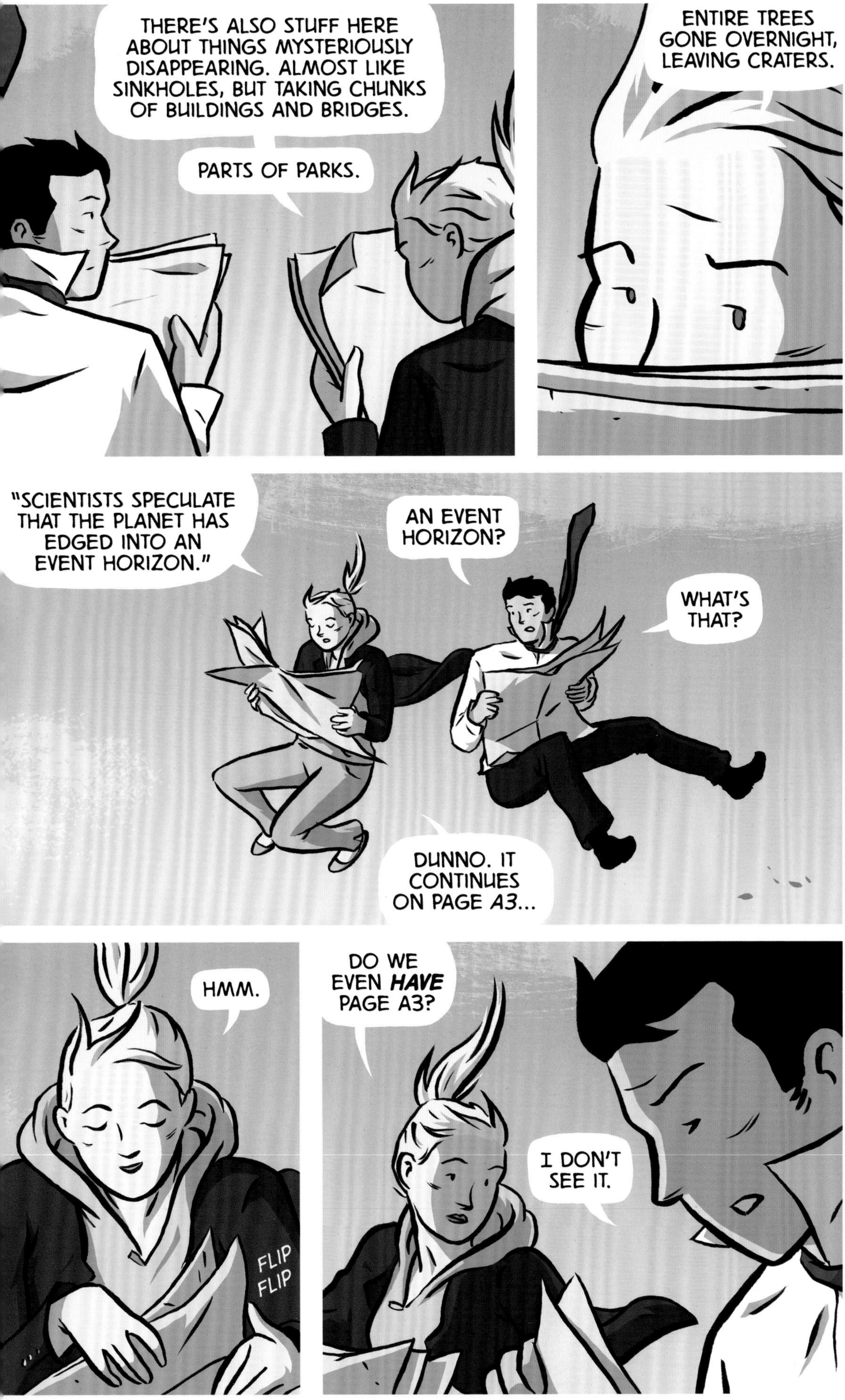
THERE'S ALSO STUFF HERE ABOUT THINGS MYSTERIOUSLY DISAPPEARING. ALMOST LIKE SINKHOLES, BUT TAKING CHUNKS OF BUILDINGS AND BRIDGES.
PARTS OF PARKS.
ENTIRE TREES GONE OVERNIGHT, LEAVING CRATERS.
"SCIENTISTS SPECULATE THAT THE PLANET HAS EDGED INTO AN EVENT HORIZON."
AN EVENT HORIZON?
WHAT'S THAT?
DUNNO. IT CONTINUES ON PAGE A3...
HMM.
FLIP FLIP
DO WE EVEN ***HAVE*** PAGE A3?
I DON'T SEE IT.

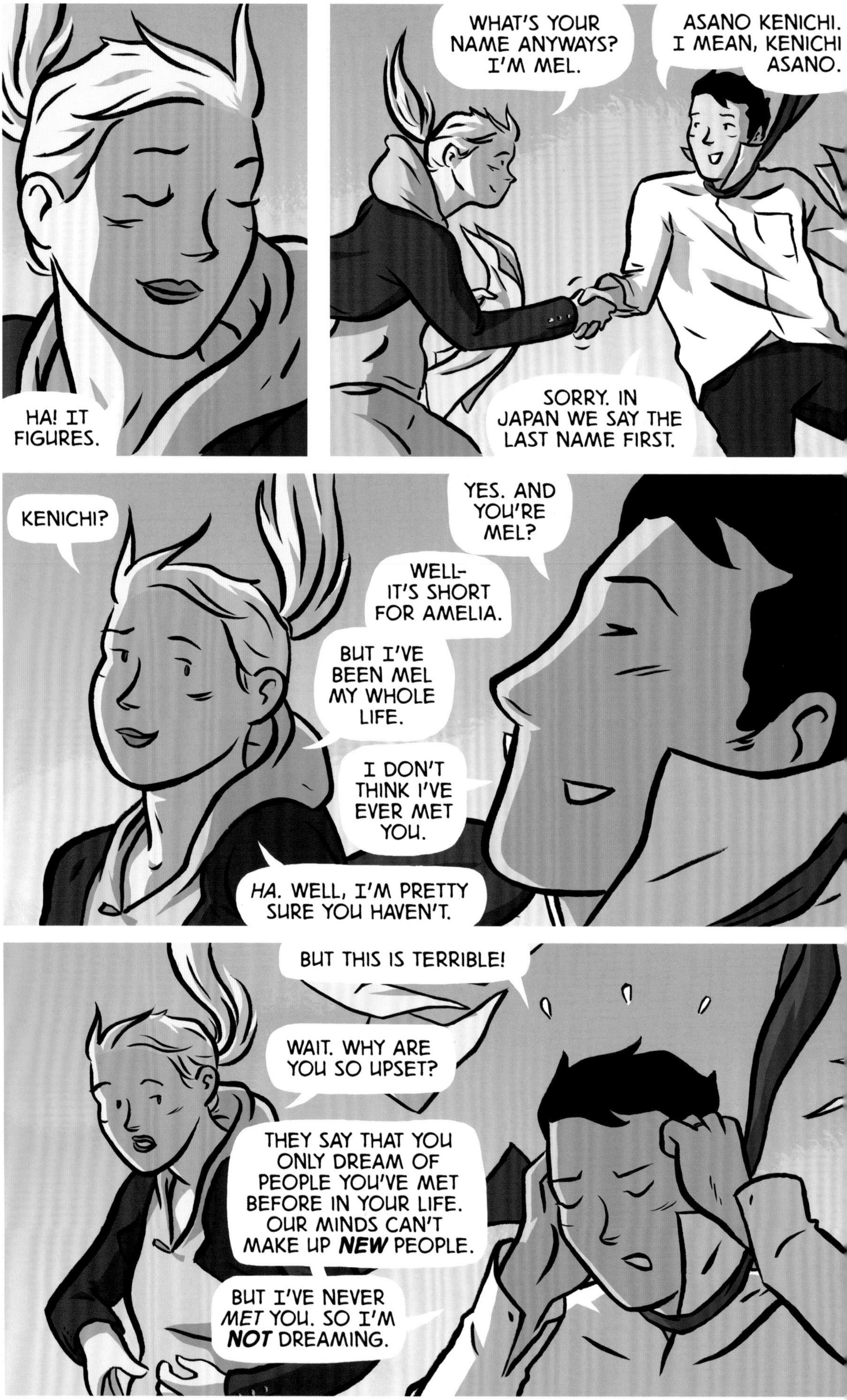
HA! IT FIGURES.
WHAT'S YOUR NAME ANYWAYS? I'M MEL.
ASANO KENICHI. I MEAN, KENICHI ASANO.
SORRY. IN JAPAN WE SAY THE LAST NAME FIRST.
KENICHI?
YES. AND YOU'RE MEL?
WELL- IT'S SHORT FOR AMELIA.
BUT I'VE BEEN MEL MY WHOLE LIFE.
I DON'T THINK I'VE EVER MET YOU.
HA. WELL, I'M PRETTY SURE YOU HAVEN'T.
BUT THIS IS TERRIBLE!
WAIT. WHY ARE YOU SO UPSET?
THEY SAY THAT YOU ONLY DREAM OF PEOPLE YOU'VE MET BEFORE IN YOUR LIFE. OUR MINDS CAN'T MAKE UP ***NEW*** PEOPLE.
BUT I'VE NEVER *MET* YOU. SO I'M ***NOT*** DREAMING.

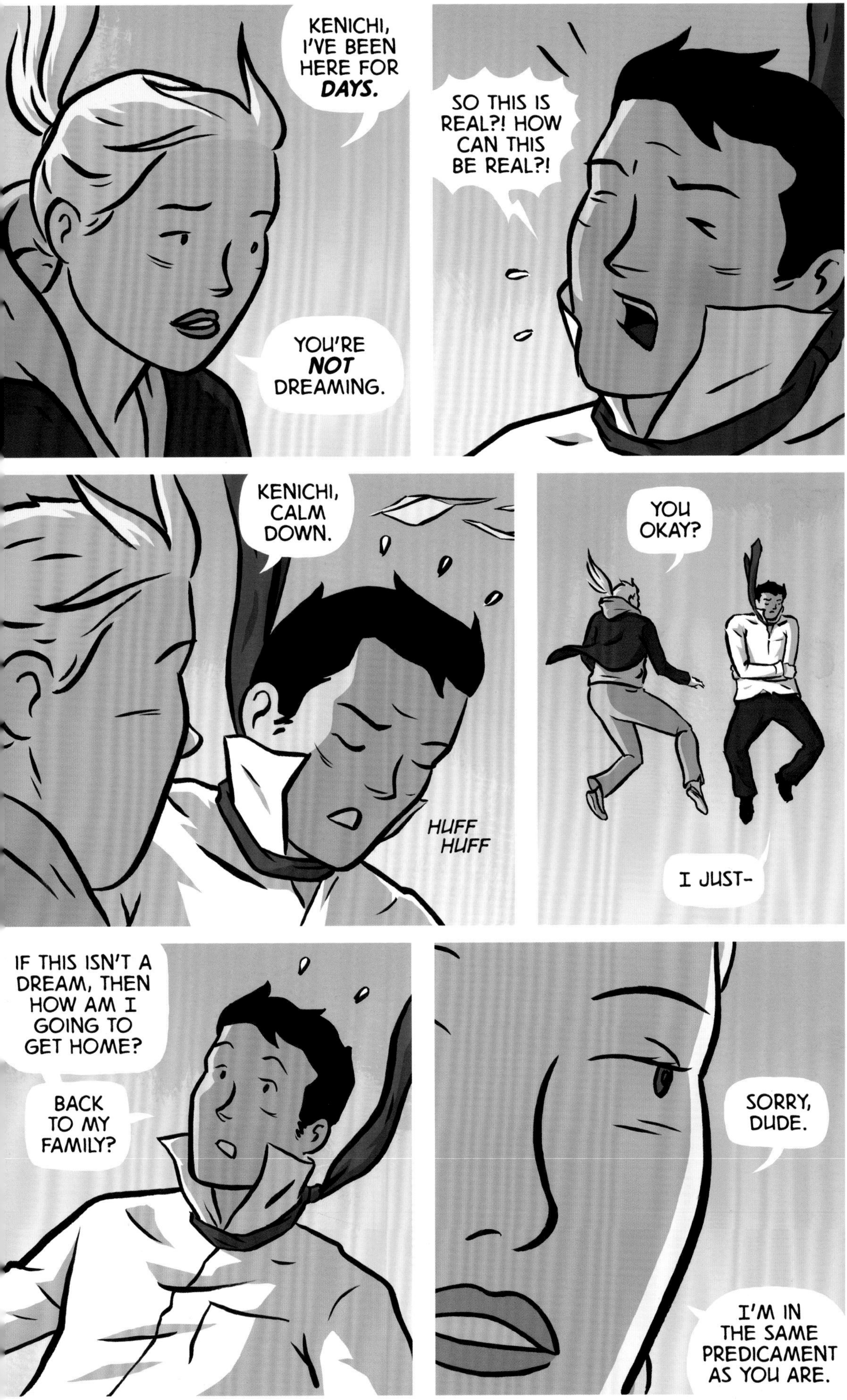
KENICHI, I'VE BEEN HERE FOR DAYS.
YOU'RE NOT DREAMING.
SO THIS IS REAL?! HOW CAN THIS BE REAL?!
KENICHI, CALM DOWN.
HUFF HUFF
YOU OKAY?
I JUST-
IF THIS ISN'T A DREAM, THEN HOW AM I GOING TO GET HOME?
BACK TO MY FAMILY?
SORRY, DUDE.
I'M IN THE SAME PREDICAMENT AS YOU ARE.

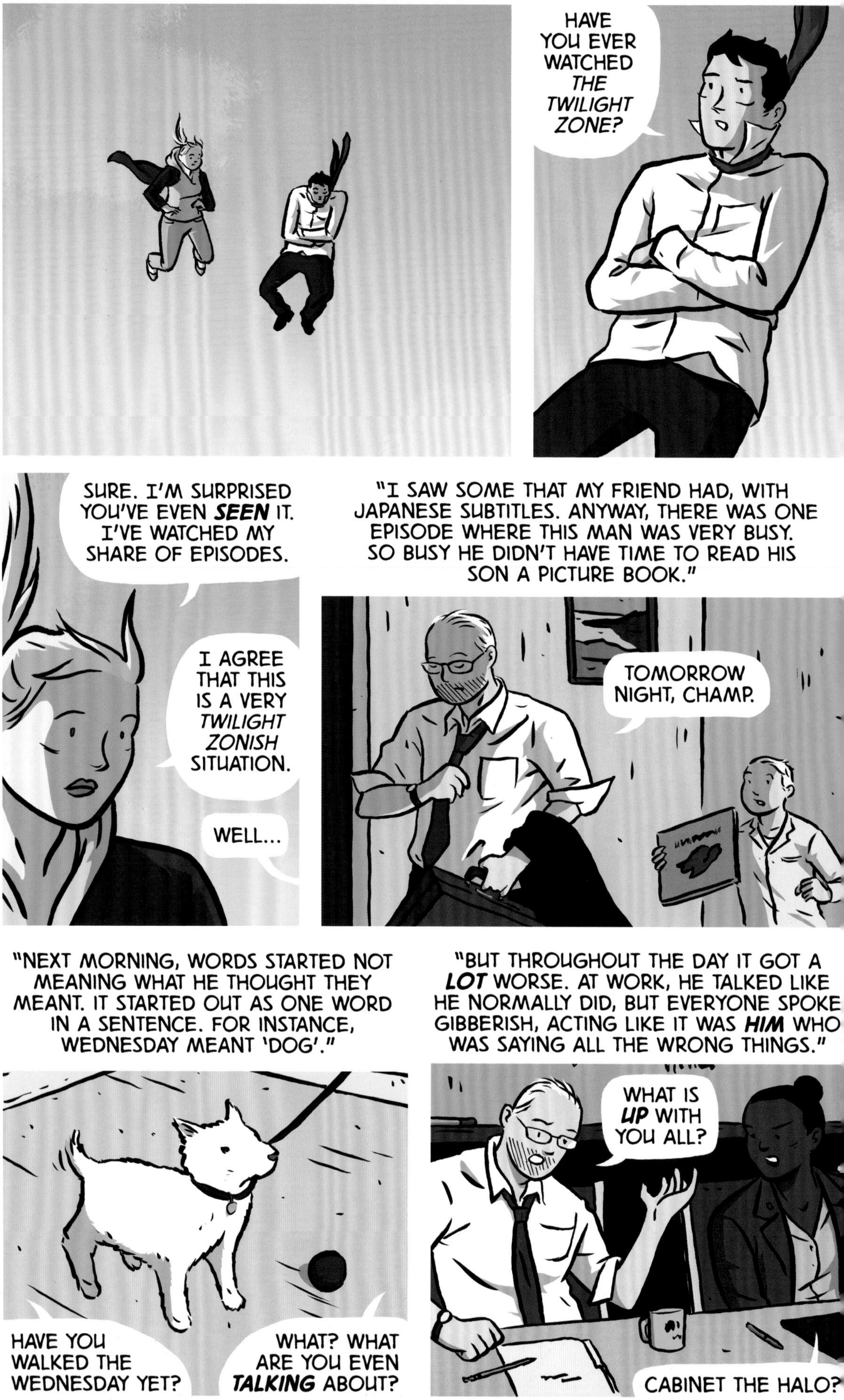
HAVE YOU EVER WATCHED *THE TWILIGHT ZONE?*
SURE. I'M SURPRISED YOU'VE EVEN ***SEEN*** IT. I'VE WATCHED MY SHARE OF EPISODES.
I AGREE THAT THIS IS A VERY *TWILIGHT ZONISH* SITUATION.
WELL...
"I SAW SOME THAT MY FRIEND HAD, WITH JAPANESE SUBTITLES. ANYWAY, THERE WAS ONE EPISODE WHERE THIS MAN WAS VERY BUSY. SO BUSY HE DIDN'T HAVE TIME TO READ HIS SON A PICTURE BOOK."
TOMORROW NIGHT, CHAMP.
"NEXT MORNING, WORDS STARTED NOT MEANING WHAT HE THOUGHT THEY MEANT. IT STARTED OUT AS ONE WORD IN A SENTENCE. FOR INSTANCE, WEDNESDAY MEANT 'DOG'."
HAVE YOU WALKED THE WEDNESDAY YET?
WHAT? WHAT ARE YOU EVEN ***TALKING*** ABOUT?
"BUT THROUGHOUT THE DAY IT GOT A ***LOT*** WORSE. AT WORK, HE TALKED LIKE HE NORMALLY DID, BUT EVERYONE SPOKE GIBBERISH, ACTING LIKE IT WAS ***HIM*** WHO WAS SAYING ALL THE WRONG THINGS."
WHAT IS ***UP*** WITH YOU ALL?
CABINET THE HALO?

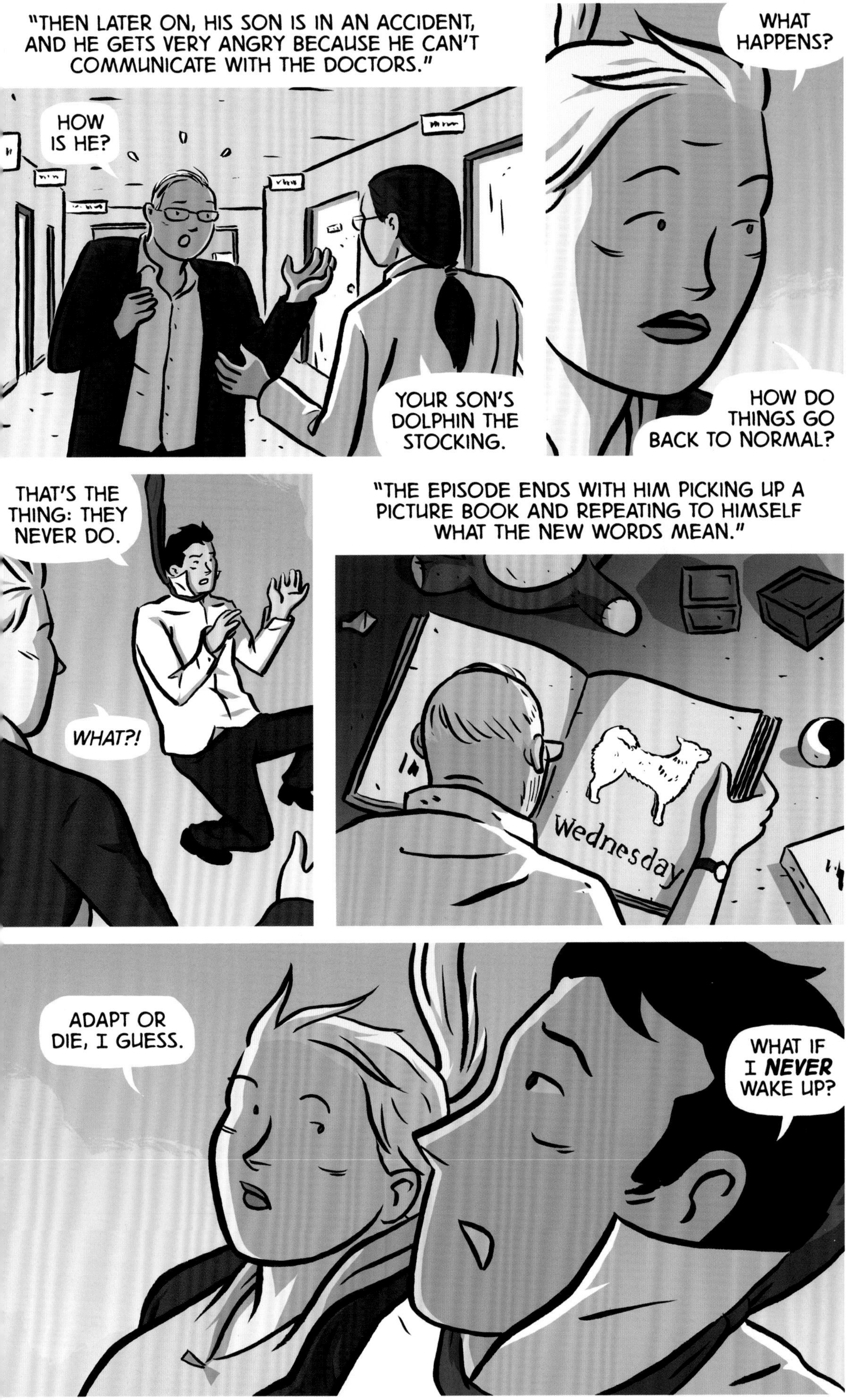
"THEN LATER ON, HIS SON IS IN AN ACCIDENT, AND HE GETS VERY ANGRY BECAUSE HE CAN'T COMMUNICATE WITH THE DOCTORS."
HOW IS HE?
YOUR SON'S DOLPHIN THE STOCKING.
WHAT HAPPENS?
HOW DO THINGS GO BACK TO NORMAL?
THAT'S THE THING: THEY NEVER DO.
WHAT?!
"THE EPISODE ENDS WITH HIM PICKING UP A PICTURE BOOK AND REPEATING TO HIMSELF WHAT THE NEW WORDS MEAN."
Wednesday
ADAPT OR DIE, I GUESS.
WHAT IF I ***NEVER*** WAKE UP?

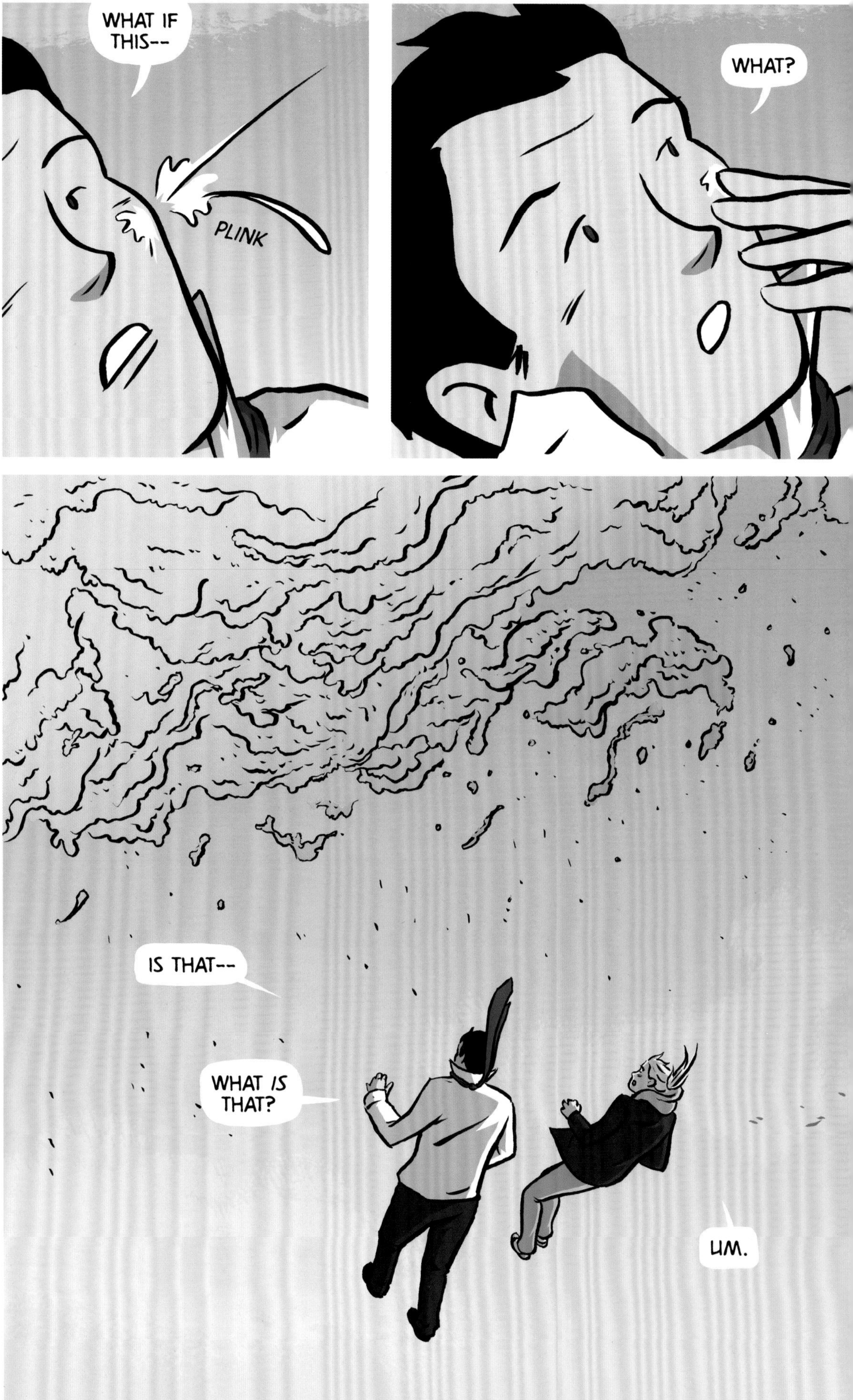
WHAT IF THIS--
PLINK
WHAT?
IS THAT--
WHAT *IS* THAT?
UM.

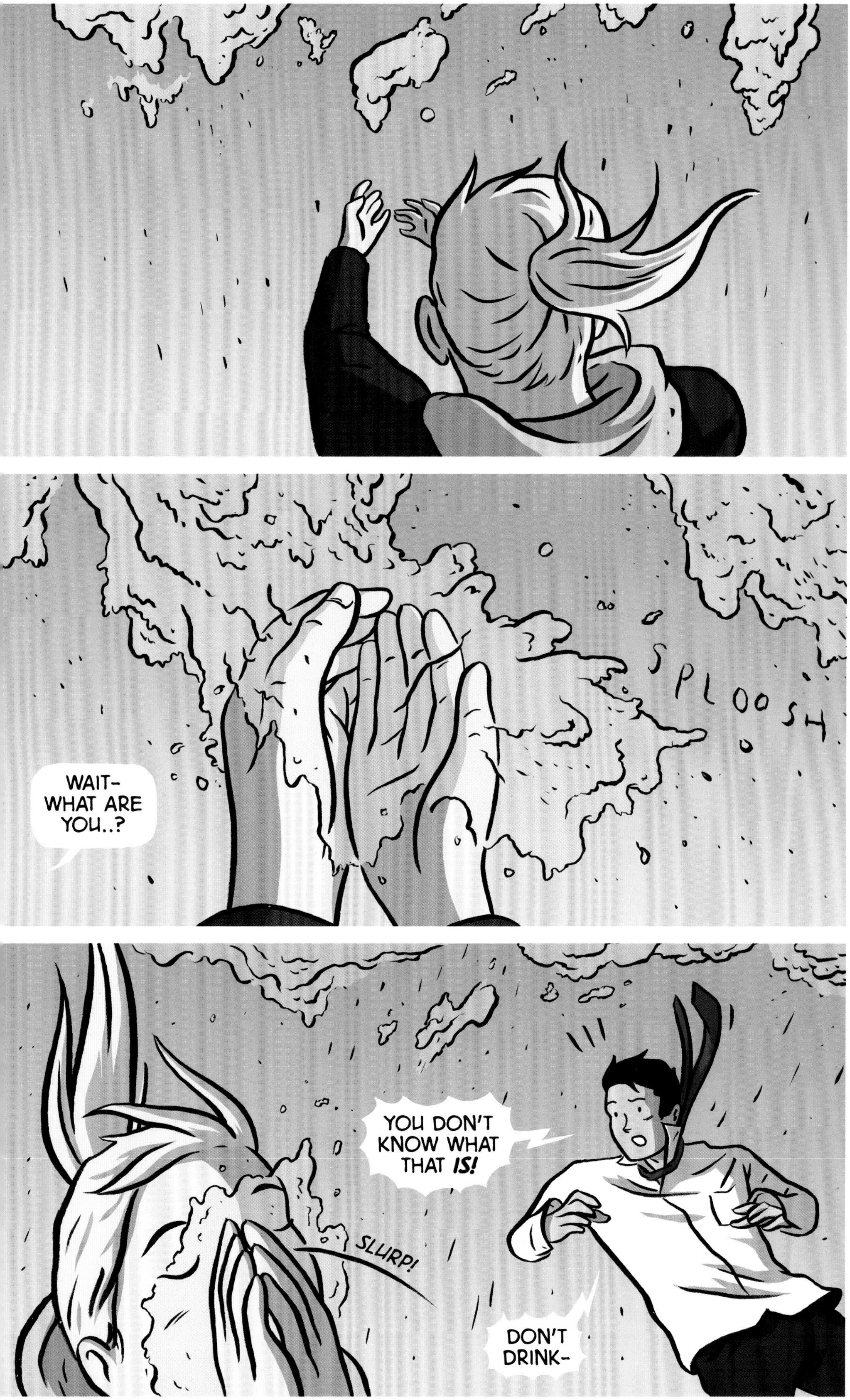
SPLOOSH
WAIT- WHAT ARE YOU..?
YOU DON'T KNOW WHAT THAT *IS!*
SLURP!
DON'T DRINK-

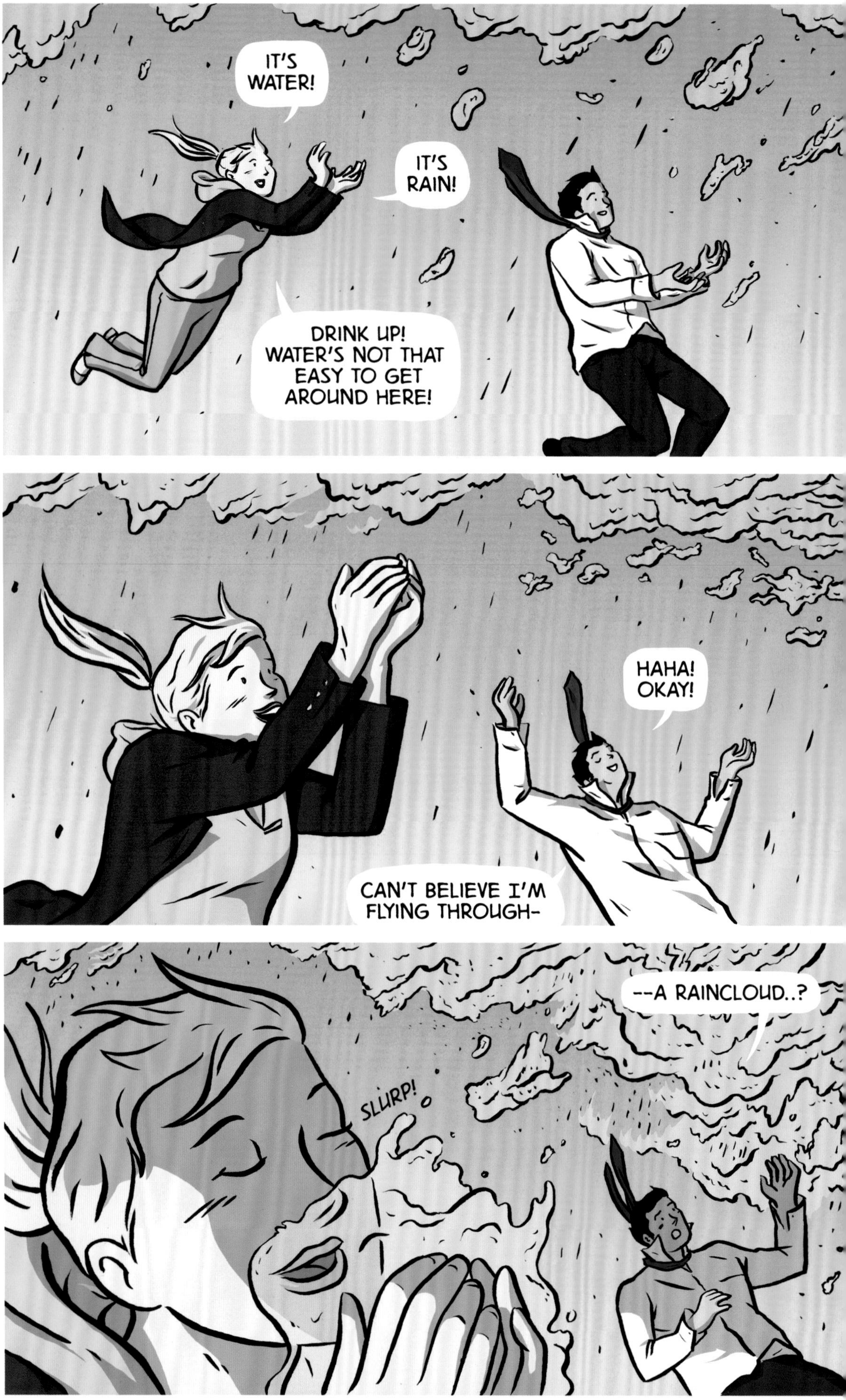
IT'S WATER!
IT'S RAIN!
DRINK UP! WATER'S NOT THAT EASY TO GET AROUND HERE!
HAHA! OKAY!
CAN'T BELIEVE I'M FLYING THROUGH-
SLURP!
--A RAINCLOUD..?

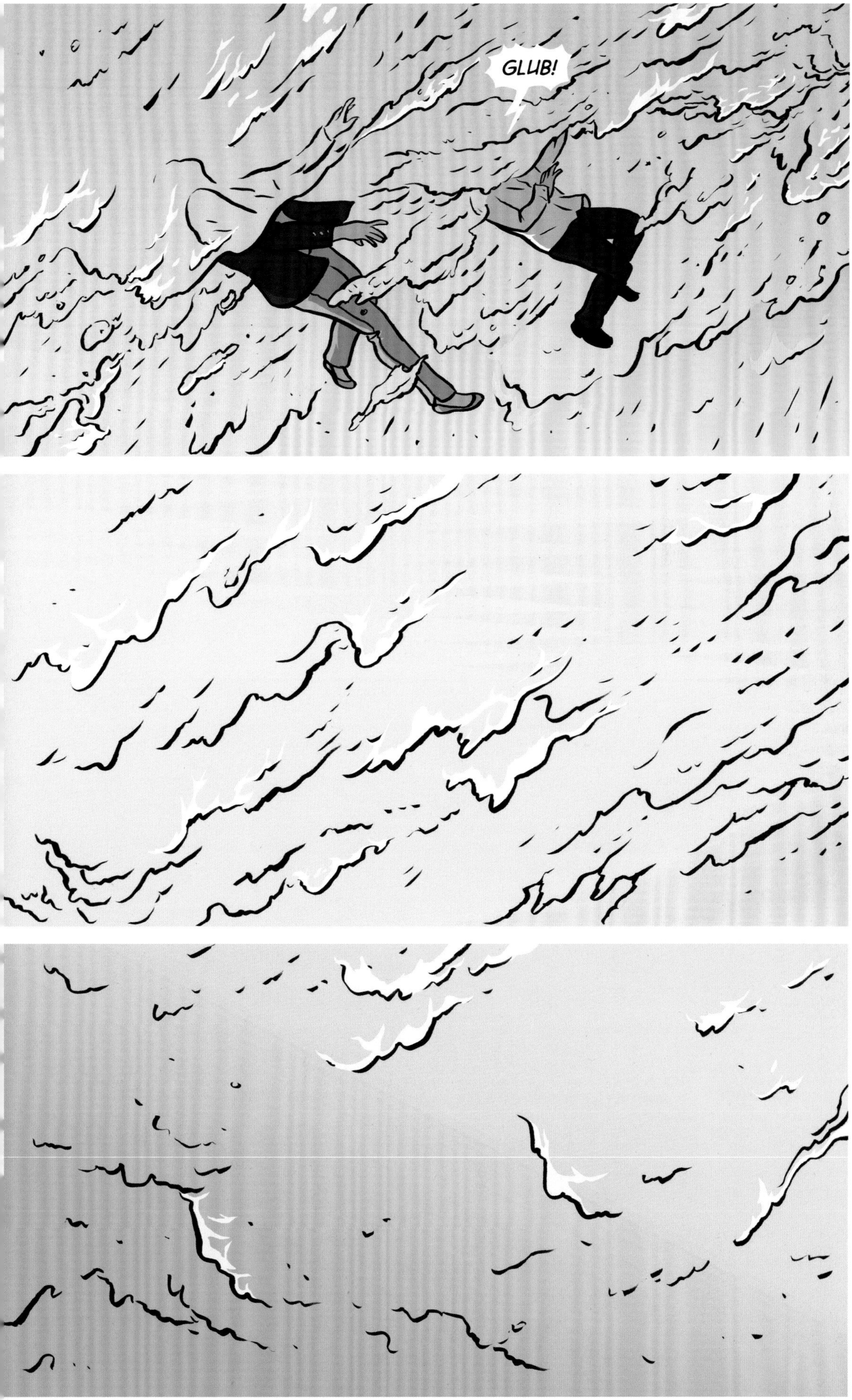
GLUB!

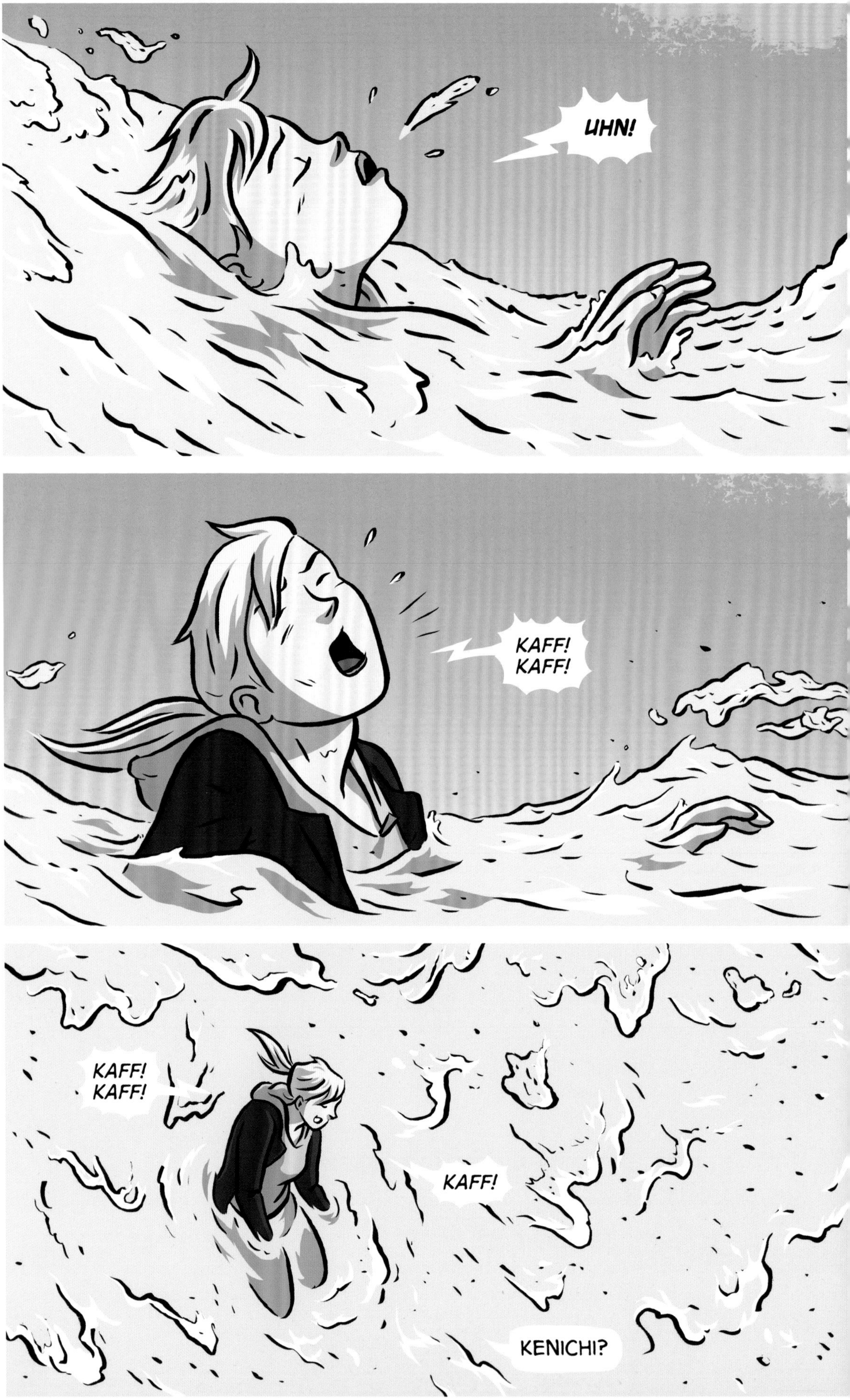
UHN!
KAFF!
KAFF!
KAFF!
KAFF!
KAFF!
KENICHI?

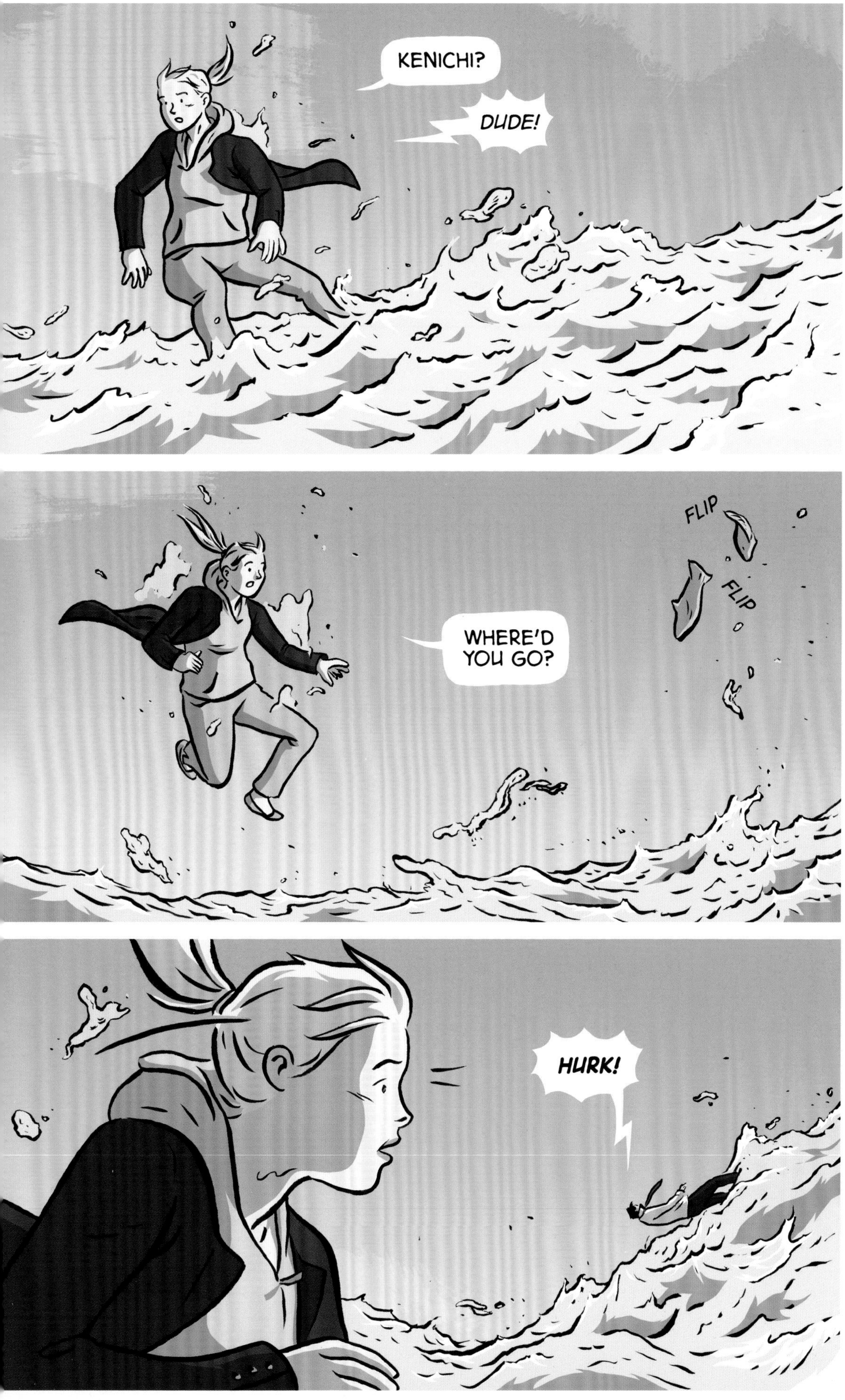
KENICHI?
DUDE!
FLIP
FLIP
WHERE'D YOU GO?
HURK!

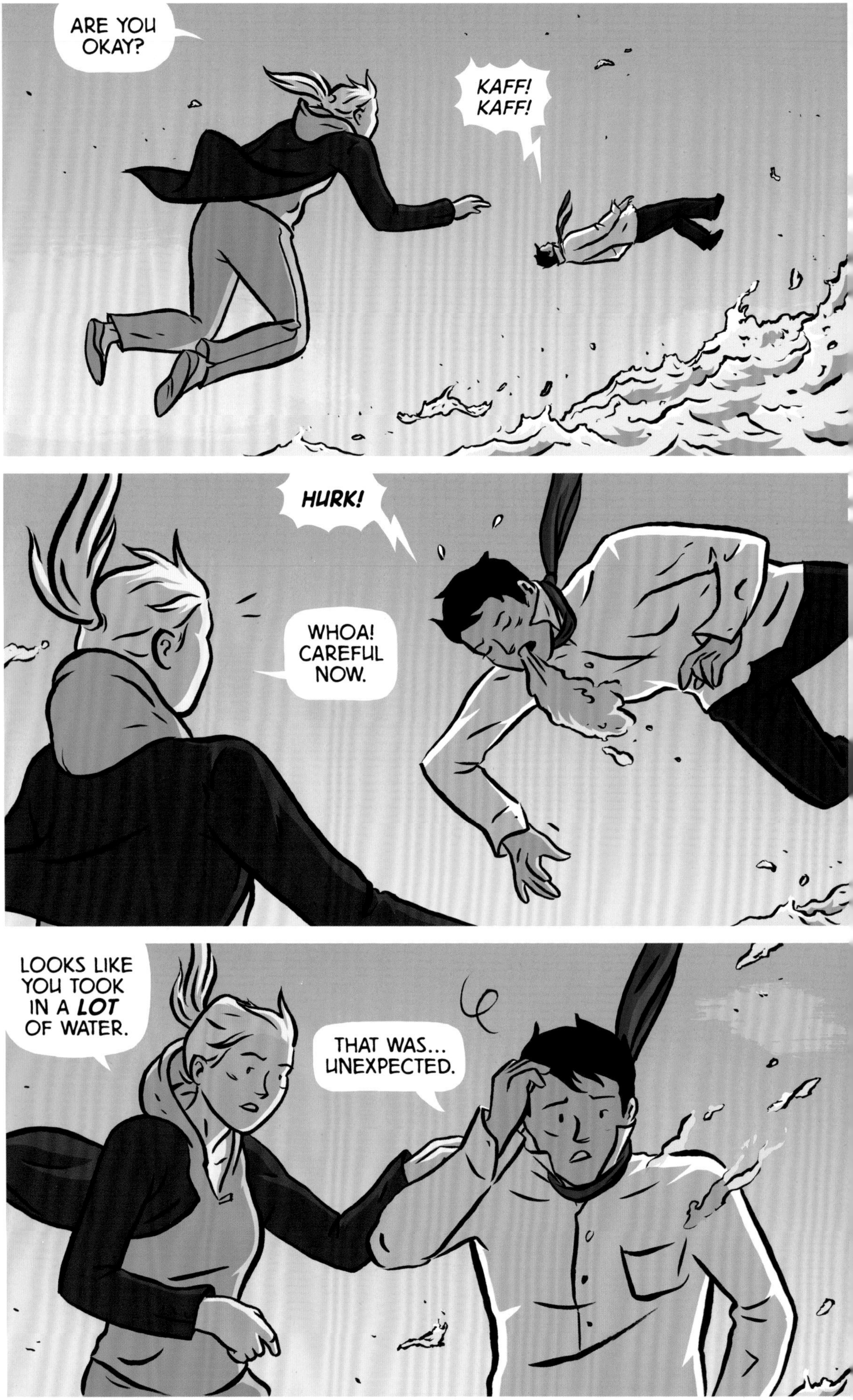
ARE YOU OKAY?
KAFF! KAFF!
HURK!
WHOA! CAREFUL NOW.
LOOKS LIKE YOU TOOK IN A ***LOT*** OF WATER.
THAT WAS... UNEXPECTED.

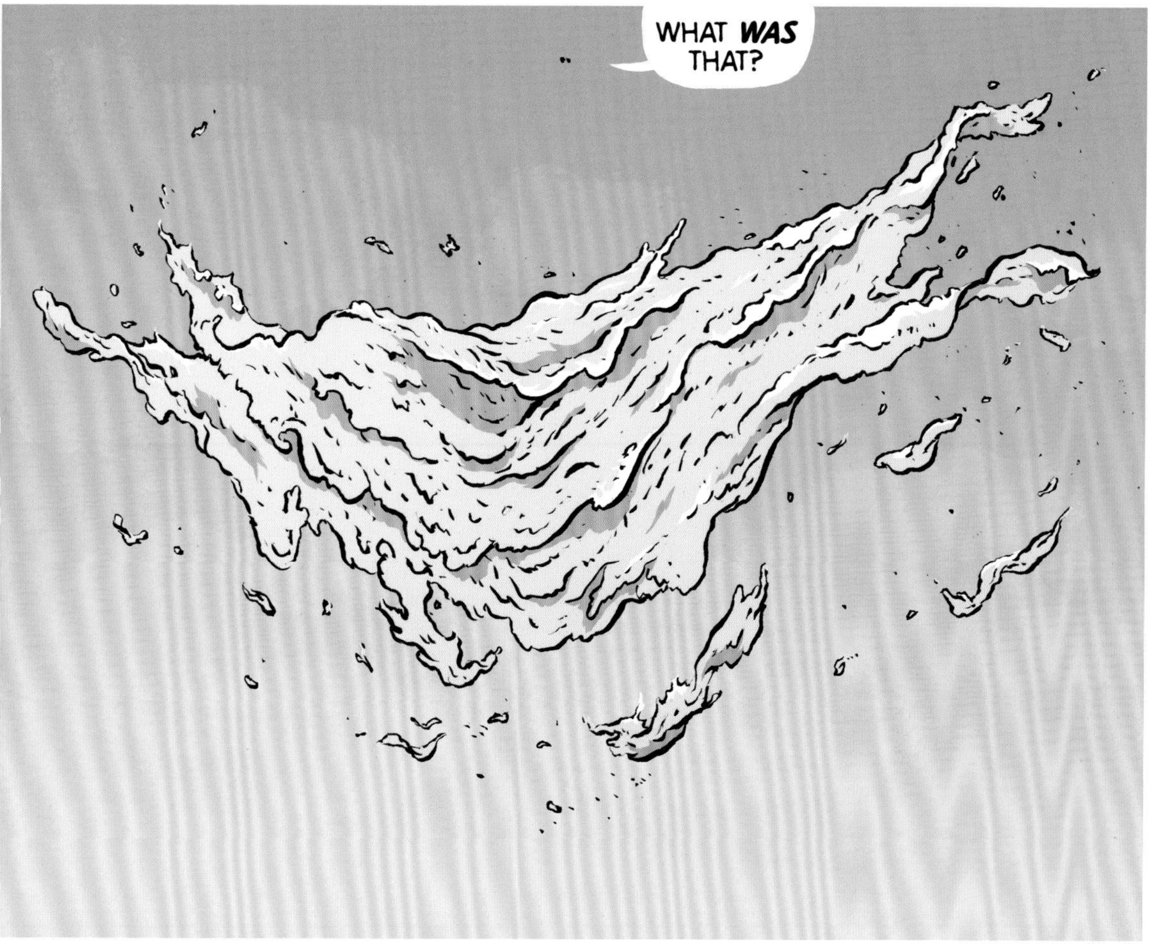
WHAT WAS THAT?

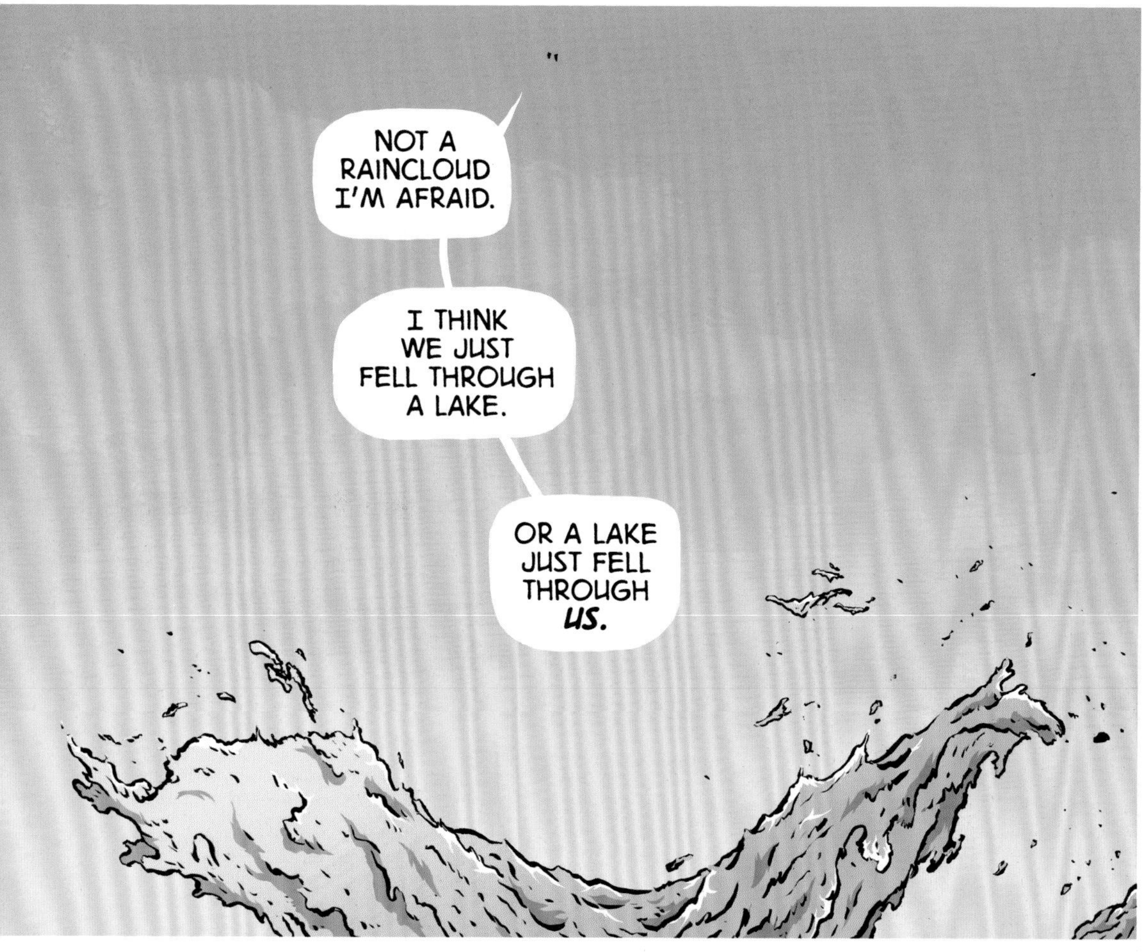
NOT A RAINCLOUD I'M AFRAID.
I THINK WE JUST FELL THROUGH A LAKE.
OR A LAKE JUST FELL THROUGH US.

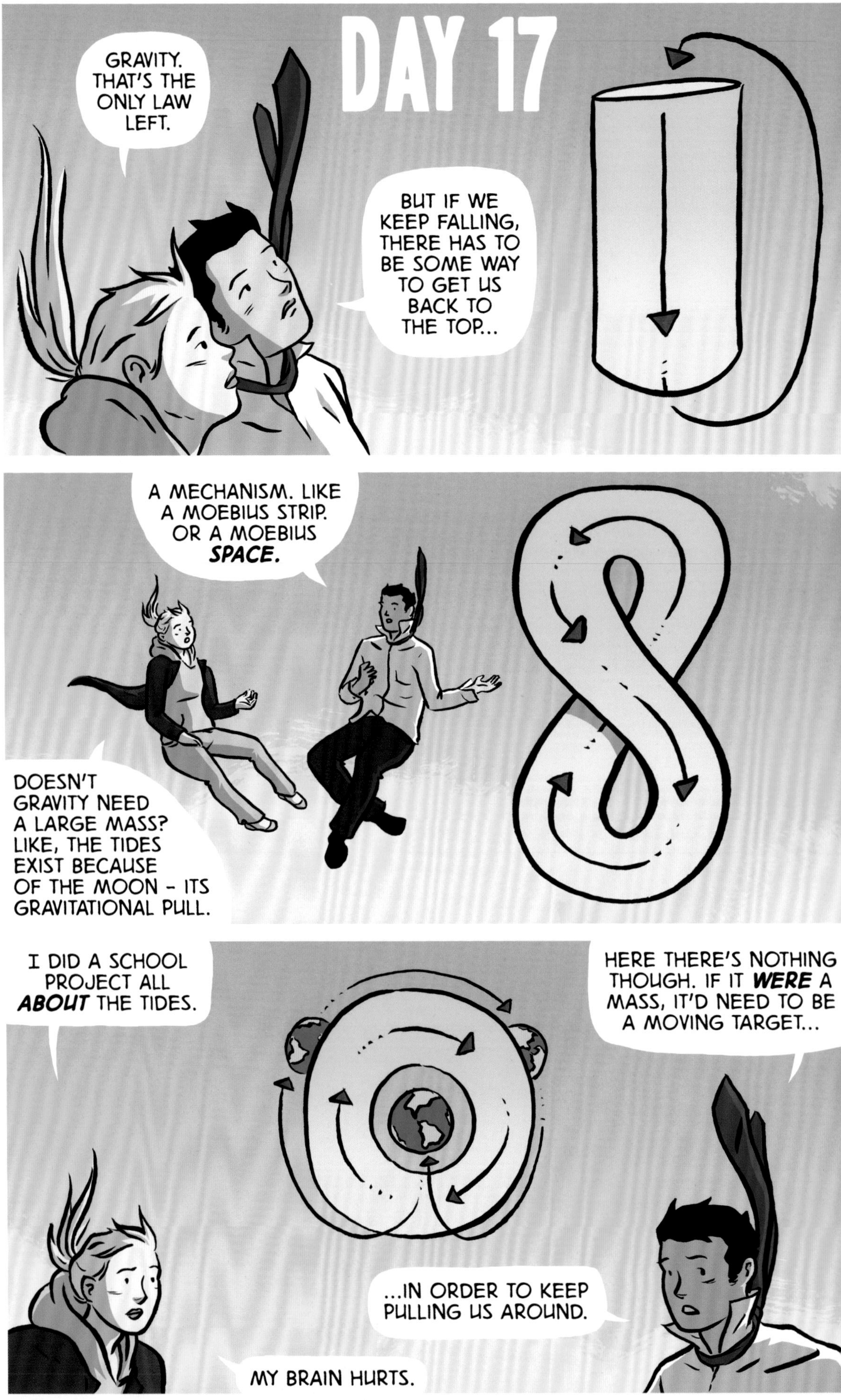
DAY 17
GRAVITY. THAT'S THE ONLY LAW LEFT.
BUT IF WE KEEP FALLING, THERE HAS TO BE SOME WAY TO GET US BACK TO THE TOP...
A MECHANISM. LIKE A MOEBIUS STRIP. OR A MOEBIUS *SPACE.*
DOESN'T GRAVITY NEED A LARGE MASS? LIKE, THE TIDES EXIST BECAUSE OF THE MOON - ITS GRAVITATIONAL PULL.
I DID A SCHOOL PROJECT ALL *ABOUT* THE TIDES.
HERE THERE'S NOTHING THOUGH. IF IT *WERE* A MASS, IT'D NEED TO BE A MOVING TARGET...
...IN ORDER TO KEEP PULLING US AROUND.
MY BRAIN HURTS.

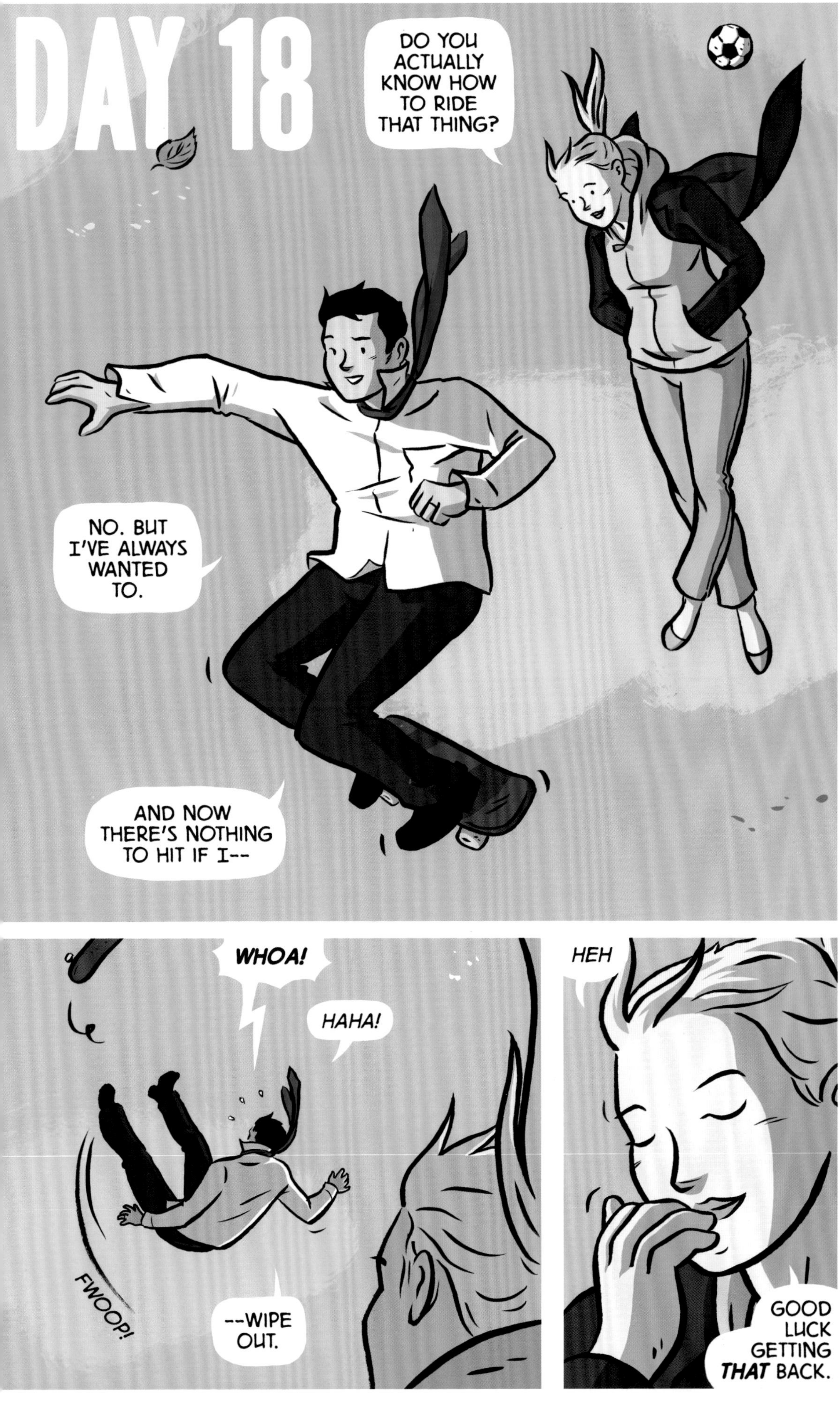
DAY 18
DO YOU ACTUALLY KNOW HOW TO RIDE THAT THING?
NO. BUT I'VE ALWAYS WANTED TO.
AND NOW THERE'S NOTHING TO HIT IF I--
WHOA!
HAHA!
FWOOP!
--WIPE OUT.
HEH
GOOD LUCK GETTING ***THAT*** BACK.

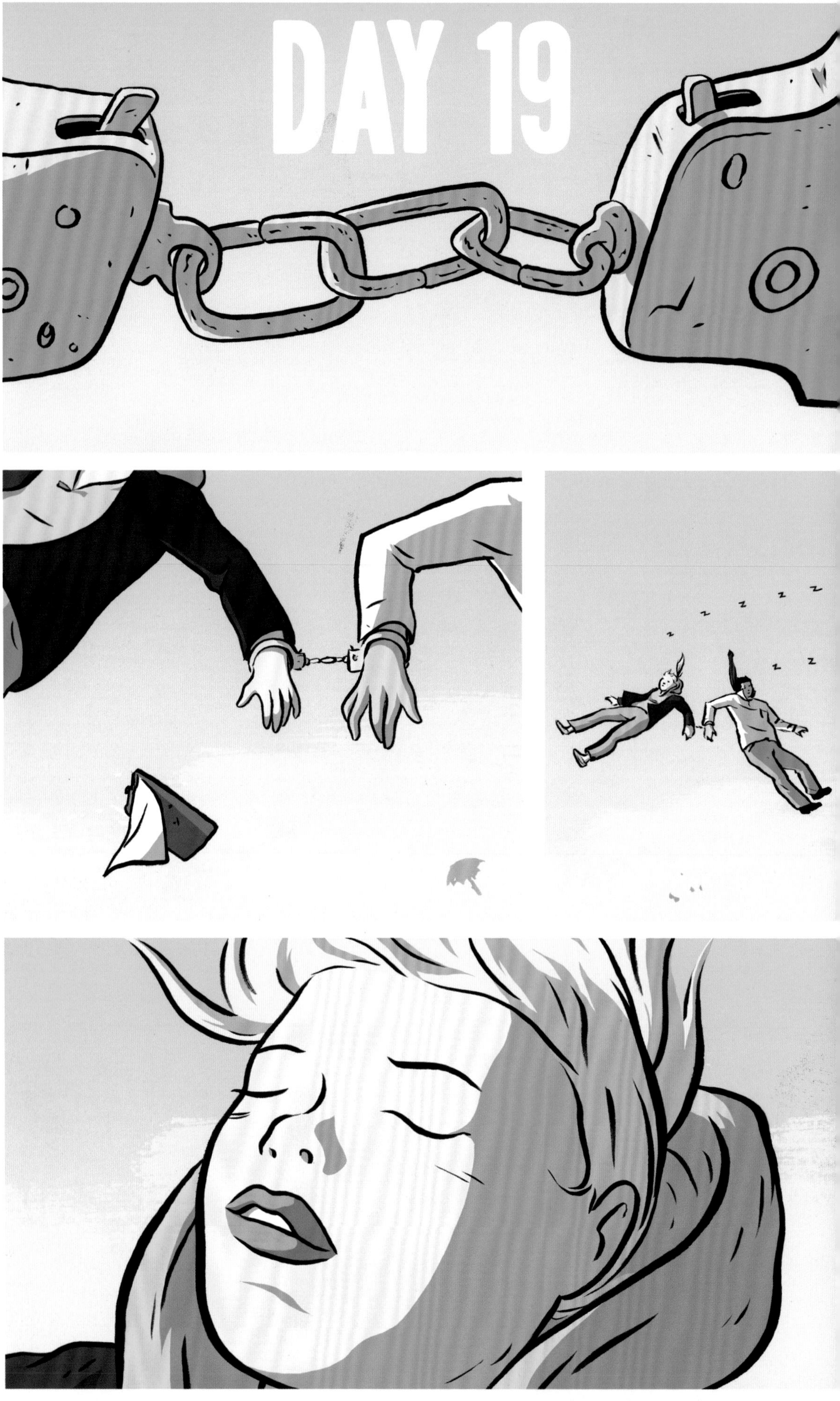
DAY 19
z z z z z
z z

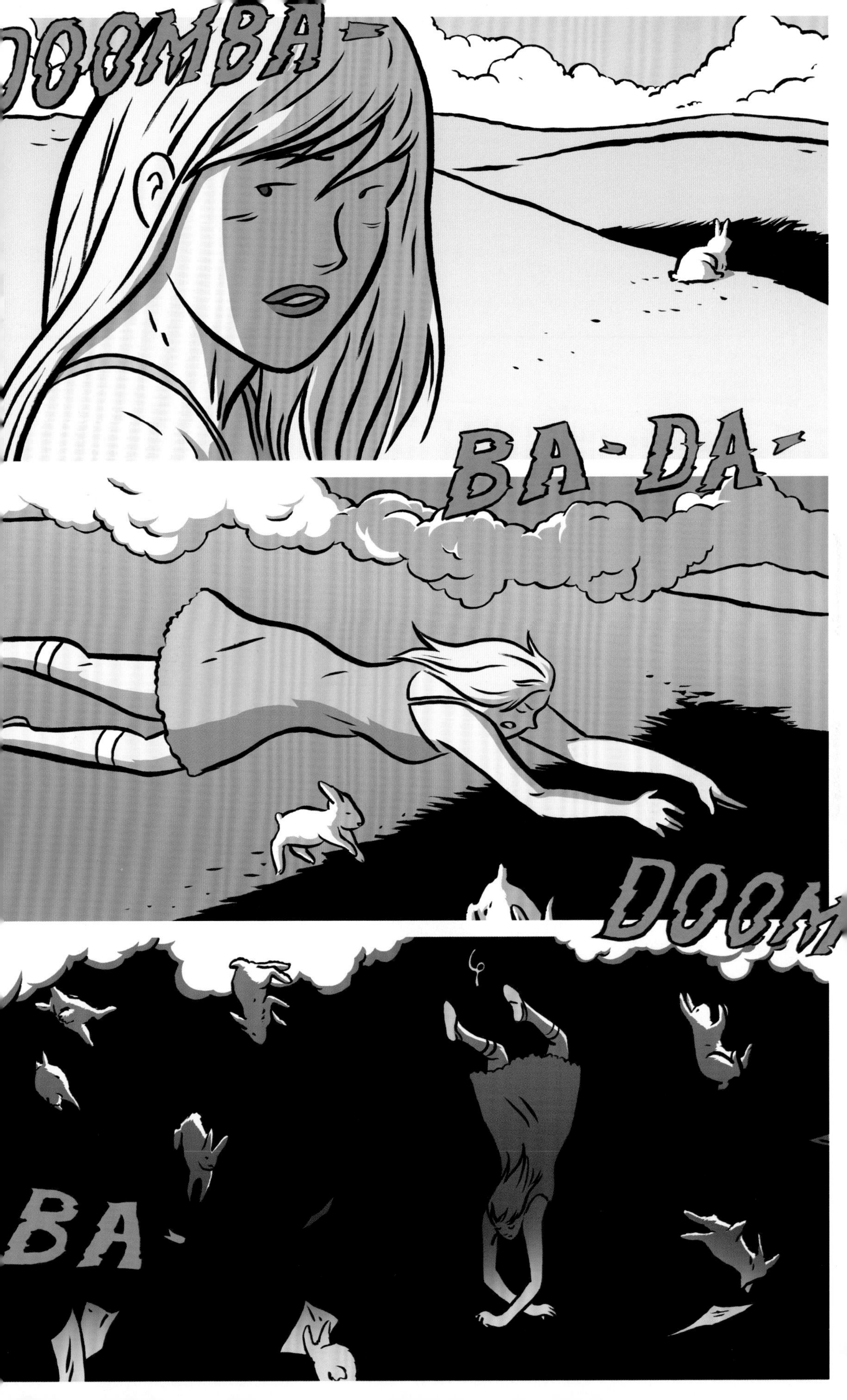

OOOMBA-
BA-DA-
DOOM
BA-

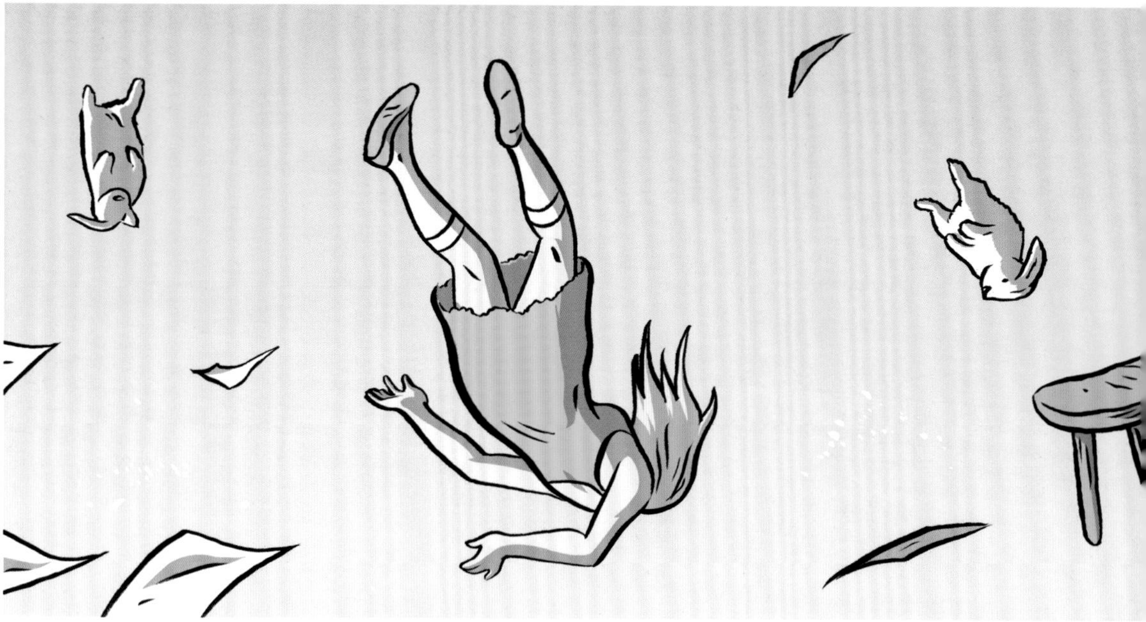
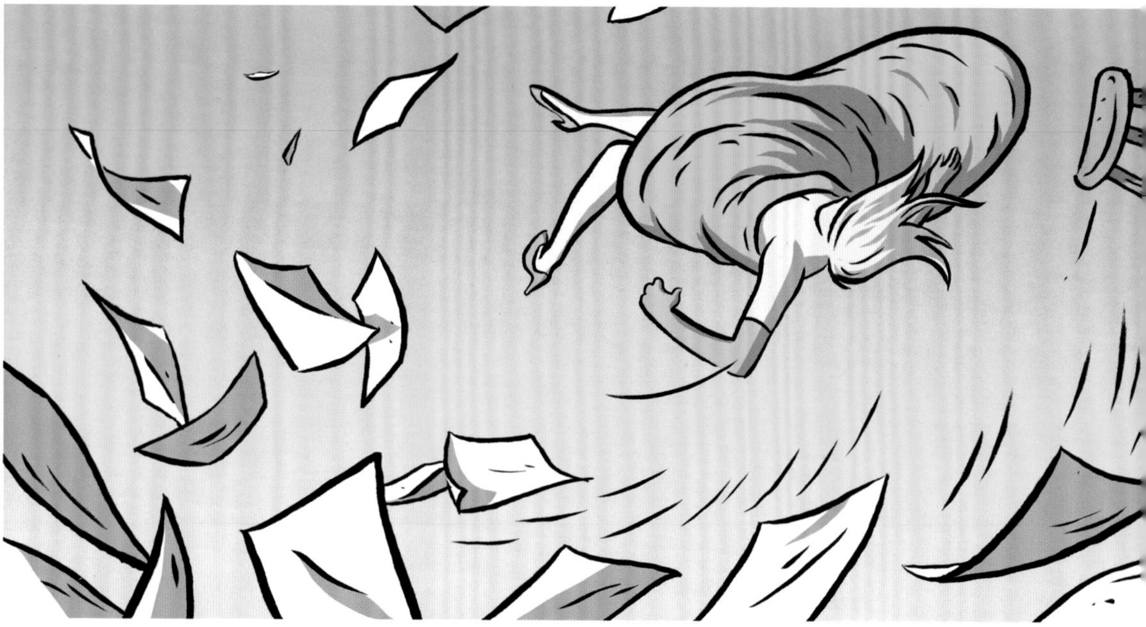
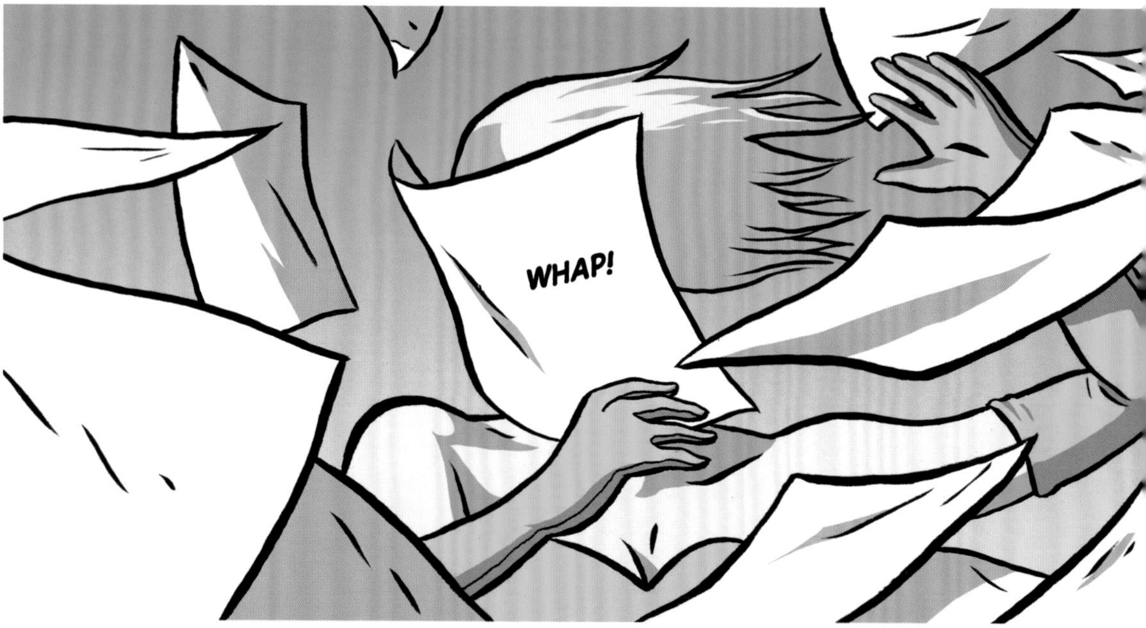
WHAP!

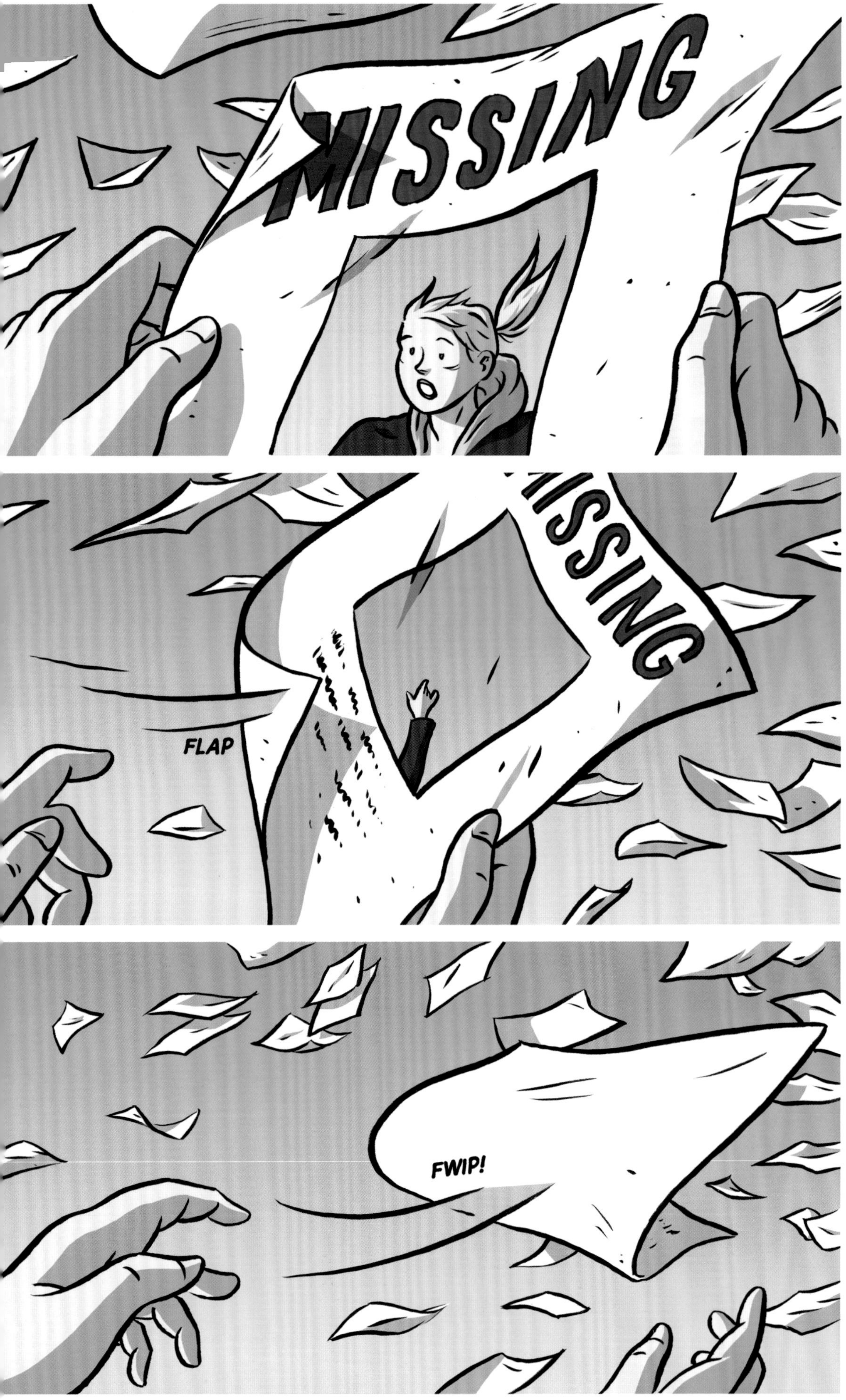
MISSING
ISSING
FLAP
FWIP!

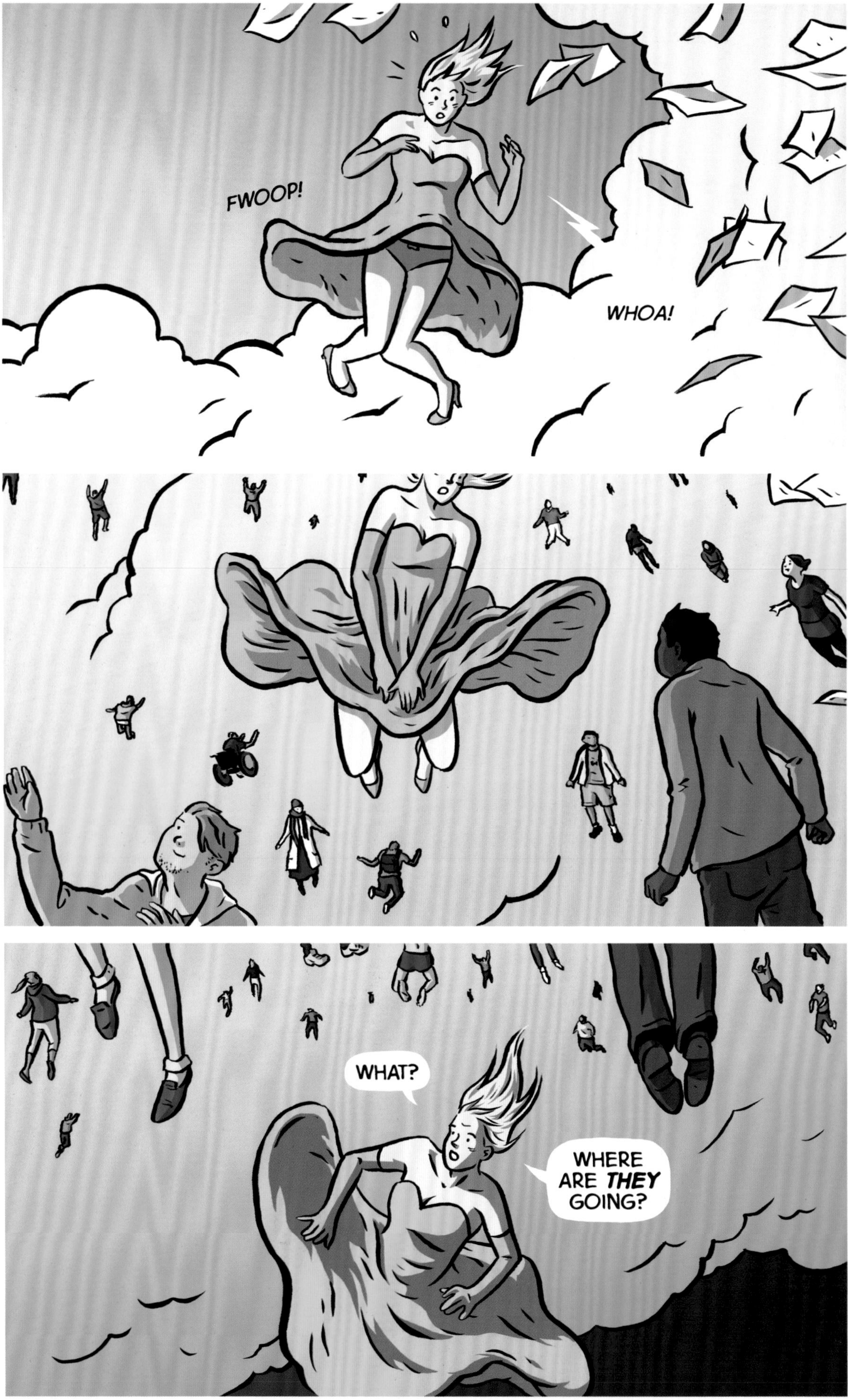
FWOOP!
WHOA!
WHAT?
WHERE ARE THEY GOING?

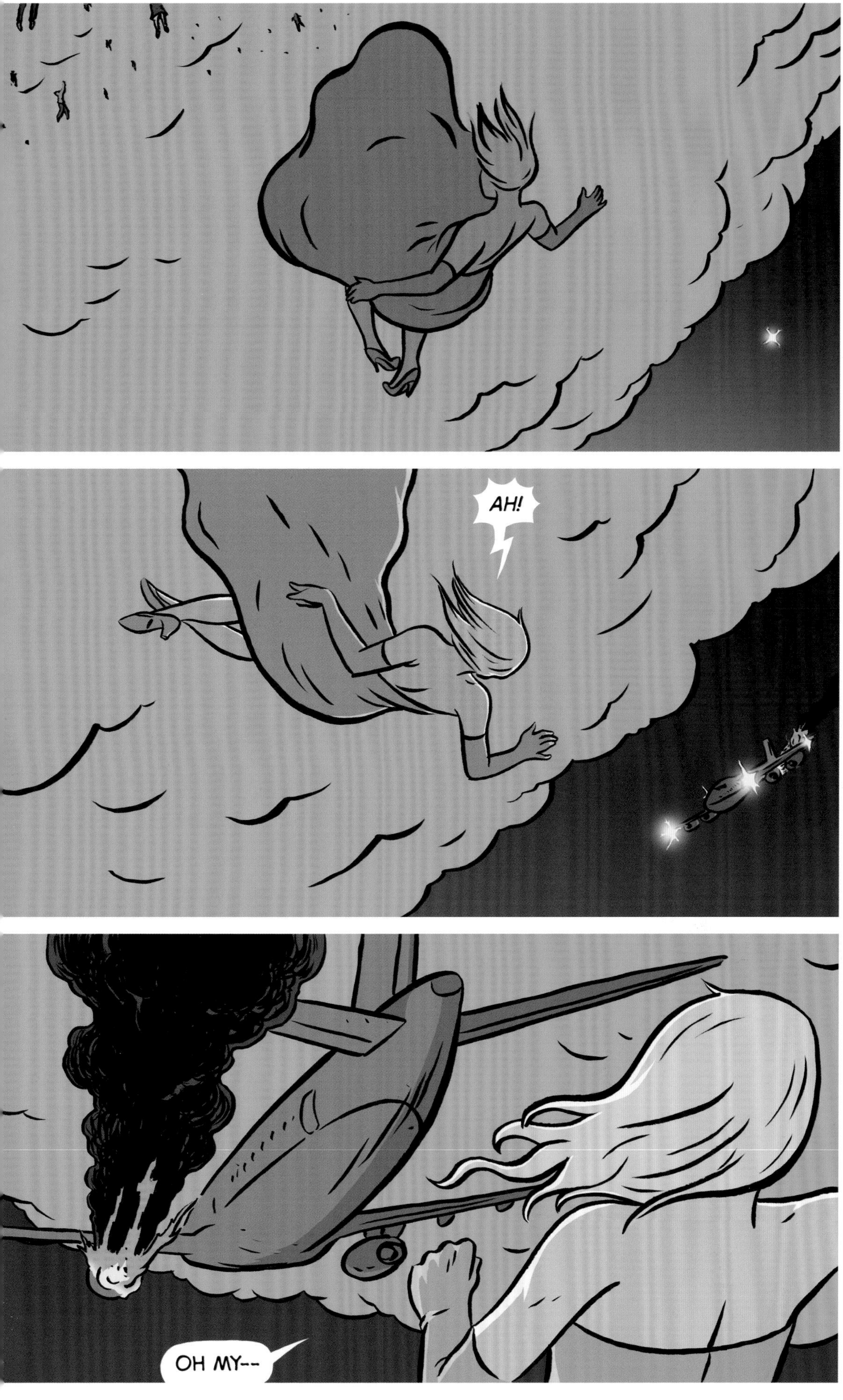
AH!
OH MY--

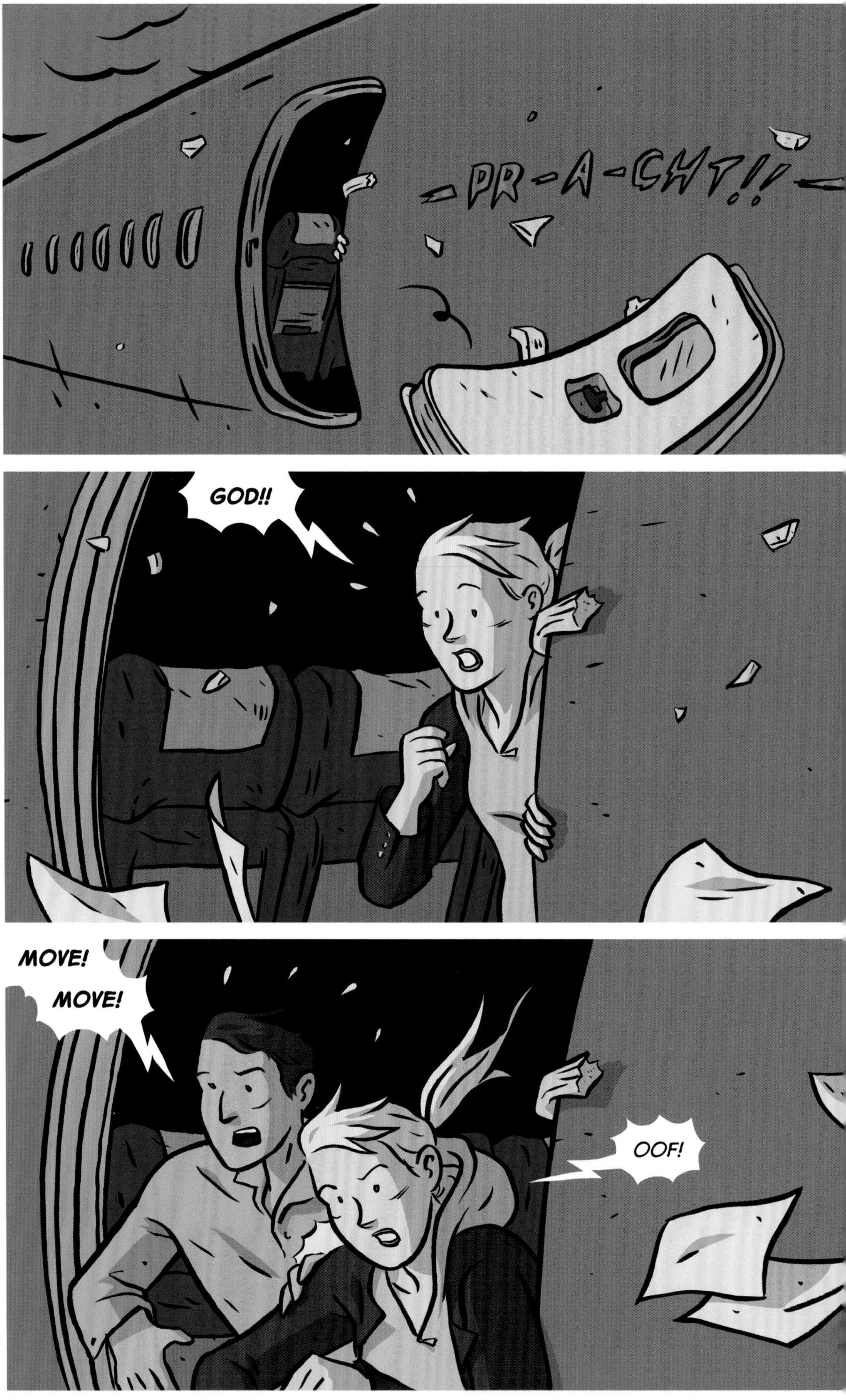
-PR-A-CHT!!-
GOD!!
MOVE!
MOVE!
OOF!

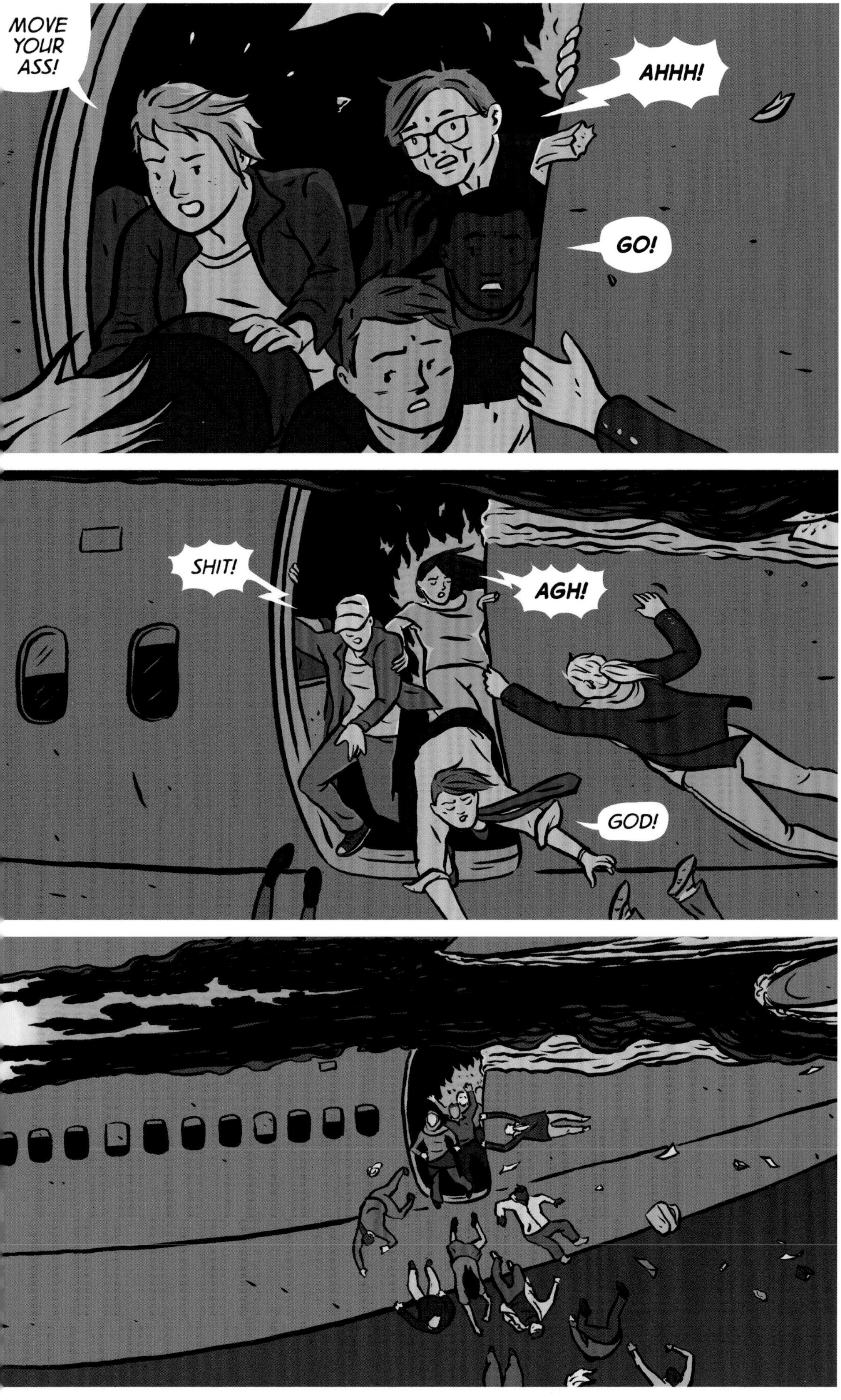
MOVE YOUR ASS!
AHHH!
GO!
SHIT!
AGH!
GOD!

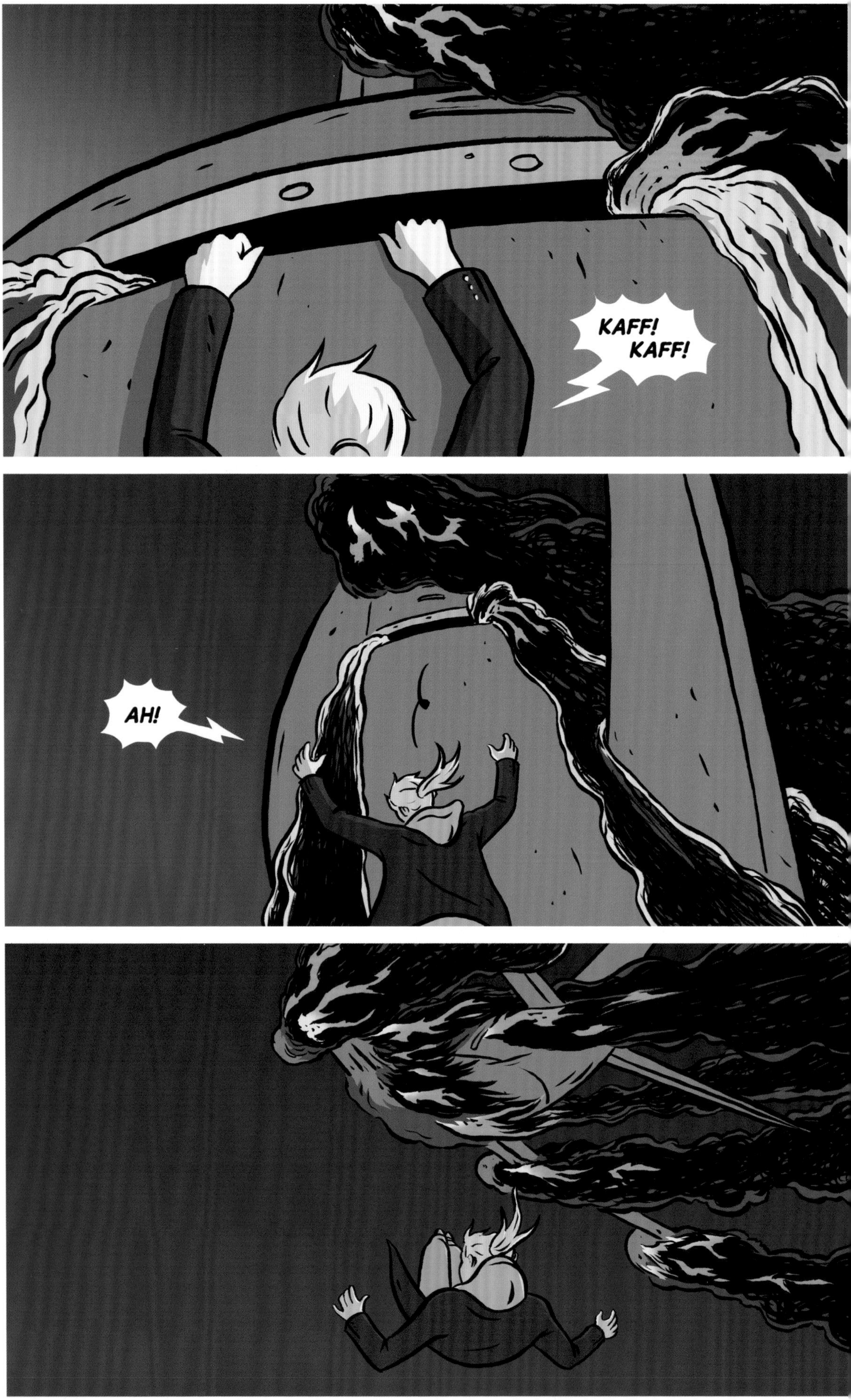
KAFF!
KAFF!
AH!

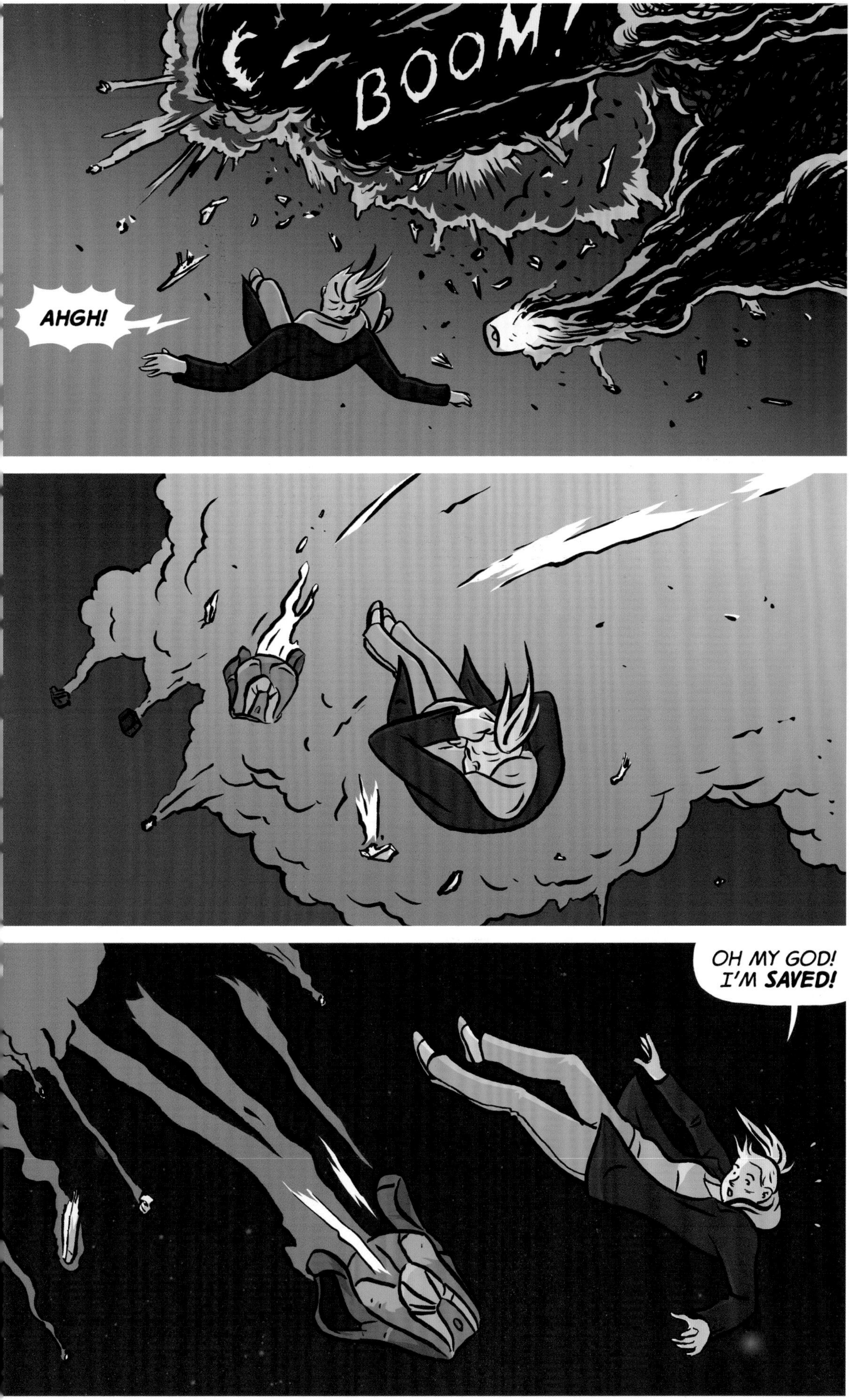
BOOM!
AHGH!
OH MY GOD!
I'M SAVED!

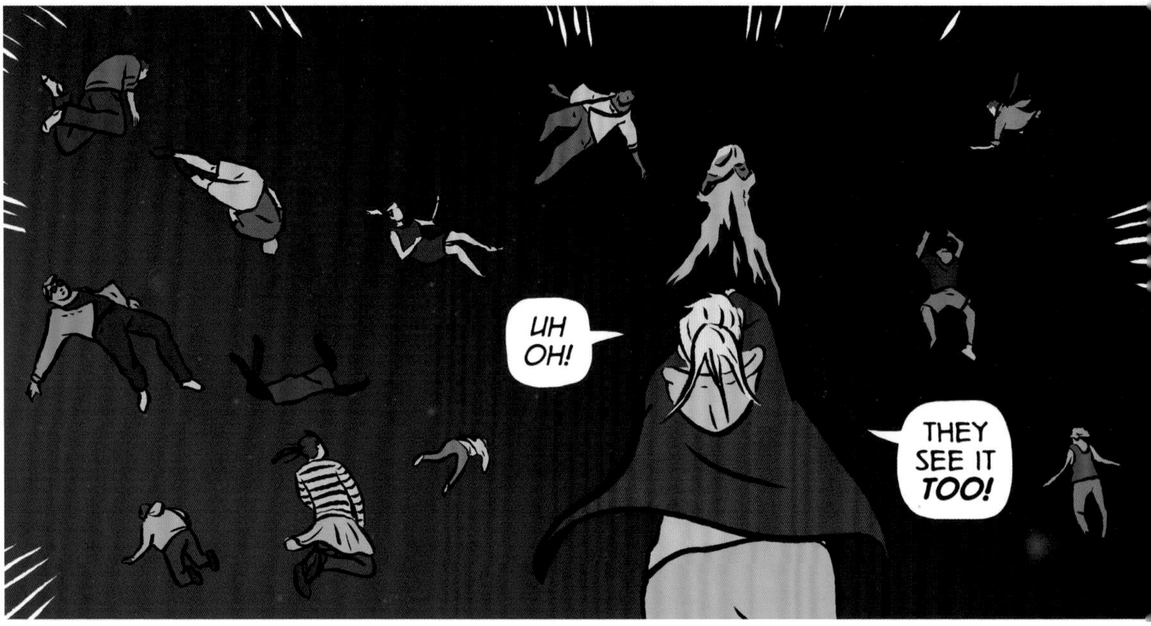
UH OH!
THEY SEE IT ***TOO!***
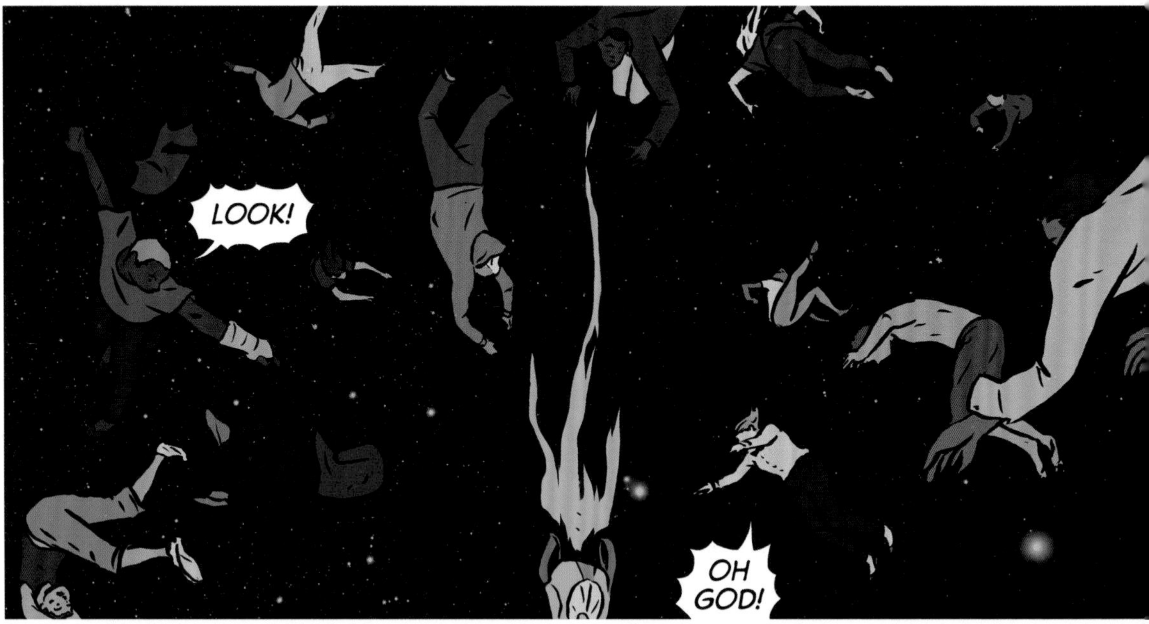
LOOK!
OH GOD!
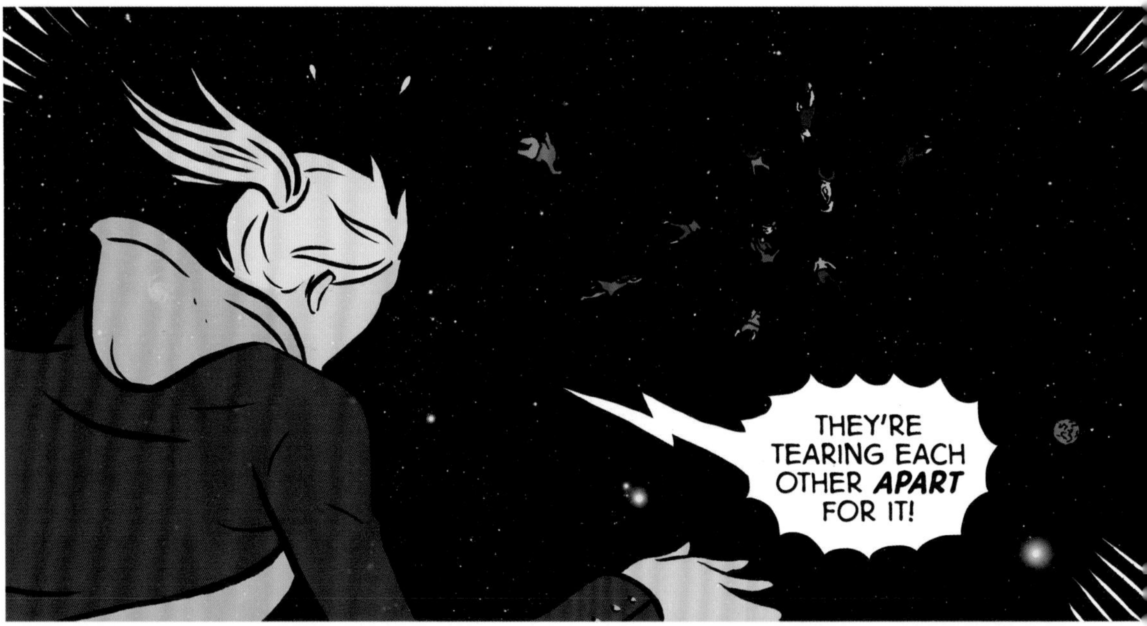
THEY'RE TEARING EACH OTHER ***APART*** FOR IT!

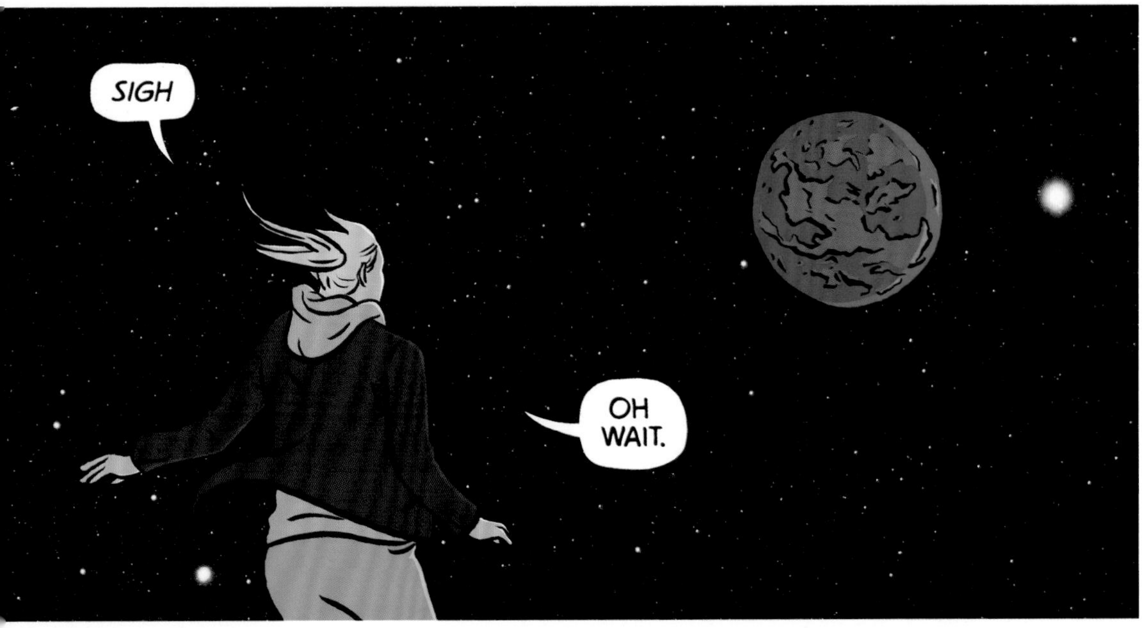
SIGH
OH WAIT.
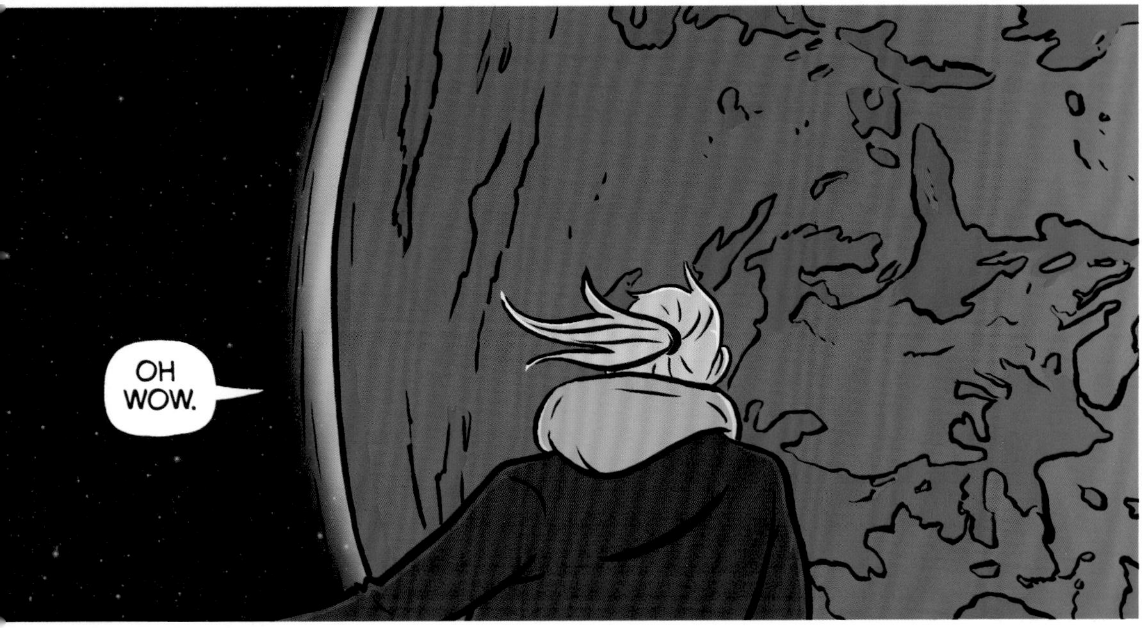
OH WOW.
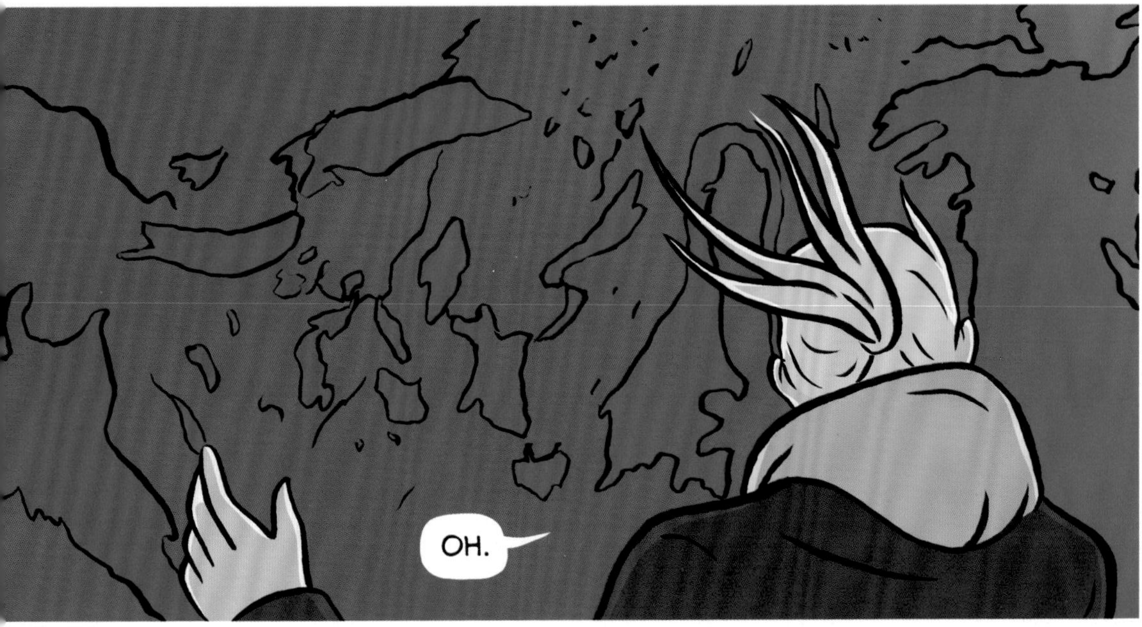
OH.

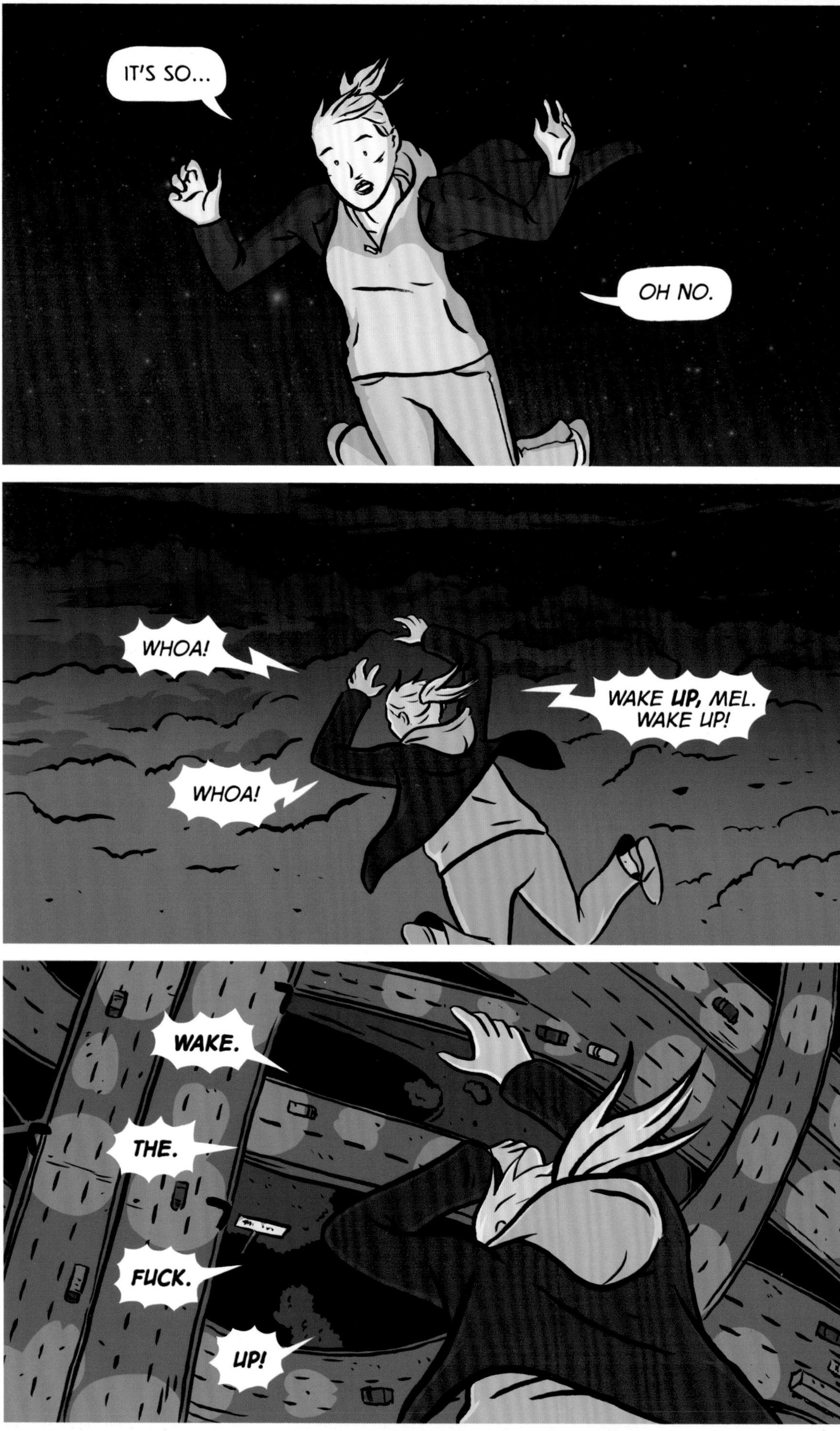
IT'S SO...
OH NO.
WHOA!
WAKE UP, MEL. WAKE UP!
WHOA!
WAKE.
THE.
FUCK.
UP!

WAKE UP!

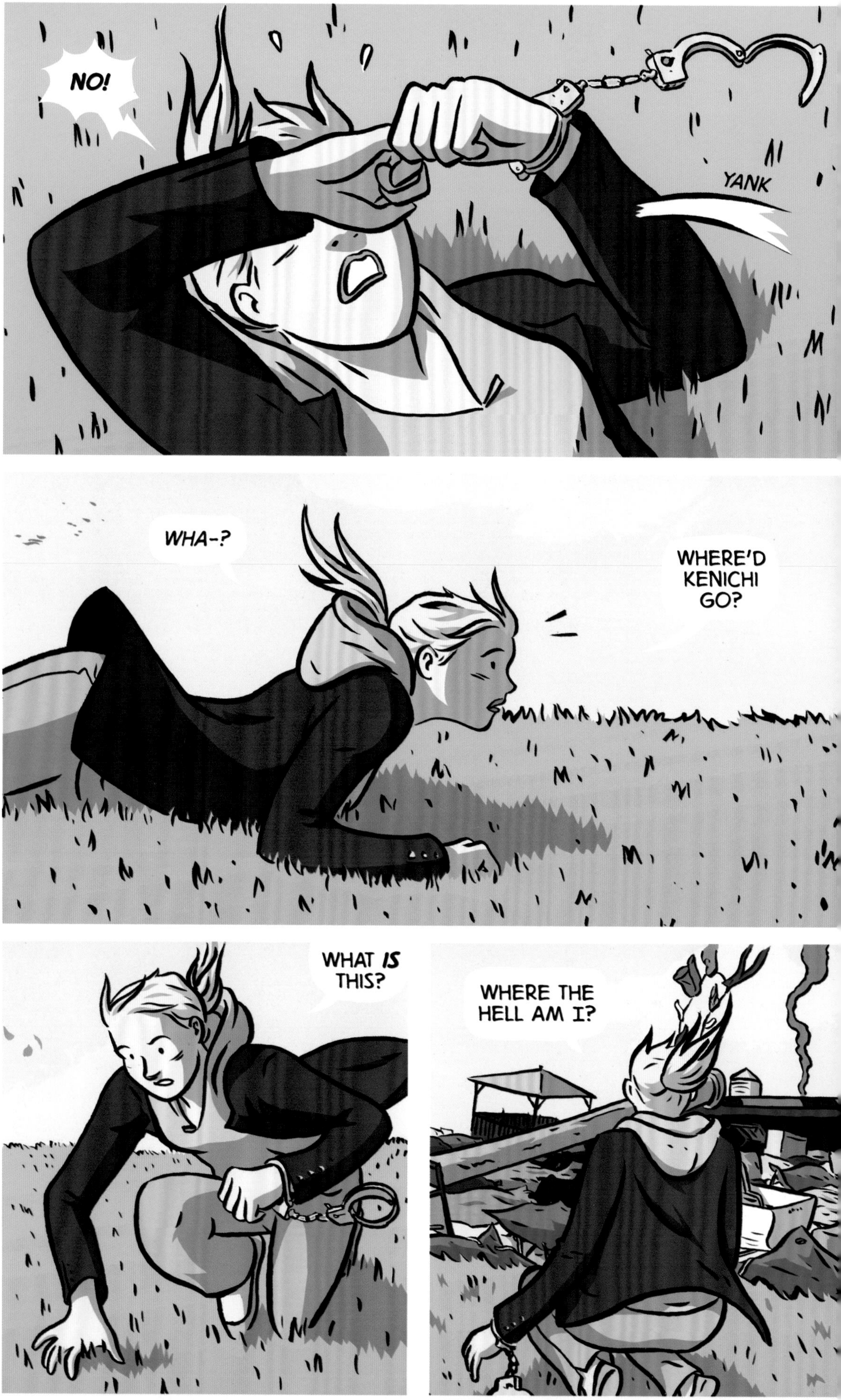
NO!
YANK
WHA-?
WHERE'D KENICHI GO?
WHAT *IS* THIS?
WHERE THE HELL AM I?

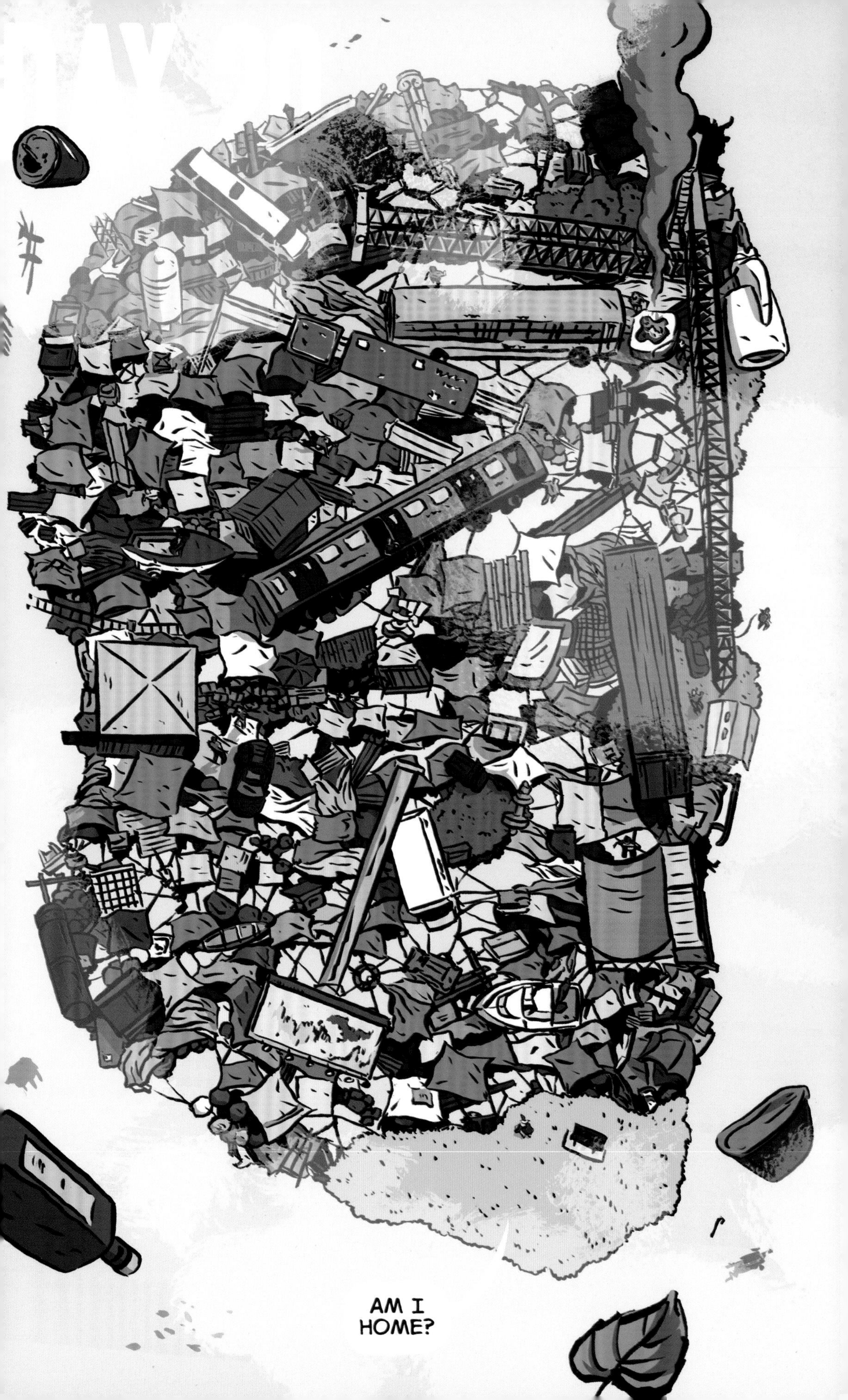
AM I
HOME?

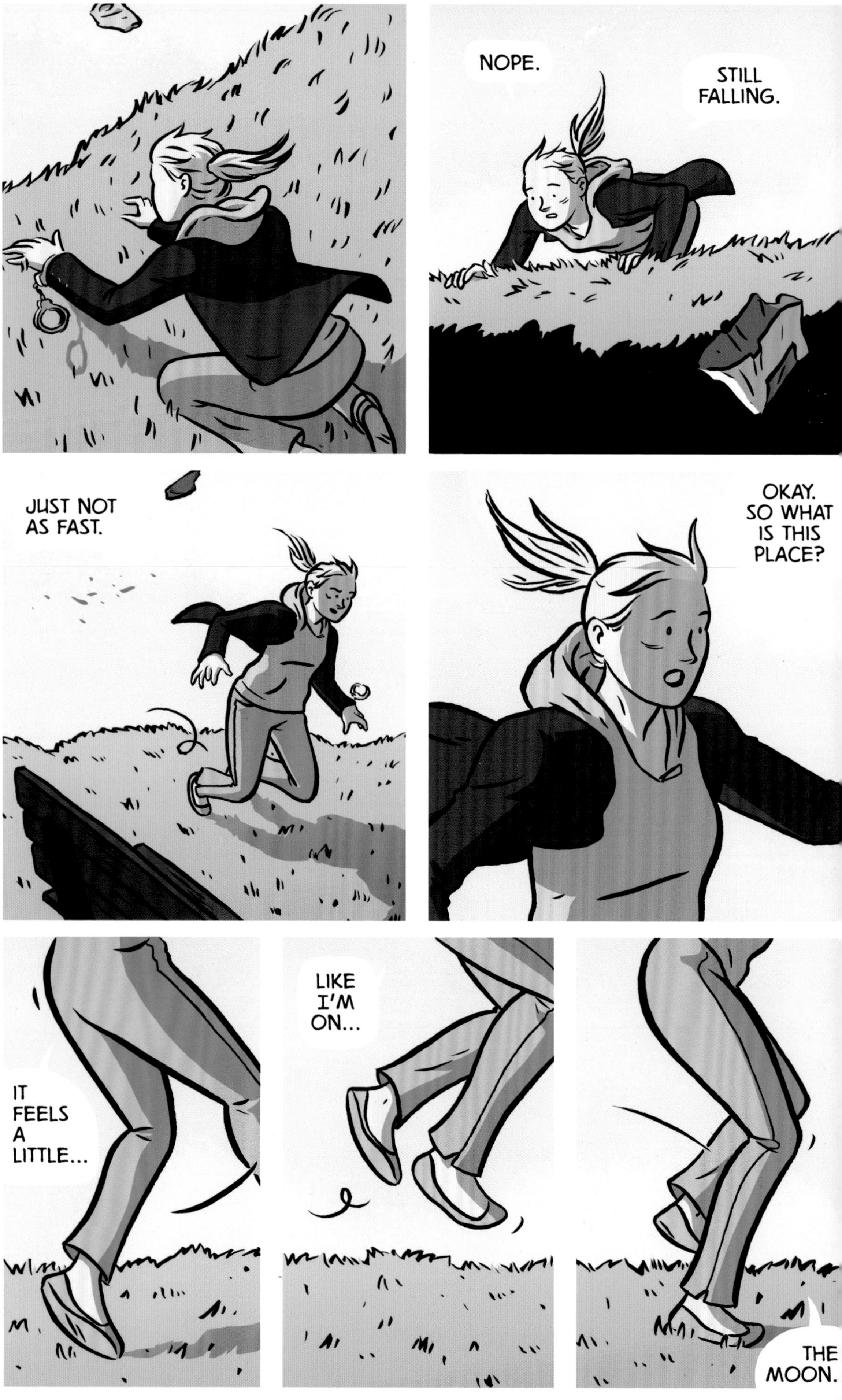
NOPE.
STILL FALLING.
JUST NOT AS FAST.
OKAY. SO WHAT IS THIS PLACE?
IT FEELS A LITTLE...
LIKE I'M ON...
THE MOON.

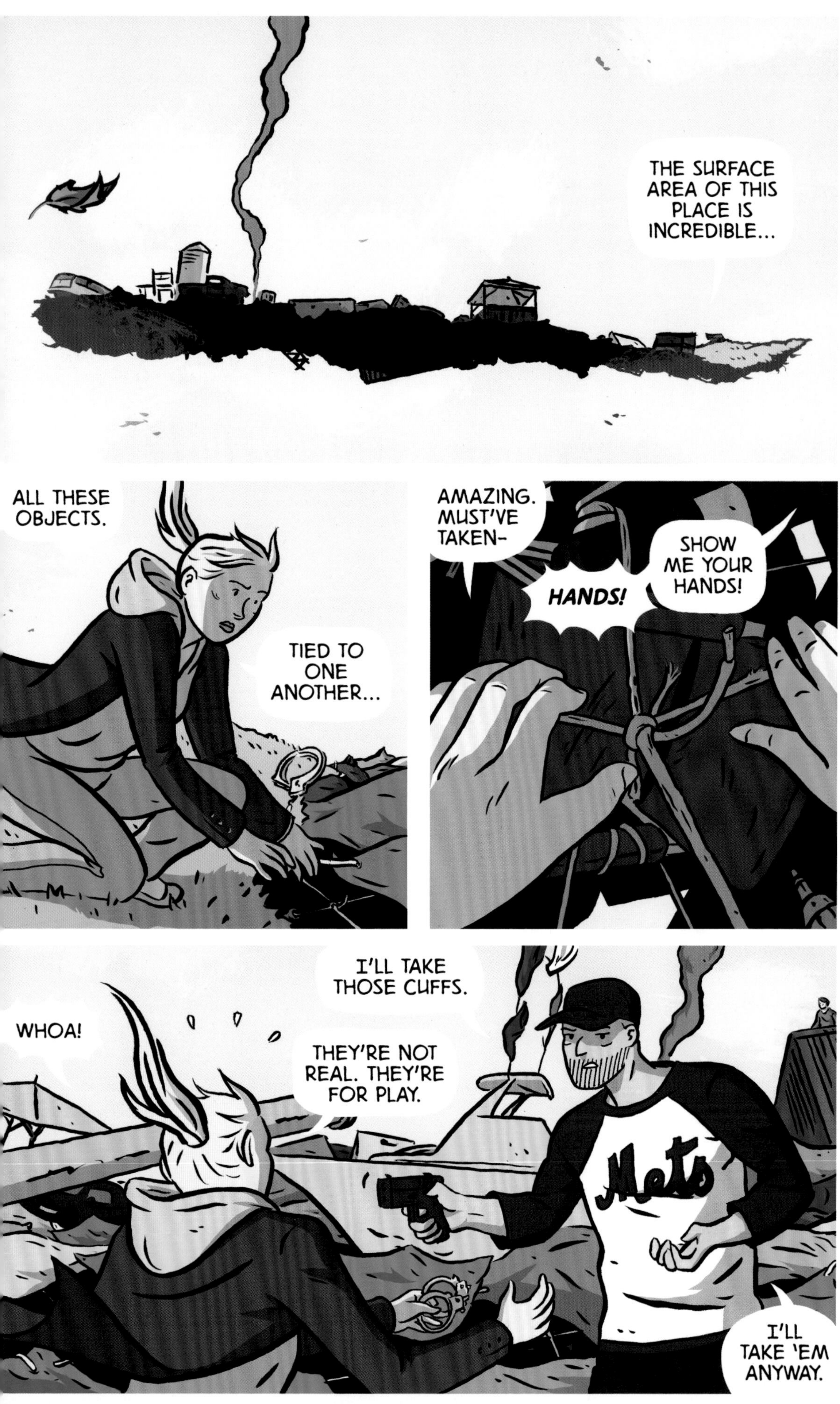
THE SURFACE AREA OF THIS PLACE IS INCREDIBLE...
ALL THESE OBJECTS.
TIED TO ONE ANOTHER...
AMAZING. MUST'VE TAKEN-
HANDS!
SHOW ME YOUR HANDS!
WHOA!
I'LL TAKE THOSE CUFFS.
THEY'RE NOT REAL. THEY'RE FOR PLAY.
I'LL TAKE 'EM ANYWAY.

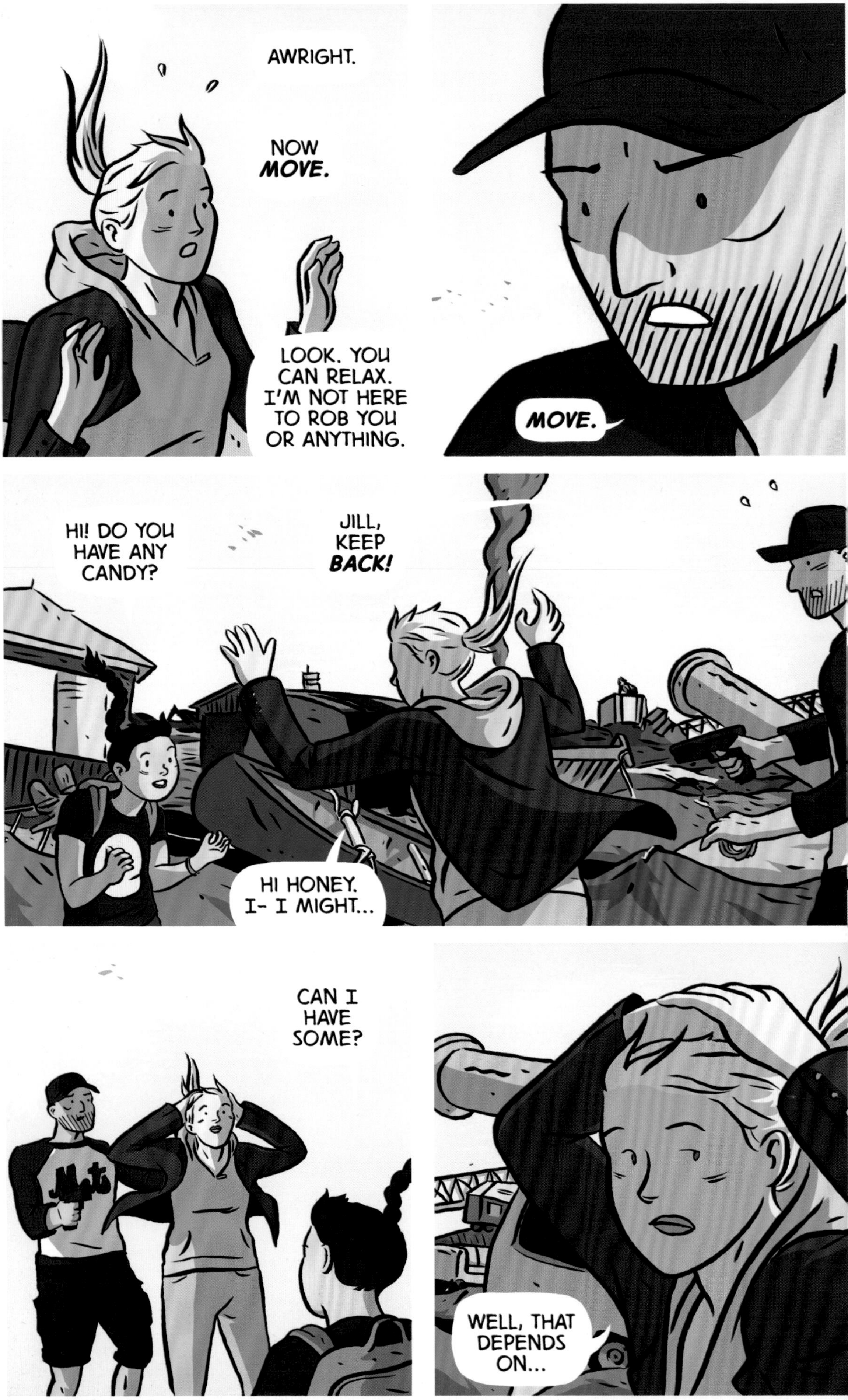
AWRIGHT.
NOW MOVE.
LOOK. YOU CAN RELAX. I'M NOT HERE TO ROB YOU OR ANYTHING.
MOVE.
HI! DO YOU HAVE ANY CANDY?
JILL, KEEP BACK!
HI HONEY. I- I MIGHT...
CAN I HAVE SOME?
WELL, THAT DEPENDS ON...

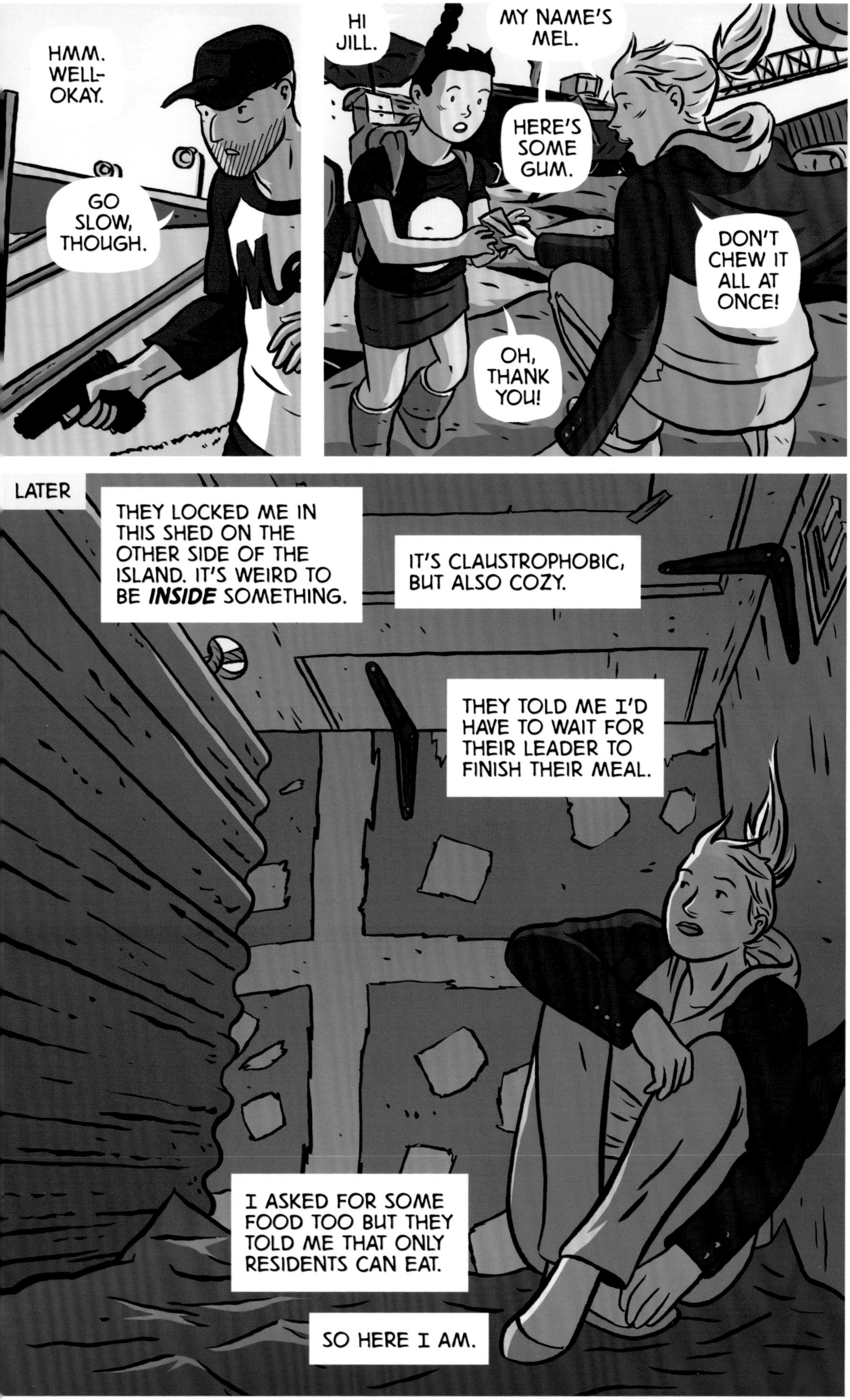
HMM. WELL- OKAY.
GO SLOW, THOUGH.
HI JILL.
MY NAME'S MEL.
HERE'S SOME GUM.
DON'T CHEW IT ALL AT ONCE!
OH, THANK YOU!
LATER
THEY LOCKED ME IN THIS SHED ON THE OTHER SIDE OF THE ISLAND. IT'S WEIRD TO BE *INSIDE* SOMETHING.
IT'S CLAUSTROPHOBIC, BUT ALSO COZY.
THEY TOLD ME I'D HAVE TO WAIT FOR THEIR LEADER TO FINISH THEIR MEAL.
I ASKED FOR SOME FOOD TOO BUT THEY TOLD ME THAT ONLY RESIDENTS CAN EAT.
SO HERE I AM.

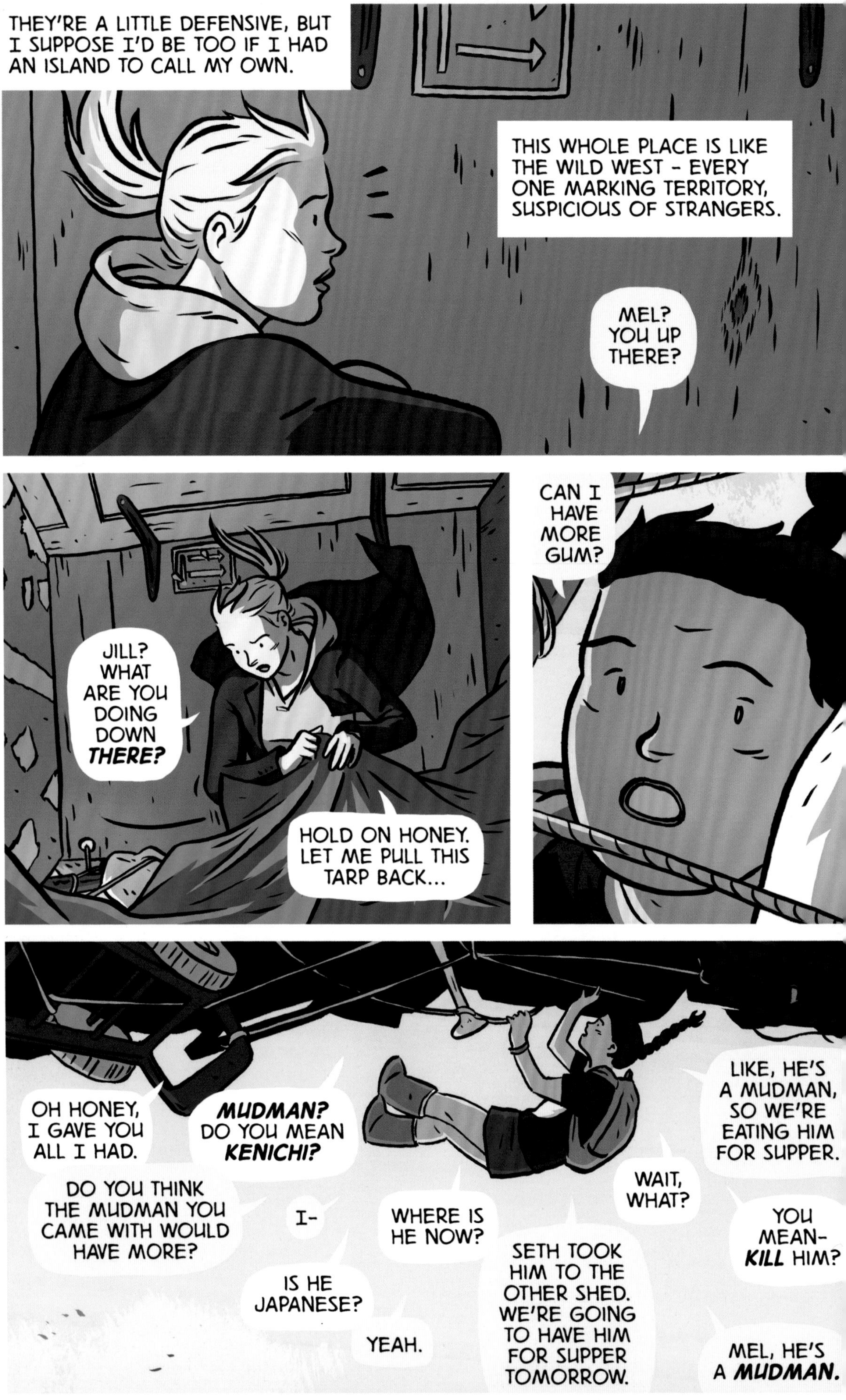

THEY'RE A LITTLE DEFENSIVE, BUT I SUPPOSE I'D BE TOO IF I HAD AN ISLAND TO CALL MY OWN.
THIS WHOLE PLACE IS LIKE THE WILD WEST - EVERY ONE MARKING TERRITORY, SUSPICIOUS OF STRANGERS.
MEL? YOU UP THERE?
JILL? WHAT ARE YOU DOING DOWN ***THERE?***
HOLD ON HONEY. LET ME PULL THIS TARP BACK...
CAN I HAVE MORE GUM?
OH HONEY, I GAVE YOU ALL I HAD.
DO YOU THINK THE MUDMAN YOU CAME WITH WOULD HAVE MORE?
MUDMAN? DO YOU MEAN ***KENICHI?***
I-
IS HE JAPANESE?
YEAH.
WHERE IS HE NOW?
SETH TOOK HIM TO THE OTHER SHED. WE'RE GOING TO HAVE HIM FOR SUPPER TOMORROW.
WAIT, WHAT?
MEL, HE'S A ***MUDMAN.***
YOU MEAN- ***KILL*** HIM?
LIKE, HE'S A MUDMAN, SO WE'RE EATING HIM FOR SUPPER.

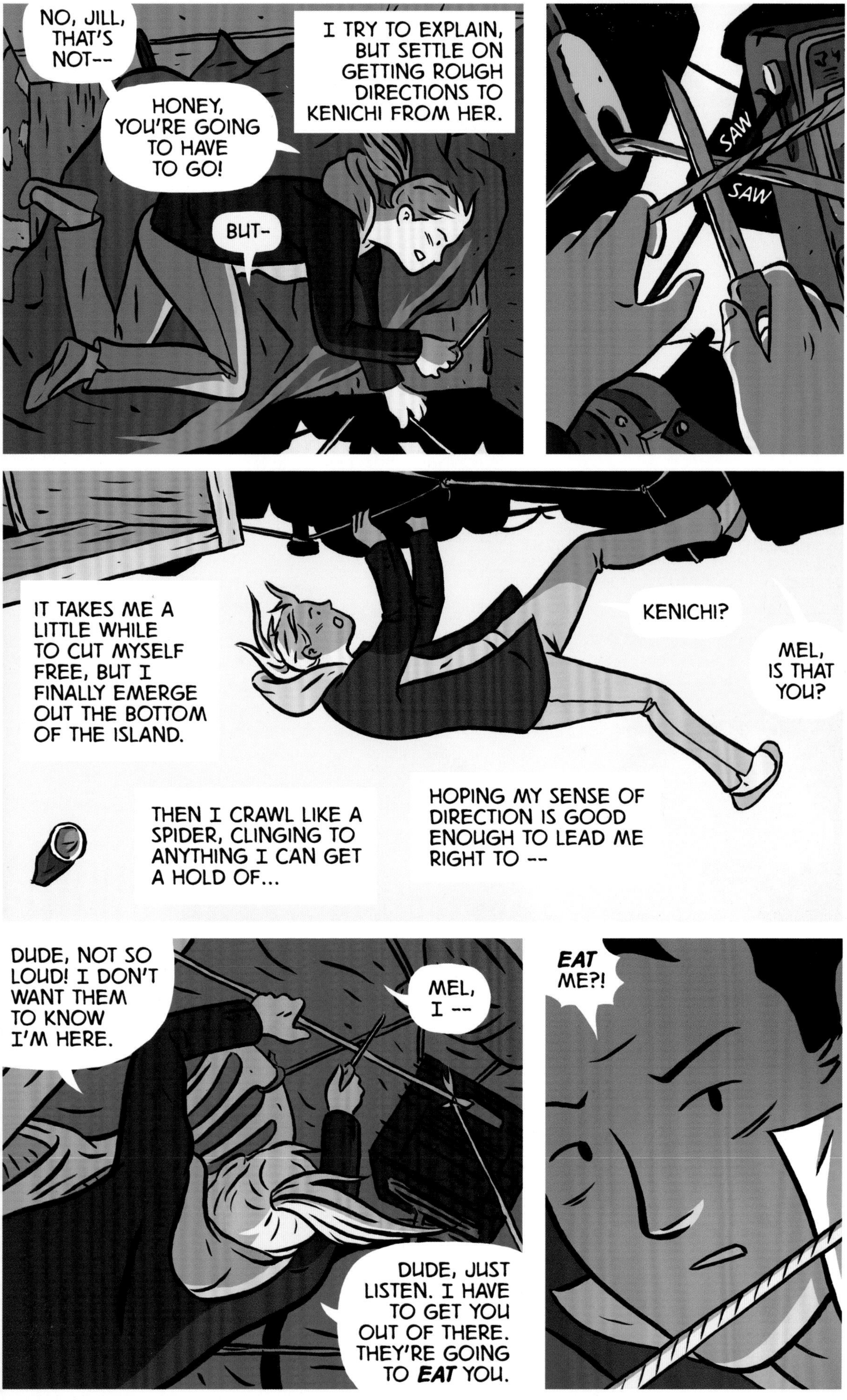
NO, JILL, THAT'S NOT--
HONEY, YOU'RE GOING TO HAVE TO GO!
I TRY TO EXPLAIN, BUT SETTLE ON GETTING ROUGH DIRECTIONS TO KENICHI FROM HER.
BUT-
SAW
SAW
IT TAKES ME A LITTLE WHILE TO CUT MYSELF FREE, BUT I FINALLY EMERGE OUT THE BOTTOM OF THE ISLAND.
KENICHI?
MEL, IS THAT YOU?
THEN I CRAWL LIKE A SPIDER, CLINGING TO ANYTHING I CAN GET A HOLD OF...
HOPING MY SENSE OF DIRECTION IS GOOD ENOUGH TO LEAD ME RIGHT TO --
DUDE, NOT SO LOUD! I DON'T WANT THEM TO KNOW I'M HERE.
MEL, I --
DUDE, JUST LISTEN. I HAVE TO GET YOU OUT OF THERE. THEY'RE GOING TO ***EAT*** YOU.
EAT ME?!

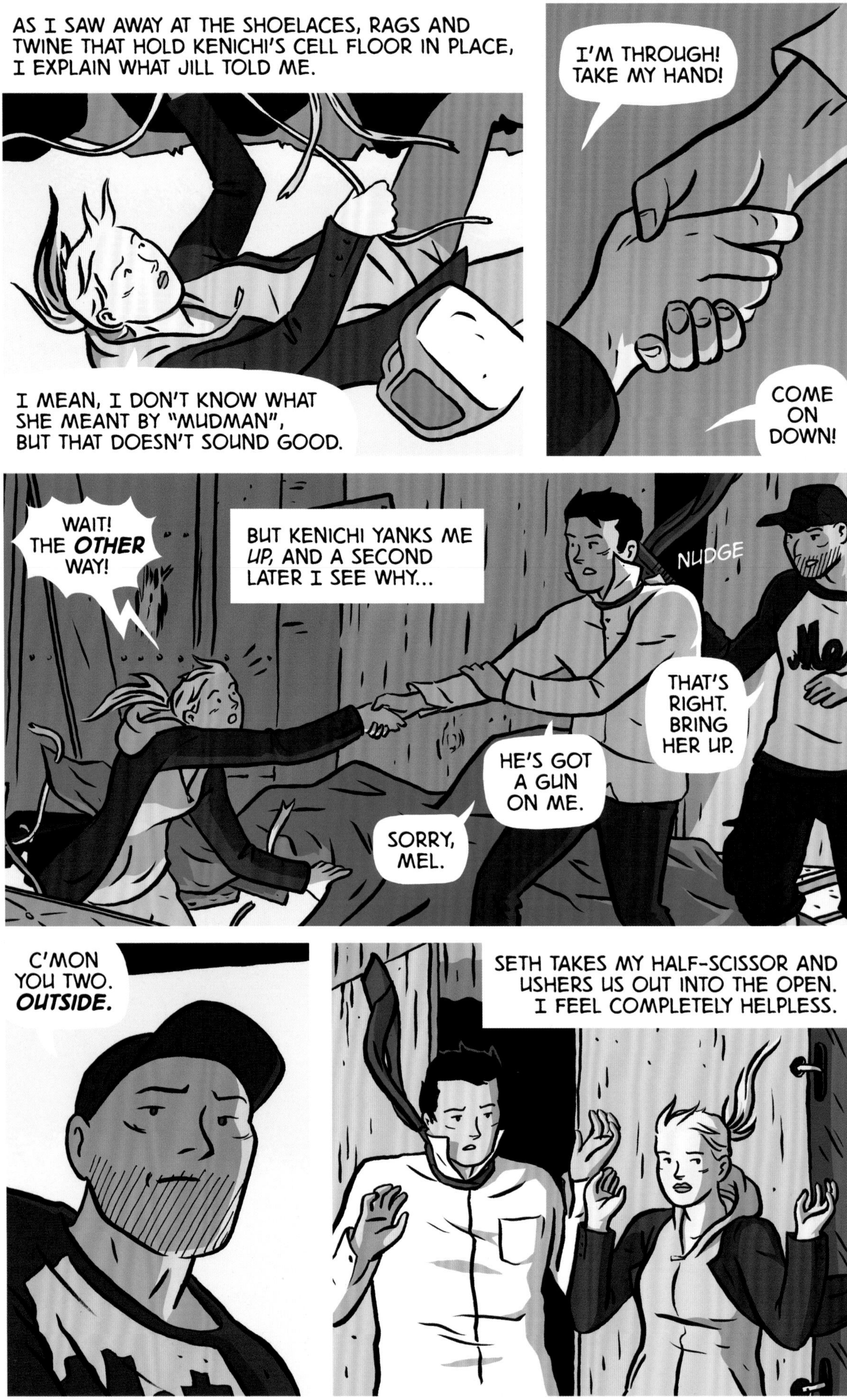

AS I SAW AWAY AT THE SHOELACES, RAGS AND TWINE THAT HOLD KENICHI'S CELL FLOOR IN PLACE, I EXPLAIN WHAT JILL TOLD ME.
I MEAN, I DON'T KNOW WHAT SHE MEANT BY "MUDMAN", BUT THAT DOESN'T SOUND GOOD.
I'M THROUGH! TAKE MY HAND!
COME ON DOWN!
WAIT! THE *OTHER* WAY!
BUT KENICHI YANKS ME *UP*, AND A SECOND LATER I SEE WHY...
NUDGE
THAT'S RIGHT. BRING HER UP.
HE'S GOT A GUN ON ME.
SORRY, MEL.
C'MON YOU TWO. ***OUTSIDE.***
SETH TAKES MY HALF-SCISSOR AND USHERS US OUT INTO THE OPEN. I FEEL COMPLETELY HELPLESS.

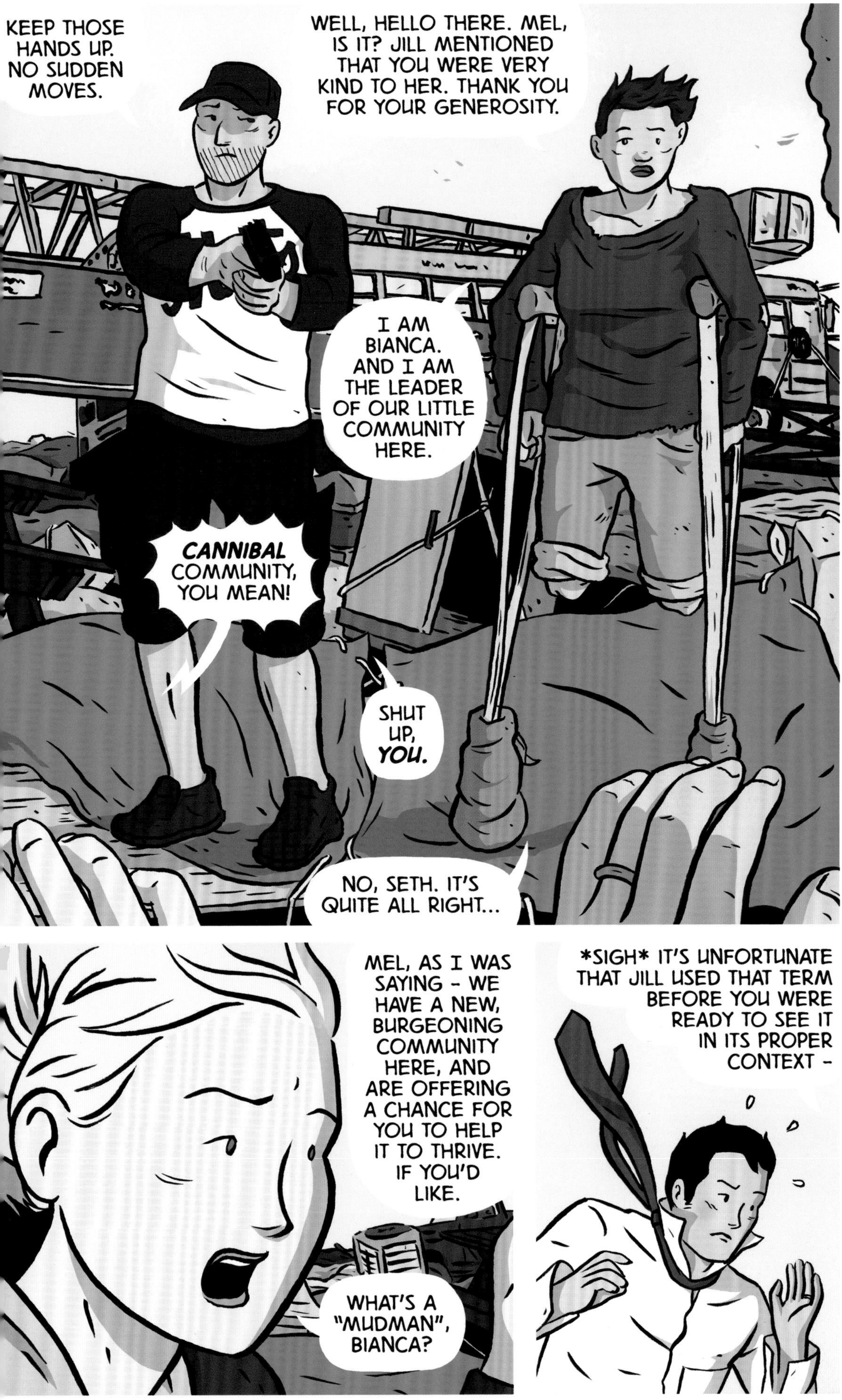
KEEP THOSE HANDS UP. NO SUDDEN MOVES.
WELL, HELLO THERE. MEL, IS IT? JILL MENTIONED THAT YOU WERE VERY KIND TO HER. THANK YOU FOR YOUR GENEROSITY.
I AM BIANCA. AND I AM THE LEADER OF OUR LITTLE COMMUNITY HERE.
CANNIBAL COMMUNITY, YOU MEAN!
SHUT UP, *YOU.*
NO, SETH. IT'S QUITE ALL RIGHT...
MEL, AS I WAS SAYING - WE HAVE A NEW, BURGEONING COMMUNITY HERE, AND ARE OFFERING A CHANCE FOR YOU TO HELP IT TO THRIVE. IF YOU'D LIKE.
WHAT'S A "MUDMAN", BIANCA?
SIGH IT'S UNFORTUNATE THAT JILL USED THAT TERM BEFORE YOU WERE READY TO SEE IT IN ITS PROPER CONTEXT -

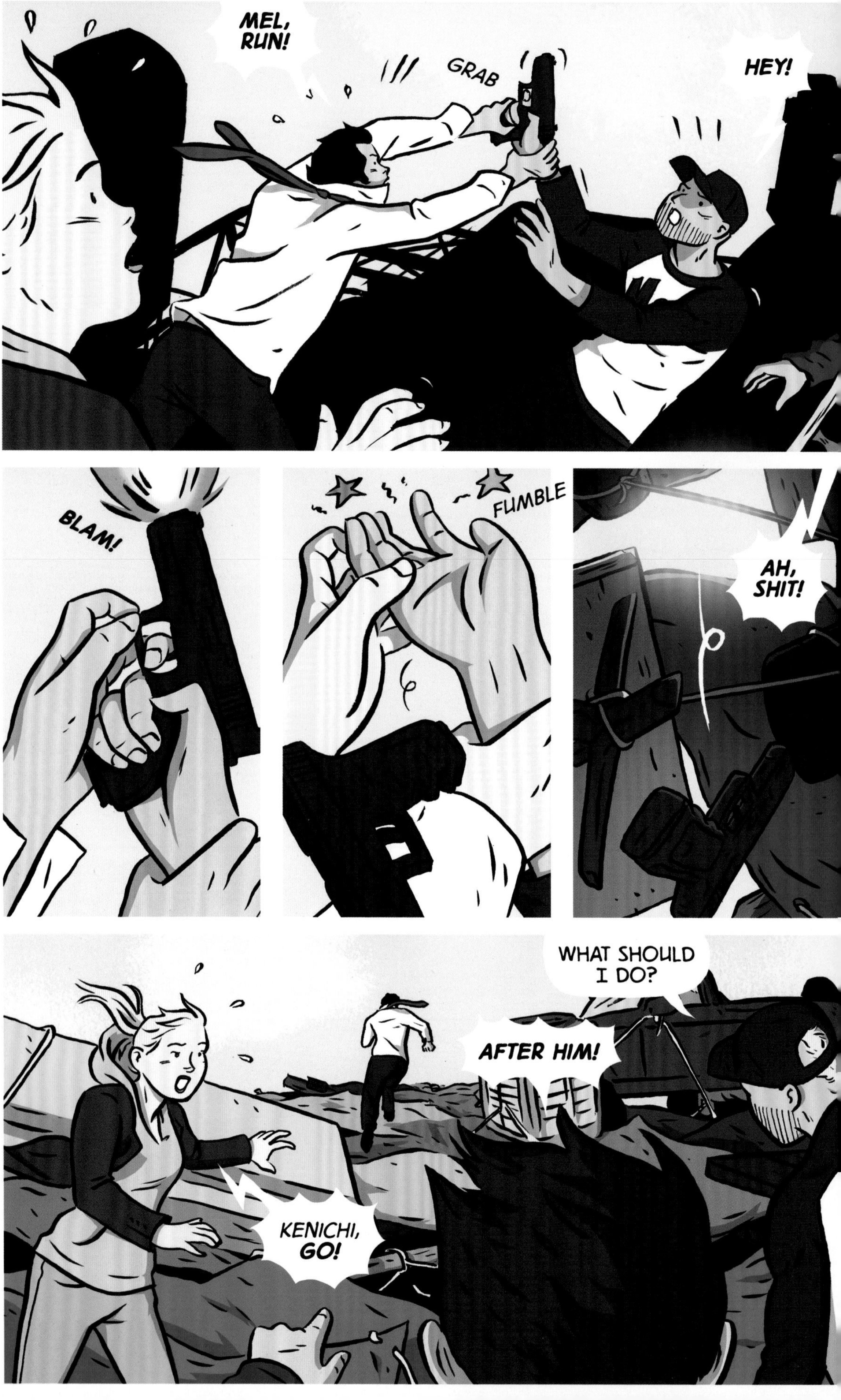
MEL, RUN!
GRAB
HEY!
BLAM!
FUMBLE
AH, SHIT!
WHAT SHOULD I DO?
AFTER HIM!
KENICHI, GO!

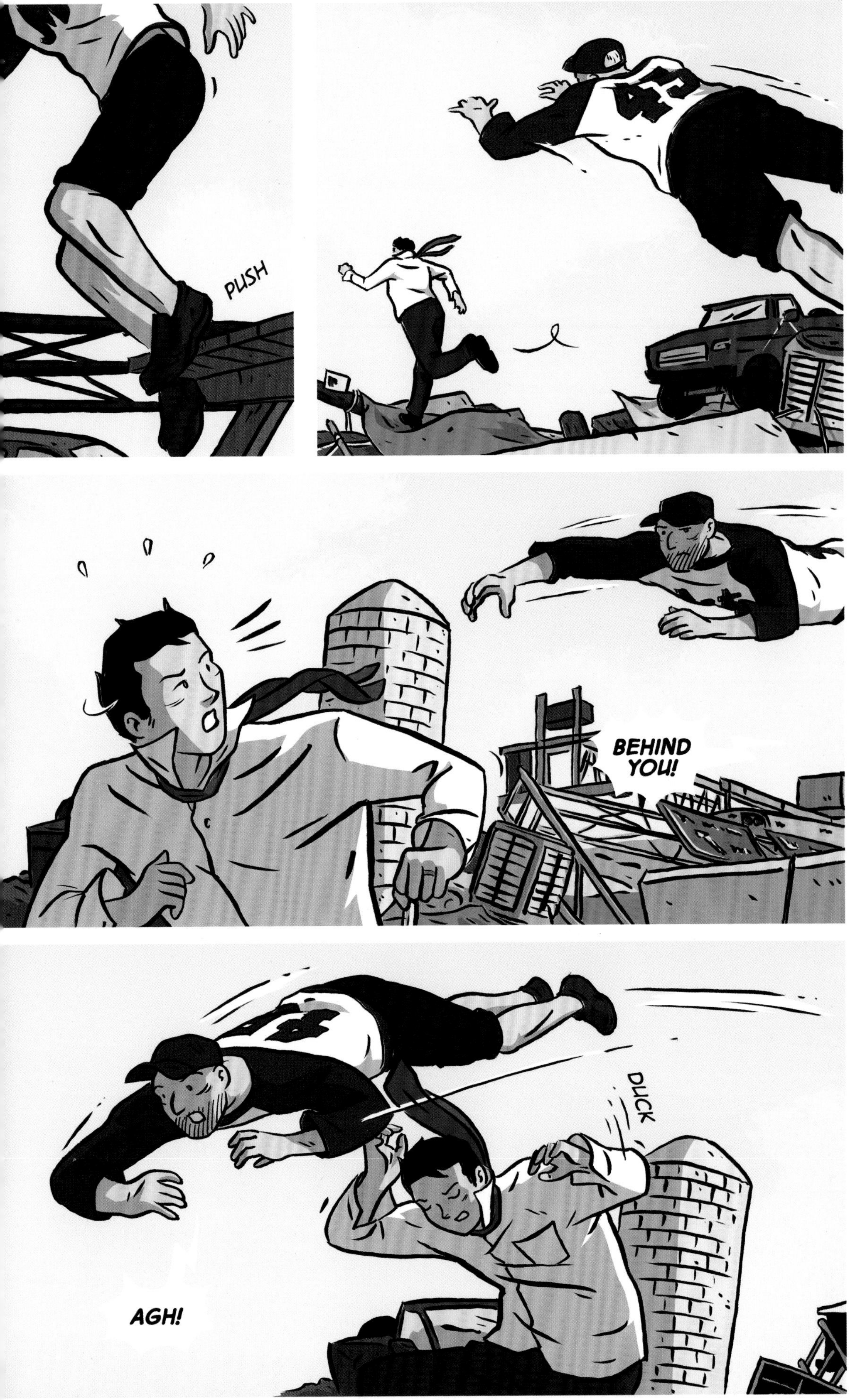
PUSH
BEHIND YOU!
DUCK
AGH!

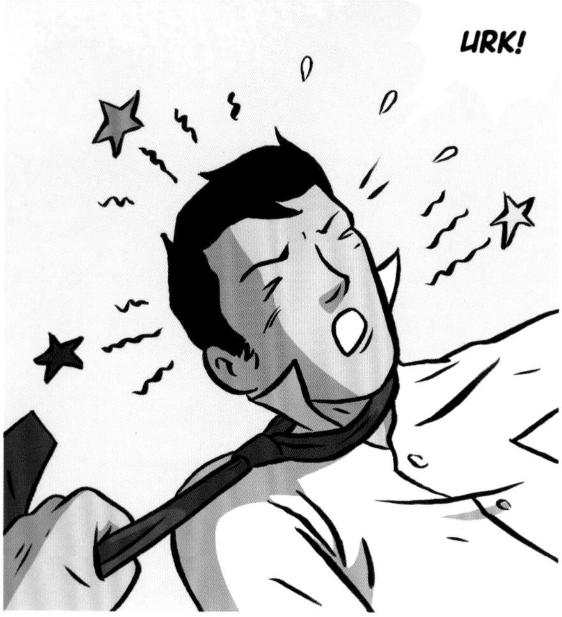
URK!
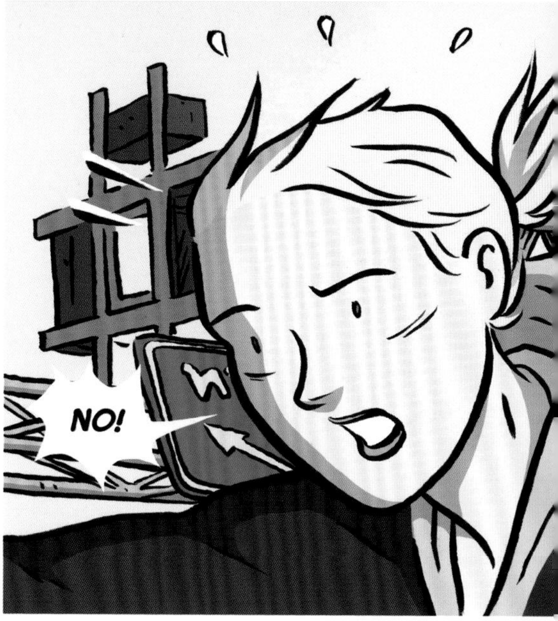
NO!
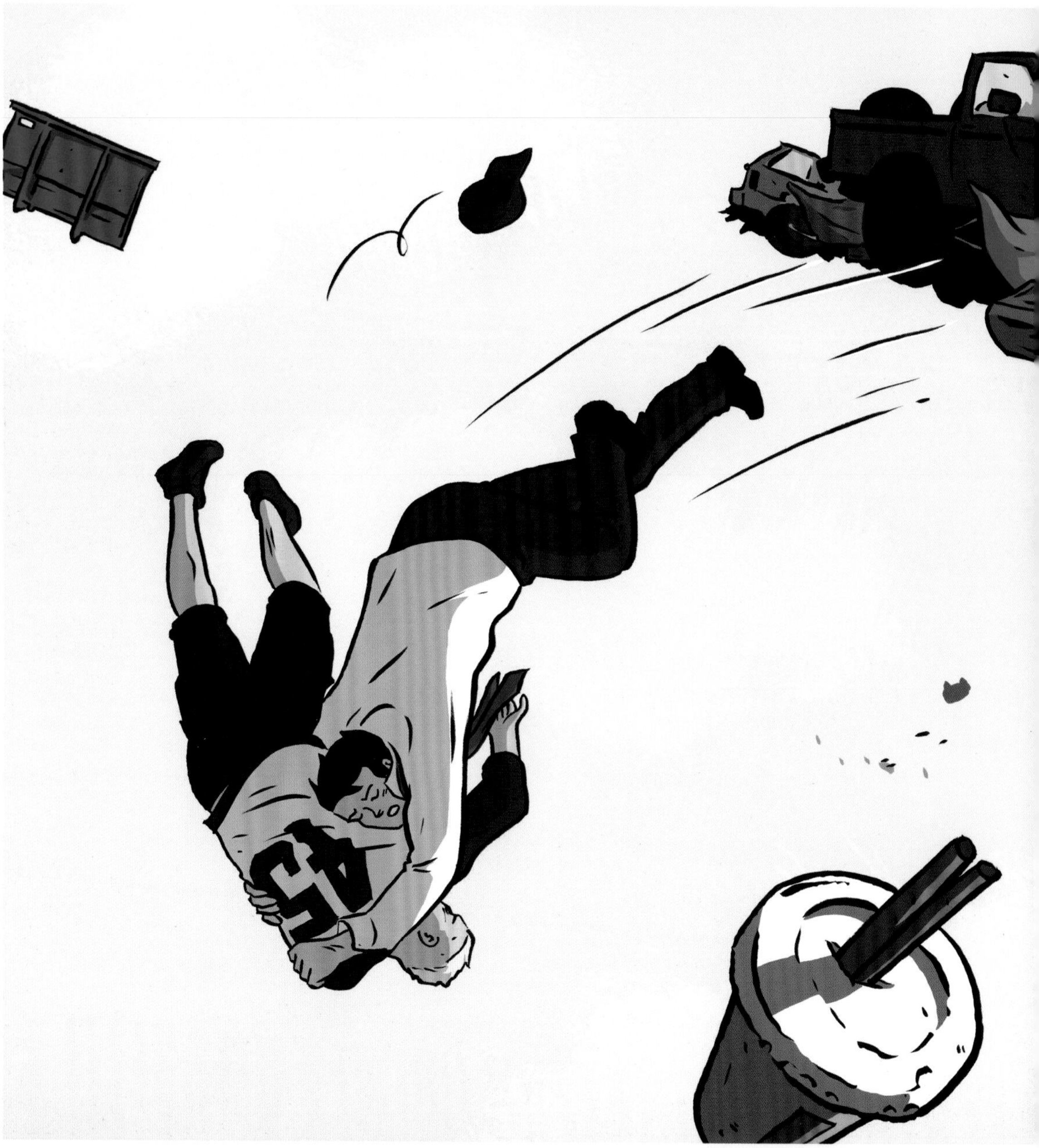

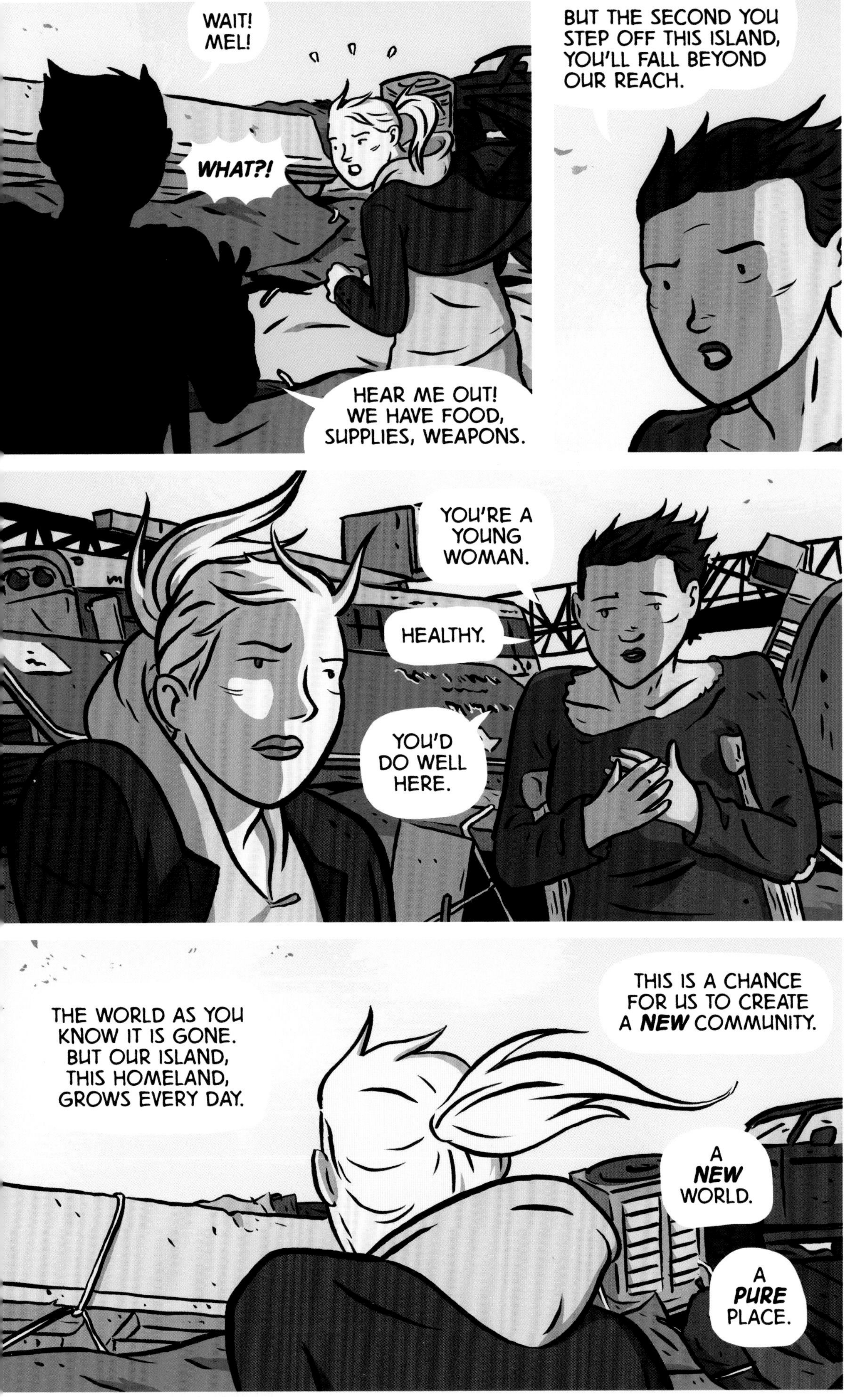
WAIT! MEL!
WHAT?!
HEAR ME OUT! WE HAVE FOOD, SUPPLIES, WEAPONS.
BUT THE SECOND YOU STEP OFF THIS ISLAND, YOU'LL FALL BEYOND OUR REACH.
YOU'RE A YOUNG WOMAN.
HEALTHY.
YOU'D DO WELL HERE.
THE WORLD AS YOU KNOW IT IS GONE. BUT OUR ISLAND, THIS HOMELAND, GROWS EVERY DAY.
THIS IS A CHANCE FOR US TO CREATE A ***NEW*** COMMUNITY.
A ***NEW*** WORLD.
A ***PURE*** PLACE.

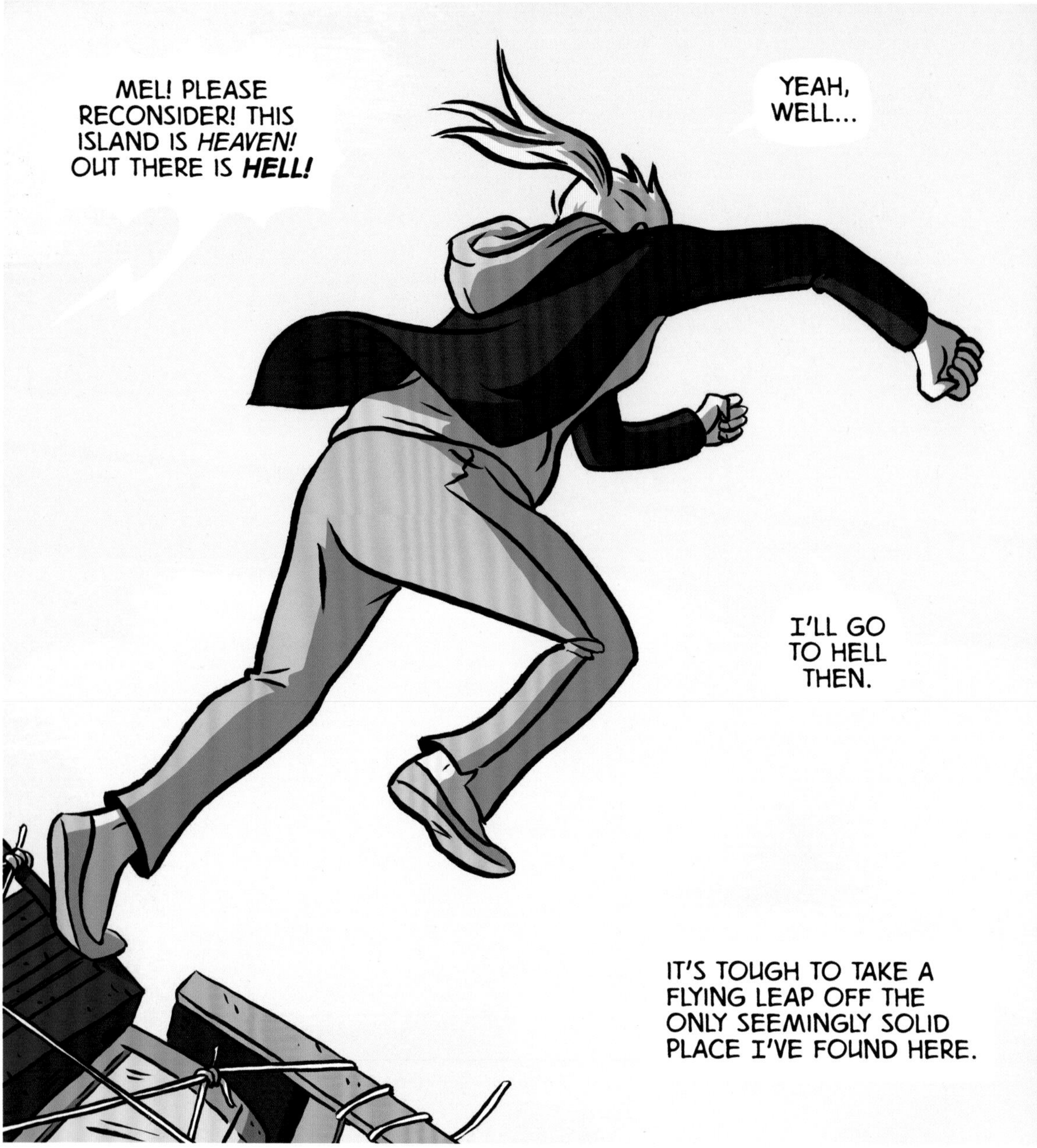
MEL! PLEASE RECONSIDER! THIS ISLAND IS HEAVEN! OUT THERE IS HELL!
YEAH, WELL...
I'LL GO TO HELL THEN.
IT'S TOUGH TO TAKE A FLYING LEAP OFF THE ONLY SEEMINGLY SOLID PLACE I'VE FOUND HERE.
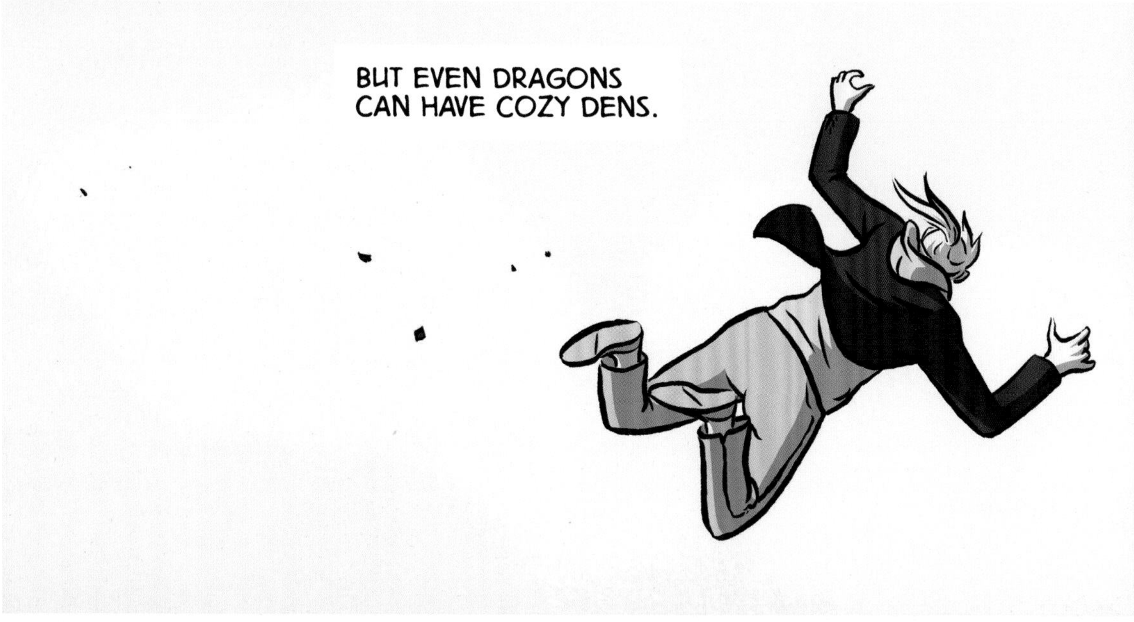
BUT EVEN DRAGONS CAN HAVE COZY DENS.

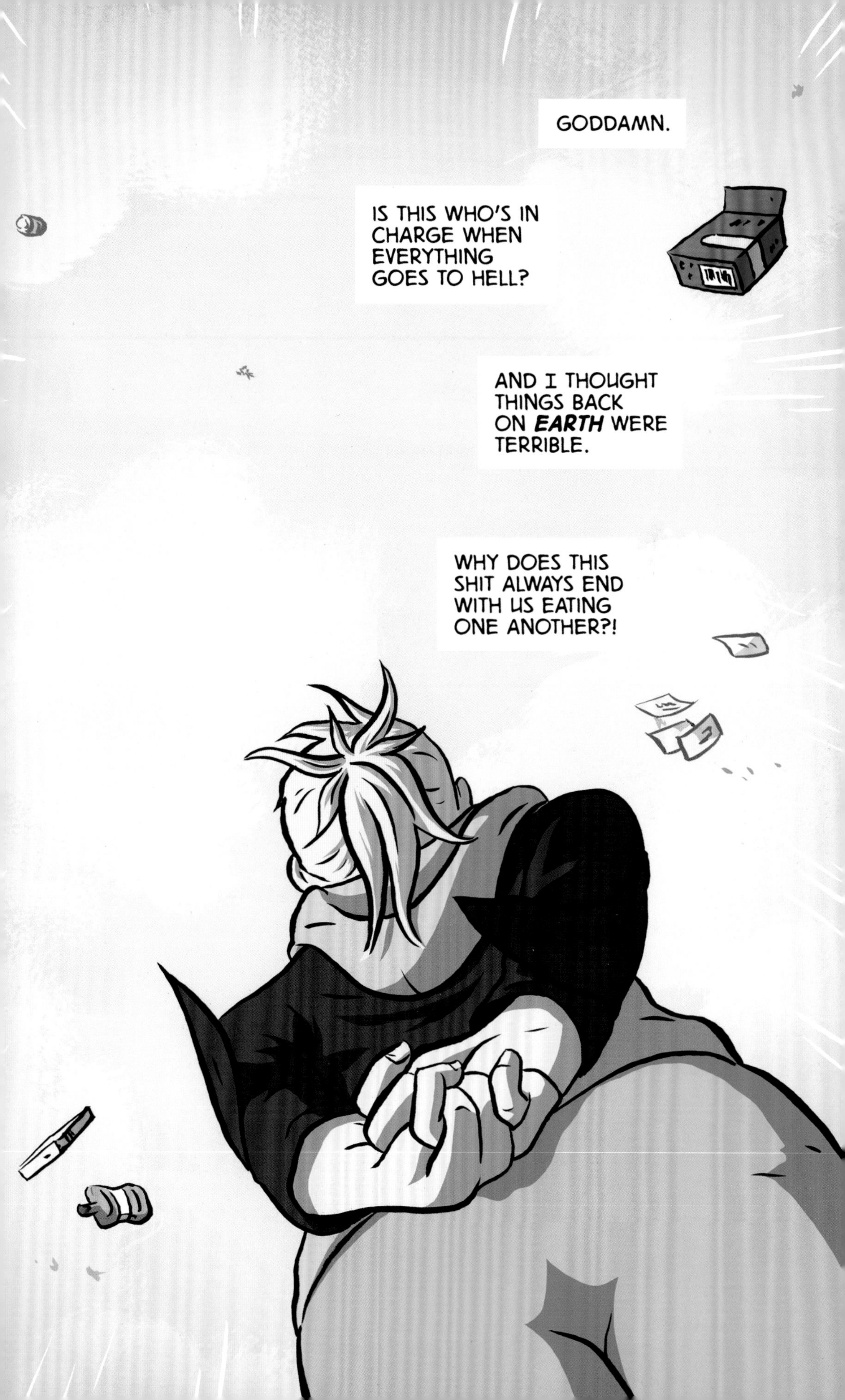
GODDAMN.
IS THIS WHO'S IN CHARGE WHEN EVERYTHING GOES TO HELL?
AND I THOUGHT THINGS BACK ON ***EARTH*** WERE TERRIBLE.
WHY DOES THIS SHIT ALWAYS END WITH US EATING ONE ANOTHER?!

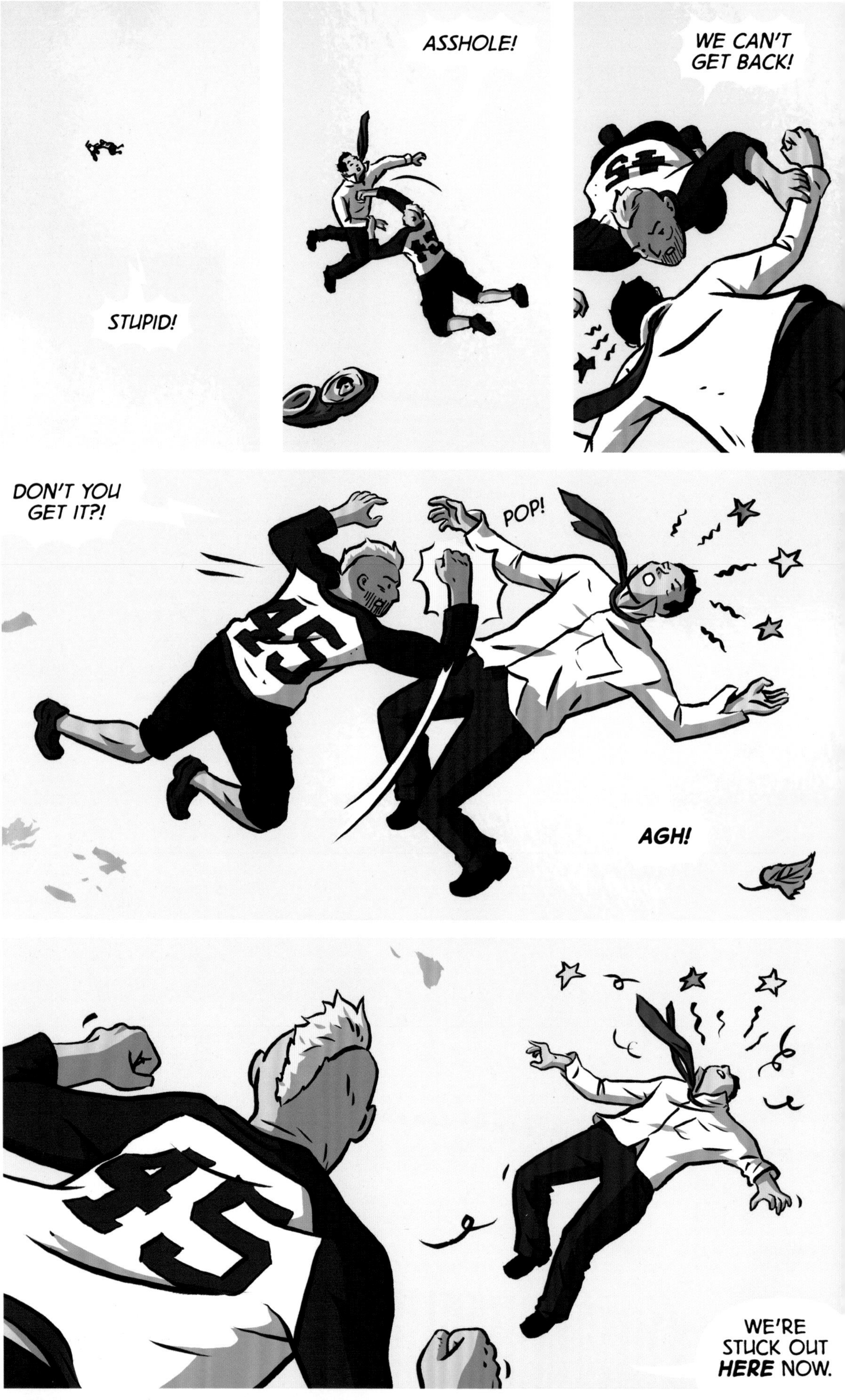
STUPID!
ASSHOLE!
WE CAN'T GET BACK!
DON'T YOU GET IT?!
POP!
AGH!
WE'RE STUCK OUT HERE NOW.

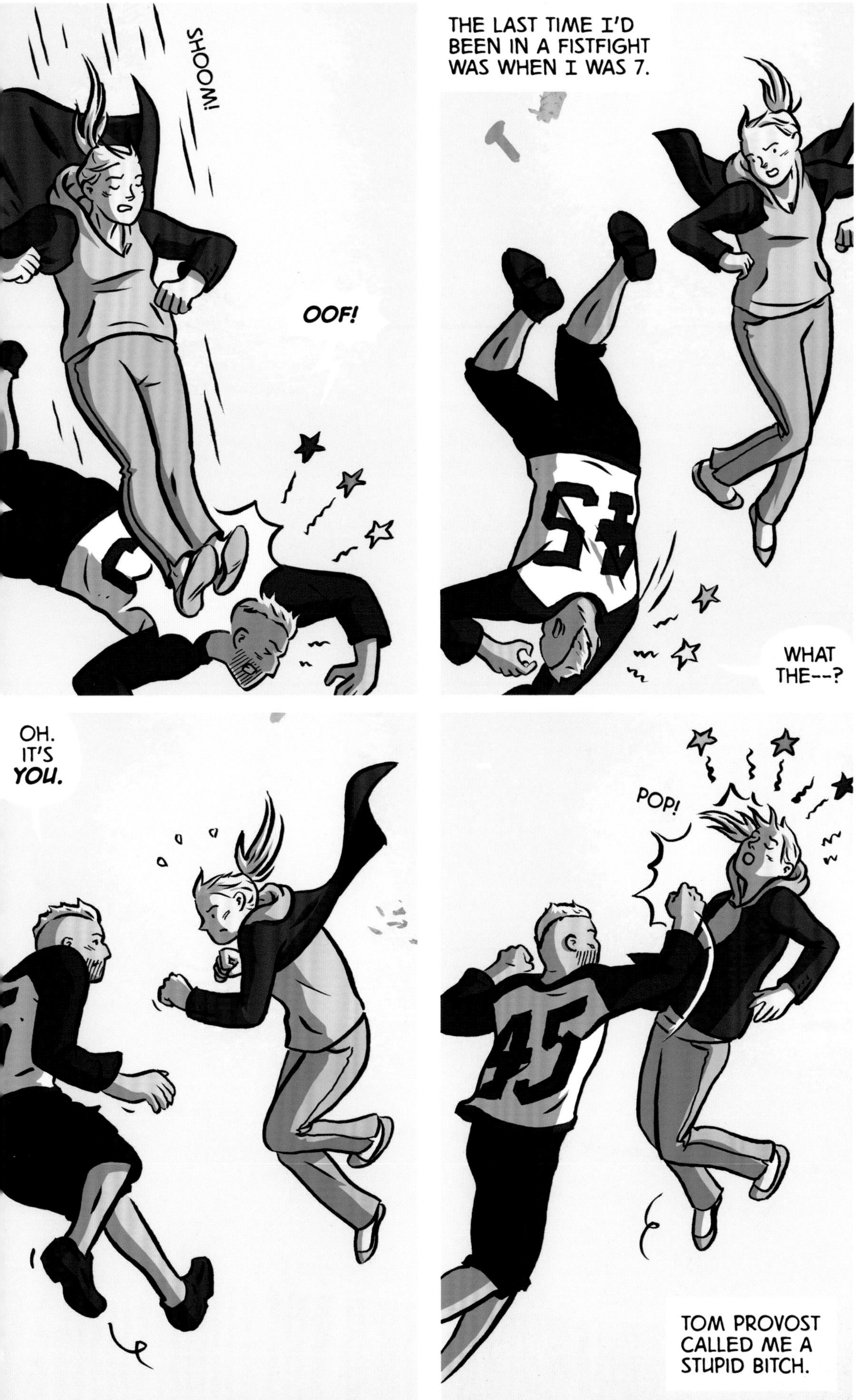
SHOOM!
OOF!
THE LAST TIME I'D BEEN IN A FISTFIGHT WAS WHEN I WAS 7.
WHAT THE--?
OH. IT'S *YOU.*
POP!
TOM PROVOST CALLED ME A STUPID BITCH.

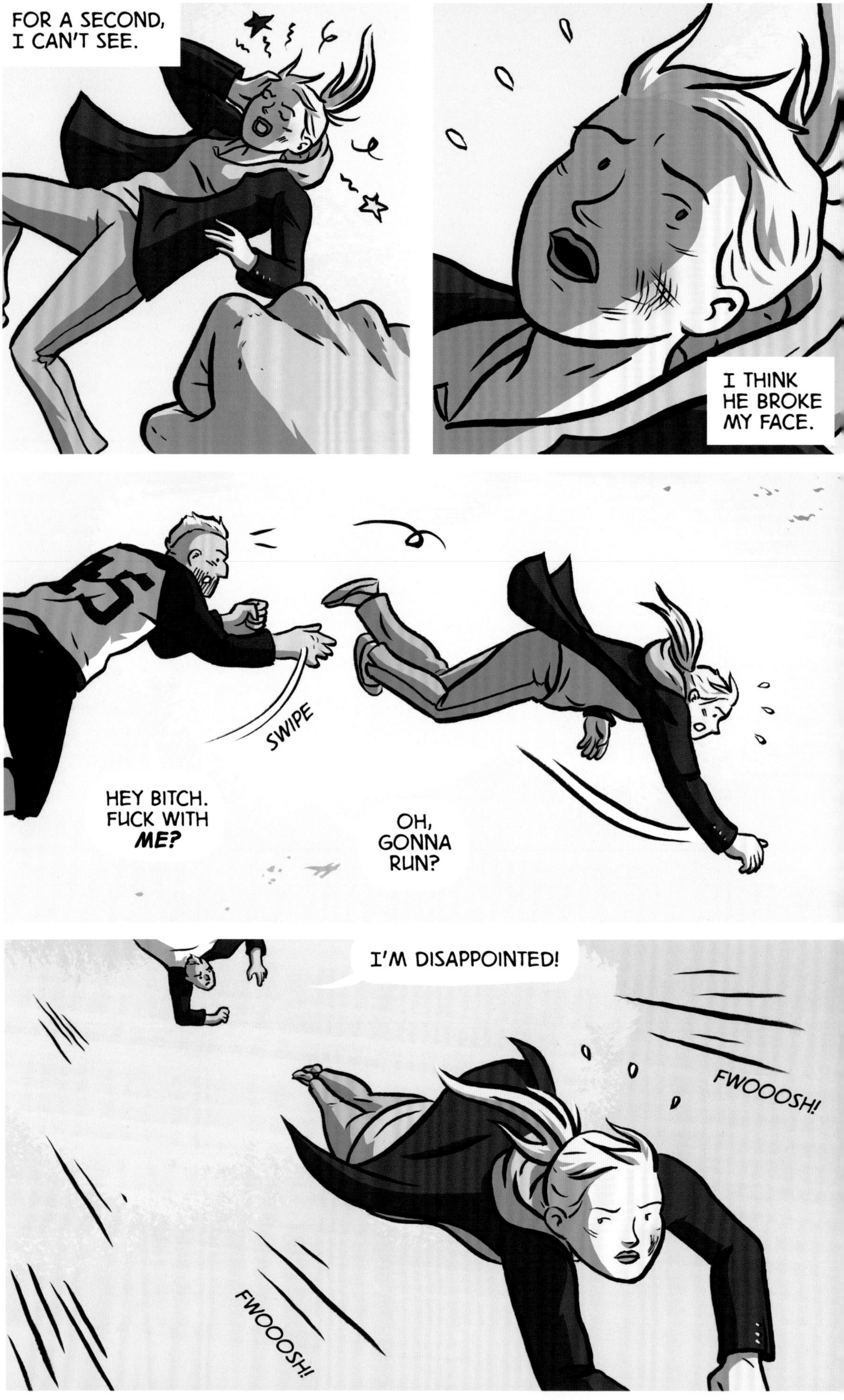
FOR A SECOND, I CAN'T SEE.
I THINK HE BROKE MY FACE.
SWIPE
HEY BITCH. FUCK WITH ***ME?***
OH, GONNA RUN?
I'M DISAPPOINTED!
FWOOOSH!
FWOOOSH!

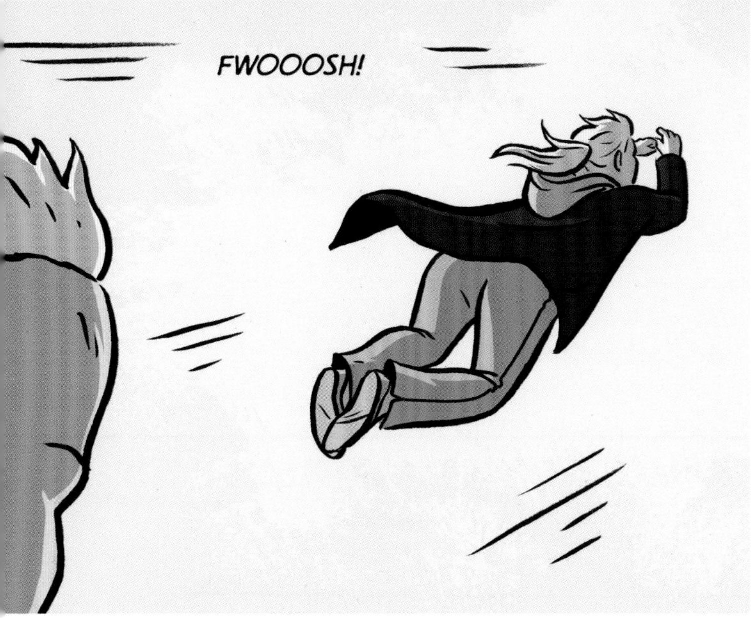
FWOOOSH!

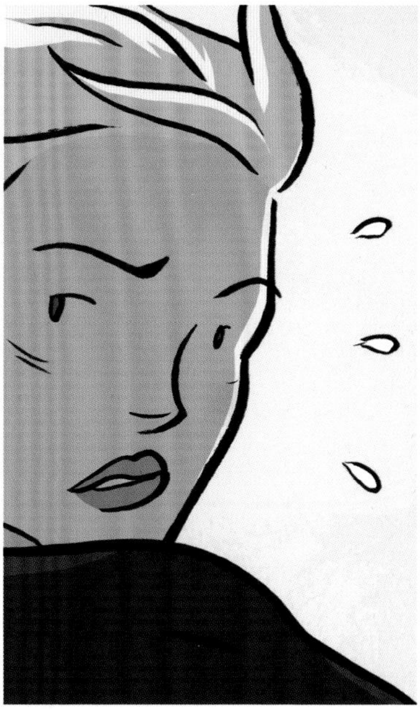

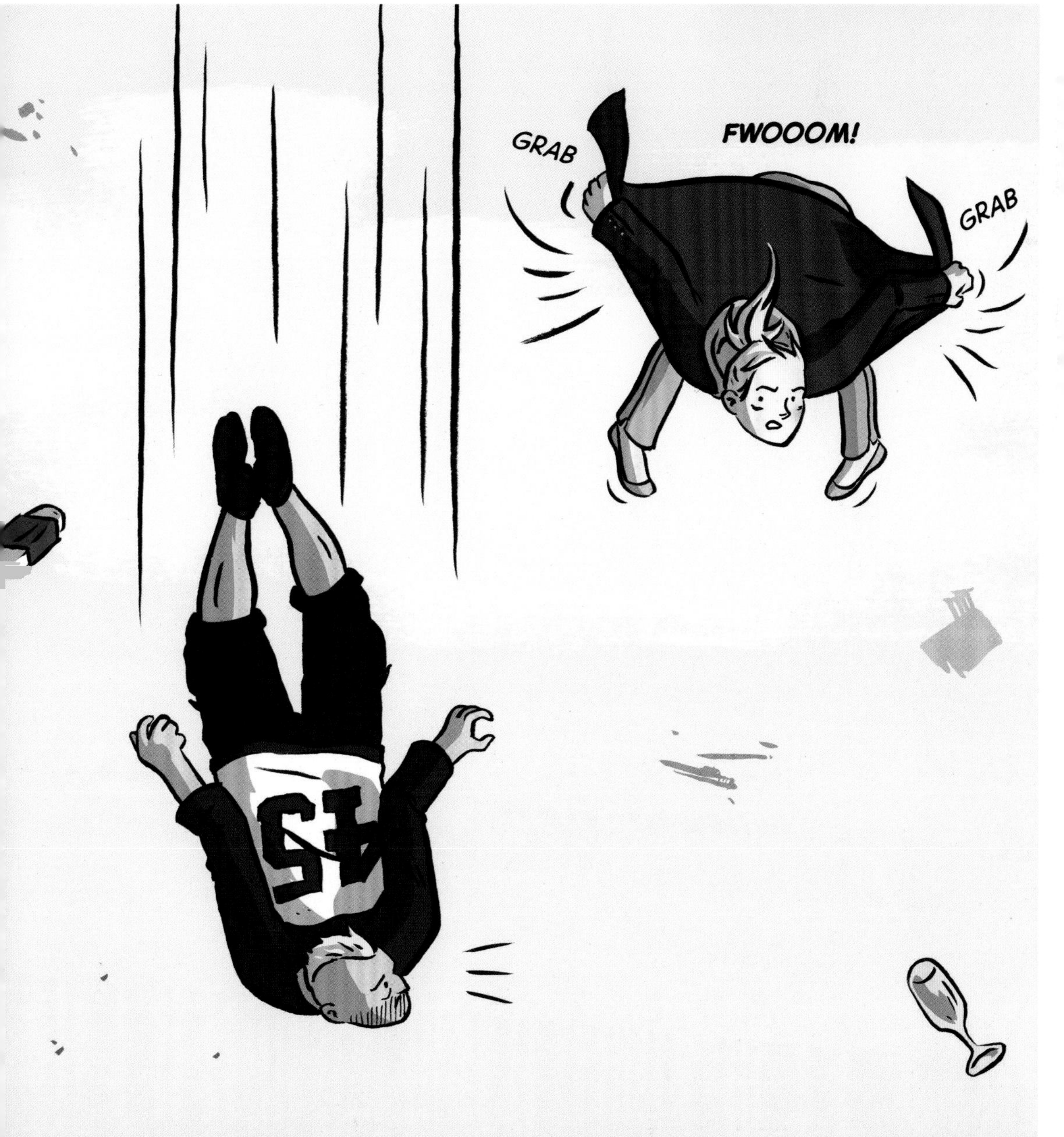
GRAB
FWOOOM!
GRAB

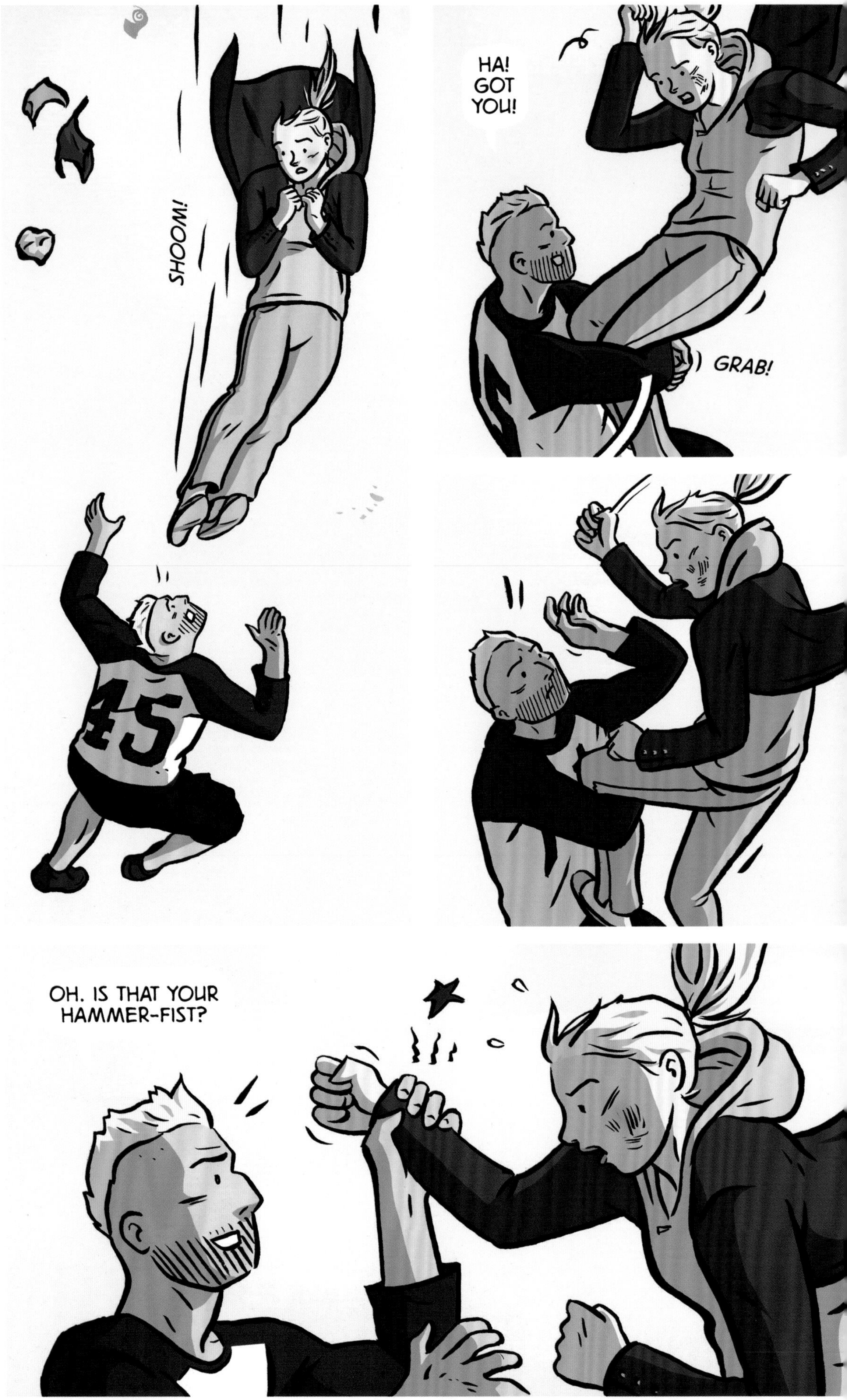
SHOOM!
HA! GOT YOU!
GRAB!
OH. IS THAT YOUR HAMMER-FIST?

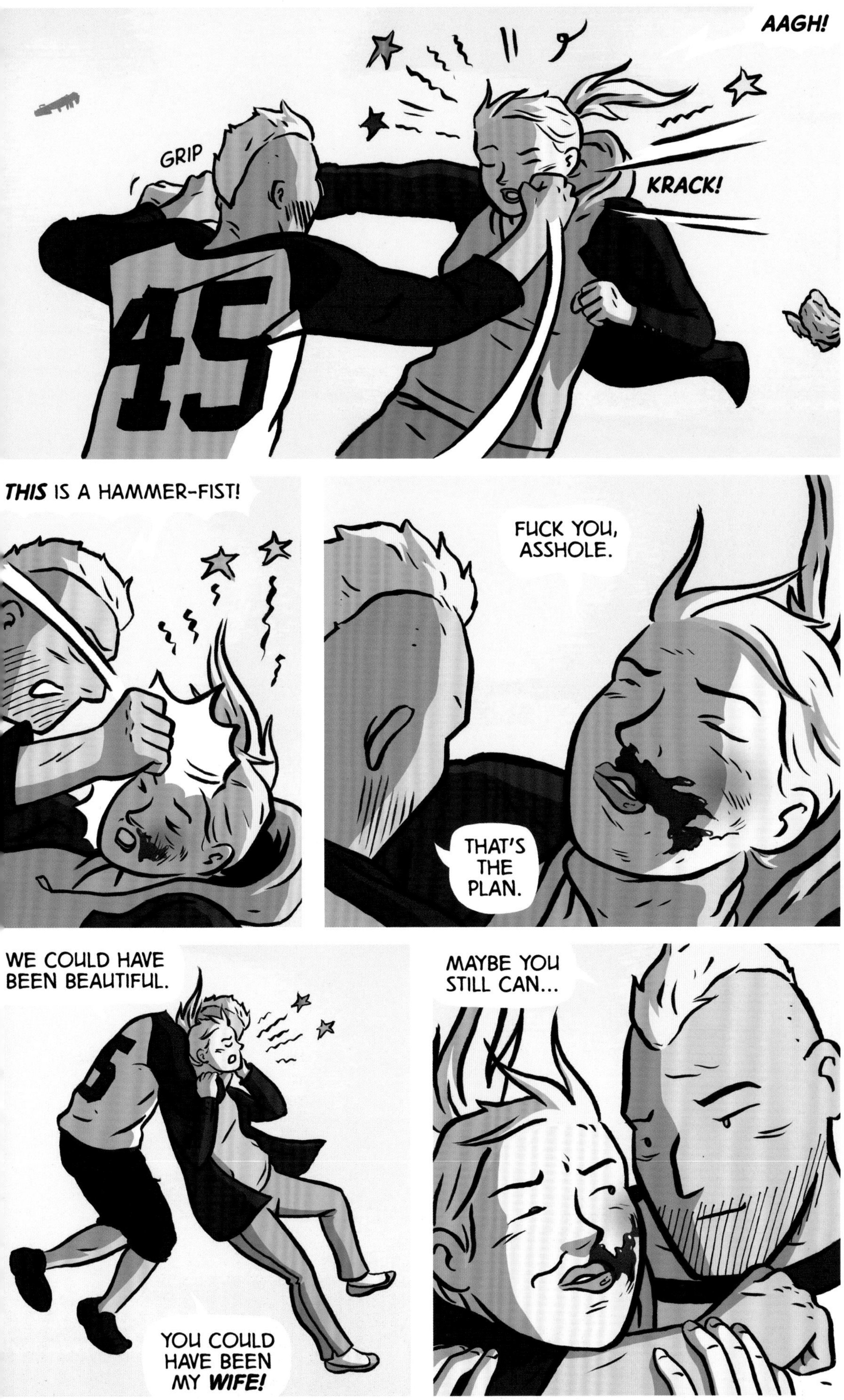
AAGH!
GRIP
KRACK!
45
THIS IS A HAMMER-FIST!
FUCK YOU, ASSHOLE.
THAT'S THE PLAN.
WE COULD HAVE BEEN BEAUTIFUL.
YOU COULD HAVE BEEN MY **WIFE!**
MAYBE YOU STILL CAN...

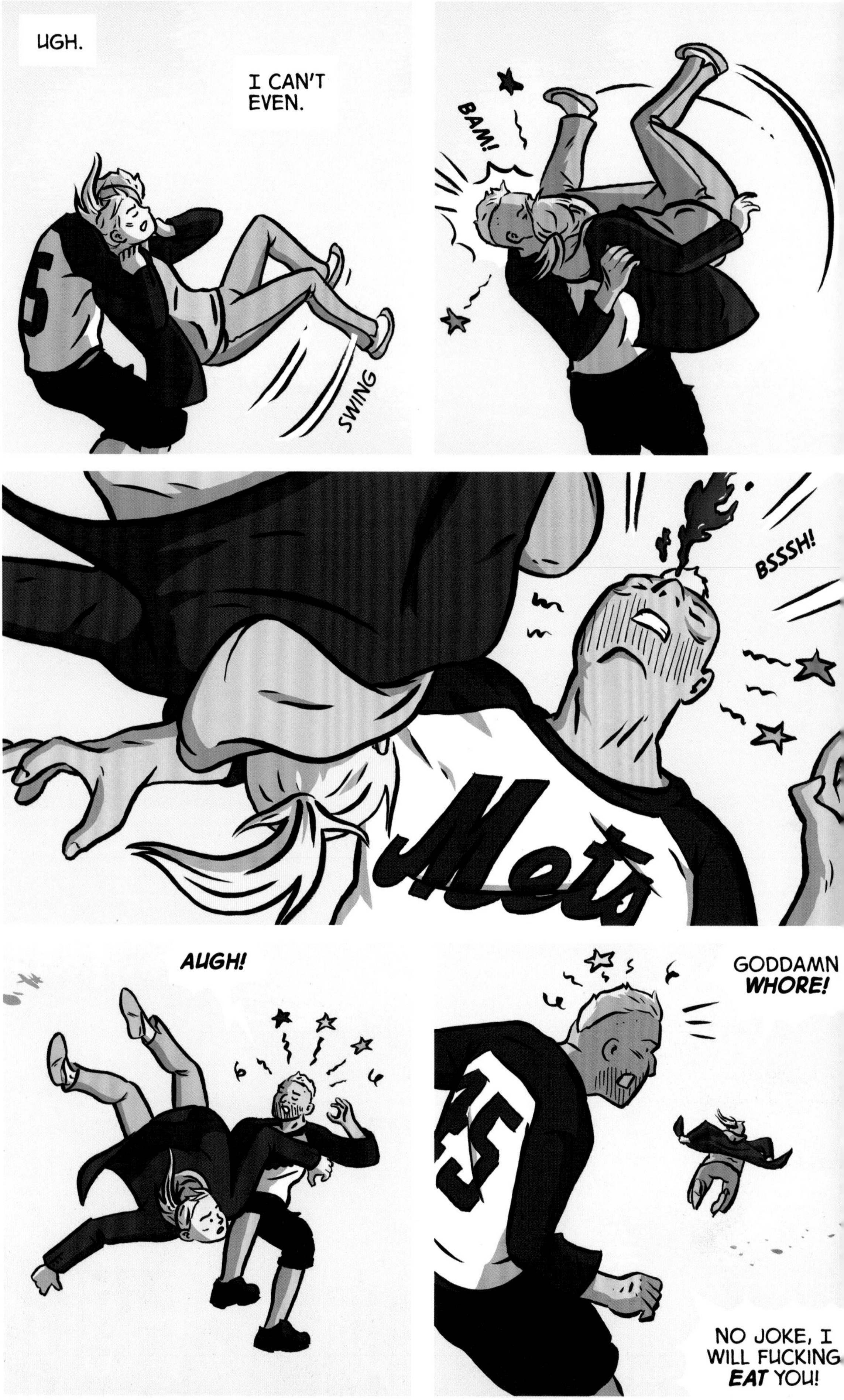

UGH.
I CAN'T EVEN.
SWING
BAM!
BSSSH!
Mets
AUGH!
GODDAMN WHORE!
NO JOKE, I WILL FUCKING EAT YOU!

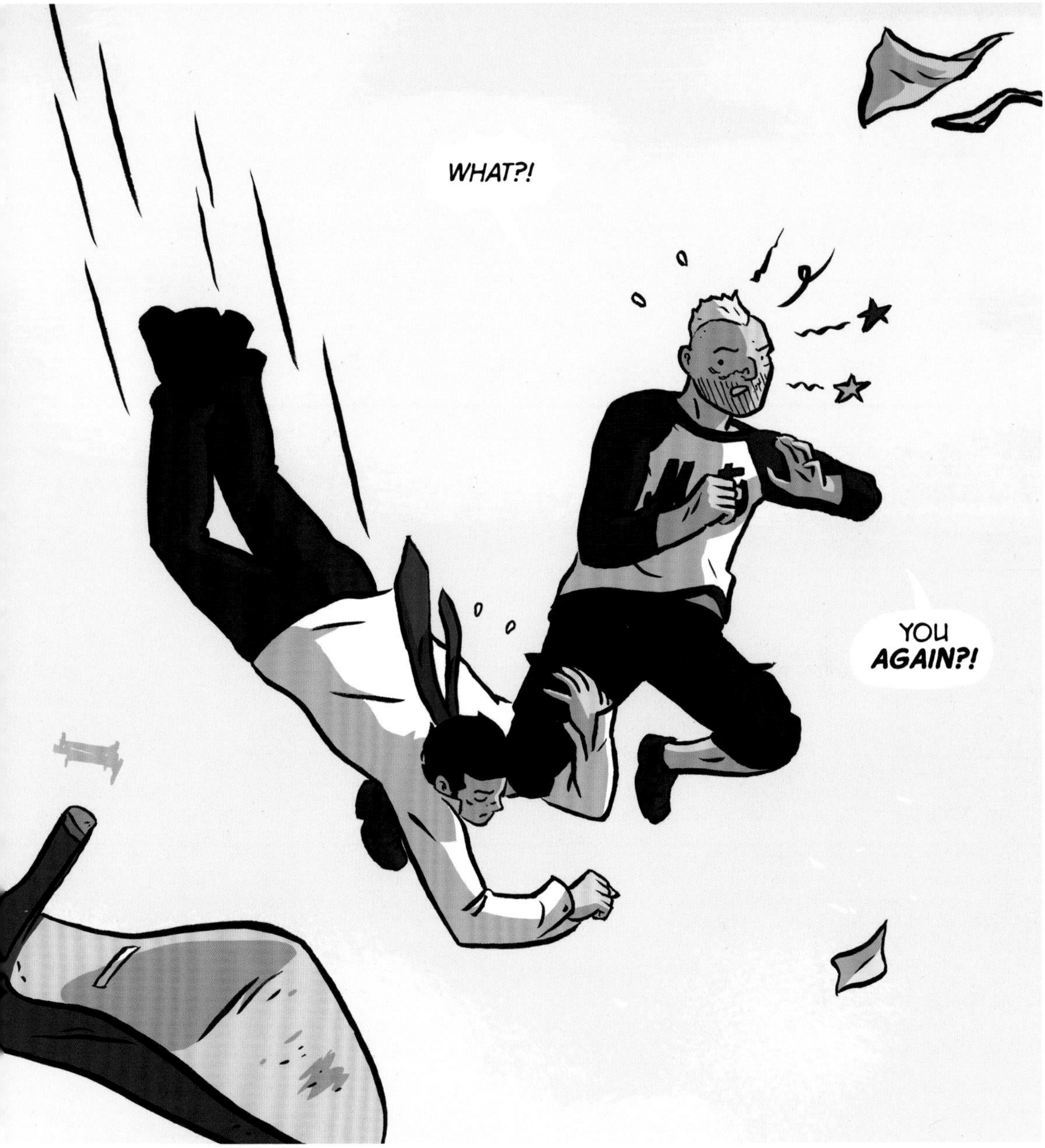
WHAT?!
YOU AGAIN?!

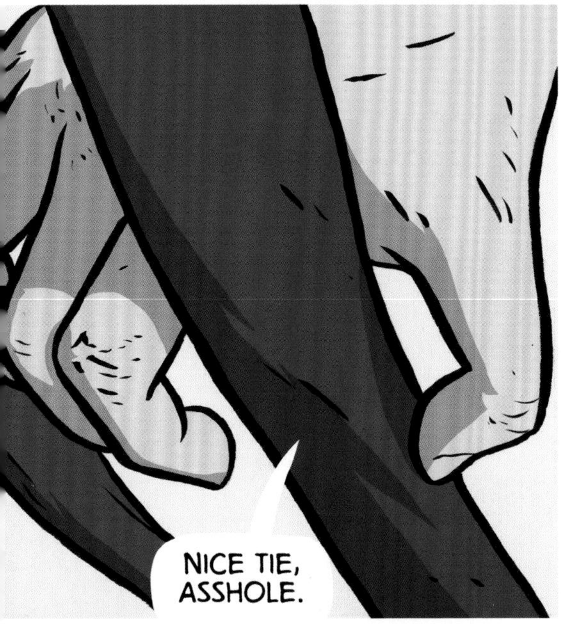
NICE TIE, ASSHOLE.

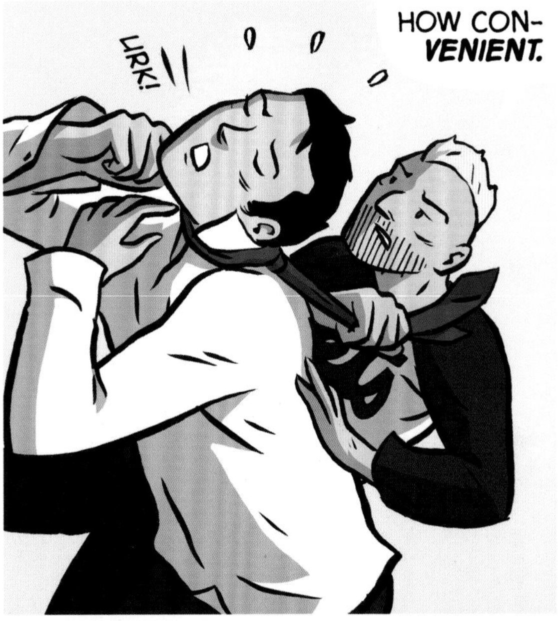
URK!
HOW CON-VENIENT.

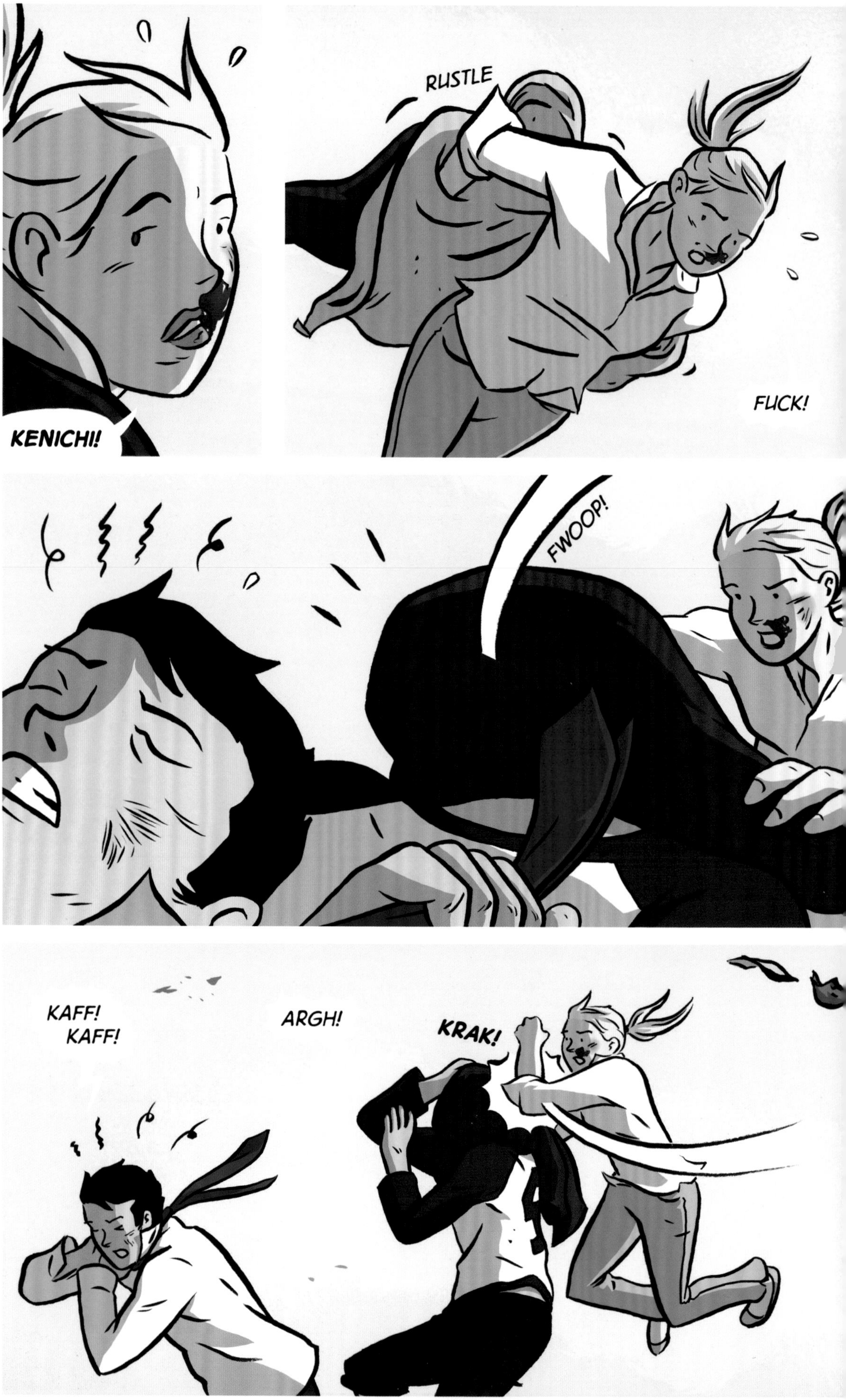
KENICHI!
RUSTLE
FUCK!
FWOOP!
KAFF!
KAFF!
ARGH!
KRAK!

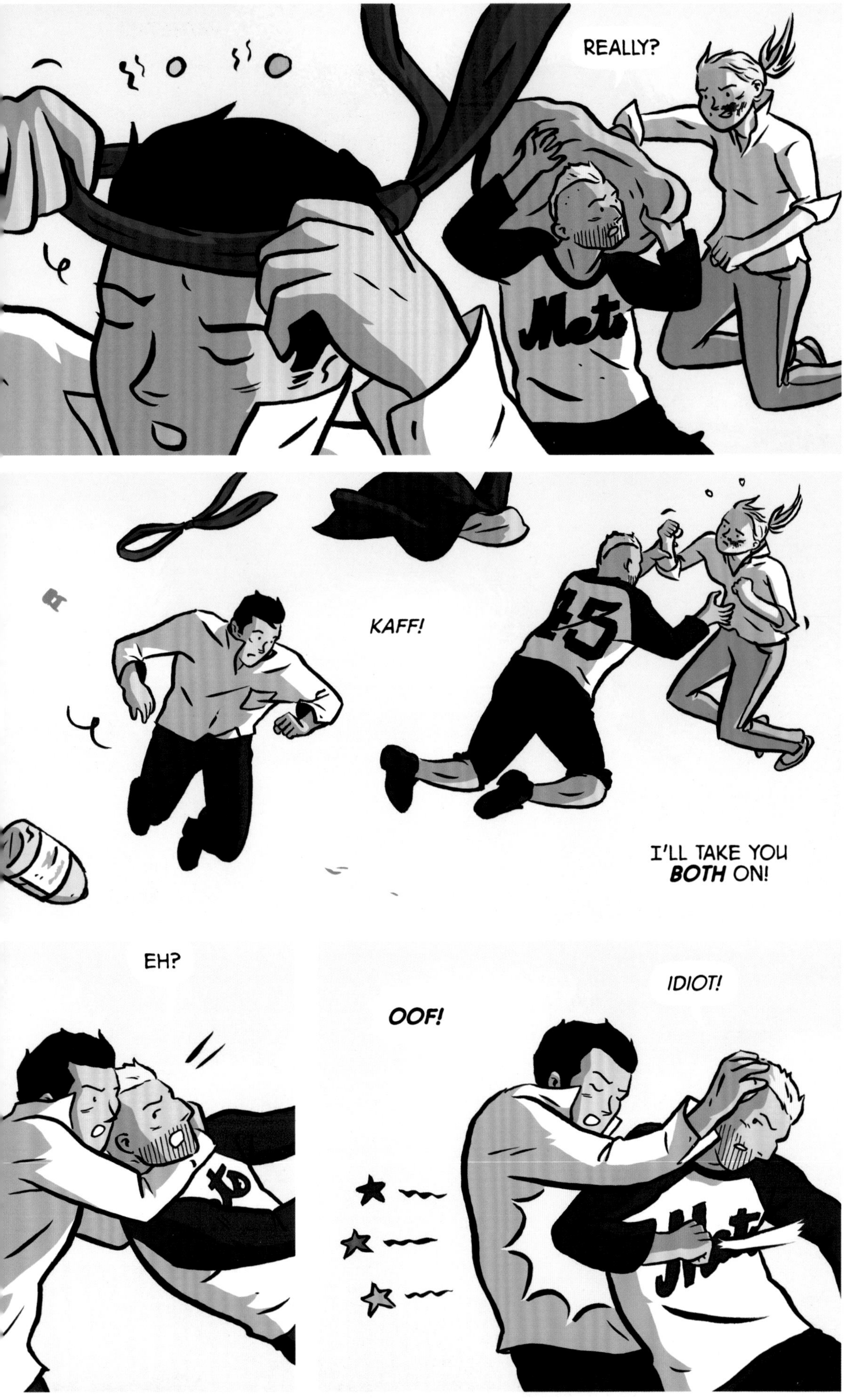
REALLY?
KAFF!
I'LL TAKE YOU *BOTH* ON!
EH?
OOF!
IDIOT!

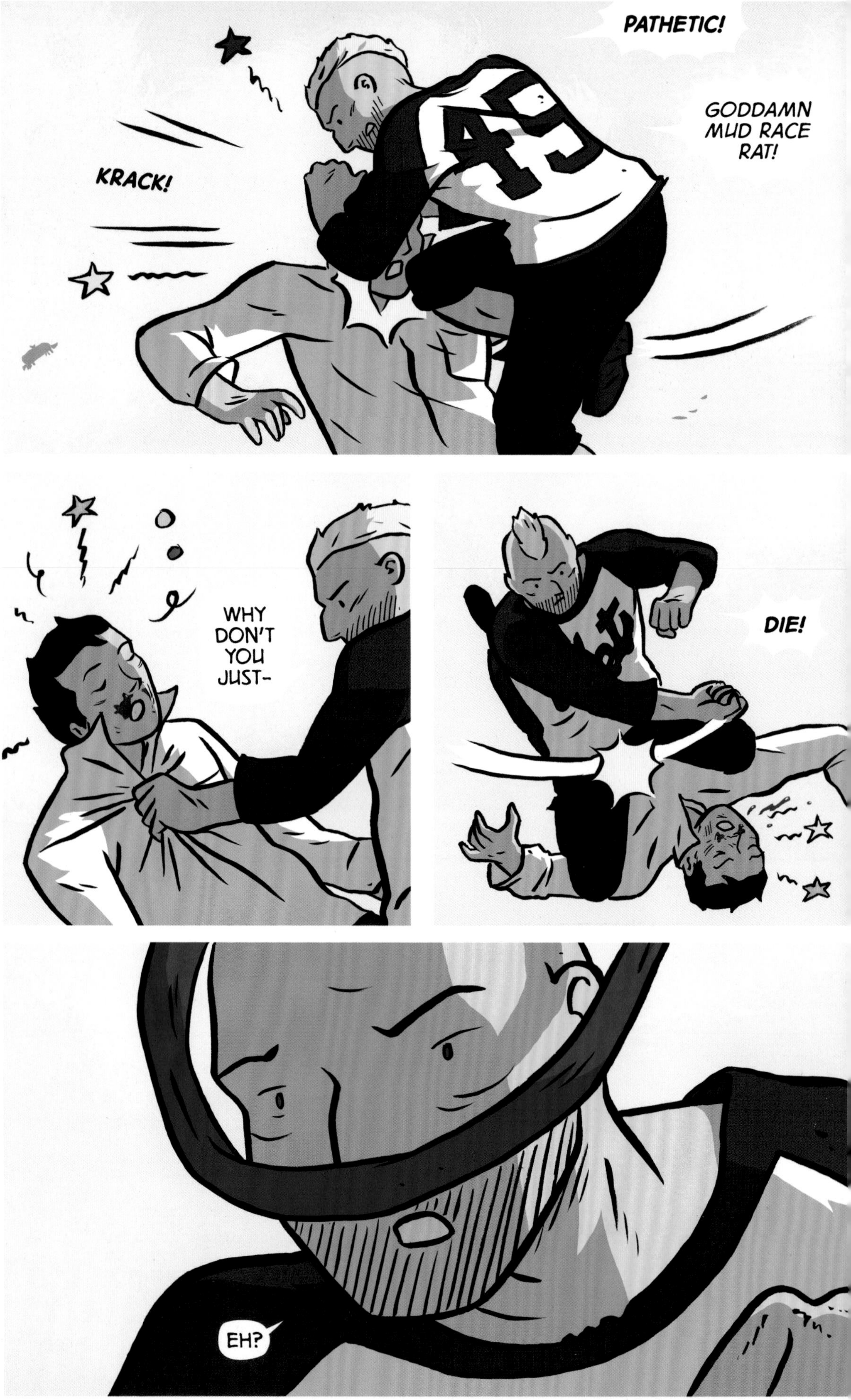
PATHETIC!
GODDAMN MUD RACE RAT!
KRACK!
WHY DON'T YOU JUST-
DIE!
EH?

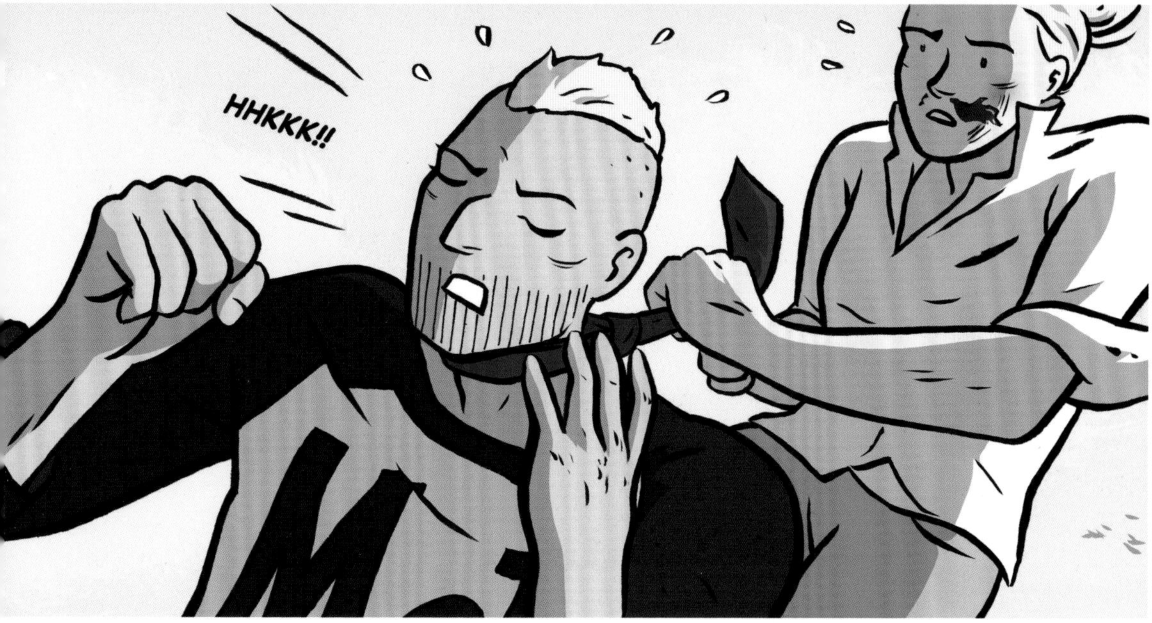
HHKKK!!

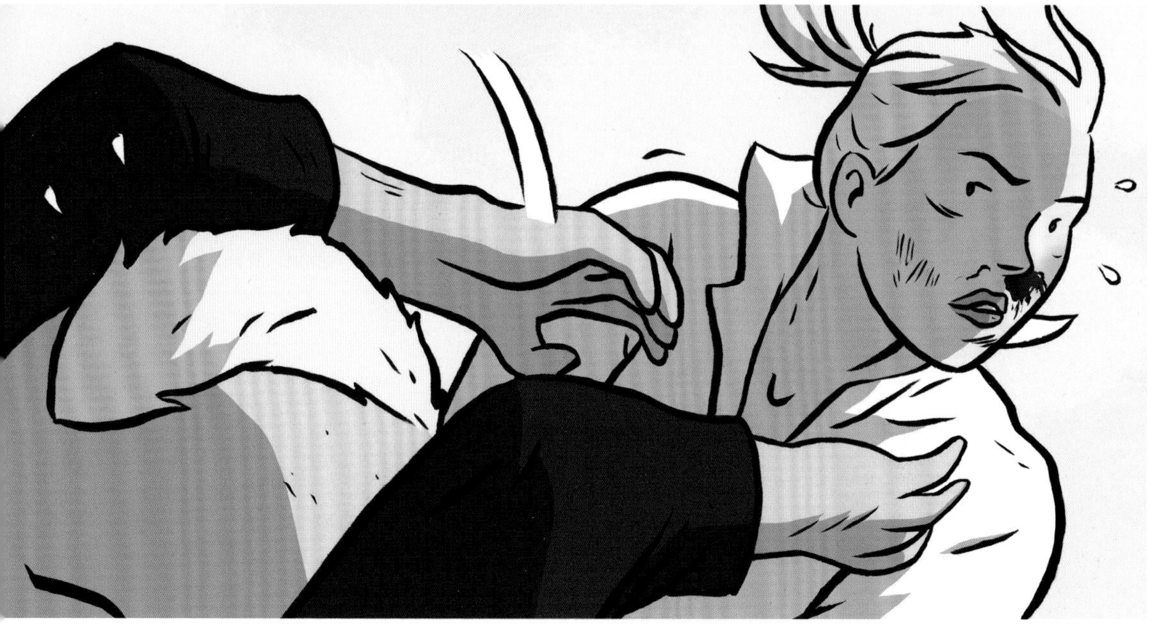

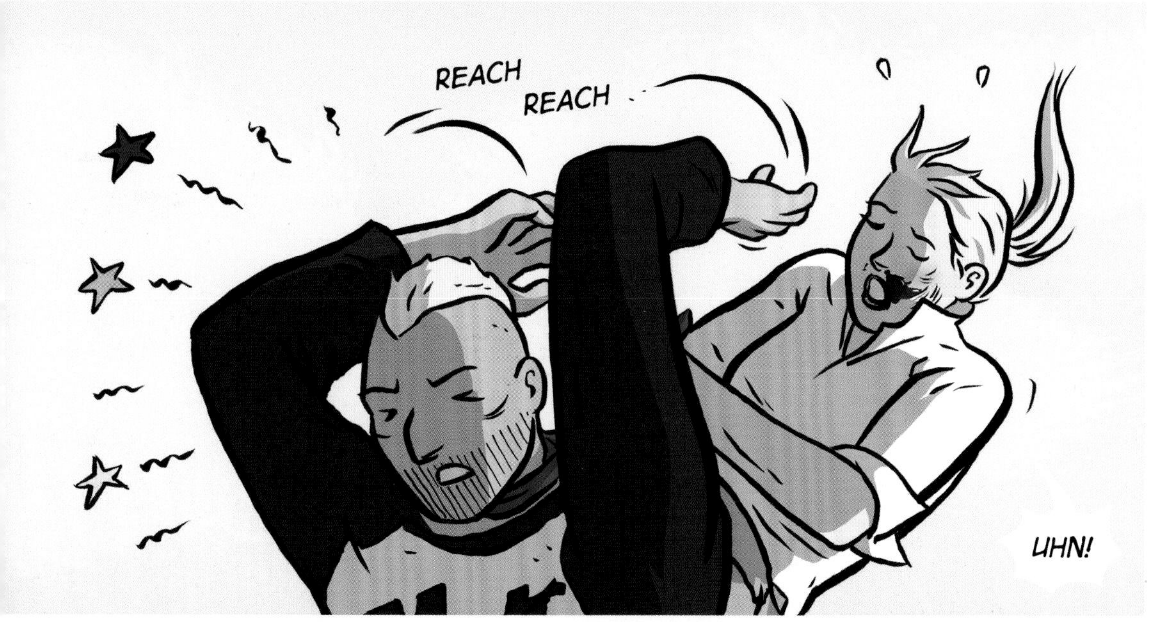
REACH
REACH
UHN!

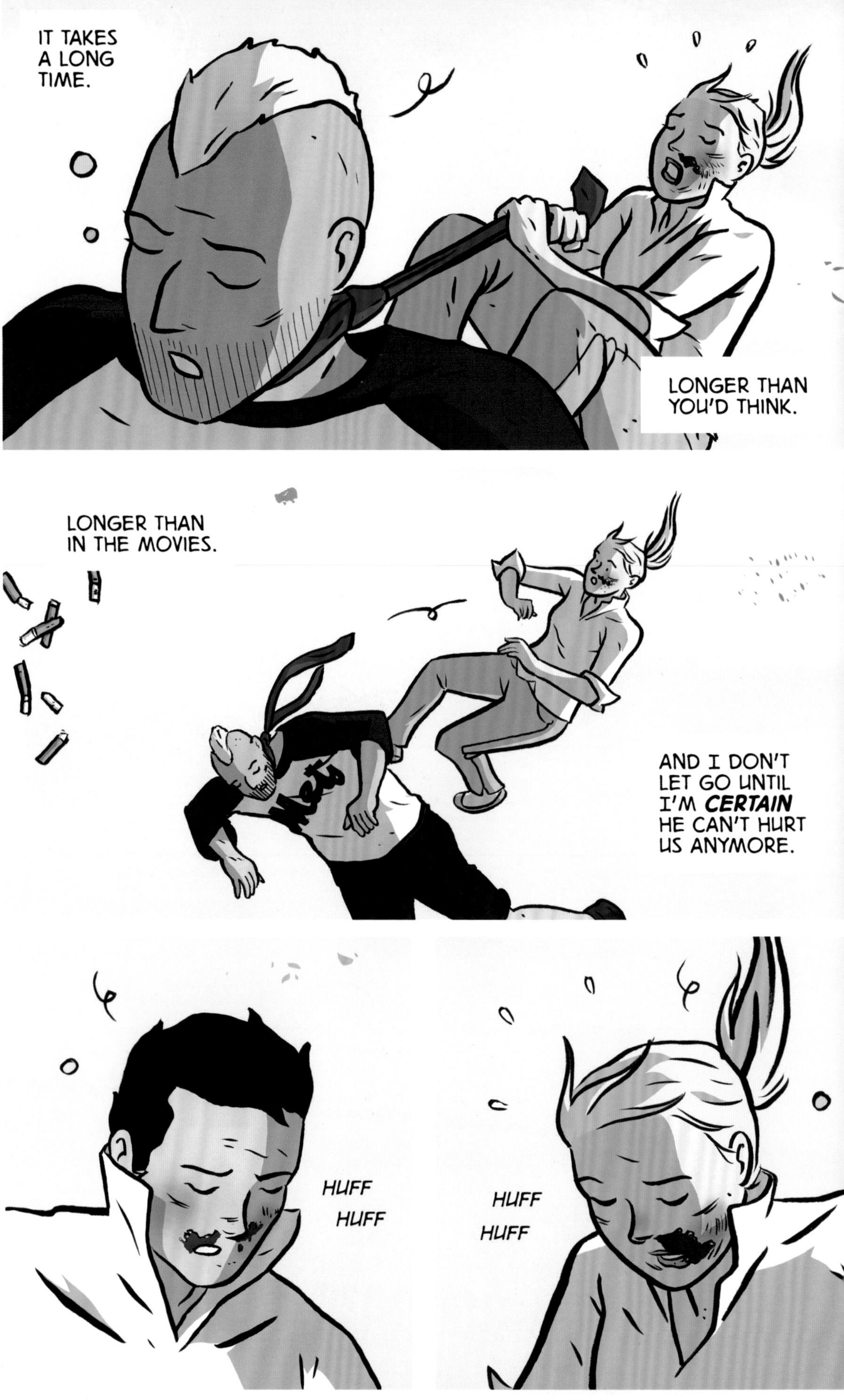
IT TAKES A LONG TIME.
LONGER THAN YOU'D THINK.
LONGER THAN IN THE MOVIES.
Mets
AND I DON'T LET GO UNTIL I'M **CERTAIN** HE CAN'T HURT US ANYMORE.
HUFF HUFF
HUFF HUFF

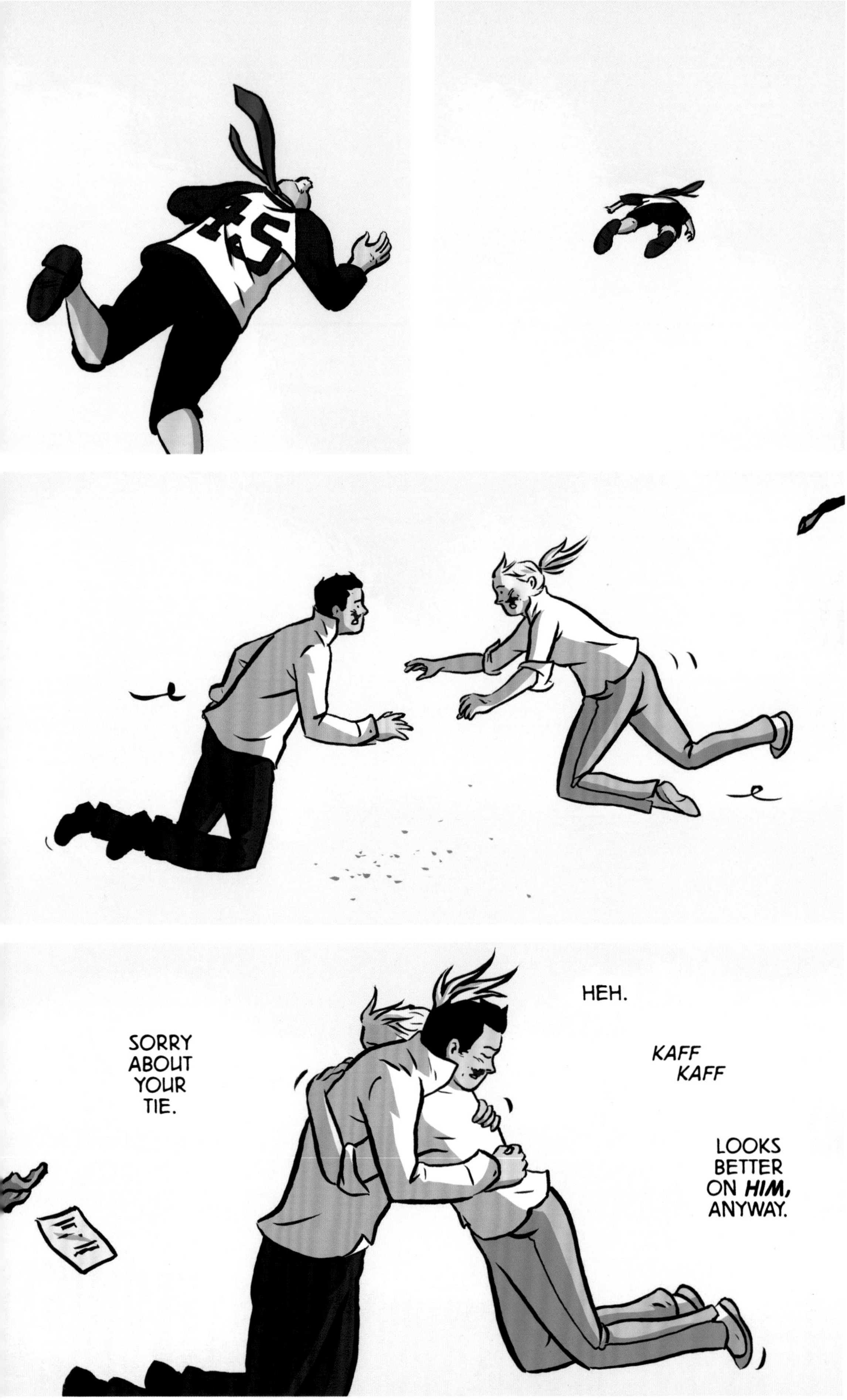
SORRY ABOUT YOUR TIE.
HEH.
KAFF KAFF
LOOKS BETTER ON ***HIM,*** ANYWAY.

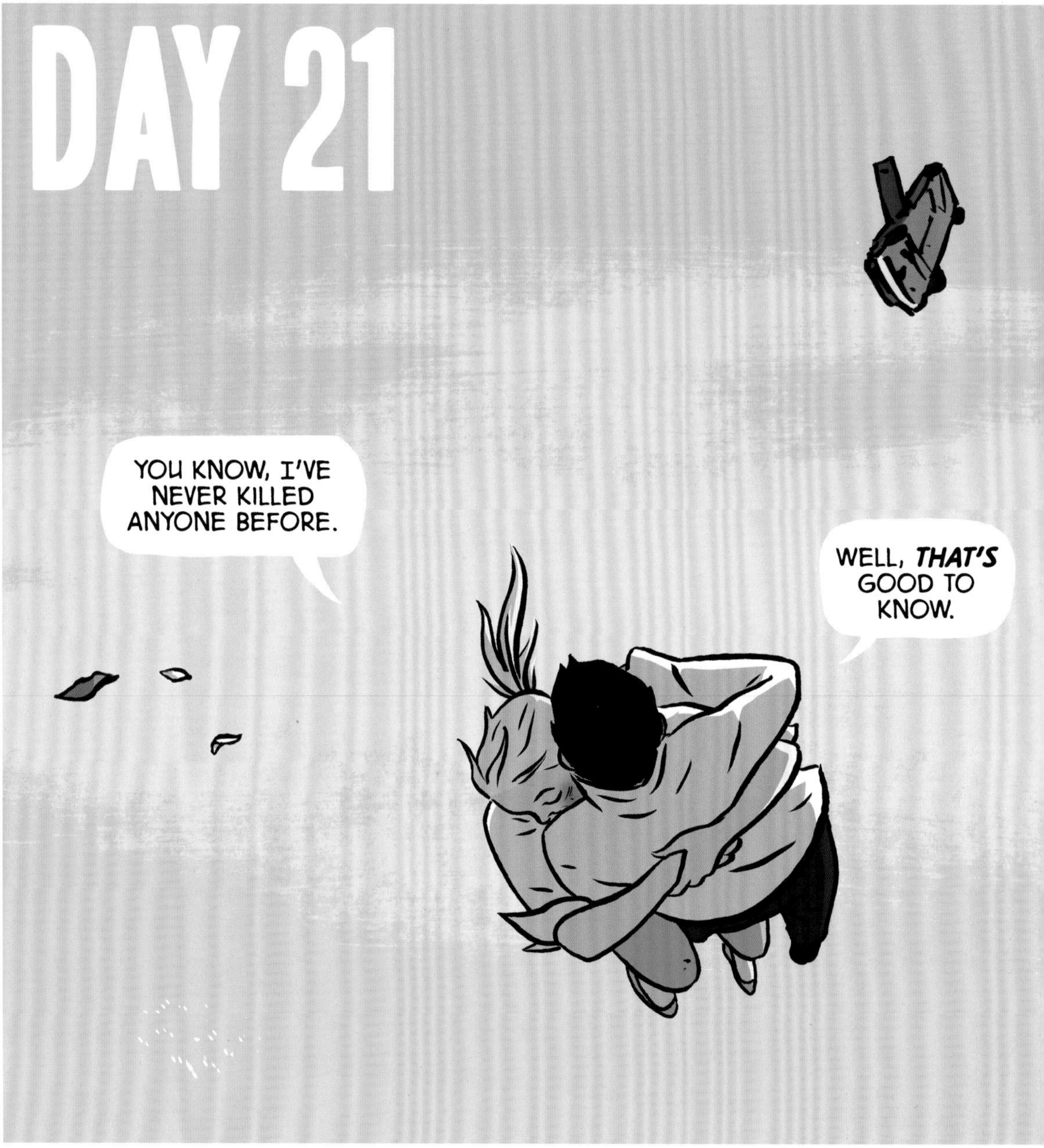
DAY 21
YOU KNOW, I'VE NEVER KILLED ANYONE BEFORE.
WELL, ***THAT'S*** GOOD TO KNOW.

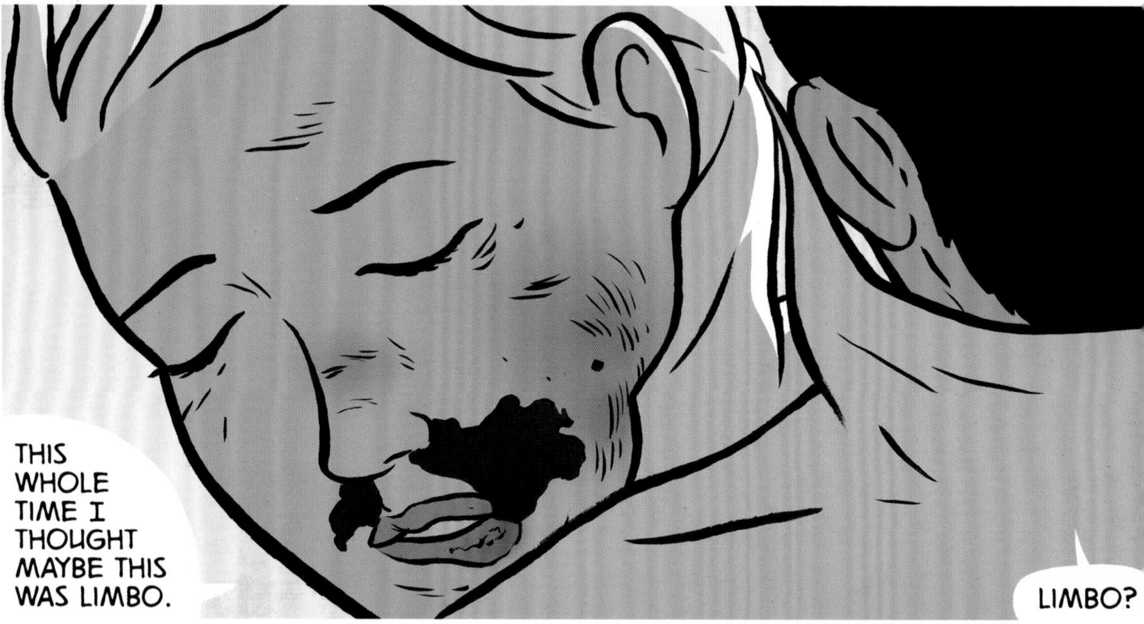
THIS WHOLE TIME I THOUGHT MAYBE THIS WAS LIMBO.
LIMBO?

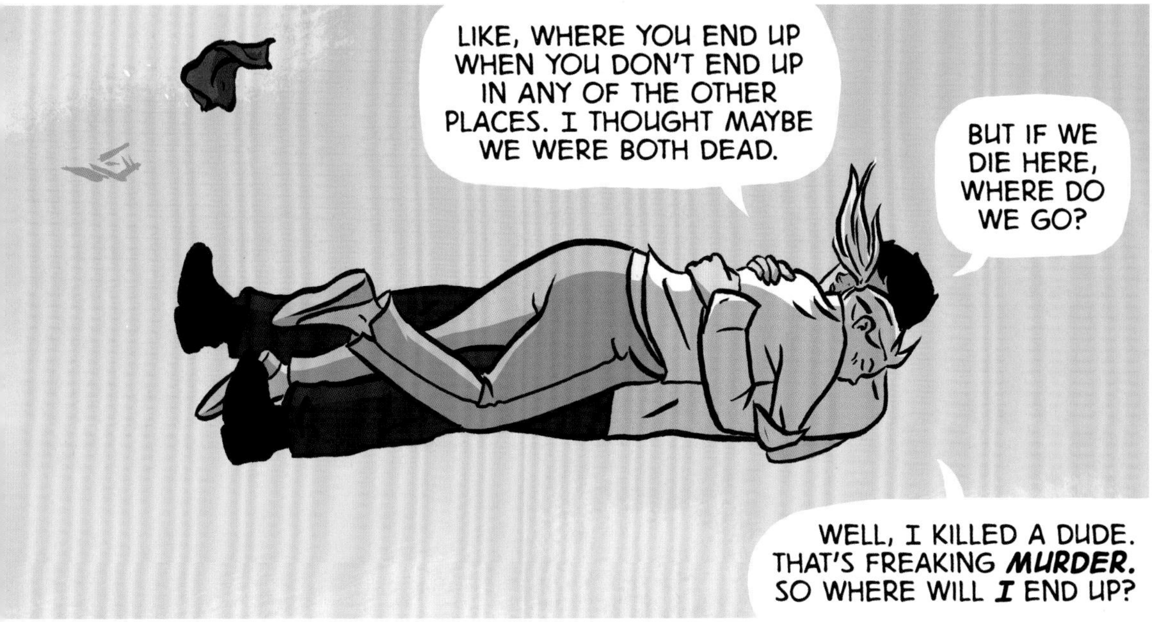
LIKE, WHERE YOU END UP WHEN YOU DON'T END UP IN ANY OF THE OTHER PLACES. I THOUGHT MAYBE WE WERE BOTH DEAD.
BUT IF WE DIE HERE, WHERE DO WE GO?
WELL, I KILLED A DUDE. THAT'S FREAKING MURDER. SO WHERE WILL I END UP?
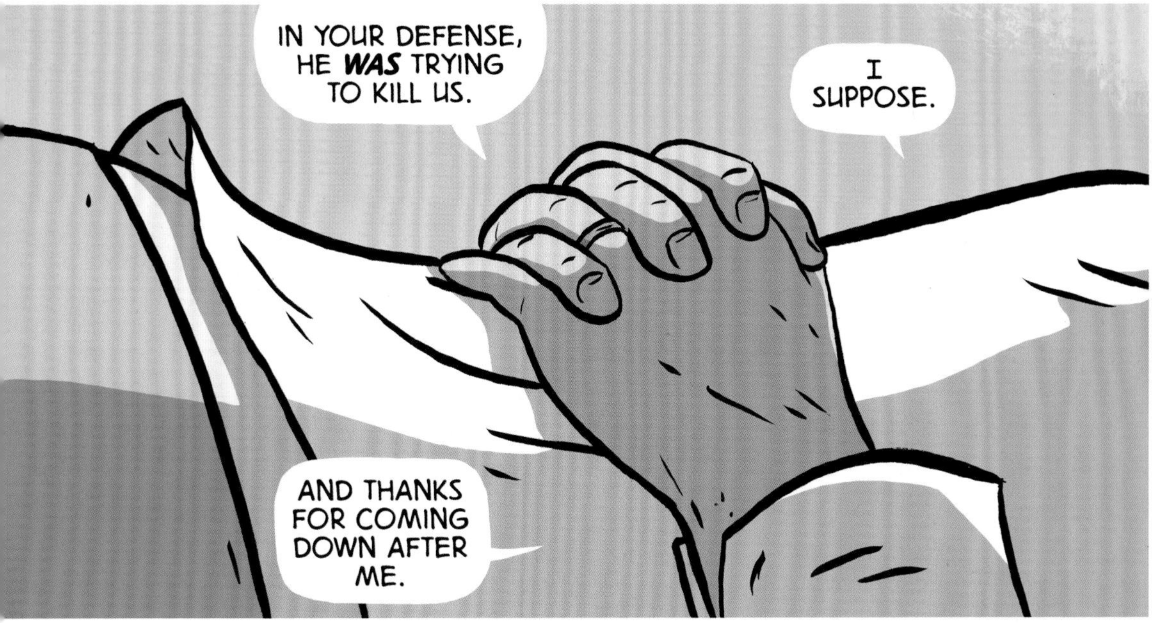
IN YOUR DEFENSE, HE WAS TRYING TO KILL US.
I SUPPOSE.
AND THANKS FOR COMING DOWN AFTER ME.
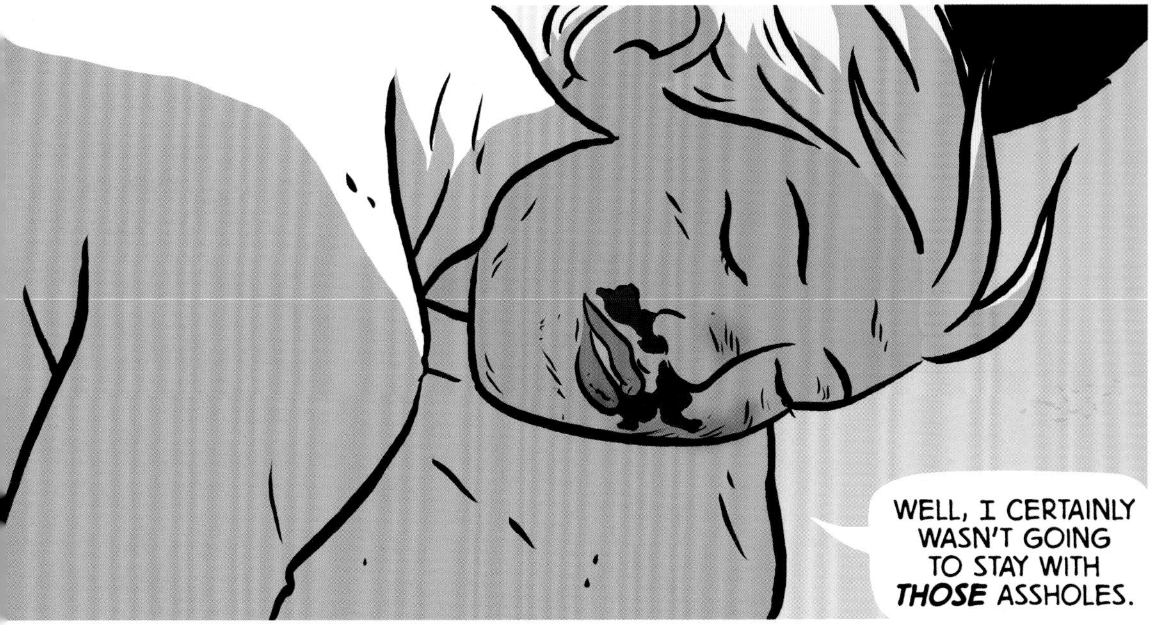
WELL, I CERTAINLY WASN'T GOING TO STAY WITH THOSE ASSHOLES.

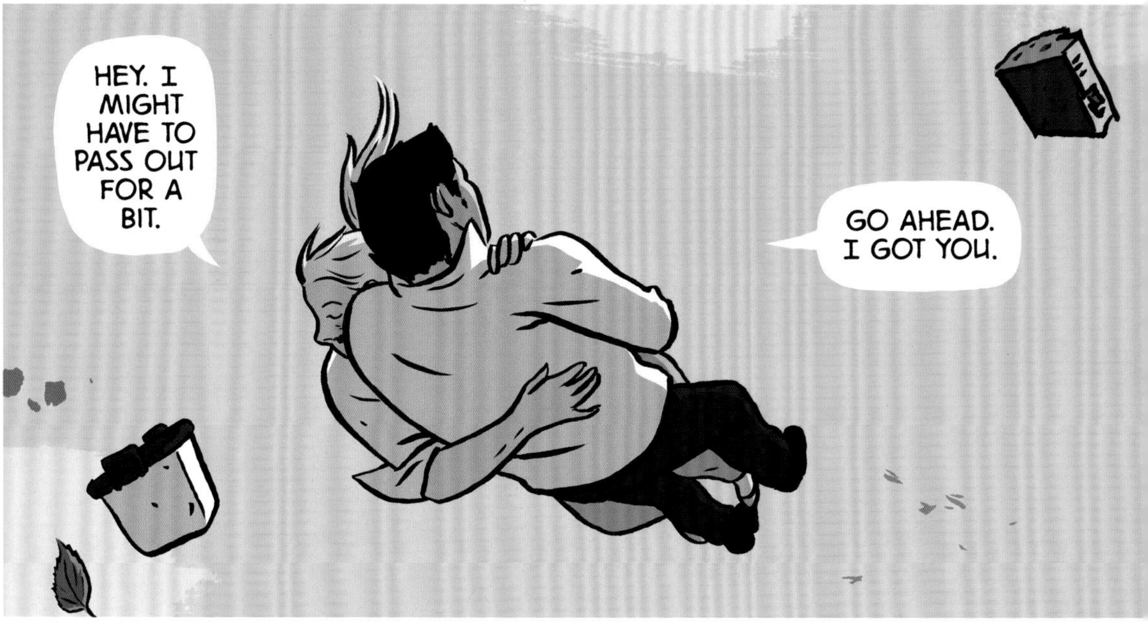
HEY. I MIGHT HAVE TO PASS OUT FOR A BIT.
GO AHEAD. I GOT YOU.
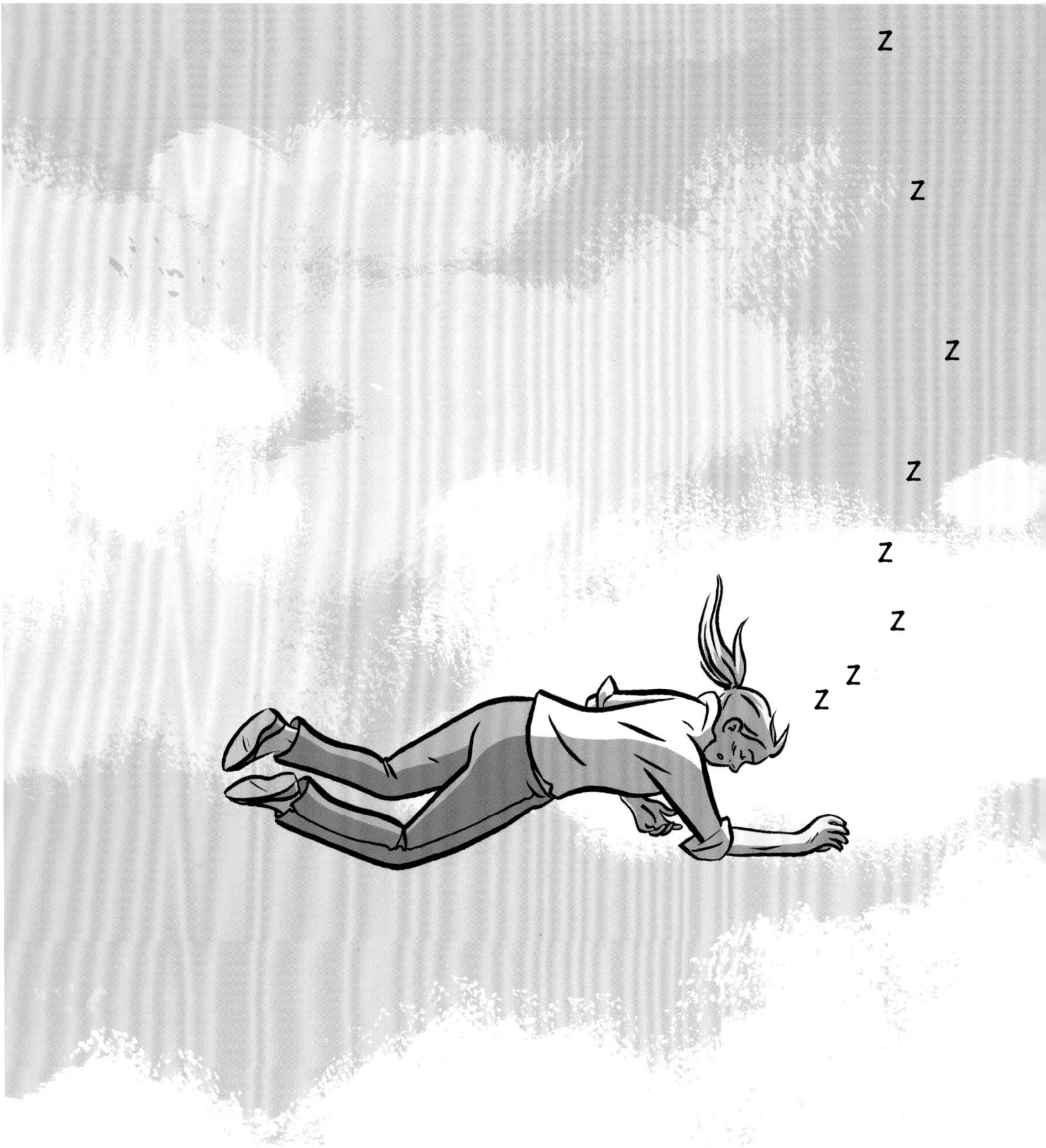
Z
Z
Z
Z
Z
Z
Z
Z

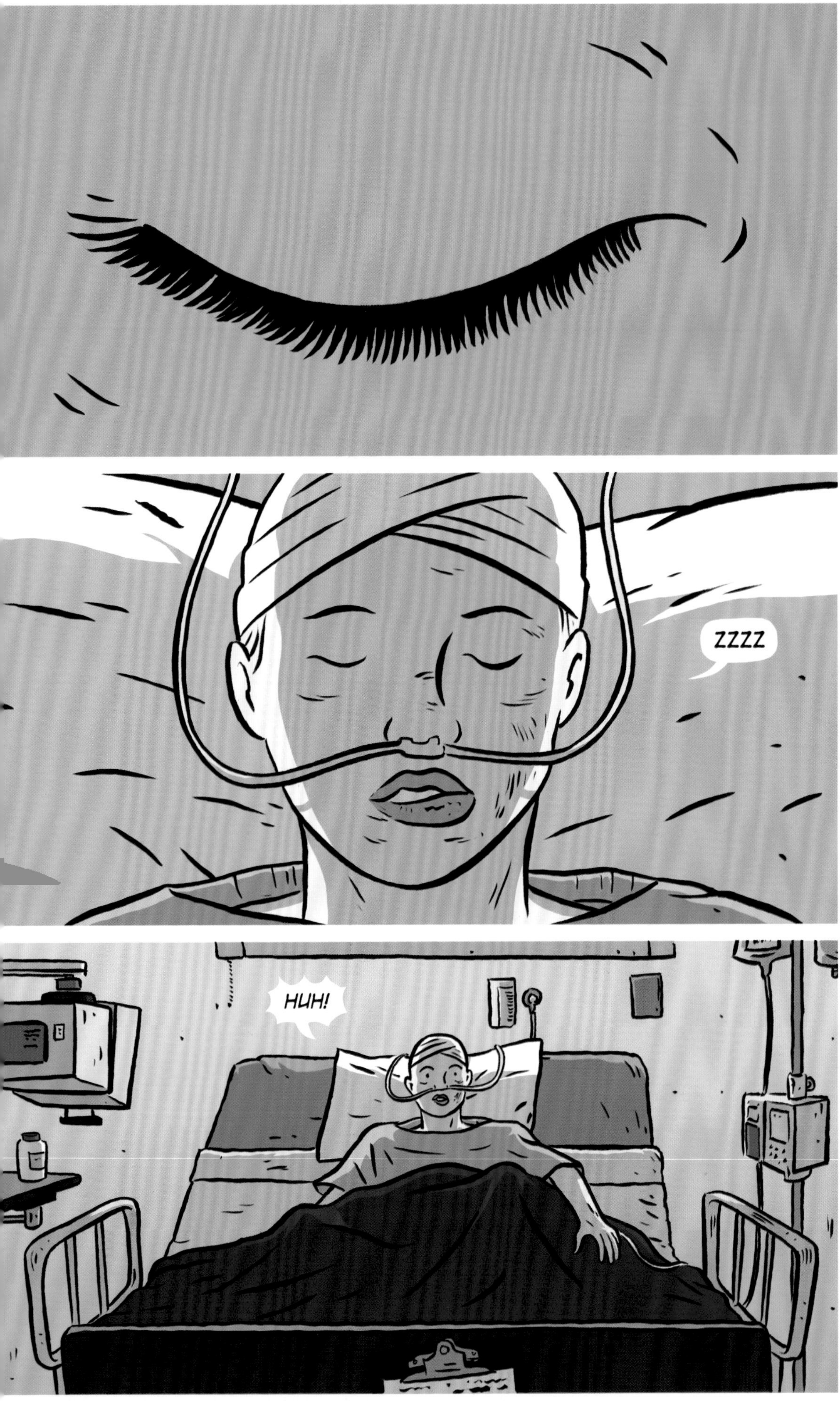
ZZZZ
HUH!

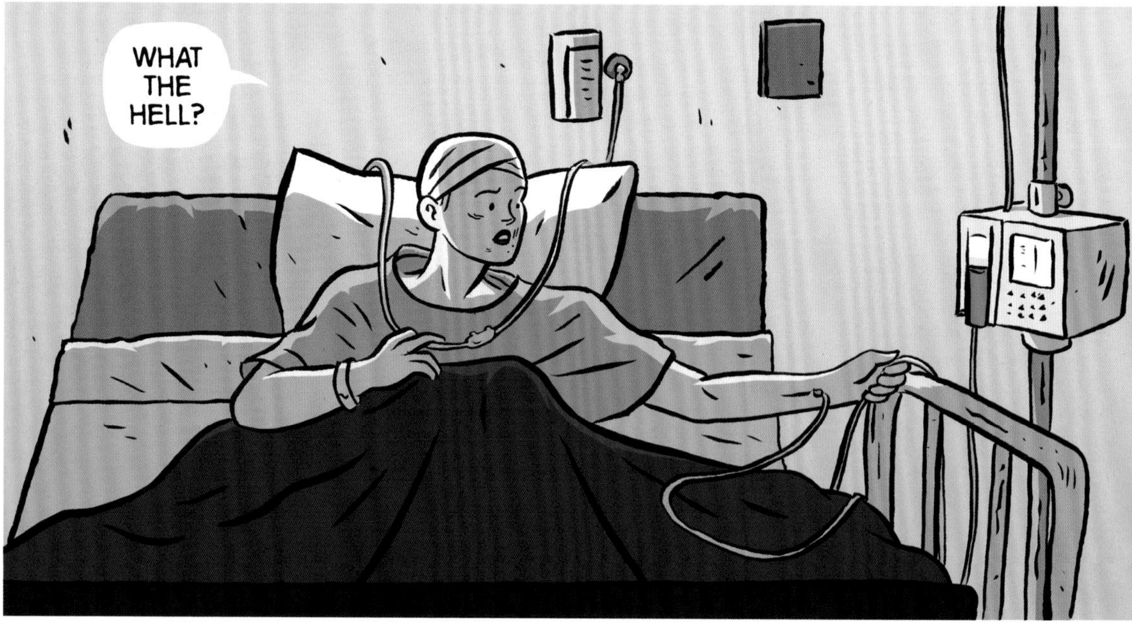
WHAT THE HELL?

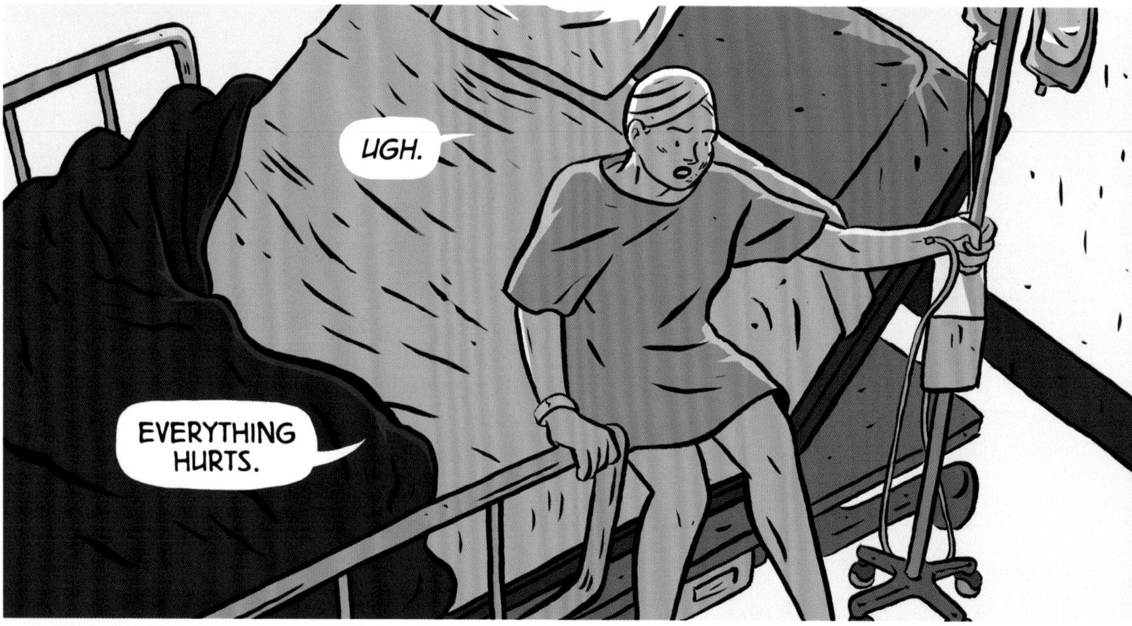
UGH.
EVERYTHING HURTS.

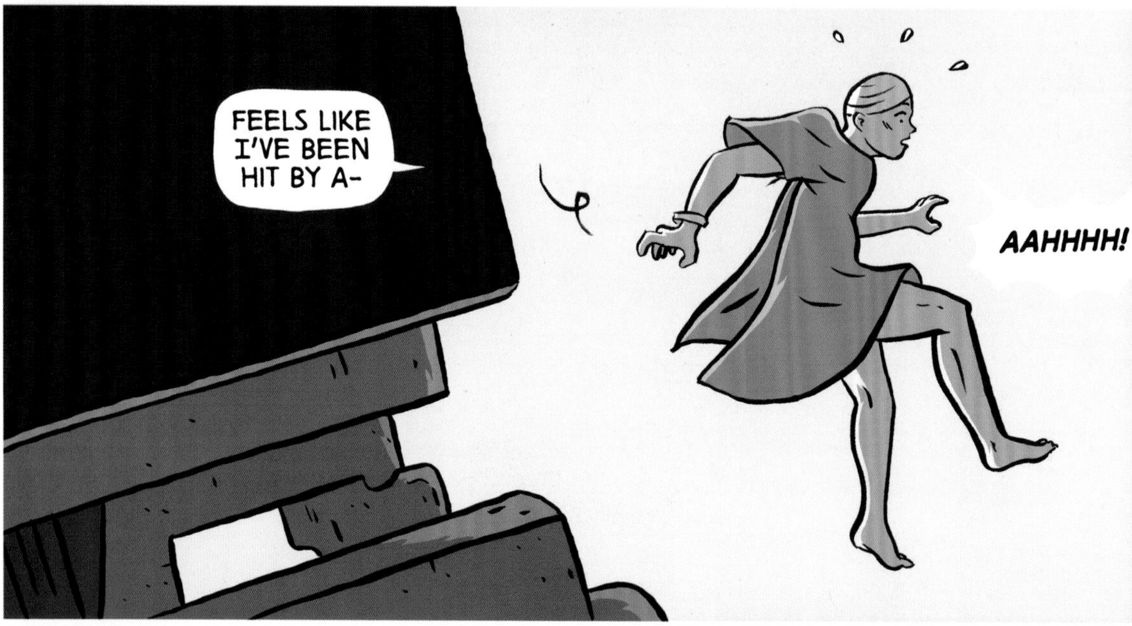
FEELS LIKE I'VE BEEN HIT BY A-
AAHHHH!

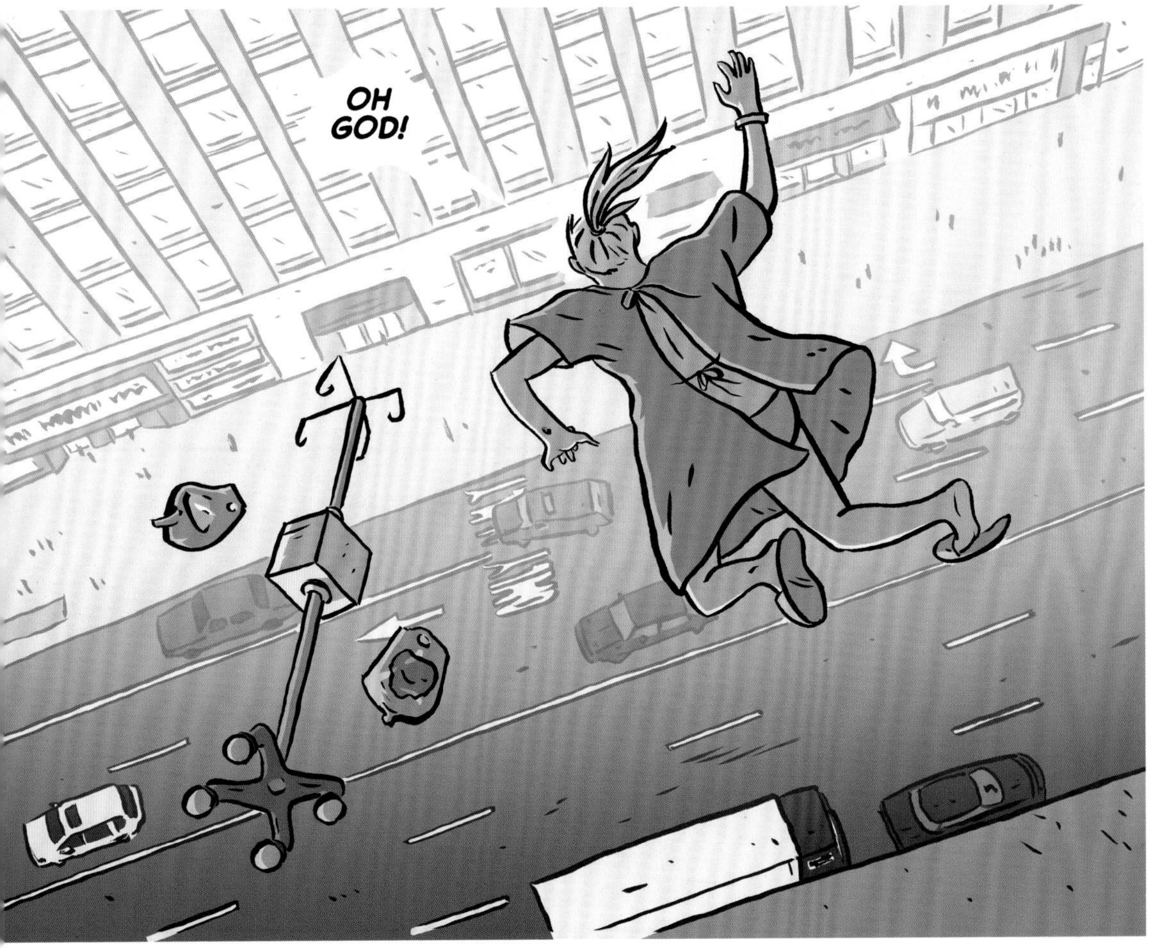
OH GOD!
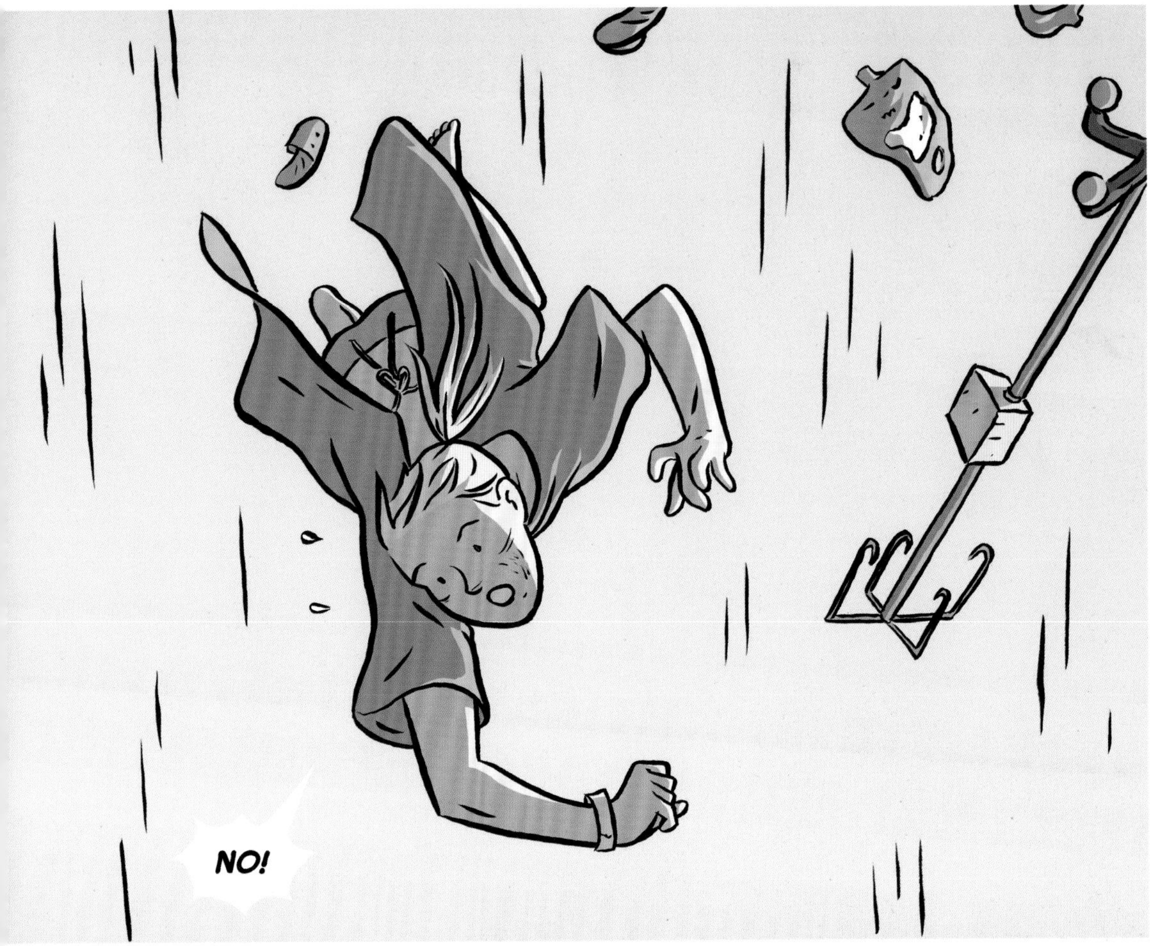
NO!

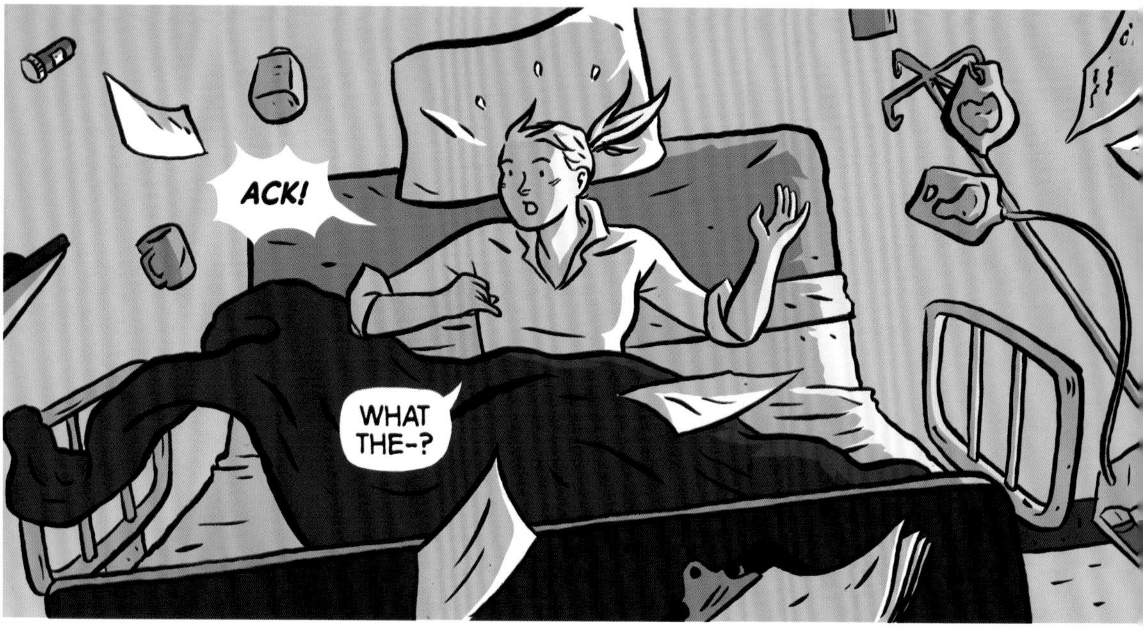
ACK!
WHAT THE-?
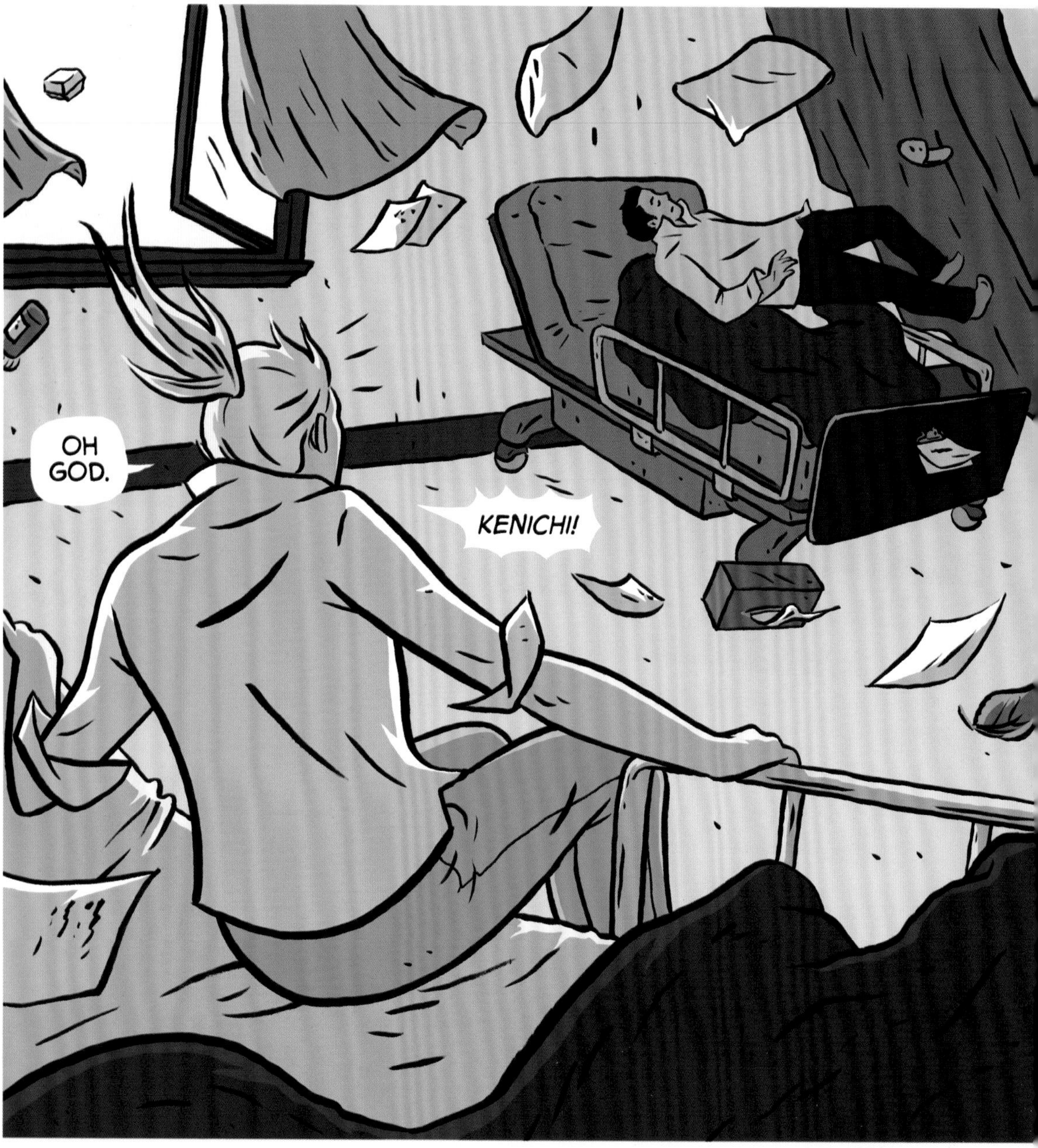
OH GOD.
KENICHI!

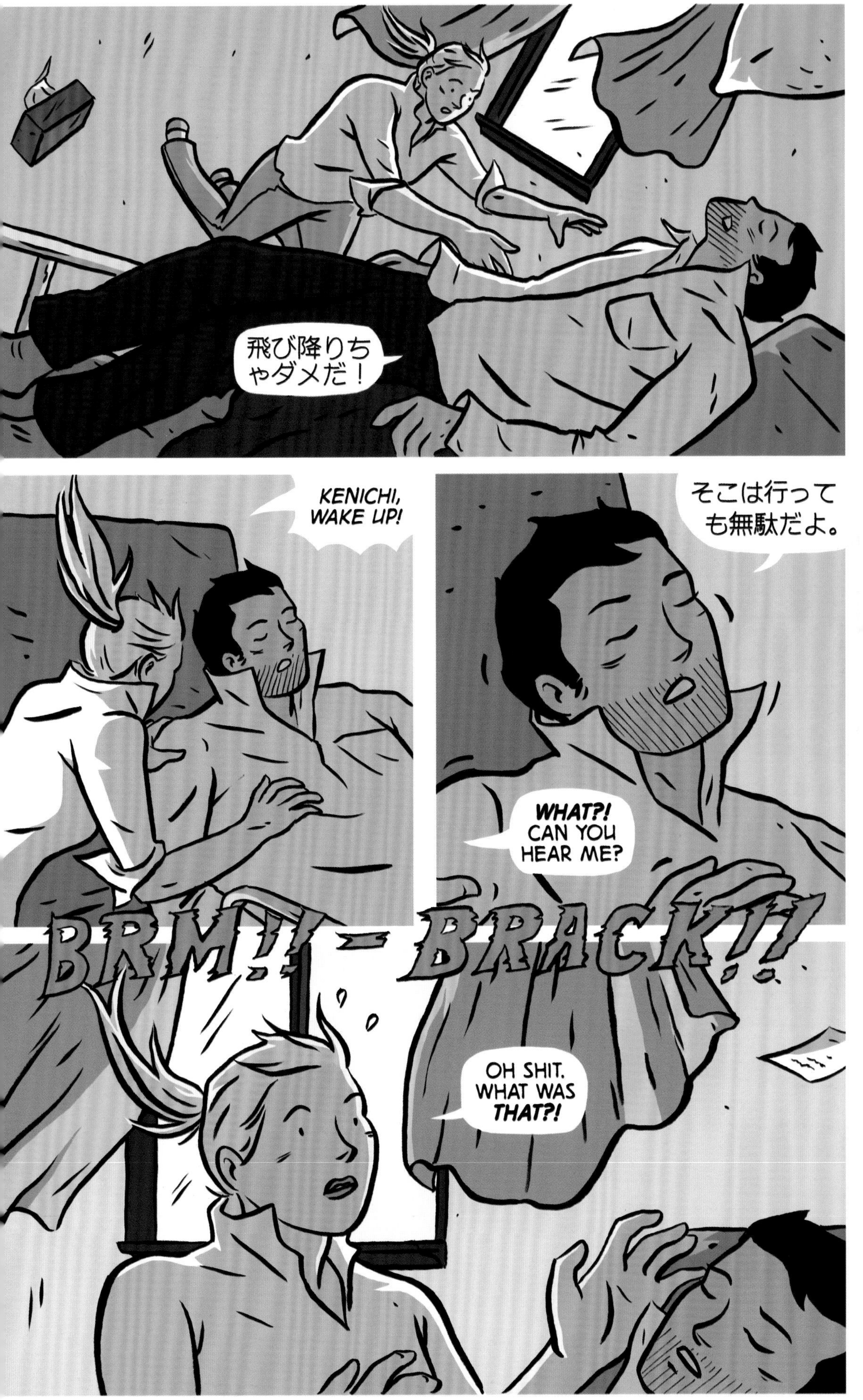
飛び降りちゃダメだ！
KENICHI, WAKE UP!
そこは行っても無駄だよ。
WHAT?! CAN YOU HEAR ME?
BRM!! - BRACK!!
OH SHIT. WHAT WAS THAT?!

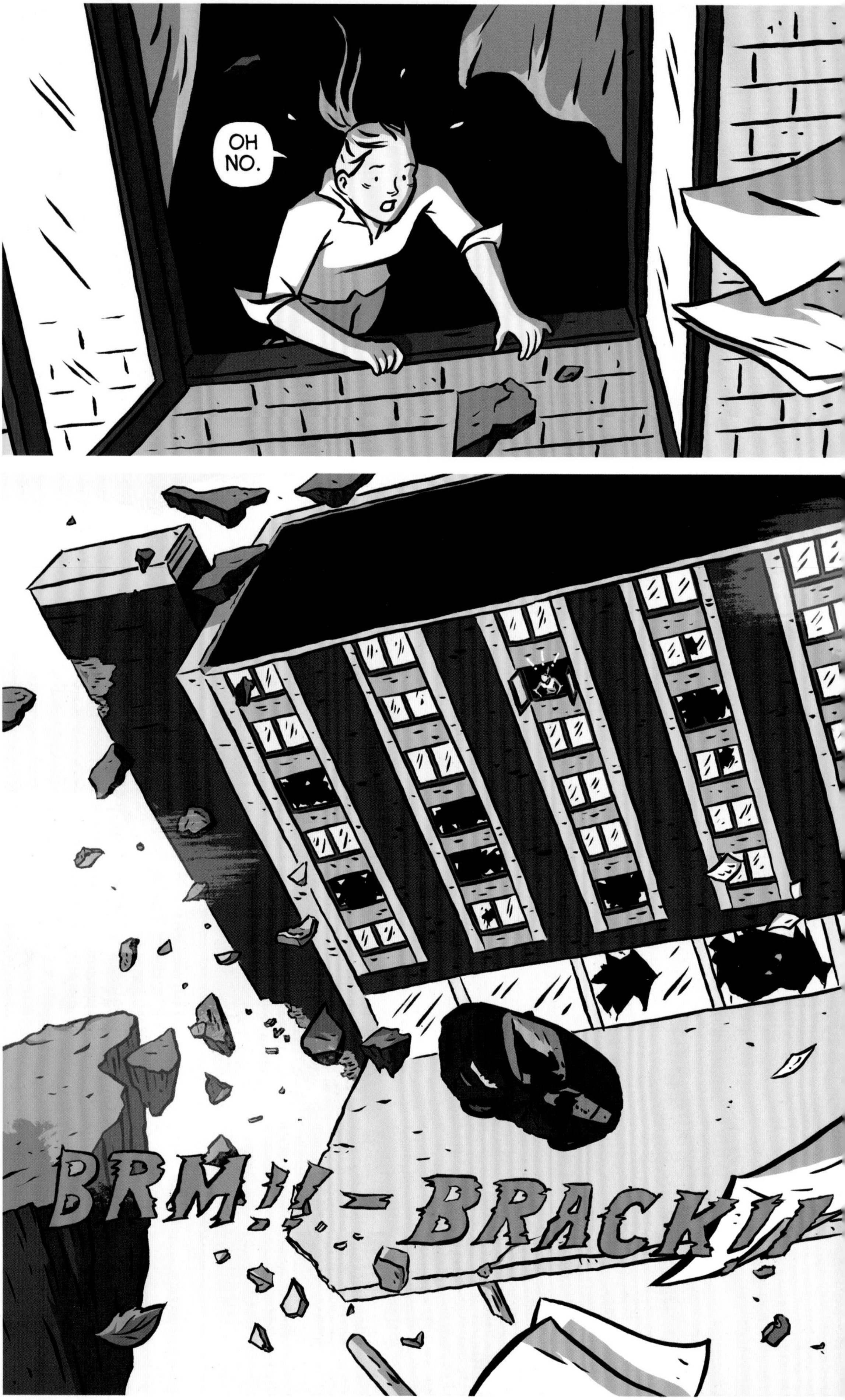
OH NO.
BRM!! - BRACK!!

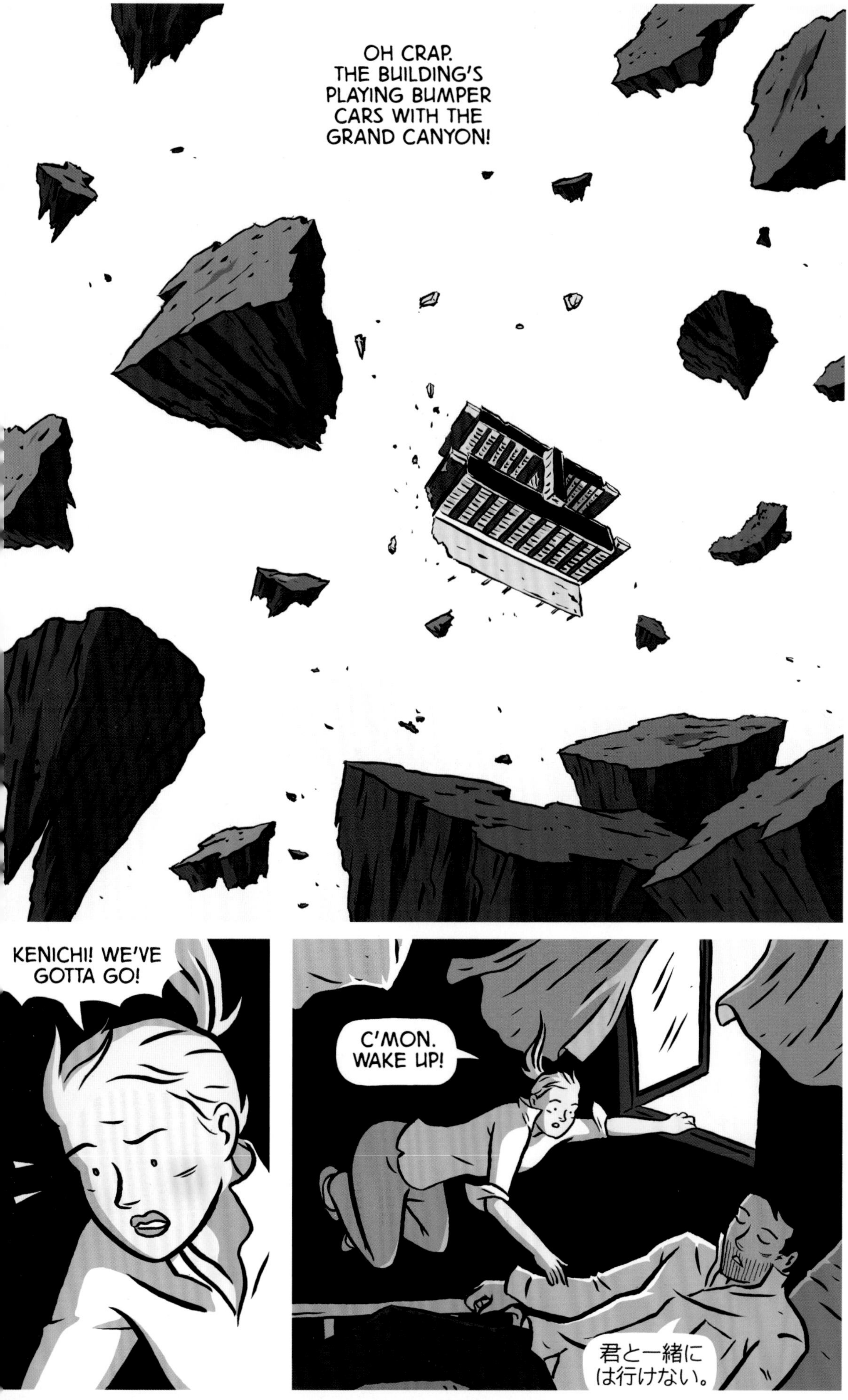
OH CRAP. THE BUILDING'S PLAYING BUMPER CARS WITH THE GRAND CANYON!
KENICHI! WE'VE GOTTA GO!
C'MON. WAKE UP!
君と一緒には行けない。

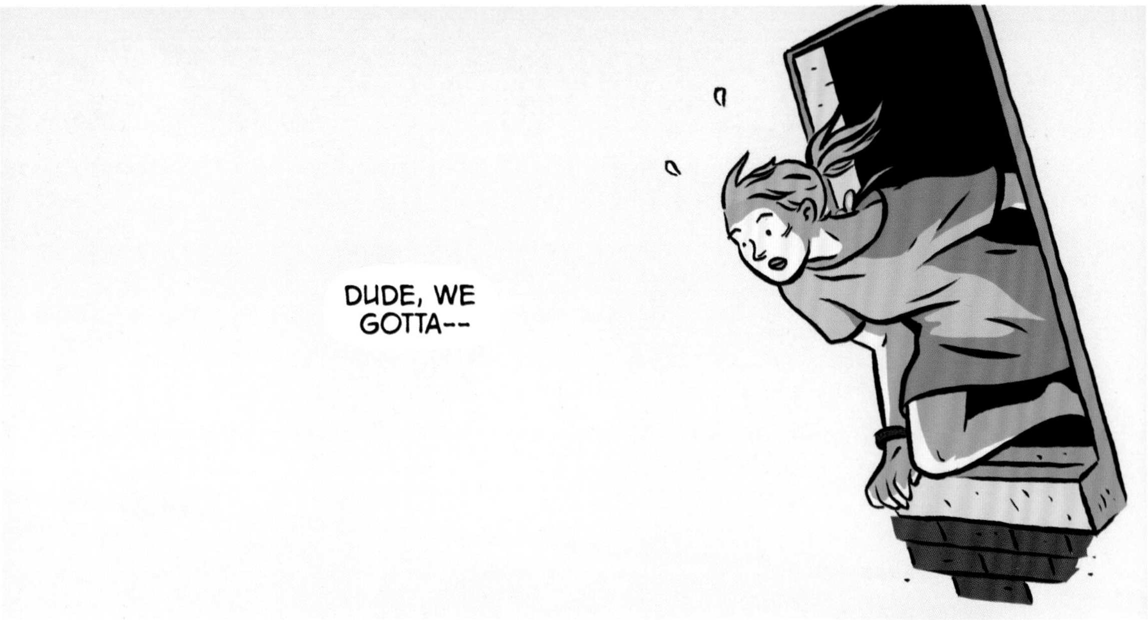
DUDE, WE GOTTA--
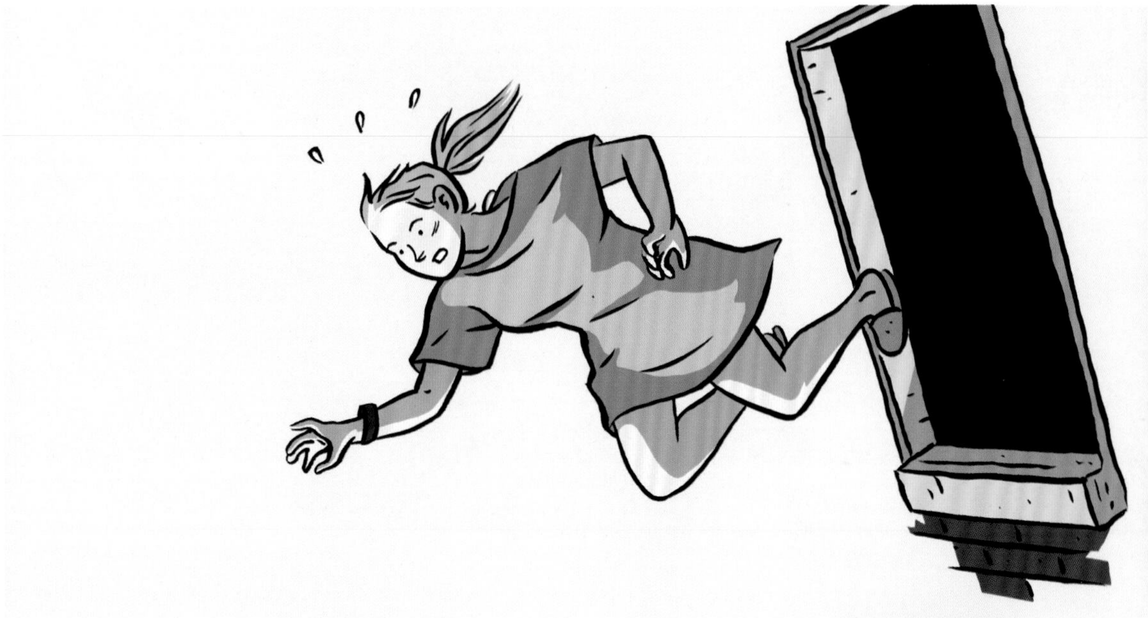
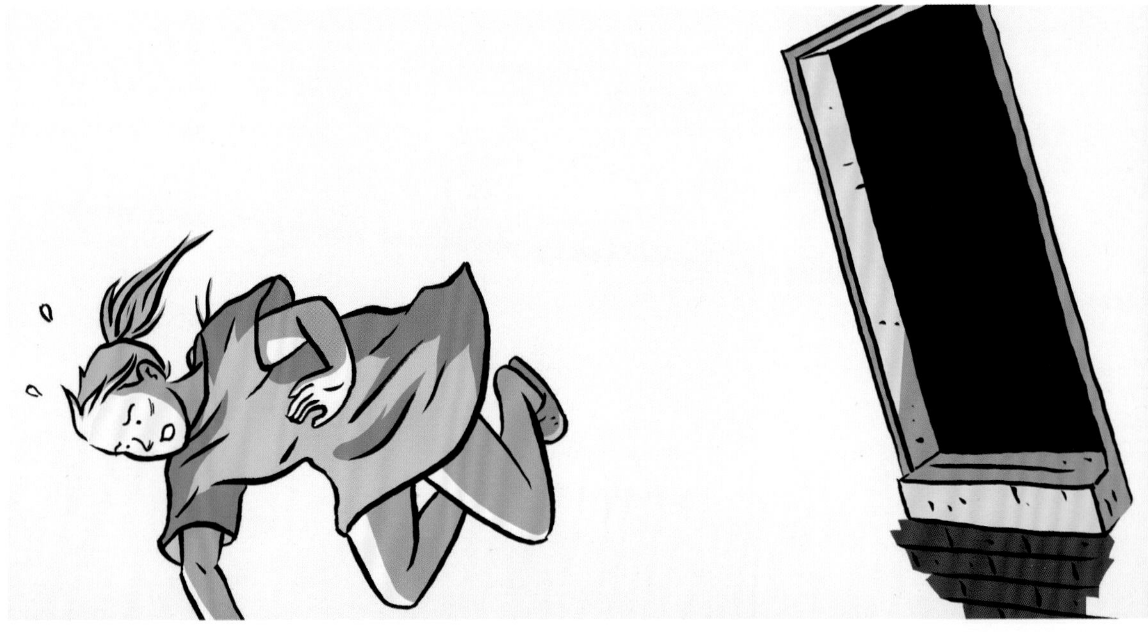

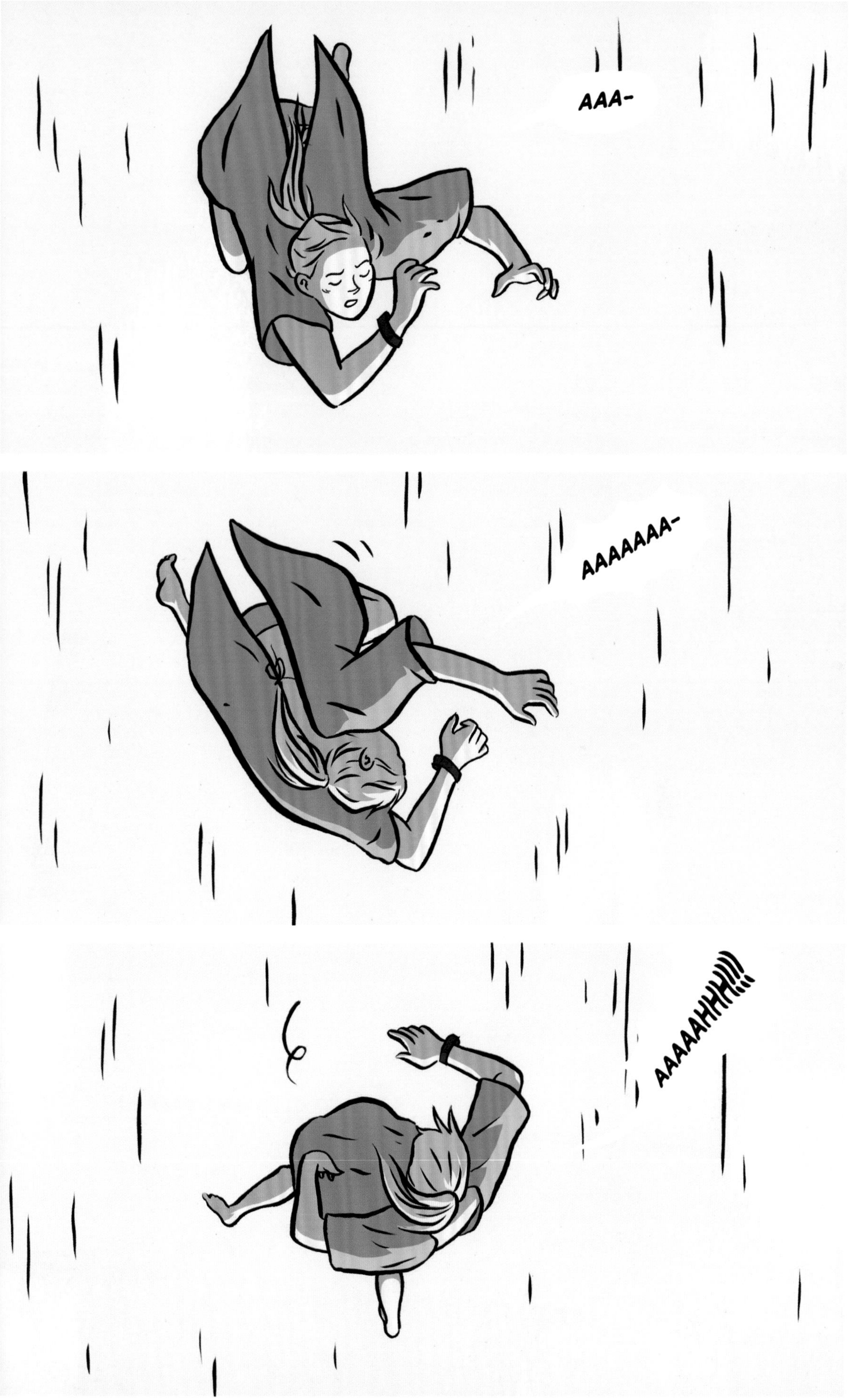
AAA-
AAAAAAA-
AAAAAHHH!!!

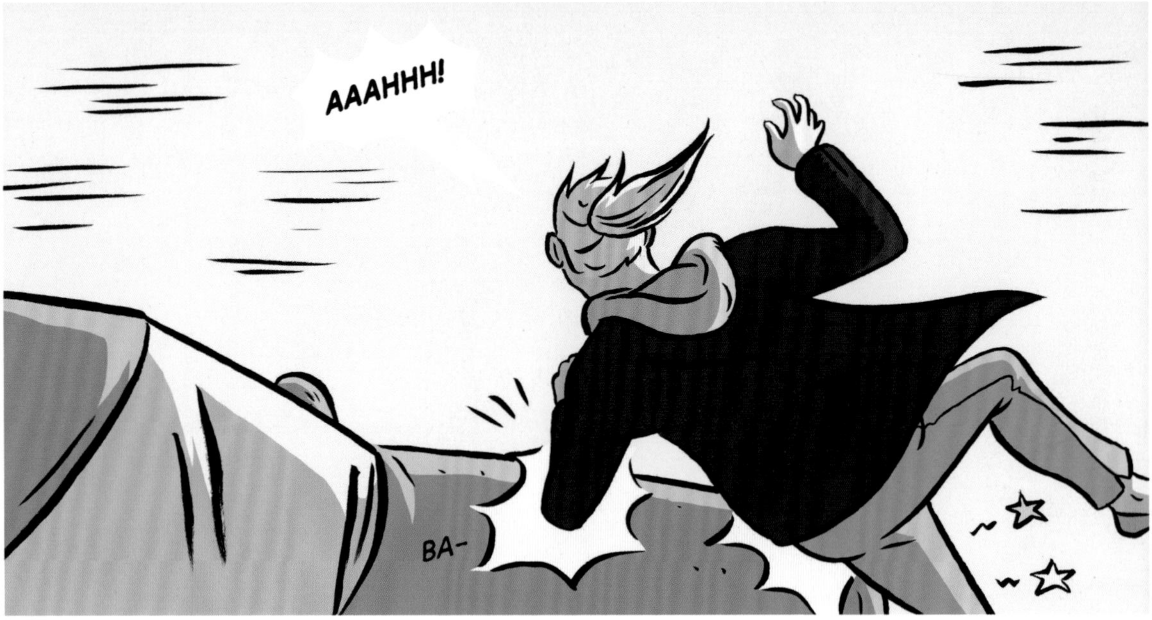
AAAHHH!
BA-
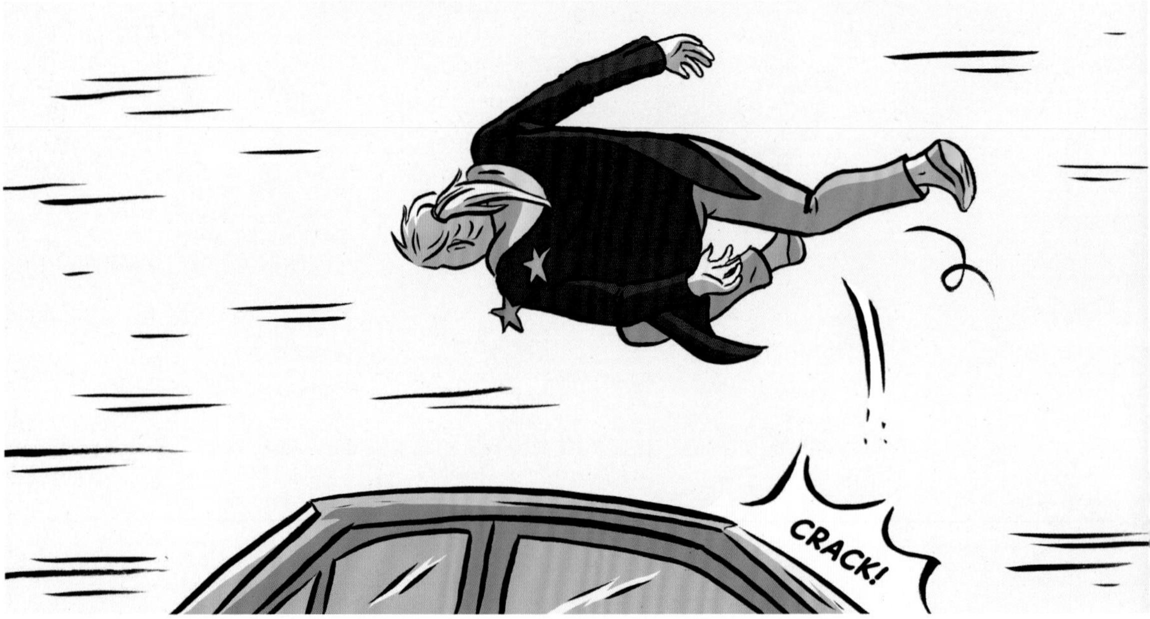
CRACK!
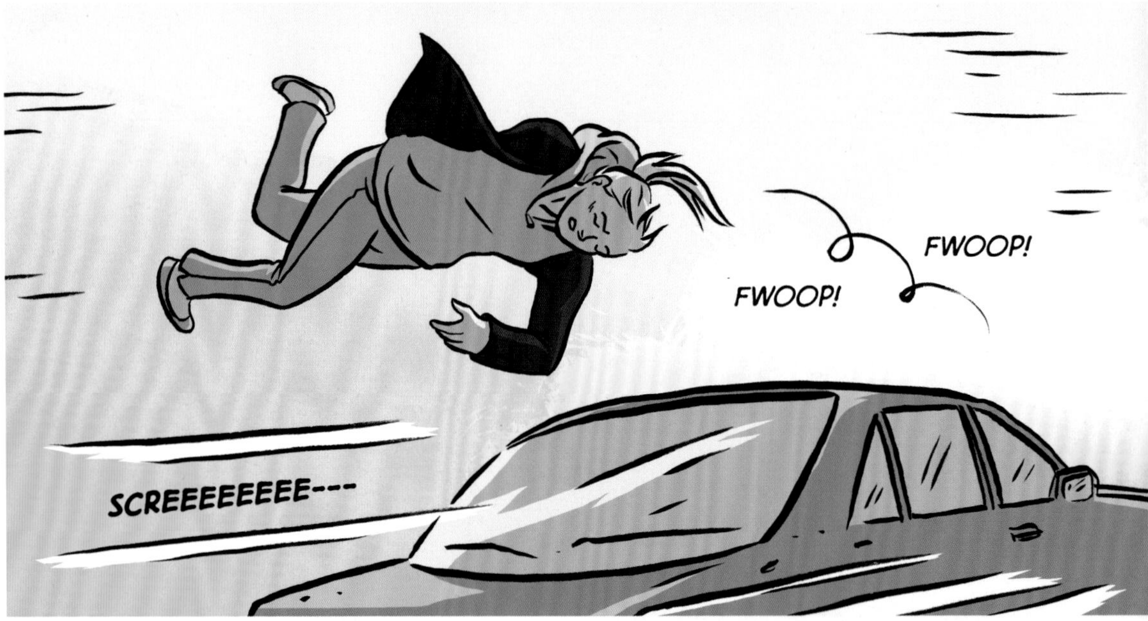
FWOOP!
FWOOP!
SCREEEEEEEE---

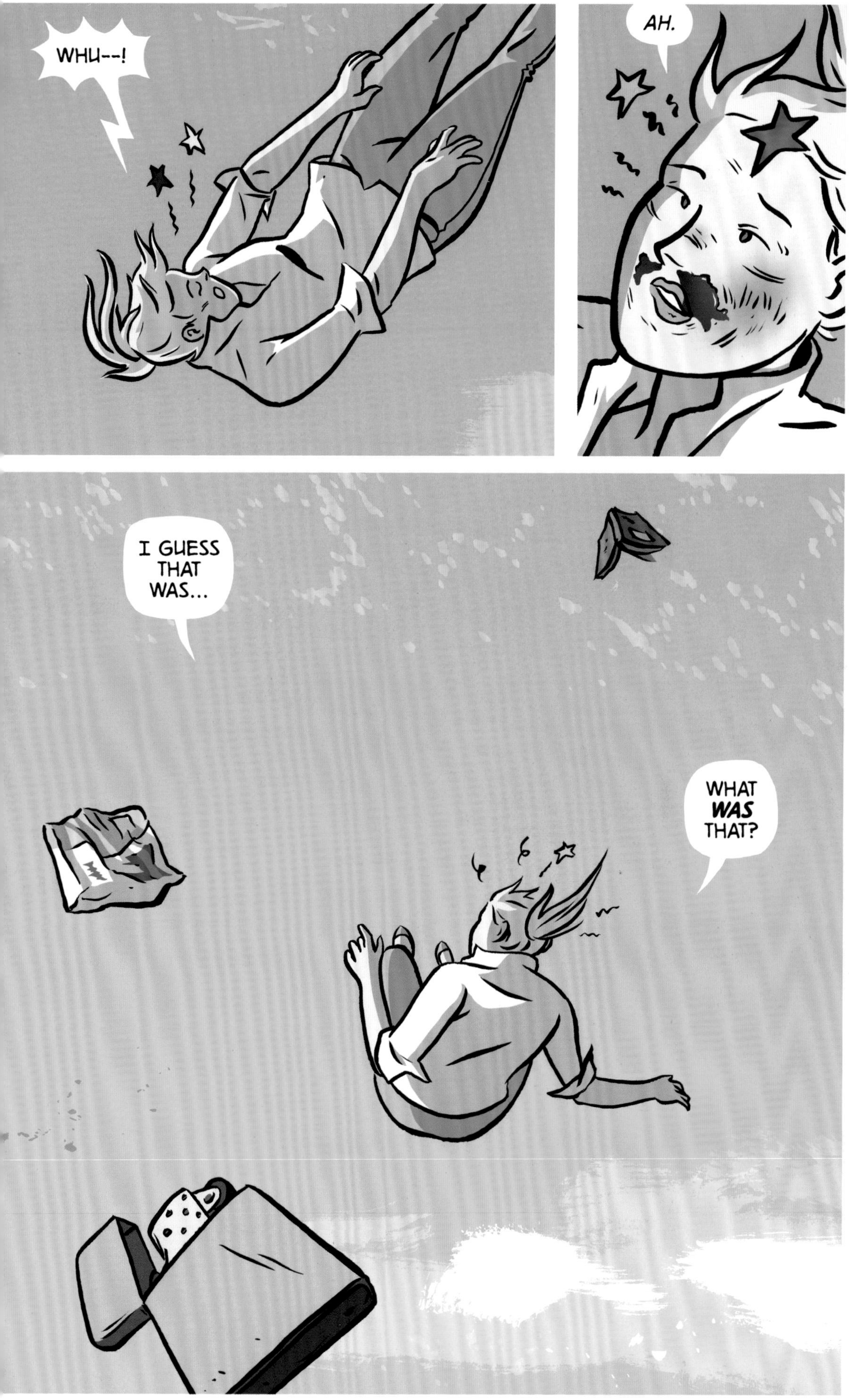
WHU--!
AH.
I GUESS THAT WAS...
WHAT *WAS* THAT?

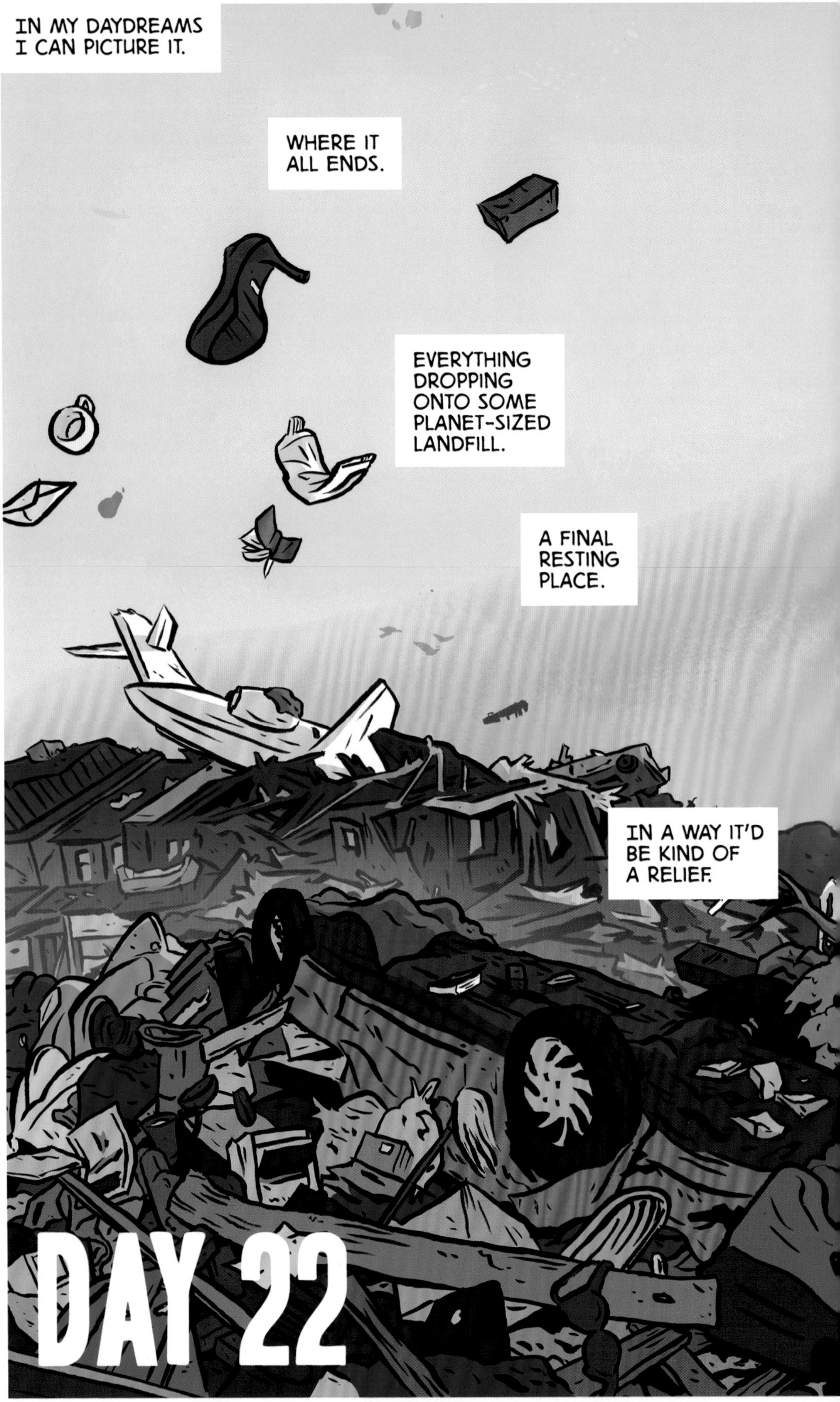
IN MY DAYDREAMS I CAN PICTURE IT.
WHERE IT ALL ENDS.
EVERYTHING DROPPING ONTO SOME PLANET-SIZED LANDFILL.
A FINAL RESTING PLACE.
IN A WAY IT'D BE KIND OF A RELIEF.
DAY 22

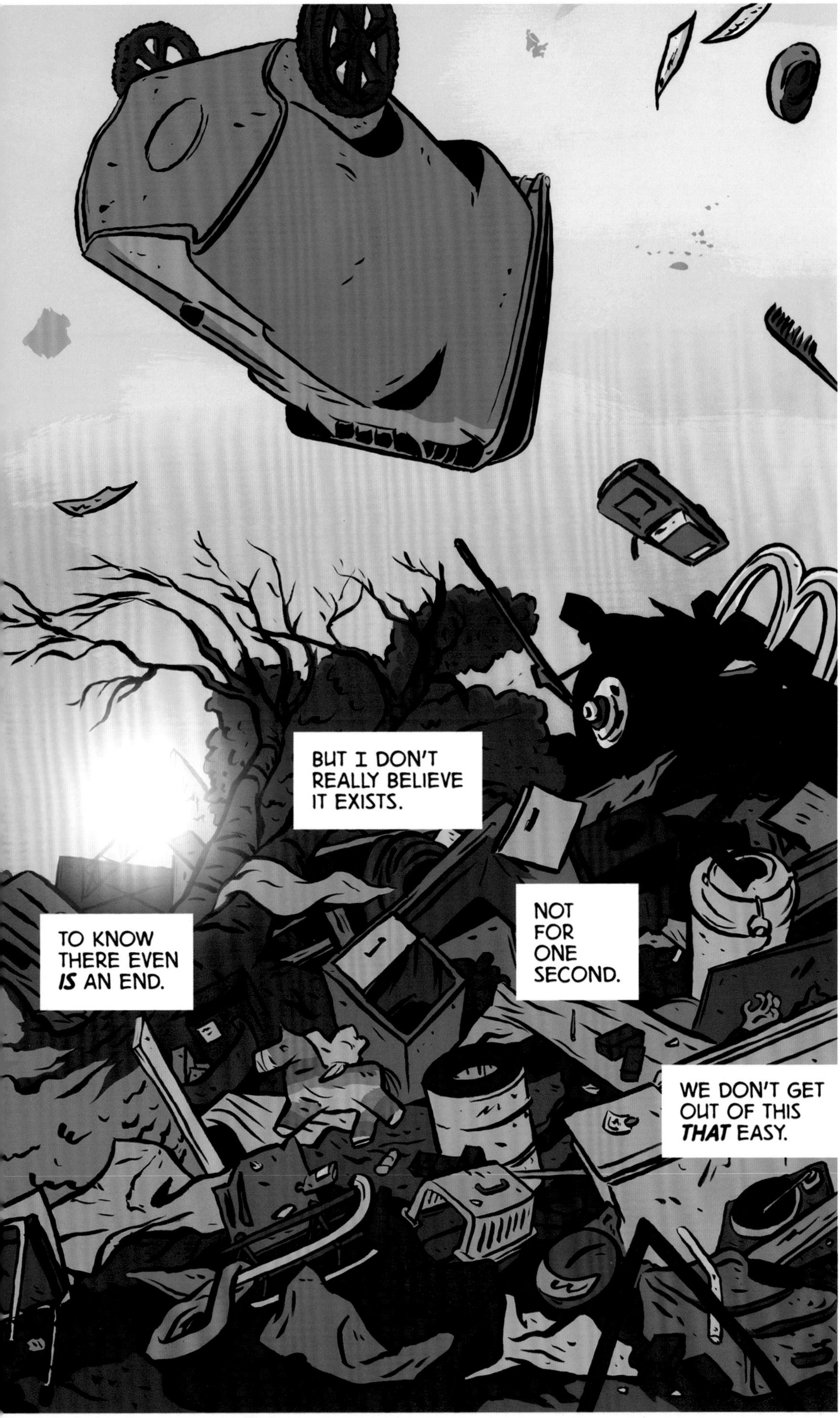
BUT I DON'T REALLY BELIEVE IT EXISTS.
TO KNOW THERE EVEN *IS* AN END.
NOT FOR ONE SECOND.
WE DON'T GET OUT OF THIS *THAT* EASY.

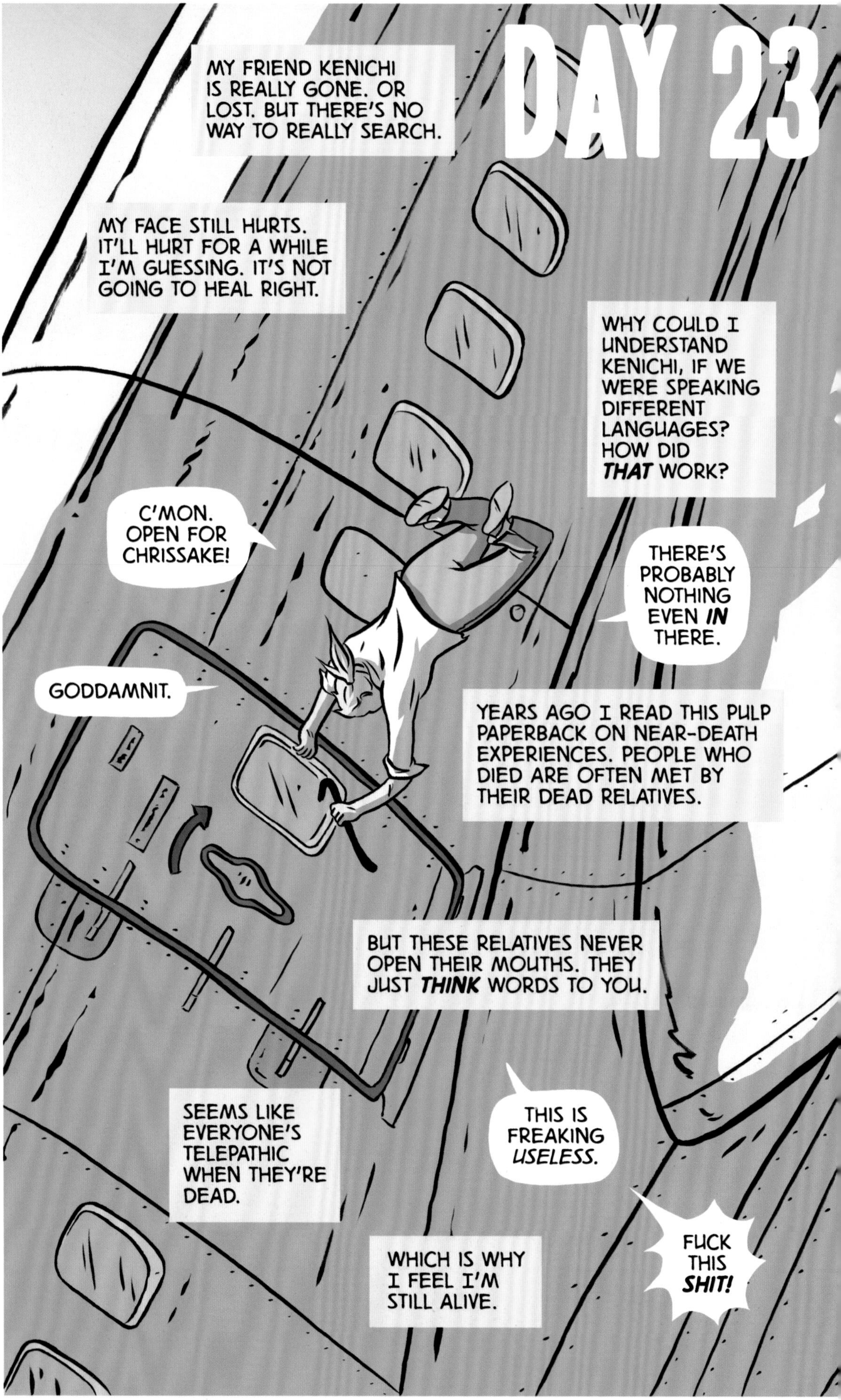
DAY 23
MY FRIEND KENICHI IS REALLY GONE. OR LOST. BUT THERE'S NO WAY TO REALLY SEARCH.
MY FACE STILL HURTS. IT'LL HURT FOR A WHILE I'M GUESSING. IT'S NOT GOING TO HEAL RIGHT.
WHY COULD I UNDERSTAND KENICHI, IF WE WERE SPEAKING DIFFERENT LANGUAGES? HOW DID ***THAT*** WORK?
C'MON. OPEN FOR CHRISSAKE!
THERE'S PROBABLY NOTHING EVEN ***IN*** THERE.
GODDAMNIT.
YEARS AGO I READ THIS PULP PAPERBACK ON NEAR-DEATH EXPERIENCES. PEOPLE WHO DIED ARE OFTEN MET BY THEIR DEAD RELATIVES.
BUT THESE RELATIVES NEVER OPEN THEIR MOUTHS. THEY JUST ***THINK*** WORDS TO YOU.
SEEMS LIKE EVERYONE'S TELEPATHIC WHEN THEY'RE DEAD.
THIS IS FREAKING *USELESS.*
WHICH IS WHY I FEEL I'M STILL ALIVE.
FUCK THIS ***SHIT!***

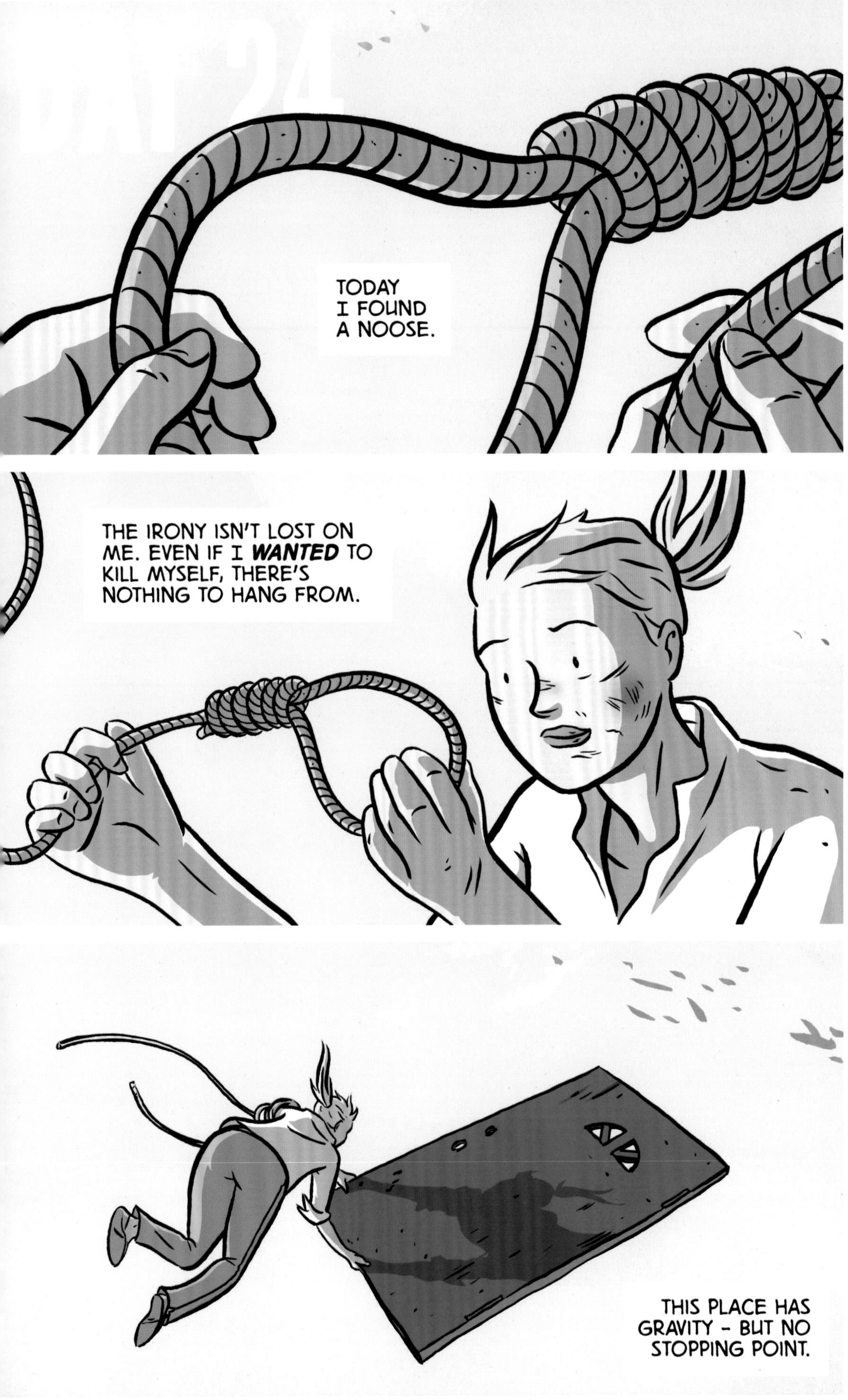
DAY 24
TODAY I FOUND A NOOSE.
THE IRONY ISN'T LOST ON ME. EVEN IF I **WANTED** TO KILL MYSELF, THERE'S NOTHING TO HANG FROM.
THIS PLACE HAS GRAVITY - BUT NO STOPPING POINT.

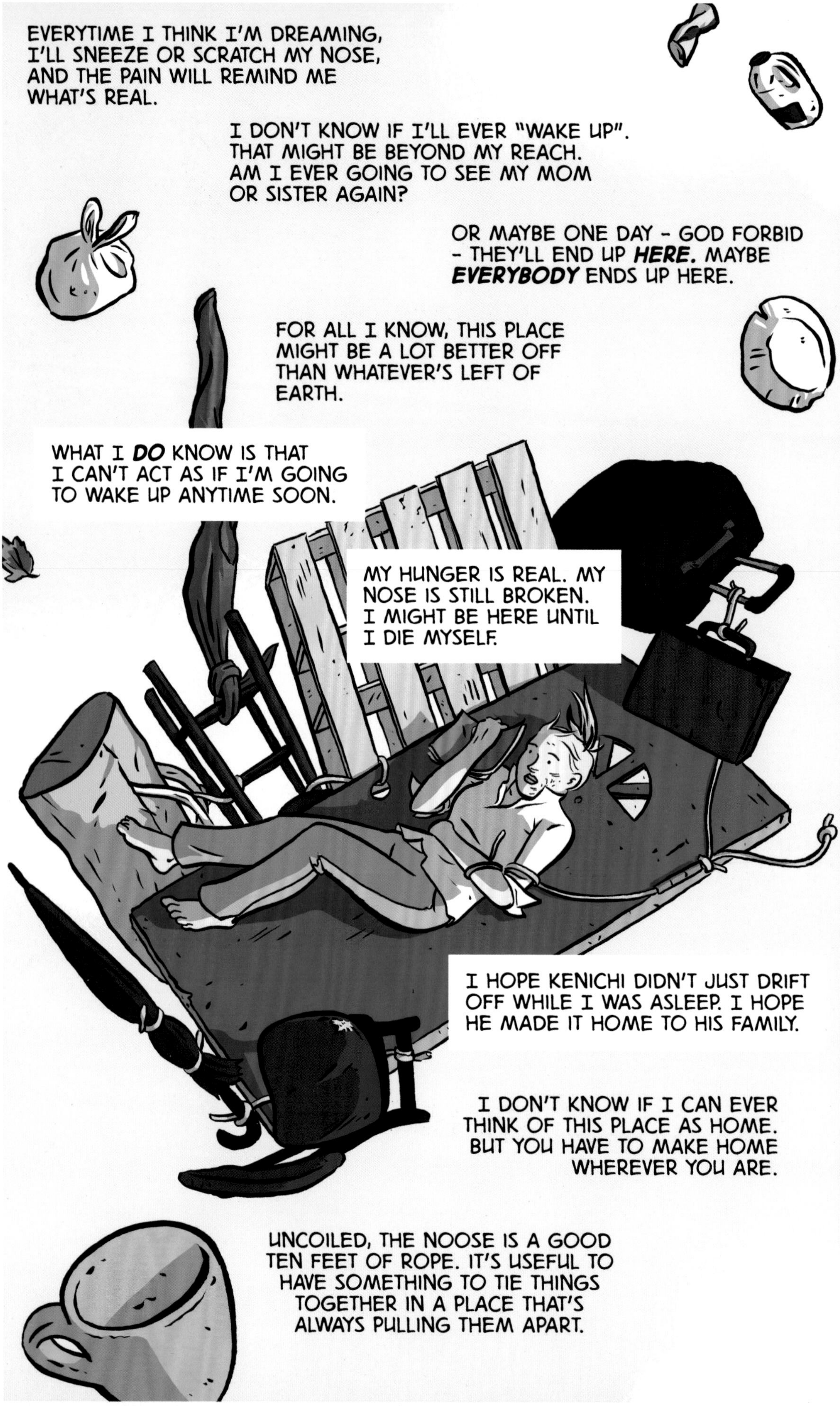
EVERYTIME I THINK I'M DREAMING, I'LL SNEEZE OR SCRATCH MY NOSE, AND THE PAIN WILL REMIND ME WHAT'S REAL.
I DON'T KNOW IF I'LL EVER "WAKE UP". THAT MIGHT BE BEYOND MY REACH. AM I EVER GOING TO SEE MY MOM OR SISTER AGAIN?
OR MAYBE ONE DAY - GOD FORBID - THEY'LL END UP ***HERE.*** MAYBE ***EVERYBODY*** ENDS UP HERE.
FOR ALL I KNOW, THIS PLACE MIGHT BE A LOT BETTER OFF THAN WHATEVER'S LEFT OF EARTH.
WHAT I ***DO*** KNOW IS THAT I CAN'T ACT AS IF I'M GOING TO WAKE UP ANYTIME SOON.
MY HUNGER IS REAL. MY NOSE IS STILL BROKEN. I MIGHT BE HERE UNTIL I DIE MYSELF.
I HOPE KENICHI DIDN'T JUST DRIFT OFF WHILE I WAS ASLEEP. I HOPE HE MADE IT HOME TO HIS FAMILY.
I DON'T KNOW IF I CAN EVER THINK OF THIS PLACE AS HOME. BUT YOU HAVE TO MAKE HOME WHEREVER YOU ARE.
UNCOILED, THE NOOSE IS A GOOD TEN FEET OF ROPE. IT'S USEFUL TO HAVE SOMETHING TO TIE THINGS TOGETHER IN A PLACE THAT'S ALWAYS PULLING THEM APART.

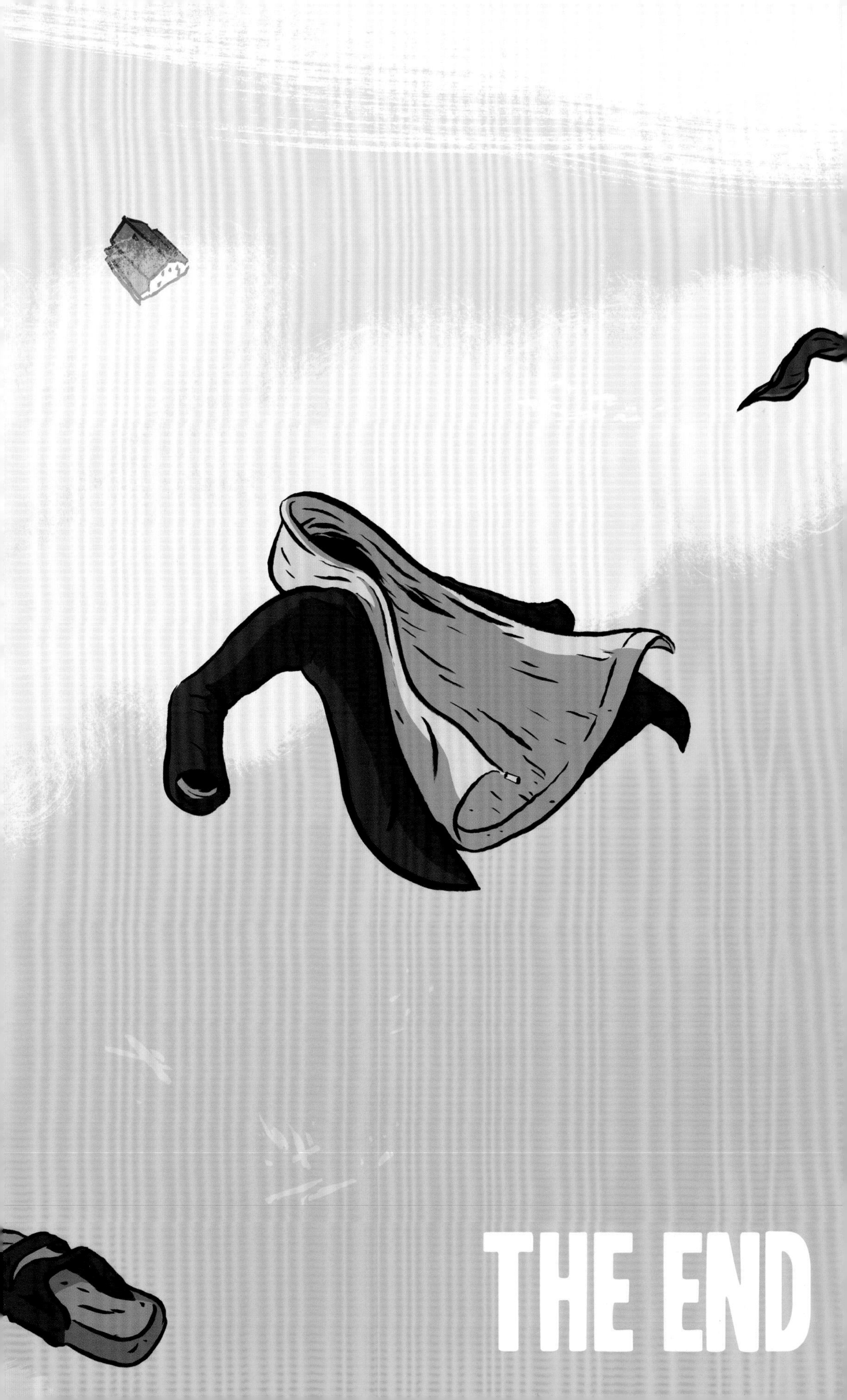
THE END

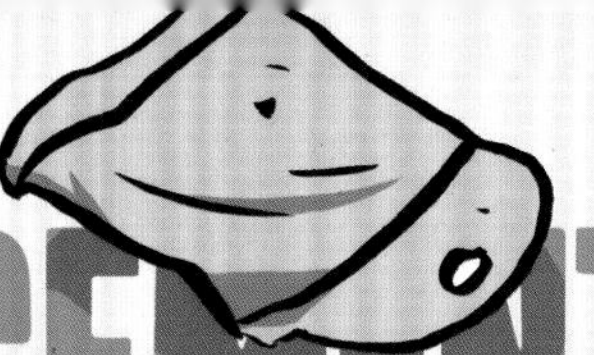

ACKNOWLEDGEMENTS

OF EVERYTHING I'VE EVER MADE, I'VE PROBABLY STRUGGLED WITH THIS BOOK THE MOST. AS YOU CAN IMAGINE, IT'S TOUGH TO TELL A STORY WHEN YOUR PROTAGONIST PLUMMETS PERPETUALLY. IN MANY WAYS, ***PLUMMET*** RESEMBLES A ROAD TRIP, BUT WITHOUT THE ABILITY TO PARK OR REVERSE. IT'S A STORY TOLD ON THE OUTSIDE OF A MOVING TRAIN. IT'S PROPULSIVE, LIKE SHEET MUSIC, OR A RAFT ON A RIVER. IT TOOK ME YEARS TO BOIL THIS NOTION DOWN INTO AN ACTIONABLE STORY, WHICH IS WHY I HAVE SO MANY PERSONS, PLACES AND THINGS TO THANK NOW.

PROBABLY THE FIRST PEOPLE I WANT TO THANK ARE THOSE WHO TRIGGERED THIS IDEA IN THE FIRST PLACE — THE TRAGIC, FALLING FIGURES OF SEPTEMBER 11, 2001. I WAS RAPT BY THE PEOPLE CAUGHT IN THAT TERRIBLE DILEMMA BETWEEN BURNING OR FALLING. SOME JUMPED TOGETHER, HOLDING HANDS. OTHERS DIVED HEADFIRST. I KNOW THAT MOMENTS OF TRAUMA CAN DILATE TIME AND STRETCH OUT SECONDS ARTIFICIALLY. I WONDERED IF THEIR TIME IN THE AIR FELT LIKE FOREVER. I WISHED I COULD REMOVE THE GROUND, SO THAT THEY WOULD NEVER HIT.

IN THE TIME IT TOOK TO MAKE THIS BOOK, I NOTED THAT THERE SEEMED TO BE LOTS OF BOOKS WITH FALLING FIGURES ON THEIR COVERS. IT'S THE WORST NIGHTMARE OF ANY STORYTELLER THAT WHILE YOU'RE WORKING SO DILIGENTLY ON YOUR WONDERFUL IDEA, SOMEONE *ELSE* IS OUT THERE DOING THE SAME *THING*, BUT EXECUTING IT BETTER, WI… MORE PANACHE, WITH THINGS YOU NEVE… THOUGHT OF. *AND* THEY'RE MORE FAM… THAN YOU ARE. MAYBE THAT'S WHY E… THING I'VE EVER DONE IS SO OUTL… FREAKISH OR WEIRD. YOU HAVE TO … …LD TO ARRIVE AT AN IDEA NO … TO WORK ON.

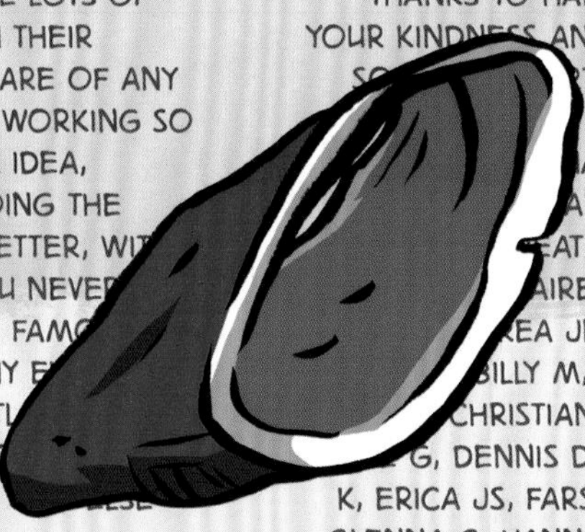

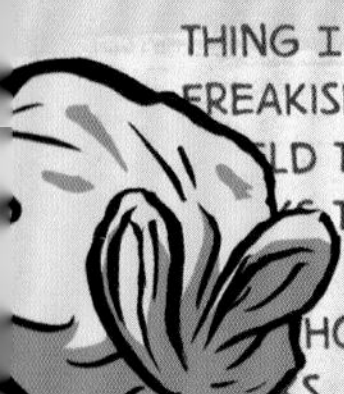

…HOUGH I PICKED UP A LOT OF THOSE …KS, NONE SEEMED TO DELIVER ON THE VERY SIMPLE IDEA THAT THERE'S SOMETHING ELEGANTLY EUPHORIC ABOUT WATCHING PEOPLE IN FREEFALL. HENCE - THOSE COVERS. BUT IN THOSE BOOKS FALLING PEOPLE WERE AN EYE-CATCHING METAPHOR, RATHER THAN A TRENCHANT REALITY.

OF ALL MY INFLUENCES FOR THIS WORK, I WANT TO ACKNOWLEDGE THE DREAMLIKE WORLDS OF ***WINSOR MCCAY*** AND HIS ASTONISHING *LITTLE NEMO IN SLUMBERLAND,* FULL OF ELASTIC, ANTI-GRAVITY ADVENTURES. SO RACIST IN CERTAIN DEPICTIONS, BUT SO RAVISHING. I WANT TO THANK THE SUFFUSED AND PLAYFUL ENAMEL PAINTINGS OF ***INKA ESSENHIGH***. NOT HER RECENT STUFF, BUT EARLY 2K, WHICH SO DEFTLY MANAGE TO CAPTURE THE FEELING OF BIRDS IN FLIGHT, IF ALL THOSE BIRDS WERE BLOATED, SOMERSAULTING TEAPOTS. AND OF COURSE I WANT TO THANK ***HERGE***, WHOSE CLEAR LINE WAS SOMETHING I ASPIRED TO, BUT NEVER QUITE ASCENDED TO, AND WHOSE VISUAL LANGUAGE I HEARTILY ACKNOWLEDGE, LOVE, AND RAIDED SHAMELESSLY FOR THIS STORY.

I WANT TO THANK ALL THE SKYDIVERS, BASE-JUMPERS, INDOOR SKYDIVERS, BED JUMPERS, HIGH DIVERS AND OTHER FREEFALLERS I LOOKED AT TO GET A SENSE OF FALLING BODIES. I C…D NEVER DO WHAT YOU DO - BUT THEN THAT'S PROBABLY WHY YOU DO IT.

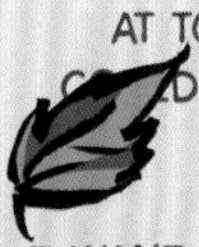

I WANT TO THANK MY FAMILY — MY BROTHER SEAN, HIS GIRLFRIEND STEPH, MY MOM AND MY DAD, MY LATE UNCLE SIE GIE AND MY EXTENDED FAMILY FOR THEIR SUPPORT AND LOVE OVER THE YEARS AND INTO THE FUTURE. AS WELL AS THANKS TO HARRY & SUE B. THANK YOU FOR YOUR KIND… AND FOR WELCOMING ME WITH SO… …T THESE LAST SEVERAL YEARS.

…ANK THE FOLLOWING PEOPLE, …ARTICULAR WAYS, CONTRIBUTED …EATION OF THIS VERY PARTICULAR …AIRE G, AMBER G, AMY B, AMY D, …REA JR, ANDREW B, ANDY H, BRUCE …BILLY M, BRIONY S, BRYANNA R, CARO …CHRISTIAN M, CINDY L, DAN S, DAWN K, …G, DENNIS D, ELENA T, EMILIE O'B, EMMA K, ERICA JS, FARSHID E, GEOFF A, GEORGIA W, GLENNA G, HANNAH E, IAN SC, IAN F, INDIGO E, JAMES F, JENNY L, JENNY LG, JIM M, JOE O, JOEY D, JOHN D, JULIAN P, KELLY M, KENNY S, LARISSA P, LORRAINE D, LOUIS R, LUNA A, LYNN C, MARGAUX W, MARILYN T, MARK T, MARY MAC, MEGAN H, MICHELLE W, MIKE O'B, MIRIAM G, NATHAN W, PATRICIA W, REBECCA B, RYAN K, SHAYNA H, SHIE K, SOL L, SOFI P, SOFIA A, SONJA A, STEPHEN T, TAES L, TIF F, TORI A, AND VINCE T.

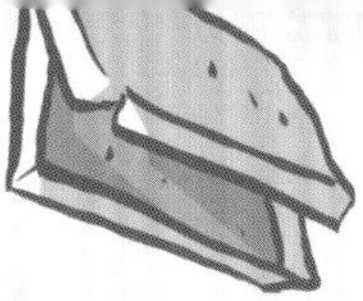

THANKS TO SHIE K, FOR FACT-CHECKING MY JAPANESE PROTAGONIST'S SPOKEN WORDS IN BOTH LANGUAGES, AND FOR YOUR FRIENDSHIP AND MANY KINDNESSES OVER THE YEARS.

THANKS TO LINDEN R AND THE ST-LAURENT BLVD. SECOND CUP, WHERE I CRANKED OUT (EVERY DAY BEFORE WORK) THE FIRST, UNWIELDY AND IMPOSSIBLE DRAFT OF WHAT WOULD EVENTUALLY BECOME THIS BOOK.

THANKS TO IAN F, WHO ALLOWED ME A FORUM TO FIRST UNVEIL IT, AND THANKS TO GEORGIA W, WHO ASKED ABOUT IT.

A BIG THANKS TO MY PERENNIAL PUBLISHER ANDY BROWN OF ***CONUNDRUM PRESS,*** FOR HAVING THE OVARIES AND THE STONES TO PRINT SOMETHING SO SILLY AND SO STRANGE. EMPIRES OF ODDITIES EXIST BECAUSE OF YOU!

THANKS TO *NASA* FOR YOUR STUPENDOUS OPEN-SOURCE STARFIELD!

THANKS TO *NATE PIEKOS* OF *BLAMBOT!* FOR YOUR BEAUTIFUL FONT, SO FRIENDLY AND WARM, AND FOR YOUR GENEROSITY TOWARDS INDIE AND SMALL PRESS CREATORS!

ALSO THANKS TO THE WRITERS OF *THE TWILIGHT ZONE* EPISODE REFERENCED IN THIS BOOK. IT'S A REAL EPISODE THAT'S HAUNTED ME FOR YEARS! YOU CAN PROBABLY GOOGLE IT AND FIND IT SOMEWHERE ONLINE. IT'S CALLED "WORDPLAY".

A BIG THANKS TO THE *CANADA COUNCIL FOR THE (HE)ARTS*, WHOSE FINANCIAL SUPPORT ALLOWED THIS BOOK TO FIND A FOOTING IN THE FIRST PLACE. YOU ARE THE "WEST WING" (TV SERIES) OF CANADIAN CULTURAL ORGANIZATIONS. SMART, SHARP, AND WELL-MEANING STEWARDS OF PUBLIC FUNDS. SOME OF WHICH WENT TO THIS PREPOSTEROUS BOOK! THANK YOU.

THANKS TO MY EARLIEST AND ARDENT *PATREON* PATRONS! FOR THOSE WHO HAVE NEVER HEARD OF IT, PATREON IS BASICALLY ONGOING CROWD-FUNDING. PEOPLE BUY ME THE EQUIVALENT OF A MONTHLY BEER IN EXCHANGE FOR BEHIND THE-SCENES GLIMPSES OF MY WORKFLOW, MY ONGOING PROJECTS, ACCESS TO VARIOUS UNRELEASED PROJECTS, AND MY FUNNY, IRREGULAR PODCAST, LATE-ONSET AWESOME. YOUR CONTRIBUTIONS DO MUCH TO HELP ME CONTINUE FINANCIALLY, BUT MORE IMPORTANTLY, EMOTIONALLY. SO MY BLESSINGS TO YOU — CEDA VERBAKEL, ADAM ANKLEWICZ, BENJAMIN HUNTING, KATE CUSHON, DAN SVATEK, DAVE BENSON, ZOE FITZGERALD, MARC NGUI, LUI RAMIREZ, DIANA DEE, JOHN LAPSLEY, MIRIAM GINESTIER, DAVID MCLEOD, KATHLEEN WINTER, BOB HETIKER, MICHAEL ROYLE, EVA DUSOME, AL LAFRANCE, TREVOR MURPHY, ERIC NOTA-RANGELO, ELENA TOEWS & TAB. I AM CONSTANTLY TOUCHED BY YOU ALL. AND IF YOU, DEAR READER, ARE SOMEONE WHO MIGHT CONSIDER HELPING ME BE THE STRANGE I WANT TO SEE IN THE WORLD, PLEASE VISIT *HTTPS://WWW.PATREON.COM/SHERWINEVENTS*

THANKS TO MY FACEBOOK "FRIENDS". I UNDERSTAND THAT A FACEBOOK RELATIONSHIP IS TENUOUS AND COMPLICATED, AND WHILE SOME PEOPLE FIND FACEBOOK INVASIVE AND SUPERFICIAL, I HAVE FOUND IT NOTHING BUT A SCINTILLATING REVELATION, AND AM PROUD TO ENGAGE IN THIS GLOBAL VILLAGE CONVERSATION EVERY DAY WITH ALL OF YOU.

THANKS TO ELENA T FOR OUR CONTINUED MADCAP ADVENTURES, EVEN ACROSS THE CONTINENT.

AND A SPECIAL THANKS TO KAILEY B, WHO HAS BEEN MY SOFT PLACE TO LAND.

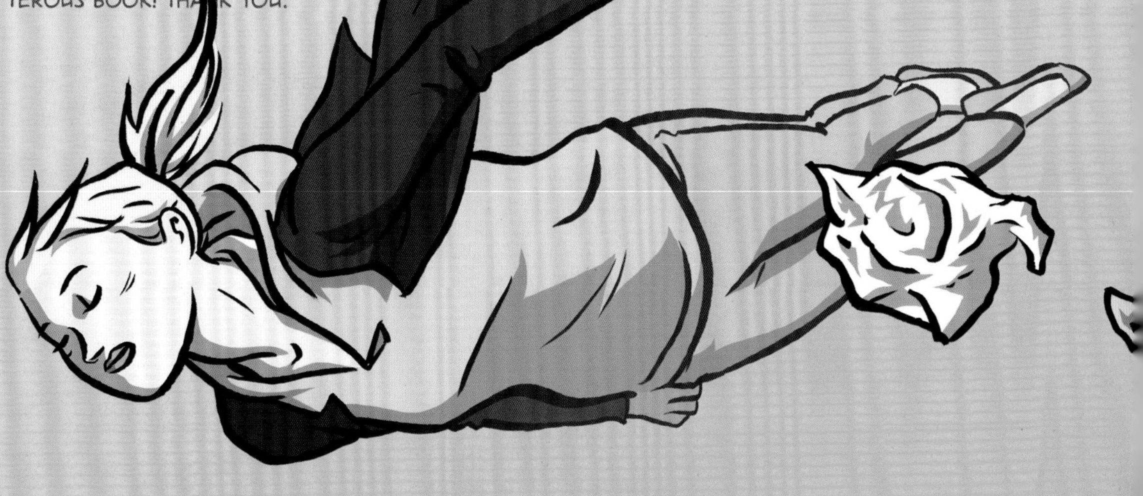

ABOUT THE AUTHOR

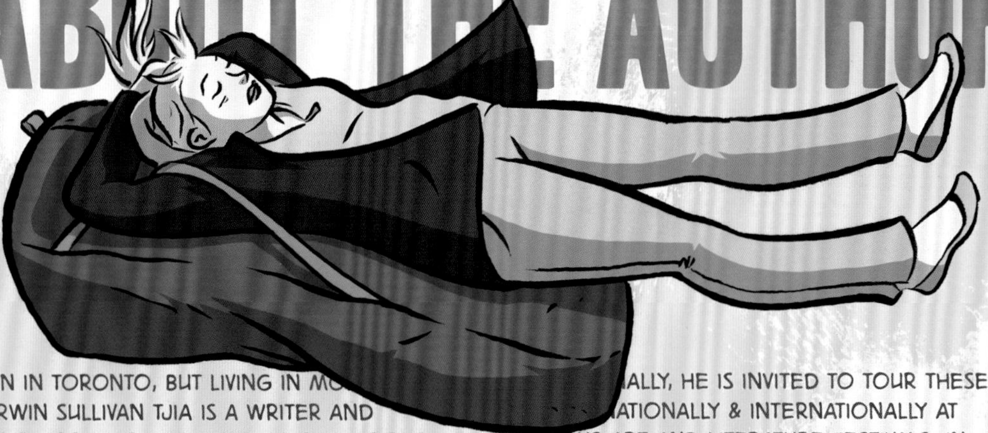

BORN IN TORONTO, BUT LIVING IN MO… SHERWIN SULLIVAN TJIA IS A WRITER AND ILLUSTRATOR WHO HAS MADE 11 ODD BOOKS, INCLUDING THIS FANCIFUL ONE.

IN 200… ***THE WORLD IS A HEARTBREAKER,*** A COLLECTION OF 1300 PSEUDOHAIKUS, WAS A FINALIST FOR THE QUEBEC WRITER'S FEDERATION'S *A.M. KLEIN POETRY AWARD.*

FIVE YEARS LATER, IN 2010, HIS GRAPHIC NOVEL, ***THE HIPLESS BOY,*** A COLLECTION OF SHORT, INTERCONNECTED STORIES, WAS A FINALIST FOR THE *DOUG WRIGHT AWARD* IN THE BEST EMERGING TALENT CATEGORY, & ALSO NOMINATED FOR 4 *IGNATZ AWARDS*.

AND THE VERY NEXT YEAR, HIS CHOOSE-YOUR-OWN-ADVENTURE STYLE BOOK FROM THE POV OF A HOUSECAT NAMED HOLDEN CATFIELD, ***YOU ARE A CAT!***, WON THE 2011 *EXPOZINE AWARD* FOR BEST ENGLISH BOOK.

FINALLY IN 2007, HE ILLUSTRATED JONARNO LAWSON'S *BLACK STARS IN A WHITE NIGHT SKY* WHICH WAS AWARDED *THE LION & THE UNICORN AWARD* FOR EXCELLENCE IN NORTH AMERICAN POETRY THAT YEAR.

AS A GRAPHIC DESIGNER AND ILLUS… VARIOUS WEBSITES AND PUBLICATIONS, … HAS APPEARED IN *MAISONNEUVE* MAGAZINE, *TORONTO THEATRE CRITICS AWARDS, OAITH, ASKMEN.COM, ASCENT MAGAZINE,* TORONTO'S *EYE WEEKLY,* MONTREAL'S … SADLY DEFUNCT) *HOUR WEEKLY,* THE QU… FEDERA-TION, COACH HOUSE… RN BOOKS.

FOR A LIVING, HE IN… ND ORGANIZES SLOWDAN…, CROWD KARAOKE SINGALONGS, STRIP SPELLING BEES, & OTHER INTIMATE AND ODD EVENTS IN AND AROUND MONTREAL AND TORONTO AS *CHAT PERDU PRODUCTIONS* AND PREVIOUSLY AS *PERPETUAL EMOTION MACHINE PRODUCTIONS*.

…ALLY, HE IS INVITED TO TOUR THESE …NATIONALLY & INTERNATIONALLY AT VARIOUS ART AND LITERATURE FESTIVALS. IN RECENT YEARS HE HAS BEEN A FEATURED ARTIST AT BIRMINGHAM, ENGLAND'S *FIERCE FESTIVAL*; AT SOPOT, POLAND'S *ARTLOOP* FESTIVAL; AUSTIN, TEXAS'S *FUSEBOX FES…*; CALGARY, ALBERTA'S *WORDFEST*; & MONTR… NADA'S *BLUE METROPOLIS LITERARY F…*.

OTHER THAT THAT, HE ALSO DJ'S WEDDINGS.

HE WOULD HAVE LIKED TO HAVE BEEN BORN A GIRL, BUT THESE DAYS IDENTIFIES AS GENDER-QUEER AND DOES NOT PERSONALLY USE A PAR-TICULAR PRONOUN. AND IN FACT SHE LIKES ALL OF THEM. JUST AS SHE LIKES POTATOES, AND REVELS IN ALL THE WAYS POTATOES CAN BE PREPARED. BAKED, MASHED, FRIED, ETC.

HER CHARMING INVENTION, THE ***E-Z-PURR: THE VIRTUAL CAT!*** (AN AUDIO RECORDING WITH OVER AN HOUR OF CATS PURRING) IS AVAILABLE FOR PURCHASE ON THE ITUNES MUSIC STORE AND ITS PROCEEDS ARE DONATED TO LOCAL NO-KILL CAT SHELTERS & ADOPTION/FOSTERING PROGRAMS, LARGELY OWING TO HER GREAT FONDNESS FOR CATS, AND BECAUSE THEY'VE OFTEN BEEN THERE FOR HER WHEN HUMANS HAVEN'T.

IF YOU HAVE ANY QUESTIONS OR COMMENTS FOR HER, FEEL FREE TO EMAIL THEM TO ***INCONSOLABLECAT@HOTMAIL.COM.***
IT'S UNLIKELY SHE'LL RESPOND, BECAUSE SHE'S A DEEP INTROVERT AND ALSO KINDA SUCKS, BUT SHE'D LIKE YOU TO KNOW THAT SHE READS AND APPRECIATES EVERY SINGLE LETTER.

AND IF YOU HAVE A MOMENT, PLEASE FOLLOW THEIR SOCIAL MEDIAS AND IRREGULAR POSTINGS:

WWW.FACEBOOK.COM / INCONSOLABLECAT
WWW.TWITTER.COM / INCONSOLABLECAT
WWW.INSTAGRAM.COM / INCONSOLABLECAT

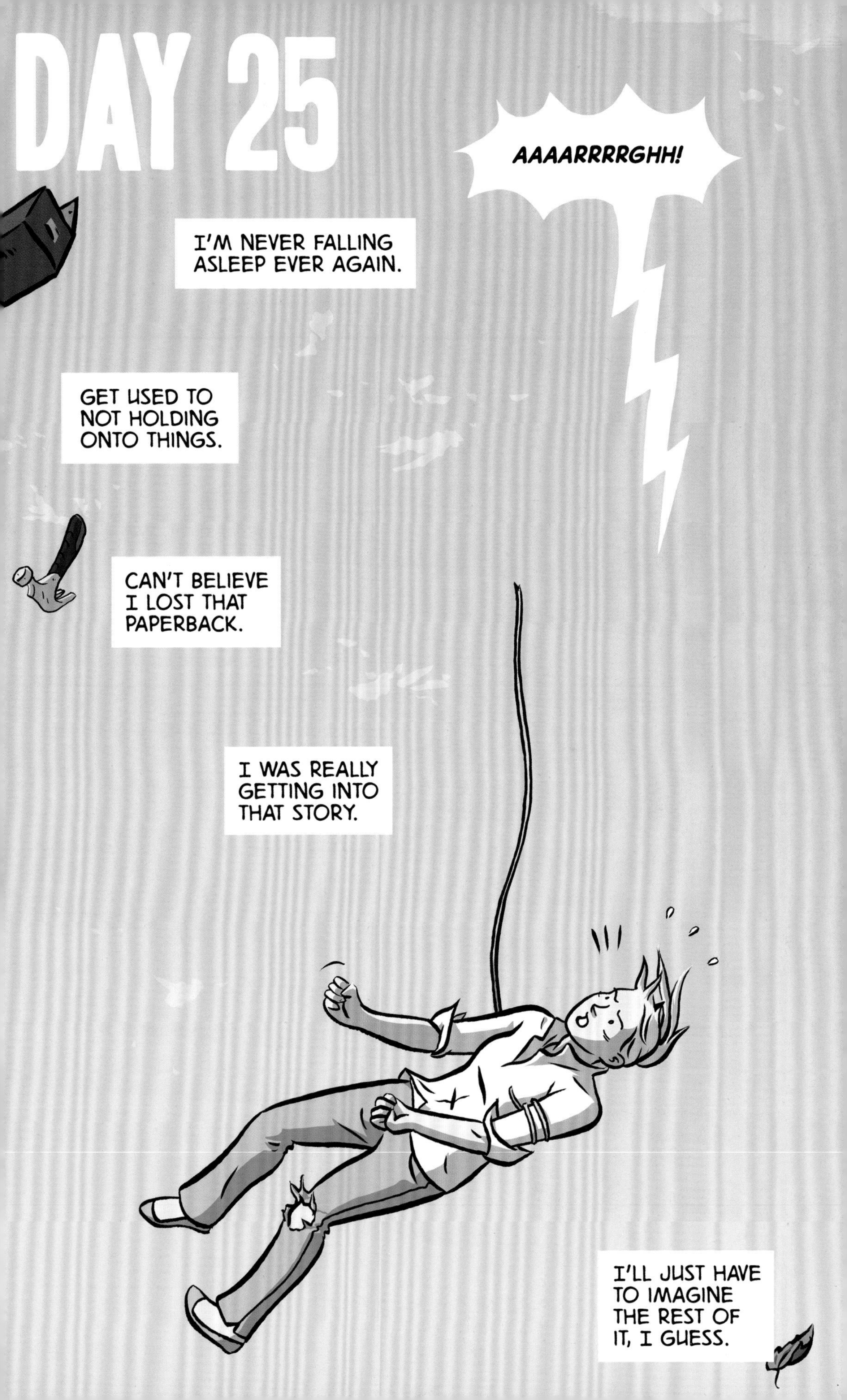

DAY 25
AAAARRRRGHH!
I'M NEVER FALLING ASLEEP EVER AGAIN.
GET USED TO NOT HOLDING ONTO THINGS.
CAN'T BELIEVE I LOST THAT PAPERBACK.
I WAS REALLY GETTING INTO THAT STORY.
I'LL JUST HAVE TO IMAGINE THE REST OF IT, I GUESS.

OTHER BOOKS BY THE SAME AUTHOR

YOU ARE ***HOLDEN CATFIELD*** IN THE FIRST 3 ***PICK-A-PLOT*** BOOKS IN THIS SERIES! GUIDE HIM AS HE FALLS IN LOVE, SURVIVES THE ZOMBIE APOCALYPSE, AND EXPERIENCES HIS FIRST LEAPS & LICKS!

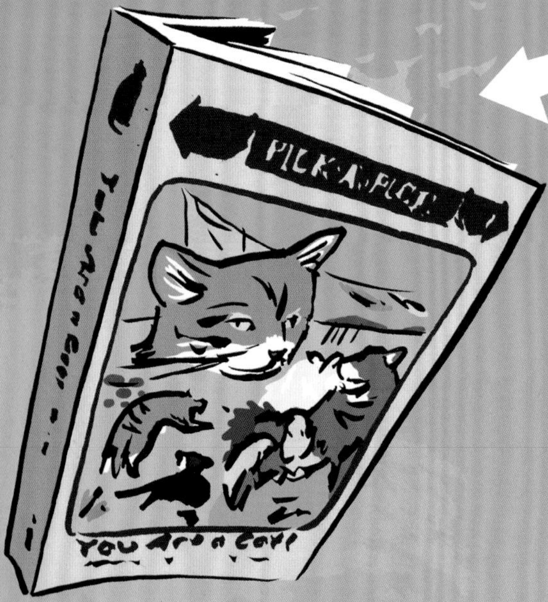

PICK-A-PLOT
You Are a Cat

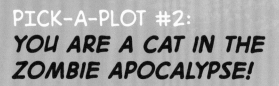

PICK-A-PLOT #1:
YOU ARE A CAT!

READ THE ORIGINAL *AND GUIDE HOLDEN CATFIELD AS HE STAYS IN THE HOUSE, OR EXPLORES HIS NEIGHBOURHOOD. HANG OUT WITH THE FAMILY! TAKE A NAP, OR INVESTIGATE THE UNUSUAL SOUNDS COMING FROM THE UPSTAIRS BATHROOM! THE CHOICE IS YOURS! EXPERIENCE THE BOOK THAT STARTED IT ALL...*

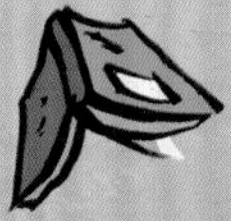

PICK-A-PLOT #2:
YOU ARE A CAT IN THE ZOMBIE APOCALYPSE!

THE EXCITING SEQUEL *THRUSTS YOU INTO THE END OF THE WORLD AS WE KNOW IT (AND YOU'RE FELINE)! TAKE OFF ON THE ROAD WITH THE GIRLS OR STAY IN YOUR NEIGHBOURHOOD AND LOOK FOR YOUR GIRLFRIEND. THE CHOICE IS YOURS! BUT YOU'LL LEARN THAT SOME THINGS AREN'T ALWAYS UP TO YOU...*

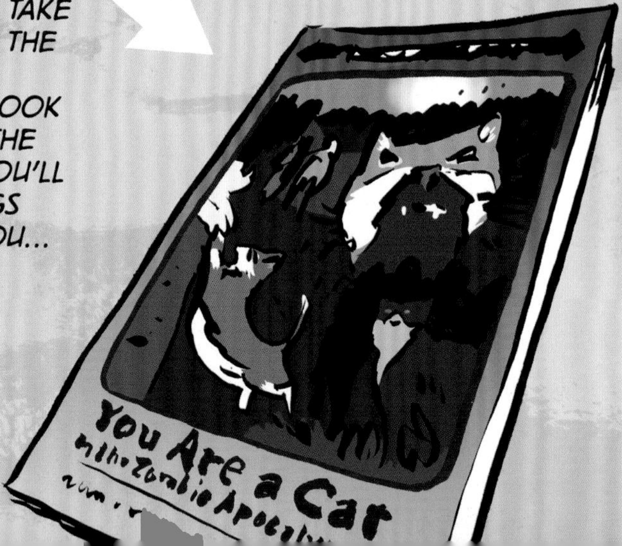

You Are a Cat

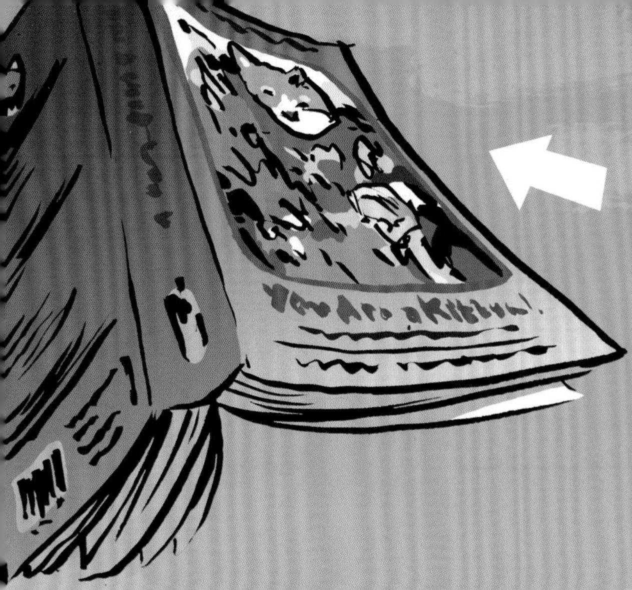

PICK-A-PLOT #3:
YOU ARE A KITTEN!

EXPLORE HOLDEN CATFIELD'S *DARK ORIGIN IN THIS ALARMINGLY CHARMING PREQUEL! FIRST LEAPS, FIRST LICKS! FIRST KIBBLE, FIRST KILLS! THEN TEAM UP WITH A PAIR OF TEEN SLEUTHS AS THEY INVESTIGATE A RASH OF MISSING NEIGHBOURHOOD PETS...*

PICK-A-PLOT #4:
YOU ARE ALICE IN WONDERLAND'S MUM!

IN 1862'S LONDON, YOU ARE ALICE'S MUM! ONE AFTERNOON, WHEN YOUR DAUGHTERS GO FOR A PICNIC, ALICE GOES ASTRAY! WHAT WILL YOU DO? HOW TO FIND A SINGLE CHILD IN THE WORLD'S LARGEST CITY?

IN A QUEST TO FIND YOUR DAUGHTER THAT WILL TAKE YOU THROUGH THE SEEDY UNDERBELLY OF LONDON'S WHITECHAPEL DISTRICT TO THE SECRET DEBAUCHED HEART OF ITS RICHEST DENIZENS, ***YOU ARE ALICE IN WONDERLAND'S MUM!*** *WILL INTRODUCE YOU TO A CAST OF UNIQUE, INTIMATE AND ODD CHARACTERS THAT CAN ALTERNATELY HELP OR HINDER YOU, DEPENDING ON YOUR CHOICES!*

IN THIS TENSE NOCTURNAL ODYSSEY ***YOU*** *PICK THE PLOT,* ***YOU*** *MAKE THE CHOICES THAT WILL BRING YOUR DEAR DAUGHTER HOME, OR LOSE HER TO WONDERLAND FOREVER!*

OVER 13 POSSIBLE MIND-BENDING ENDINGS.

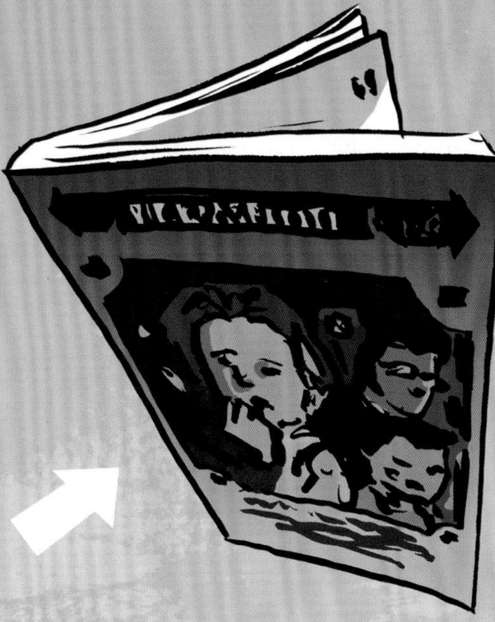

WHICH YOU MIGHT QUITE ENJOY

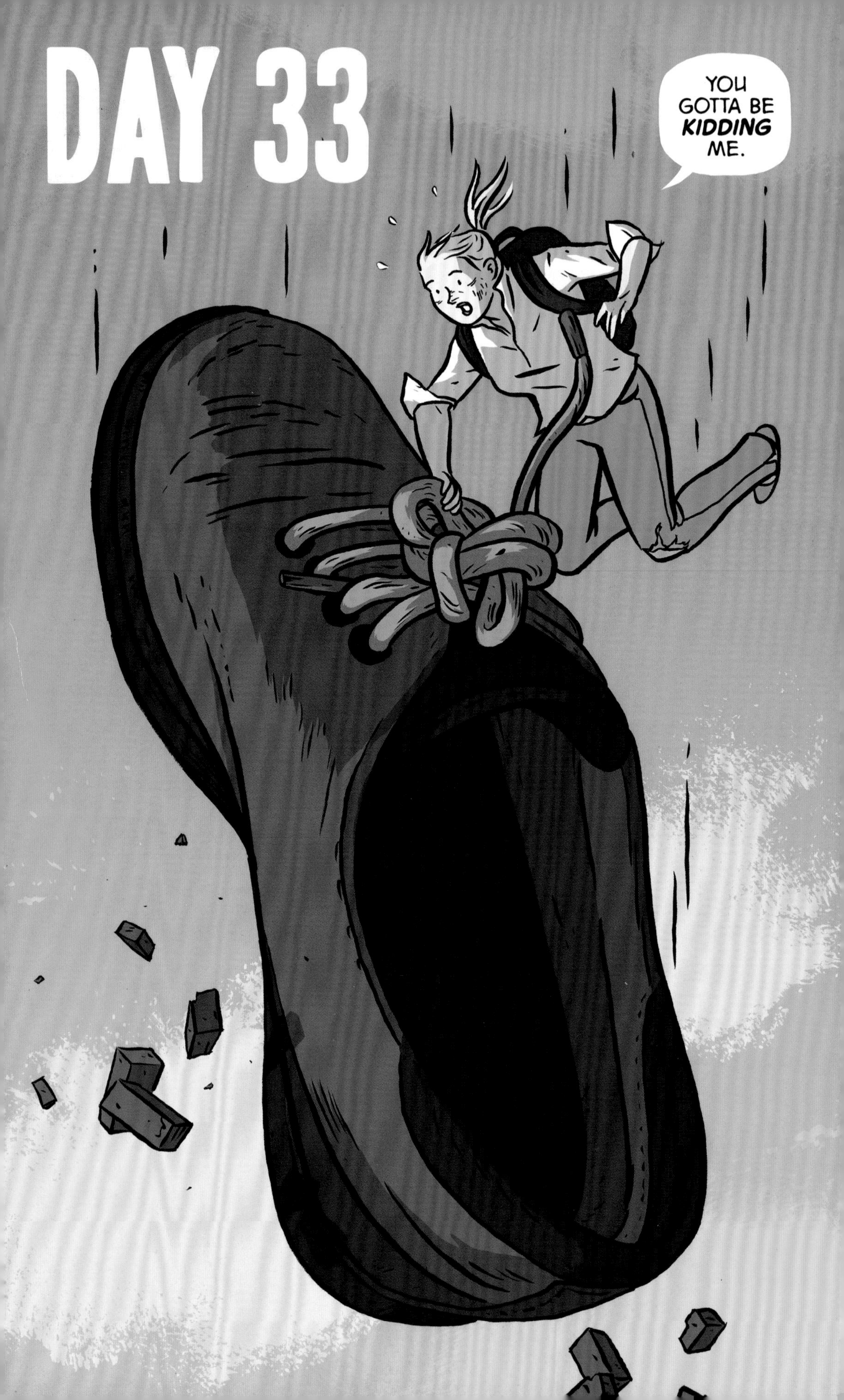
DAY 33
YOU GOTTA BE **KIDDING** ME.